NORMAN MAILER

WORKS AND DAYS

NORMAN MAILER

WORKS AND DAYS

J. MICHAEL LENNON

DONNA PEDRO LENNON

Preface
by
Norman Mailer

Sligo Press
Shavertown, Pennsylvania
2000

For

Peter Lennon

Robert F. Lucid

Gloria Taylor

Contents

Preface

by Norman Mailer

Sometimes I think that Michael Lennon and I were as designed for each other as some species of American Yin and Yang, as hot dogs, perhaps, and mustard. His talents, his discipline, and his ambition form a complement to all the slacks, voids, and indolences of my nature. Which is not to say that I see myself as untalented, unambitious and without discipline, no, it is rather that what I am good at, I am pretty good at, yes, but my interest in what I have written has a short half-life. Once I finish a piece of work, my interest moves to other matters, and all is left to my filing system. In truth, I have no system other than to throw old manuscripts and letters into manila envelopes and deposit them in cartons.

Without the participation of my good friend Mike as a pro bono archivist, my literary estate would have long ago become a dumping ground of moldering unlabelled cardboard boxes. By his efforts, however, which go back over more than two decades, my literary artifacts have since become well-organized, indeed, so well-organized by his passion for precision and documentation that the result could appear obscene to me in its perfection, if it were not for the fact that I need and use it like a bone with its marrow. Should the gods who look after posthumous literary life choose to decide in my favor—an assumption that no writer can make with confidence what with literary history flinging many a good dead writer off the road—then, for certain, if a reasonable denouement does come to my work, the materials to support this scribbler have been put in place. And should I end by occupying no larger place than a footnote in literary history, it will not be the fault of Michael Lennon. Those historic tides that carry a few authors' boats to the golden islands of posthumous investiture will have felt his hand on the tiller. So let these words serve to express the size of my debt. Three cheers for my friend, Mike Lennon, and my own private ovation for *Works and Days*.

Introduction

By J. Michael Lennon

Mailer is Proteus. Perhaps no career in American literature has been at once so brilliant, varied, controversial, improvisational, public, productive, lengthy and misunderstood. [...]
on the minds of contemporary [...]
for such an unbroken span [...]
same and so many seasons, [...]
and redundant, has never been [...]
pletely relished. Valuable [...]

been made over the years, much of it very [...] Thomas Fiske. But whatever Mailer said [...] phosing from novelist and biographer and [...] sports reporter (and also [...]
graphic scaffolding is heard [...]
became apparent. Because [...]
output has been so prolific, so [...]
many different and often contradictory [...]
lations, including my own, to prove [...]
is built upon these careers to establish [...]

Mailer has not only published [...]
written plays (and staged them himself) [...]
them), poems (for both serious readers [...]
saved every sort of adventure and has [...]
reported on six separate conventions [...]
1996), participated in countless [...]
of times on college campuses [...]
fought) in several venues [...]
and Provincetown. His [...]
tions, embarrassments and has [...]
Happily married for nearly a quarter [...]
wed five times previously [...]
radio and television talk shows [...]
more than any other writer [...]
pains, he has given abundant [...]
(mayor of New York), [...]
and has won most of America's [...]
founder of The Village Voice [...]
of a decathalon athlete if he [...]
lar, underground and [...]
periodical—Dissent, Esquire [...]
zine, Parade, Playboy and [...]
the way over to Commentary [...]
Books. Excluding interviews [...]
and symposia, Mailer has [...]

Introduction

By J. Michael Lennon

Mailer is Proteus. Perhaps no career in American literature has been at once so brilliant, varied, controversial, improvisational, public, productive, lengthy and misunderstood. Few American writers have had their careers on the minds of contemporary critics and on the anvil of public inspection for such an unbroken span; none has been so reviled and celebrated in the same and so many seasons. The Mailer record, while sometimes obvious and redundant, has never been fully compiled and therefore never completely relished. Valuable pioneering efforts to compile this record have been made over the years, notably by Robert F. Lucid, Laura Adams and Thomas Fiske. But whenever Mailer sought new opportunities, metamorphosing from novelist into biographer, theologian, politician, jeremiah or sports reporter (and always back to novelist), the need for more bibliographic scaffolding, a better vantage point for tracking his new vocations, became apparent. Because his direction has changed so often, because his output has been so prodigious, and because his words have appeared in so many different and often obscure publications, all previous Mailer compilations, including my own, are fragmentary. *Norman Mailer: Works and Days* is built upon these earlier efforts and is much indebted to them.

Mailer has not only published 39 books (including 11 novels), he has written plays (and staged them), screenplays (and directed and acted in them), poems (for both *Nugget* and *The New Yorker*, among others) and essayed every sort of narrative form (including some he invented). He has reported on six sets of political conventions (1960, 1964, 1968, 1972, 1992, 1996), participated in scores of symposia, appeared and debated hundreds of times on college campuses from the 50s through the 90s, boxed (and fought) in several venues, and enjoyed a vigorous public life in New York and Provincetown. His passions, feuds, imbroglios, generosities, litigations, embarrassments and loyalties are numerous, notorious and complex. Happily married for nearly a quarter of a century to Norris Church, he was wed five times previously and has nine children all told. A stalwart on radio and television talk shows for 40 years, he may have been interviewed more than any other writer who has ever lived. Without being paid for his pains, he has given advice to several presidents, has run for office himself (mayor of New York), served as president of the American chapter of P.E.N., and has won most of the major literary awards but for the Nobel. Cofounder of *The Village Voice*, he also named it, and has been the equivalent of a decathalon athlete in the effort to break down barriers between popular, underground and elite periodicals. He has written for every kind of periodical—*Dissent, Ladies Home Journal* and *One: The Homosexual Magazine, Parade, Playboy* and *Esquire*, from *Fuck You! A Magazine of the Arts* all the way over to *Cornhill, Commentary, Harper's* and *The New York Review of Books*. Excluding interviews, routine letters to the editor, questionnaires and symposia, Mailer has written for at least 74 different magazines.

The ambition of *Norman Mailer: Works and Days* is to chronicle Mailer's professional career, to nominate, delineate, annotate and cross-reference every significant Mailer utterance in print in English (an impossible task worth attempting), as well as the chief events of his life to date. Also included are a select secondary bibliography, an index, and four appendices. The photographs and illustrations, one for most years from 1941 through 1998, are intended to add evocative interrelations to the record. The *Chicago Manual of Style* (14th ed.) has been our regular if not exclusive guide for "Works," "Days," and the bibliography.

Works and Days is first of all a primary bibliography, one that attempts to be comprehensive. It fails of course. New Mailer poems, interviews and letters to the editor turn up regularly, and our file of leads, fragments and unidentified items bulges. But the *major* published items by Mailer have nearly all been located and described. Every named item (save one, 62.6) has been sighted and checked. It is certain, however, that there will be future discoveries.

The following have not been included: non-English language items, unpublished writings, audio and video material, including CDs, material from the Internet, blurbs for the books of other writers, letters to the editor signed by Mailer jointly with other individuals, brief and inconsequential Mailer quotations in gossip and chatter magazines. Also excluded are published drawings and sheet music—Mailer collaborated on the lyrics to "You'll Come Back (You Always Do)" for the film version of one of his novels (see 87.2). Besides the usual categories of novel, poem, play, essay, short story and interview (consisting entirely or almost so of questions and answers), we have created the categories of article-interview (reports based on interviews with Mailer, and quoting him), and of article (reports in which Mailer is quoted, but not formally interviewed). There are other categories, but their nature is self-evident—nonfiction narrative, for example.

Each item is numbered chronologically within a year. For example, 87.2 cited above refers to the second item (of 29) in 1987, a 12 January 1987 article-interview by Dinitia Smith that quoted Mailer and appeared in *New York* magazine. This simple method permits the delineation of different versions of the same item appearing several times over a span of years. All successive variants of an item are named, numbered and the changes described. *The Naked and the Dead* , for example, is listed twice after its initial 48.2 appearance: as 79.36 and as 98.6, Mailer having added a preface to the 1979 Franklin Library edition of his first published novel, and added another (dropping the first) to the 1998 Henry Holt edition. When an item was collected by an editor before Mailer collected it himself (a common occurrence), the earlier anthology is noted, e.g., his essay "The White Negro" (57.1) was collected in *The Beat Generation and the Angry Young Men* before Mailer did so in *Advertisements for Myself* (59.13).

No attempt has been made to list the vast number of reprints of Mailer's essays and other pieces (that is, reprintings containing no authorial change) in periodicals or anthologies, except in cases where the reprinting is particularly significant for some other reason. Beyond first editions in the

U.S. and U.K., no attempt has been made to list subsequent editions, impressions and states of Mailer's books, except when a hardcover edition has been *preceded* by a softcover edition, as is the case with *St. George and the Godfather* (72.17 and 83.49); or, to repeat, when Mailer has revised or added something, such as the new concluding chapter that he added to the softcover edition of *Marilyn* (75.3), published two years after the hardcover edition (73.30). When reprint information appears (after Rpt:), it is both prospective and retrospective, that is, it refers to earlier and later appearances of an item. This information, however, is confined to Mailer's work, apart from the intervening collections and significant reprintings noted above.

Annotation has been added to the majority of items. Most of this comment is descriptive, but the line is repeatedly crossed into the realm of evaluation and comparative judgment. Standard publication information for books is augmented by the addition of Mailer's dedications and "appreciations," and (in most cases) by precise dates of publication in the U.S. and U.K., number of pages and price. Other pertinent information has been added as available. A comment from Mailer on the nature, method, merit and/or compositional history of 32 major publications follows the entry for these items. These comments are taken from the item itself, from its preface or, most commonly, from a subsequent interview. Our bias has been towards inclusivity, but we have eschewed description of Mailer books as objects (bindings, dust jackets, colophons, etc.) except when such detail reveals something significant about the text. *Works and Days* is intended for both a scholarly-critical audience and for book collectors and other admirers of Mailer's work. It should be helpful to both (overlapping) groups, especially on matters of precedence and context.

The continuity of Mailer's career as a writer has thus far been insufficiently appreciated. The lead-ins of scores of articles and article-interviews present a picture of Mailer as volcano, erupting with spasmodic violence and then subsiding into periods of recovery and apparent dormancy. *Works and Days* identifies 1110 links within the sequence of his professional life and suggests, via annotation and cross-referencing, how they cohere into a mesh of craft and intentionality. The cross-referencing is for the most part topical, while the index is devoted exclusively to the names of every person named in "Works." So, for example, Mailer's theological views, as revealed most notably in several items (59.2, 75.2, 75.11, 82.15, 83.45, 89.11), are linked by cross-reference. But to learn how many times Barbara Probst Solomon has interviewed Mailer (three), or when Mailer first commented on Muhammad Ali (in 1967, when he was Cassius Clay), the index must be consulted. It is keyed to item numbers, not page numbers. The entries for his major publications serve as cross-reference hubs: you need to go there before connecting with lesser items, which are less tightly linked. But among the numbered items ("Works"), the life chronology ("Days"), the index, illustrations and appendices, a good deal of what is of interest in Mailer's career can be contextualized. Our hope is that anyone interested in his work will find in *Works and Days* a solid place to begin.

Acknowledgments and Appreciations

Without access to the Mailer archive and to Mailer himself, this volume would have been impossible. Since 1982, when it began taking shape during the editing of *Pieces and Pontifications* (82.16), Mailer has been consulted many times. His eye on the manuscript has been crucial; his generosity has been unstinting. His wife, Norris Church, has helped the project along in many ways and supplied items obtainable from no one else. The friendship and remarkable support of the Mailers has been essential from start to finish. Mailer's sister, Barbara Wasserman, and his assistant, Judith McNally, have provided unique insights and encouragement. Wasserman, the chief guide to Mailer family history, collected and preserved the photographs in the archive—some of them gratefully reproduced as yearly illustrations. McNally, Mailer's assistant since 1978, has had her finger on many of the items described and has filled in countless publication details. It was Robert F. Lucid, Mailer's friend of 40 years and his authorized biographer, who—with the help and blessing of Mailer's mother—first created the Mailer archive in the early 70s. We signed on as assistants in the early 80s. Lucid is the dean of Mailer scholar-critics. His checklist of Mailer's work in his 1971 collection, *Norman Mailer: The Man and His Work*, is the place where all Mailer bibliographers must begin. He has been our principal advisor, and his enthusiasm and counsel have been crucial to the project throughout. Indeed, the unflagging and cheerful help of this "Mailer team" has been marvelous and kept us always on task.

Laura Adams's *Norman Mailer: A Comprehensive Bibliography*, which appeared in 1974, was the first major Mailer bibliography, and as noted earlier, it has been indispensable to us in creating this volume, as it was to my earlier efforts noted in the secondary bibliography. But many new items have been discovered over the past quarter of a century, and *Works and Days* contains twice as many primary items for the period 1941 to 1974 as does Adams's compilation. Equaling Adams's volume in value is Thomas Fiske's unpublished work, "A Collector's Bibliography of Norman Mailer." Fiske's regular and thoughtful assistance on many perplexing matters has been invaluable. The *Mailer Author Price Guide, no. 114.2* (1997) by Allen and Patricia Ahearn of Quill and Brush Books, which provides reliable information on first editions in English, has been an excellent resource. Finally, B.A. Sokoloff's 1969 compilation, *A Bibliography of Norman Mailer*, has been useful, especially for early reviews of Mailer's books.

Two other people, Peter Lennon and Gloria Taylor, have played major roles in the creation of *Works and Days*. Peter, my brother, and the "mayor" of Casterbridge Books in Chicago, has sent us more items than anyone else and advised us continuously on matters of form and substance. Gloria Taylor, now retired from the Illinois State Library in Springfield, performed a huge amount of research for the project throughout the 80s. Peter's and Gloria's bibliographic fingerprints are all over this book.

Besides Norman and Norris Mailer, Robert F. Lucid, Thomas Fiske, Barbara Wasserman and Peter Lennon, the following individuals have read and commented on the manuscript: Robert Begiebing, Judith Everson (several times), Barry Leeds, Jon Lindgren, Michael Millgate, the late Willie Morris, Nancy Potter and Larry Shiner. We have been saved from errors egregious and embarrassing by these careful editors and good friends. Our sons, James, Joseph and Stephen, have also contributed greatly and listened heroically.

I am extremely grateful for the awarding of a spring 1998 sabbatical, upon the recommendation of President Christopher N. Breiseth, by the Board of Trustees of Wilkes University. Breiseth's friendship and understanding have been extraordinary and enabled us to make the final push to completion. Harold E. Cox, Director of the Wilkes University Press, has advised us on documentary editing and publication issues for seven years. His counsel and friendship have been similarly extraordinary.

Three libraries have been especially helpful: Illinois State Library, Springfield; Norris L. Brookens Library at University of Illinois, Springfield; and the Eugene S. Farley Library at Wilkes University, Wilkes-Barre, Pennsylvania. Gloria Taylor was our chief contact at the Illinois State Library; at the University of Illinois, Springfield (formerly Sangamon State University), we were greatly assisted by Brian Alley, Dick Kipp and Ned Wass; Jon Lindgren, Head Librarian at the Farley Library, has been an indefatigable and resourceful friend. We are most grateful for this professional advice and assistance.

Over the years many family members, friends and colleagues have sent us Mailer items they have stumbled on in flea markets and yard sales or clipped from periodicals. This loyal cadre has greatly augmented the number of items in *Works and Days*. Most of those on the following list have also discussed Mailer's work with us often over the past quarter of a century. Thanks to Elizabeth Adams, Peter Alson, David Antoine, Kathryn Arruda, Kathleen Arruda, John Bowers, Larsen Bowker, Jane Breiseth, Christopher Busa, Linda and Tom Bushar, Pete Capelotti, Alex Casella, Eleanor Cook, James M. Cox, John Daly, Essy Davidowitz, Pattie and Stan Davies, Cullom Davis, Jeffrey Van Davis, Michael Devine, Patrick Dickson, Steve Dykema, Barbara Ferrara, Darin Fields, Laura Forting, Bill Furry, the late Mark Goldman, Jerry Goldstein, Samuel K. Gove, Thomas Hadzor, Patricia and Robert Heaman, Kevin Heisler, Norman Hinton, Beverly and Harry Hiscox, Marilyn Huff, Kaylie Jones, Nancy and Robert Jackson, Eugene Kennedy, Robert Klaus, Lawrence Kuhar, Edward Lempenin, Hugh Lennon, Helen Lennon, Mary Mitchell Lennon, Joanne Lucid, Maureen Macedo, Warren Mason, Cliff and Ruth Melberger, the late Scott Meredith, D. F. "Joe" Mitchell, Philip Moreau, Cheryl Peck, Anthony and Mary Pedro, Susan and Wayne Penn, Diane Polachek, Jeff Posternak, James Rodechko, Kim and Richard Ross, Don Sackrider, Ray Schroeder, Barbara Probst Solomon, Tom Towers, Theresa Shypulefski, Charles Strozier, Khachig Tölölyan, Jack Scovil, Jack Van Der Slik, Rita Wolberg, Al Wasserman, John Whalen-Bridge, Sam Whitsitt and Andrew Wylie. Our deepest thanks go out to all those named and unnamed, remembered or, alas, forgotten, who have helped us build *Norman Mailer: Works and Days* over the past 18 years. Please continue to clip and send and counsel.

Works

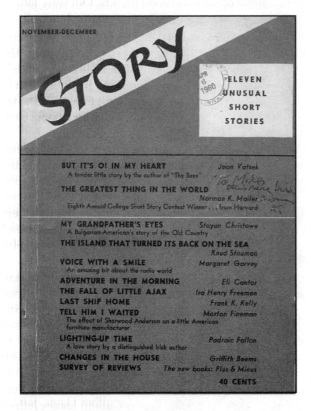

1941

See 41.1

41.1 "The Greatest Thing in the World." *Harvard Advocate*, April, 3-6, 24-28. Story. Submitted to *Story* magazine's eighth annual college contest under the name Norman K[ingsley]. Mailer, it won the first prize of $100. Mailer ceased using his middle initial and name after college, although he employed it once for his 1971 movie, "Maidstone: A Mystery" (71.28), in which the director-hero is called Norman T. Kingsley. Rpt: *Story* 19 (November-December), 17-26; *Hold Your Breath: Suspense Stories*, edited by Alfred Hitchcock. New York: Dell (no. 92), 1947; *Story: The Fiction of the Forties*, edited by Whit Burnett and Hallie Burnett. New York: E.P. Dutton, 1949; 59.13 (preceded by an introductory "advertisement"), 67.11, 82.19. See 75.14, 77.2, 83.10, 89.10, and the editorial in *Harvard Crimson*, 21 April, 2, the first published critical (and favorable) comment on Mailer's work.

Mailer: "...when I found out it had won—which was at the beginning of the summer after my sophomore year—well, that fortified me, and I sat down and wrote a novel. It was called *No Percentage*. It was just terrible. But I never questioned any longer whether I was started as a writer" (64.1).

1

42.2

42.1 "Right Shoe on Left Foot." *Harvard Advocate*, May, 12-18, 30-33. Story of racial and sexual violence in the South, never reprinted.

42.2 "Maybe Next Year." *Harvard Advocate*, June, 25-27. Story. When Mailer reprinted it in *Advertisements for Myself* (59.13), he noted that "the prose is Salinger-ish, but the inspiration was by Faulkner." Rpt: *The Harvard Advocate Anthology*, edited by Donald Hall. New York: Twayne, 1950; 59.13, 67.11, 82.19.

CROSS-
SECTION

A Collection of
New American
Writing

Novelettes. Stories. Poems;
full-length Plays

EDITED BY EDWIN SEAVER

44.1

44.1 "A Calculus at Heaven." In *Cross-Section: A Collection of New American Writing*, edited by Edwin Seaver, 317-53. New York: L.B. Fischer, May. Novella of Pacific combat, written for Robert Hillyer's English A-5 class in Mailer's senior year at Harvard. Mailer says in *Advertisements for Myself* (59.13) that it "does make an interesting contrast to *The Naked and the Dead*" (48.2). Original working title: "The Foundation," drawn from a line in André Malraux's *Man's Fate*: "All that men are willing to die for, beyond self-interest, tends...to justify that fate by giving it a foundation in dignity." Mailer's first book appearance. Rpt: 59.13, 67.11, 82.19.

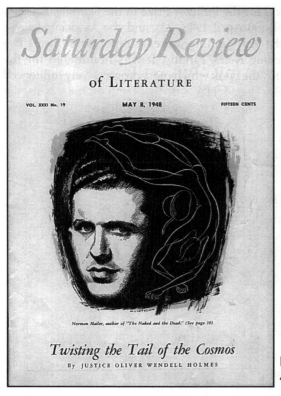

Saturday Review

of LITERATURE

VOL. XXXI No. 19   MAY 8, 1948   FIFTEEN CENTS

Norman Mailer, author of "The Naked and the Dead." (See page 10)

Twisting the Tail of the Cosmos

By JUSTICE OLIVER WENDELL HOLMES

1948

Drawing by Hal McIntosh
48.3

48.1 "The Naked and the Dead." In *Cross-Section: A Collection of New American Writing*, edited by Edwin Seaver, 392–420. New York: Simon and Schuster, April. Advance excerpt from *The Naked and the Dead* (48.2). Rpt: Appearing about a month before the novel, this excerpt (with minor variations) is the greater part of chapter 5, part 1, a description of dragging the anti-tank guns through the jungle and the following firefight at the river, an excerpt reprinted countless times in anthologies of war writing. Noted as "work in progress" on dustwrapper. See Seaver's recollections of *Cross-Section* and Mailer in his memoir, *So Far So Good: Recollections of a Life in Publishing* (Westport, Conn.: Lawrence Hill, 1986). See also Mailer's comments in *Advertisements For Myself* (59.13), 28–29.

. **48.2** *The Naked and the Dead*. New York: Rinehart, 6 May; London: Wingate, 9 May 1949. Novel, 721 pp., $4. Republished in a signed leather-bound edition with one-page preface, "A Special Message to Subscribers from Norman Mailer." Franklin Center, Pa.: Franklin Library, 1979 (79.36). Dedication and acknowledgment: "To my Mother and Bea. I would like to thank William Raney, Theodore S. Amussen, and Charles Devlin for the aid and encouragement given me at various times in the writing of this novel." The novel received a "Page One Award" from the New York Newspaper Guild (CIO affiliate) on 20 May 1949 and was chosen as one of the four best books of 1948 by *Newsweek* (13 December). Several prominent critics nominated the novel for the Pulitzer Prize in the *Saturday Review*'s annual Pulitzer Prize poll (30 April 1949, 23), and the Associated Press named Mailer "Man of the Year" in Literature, as reported in the 31 December *Asbury Park Evening News*. Finally, it was nominated for the Gutenberg Award, given to "the book which most progressively influenced American thought in 1948." The novel was on the *New York Times* bestseller list for a total of 63 weeks, until summer 1949. The novel's title was first used for an unpublished play about an insane asylum based on a one-week job Mailer held at a Boston-area asylum in the summer of 1942. Rpt: 48.1, 98.6 (new edition, with new introduction), 98.7 (partial). See other 1948 entries, 49.3, 65.21, 68.31, 74.18, 74.20, 76.21, 92.12, 95.53 and, passim, in 59.13.

Mailer: "I came out of the Army with an idea for a novel about a long patrol, an idea which had been bound in its origins to a mountain which was to serve as both an actual mass of stone and as a symbolic base for the book. The original conception was allegorical. The mountain was a consciously ambiguous symbol, something too complex, too intangible, to be defined by language" (48.4).

48.3 "The Author." Article-interview by unidentified writer. *Saturday Review*, 8 May, 10. This profile with brief comments from Mailer (on problems of characterization, his early jobs, the poverty of American letters), accompanies Maxwell Geismar's highly laudatory and influential review. *Saturday Review* was the first magazine to give Mailer a cover story; a drawing of Mailer by Hal McIntosh based on the jacket photo of 48.2 is on the cover of this issue. See 48.8.

48.4 "Life-View." *Book Find News* [July], edited by George Braziller, 6. Essay on 48.2 (a Book Find Club selection), including Mailer's plea that it be read "as a novel by a young man who immodestly or not has tried to compound his experience and imagination into something more complex than he could render in speech or by an essay."

48.5 "People Who Read and Write." Article-interview by unidentified writer. *New York Times Book Review*, 15 August, 8. Mailer is quoted in this book chat piece on the success of 48.2.

48.6 "Wonder Boy Novelist." Article-interview by Horace Sutton. *Cue*, 21 August, 17. Focuses on the success of 48.2. See 48.8.

48.7 "*The Naked* are Fanatics *and the Dead* Don't Care." Article-interview by Louise Levitas. *New York Star*, 22 August, Sec. M, pp. 3-5. Shortly after returning from Europe, Mailer discusses how he used his Army experience for 48.2, and the "growing hysteria" about a war with Russia. Longest interview given by Mailer until 1955. Accompanied by excerpt from 48.2. Rpt: 88.6.

48.8 "Norman Mailer." In *Current Biography*, edited by Anna Rothe, 408-10. New York: H.W. Wilson, October. Profile of Mailer; quotes from 48.3, 48.6, 48.7 and a Rinehart press release.

48.9 "Do Professors Have Rights?" *New York Post*, 8 October, 5, 34. Article on Indiana professor who was dismissed for his association with 1948 presidential candidate Henry Wallace. Mailer campaigned for Wallace upon his return from France in August. See 48.11, 74.20.

48.10 "Political Freedom for Teachers Urged." Article by unidentified writer. *New York Times*, 11 October, 25. At a New York rally under the auspices of the National Council of the Arts, Sciences and Professions to hear appeals for the preservation of political freedom in education, Mailer, W.E.B. DuBois and Harlow Shapley were among the speakers. Mailer: "It is a truism that fascism cannot come to America if our colleges and universities remain free."

48.11 "A Credo for the Living." *National Guardian*, 18 October. Article dealing with postwar Europe, anti-Russian hysteria in the U.S., and the 1948 Henry Wallace campaign. See 48.9, 74.20.

48.12 "Rugged Times." Article-interview [by Lillian Ross]. *New Yorker*, 23 October, 25. Mailer discusses the Wallace campaign, and 48.2, which he says "offers a good deal of hope." According to Mailer, "propositions" should be "proportions" in penultimate sentence. Contains comment on 48.2 repeated from 48.8. Rpt: 88.6.

48.13 "Books I Have Liked." Preference poll of 40 well-known writers concerning their recent reading. *New York Herald Tribune Weekly Book Review*, 5 December. Mailer lists three books: *The Castle* by Franz Kafka; *Jennie Gerhardt* by Theodore Dreiser; and *Howards End* by E.M. Forster. Seven of the 40 polled—Bartley Crum, James Hilton, Richard Lauterbach, Sinclair Lewis, Richard Match, Mary Roberts Rinehart and Irwin Shaw—named *The Naked and the Dead* (48.2). Only two other titles came close: Graham Greene's *The Heart of the Matter* and Robert E. Sherwood's *Roosevelt and Hopkins*, both with five votes. The effusive praise of Sinclair Lewis for the novel, given in an interview with Sylvia B. Richmond (*Chelsea* [Mass.] *Record*, 2 October, 5), is worth quoting in its entirety: "Speaking of newcomers in the field—one of the greatest writers of today is young Norman Mailer, author of *The Naked and the Dead*—an amazing bit of writing. That boy has talent worth preserving. His writing has great sweep and an enormous scope. There's nothing petty about Mailer—he's the author of the hour—the greatest writer to come out of his generation." Advertisements for Mailer's books carried this last phrase for many years. Mailer received the same kind of accolade in the *New York Times*, also on 5 December. Emmett Dedmon (*Chicago Sun-Times*), Lewis Gannett (*New Herald Tribune*), John Henry Jackson (*San Francisco Chronicle*), Sterling North (*New York Post*), Charles Poore (*New York Times*), Fredric Melcher (*Publishers' Weekly*), Orville Prescott (*New York Times*), Charles Rolo (*Atlantic*), and Karl Schriftgiesser (*Newsweek*) all listed the book as one of the top 10 books of the year. Jacques Barzun (*Harper's*), Norman Cousins (*Saturday Review*) and Lon Tinkle (*Dallas News*) did not. The 13 December *Newsweek* listed 48.2 as one of the top four books of the year, along with Sherwood's *Roosevelt and Hopkins*, Winston Churchill's *The Gathering Storm* and Greene's *The Heart of the Matter*. The attack on Mailer in *Life* (16 August) is also worth mentioning as a harbinger of 50 years of preponderantly negative reviews from the Time-Life organization. In a full-page editorial, Mailer was criticized for "slumming" in 48.2, for presenting an America in the "Time Machine" portions of the novel "just as ugly, arid, boring and uncomfortable as a jungle campaign." Mailer, the editorial continues, "seems to tell us...that such purposes as marrying and procreating and raising a family or mastering an art or a profession or building a business or beating the Japs are without value to anybody now living." The novel was later referred to in a *Life* editorial (16 April 1951) as "insidious slime."

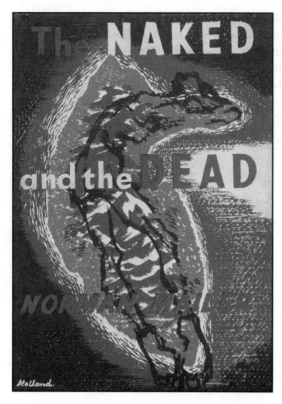

1949

Illustr. by James Holland
First British trade edition
48.2

49.1 "The Waldorf Conference." Article by Dwight Macdonald. *Politics* 6 (winter), 32A-32D. Macdonald quotes Mailer's 26 March statement to the conference concerning the state capitalism of Russia, the monopoly capitalism of the U.S. and the futility of the conference. Compare with Mailer's remembrance of the conference in *Advertisements for Myself* (59.13), 409-10; *New York Times* article, 27 March, 44; a red-baiting article in *Life*, 4 April, 39-43; and a piece sympathetic to the conferees by Cedric Belfrage in *National Guardian*, 4 April, 9.

49.2 "'48's Nine." Interview by Rochelle Girson. *Saturday Review*, 12 February, 12-14. Brief interviews with nine young authors: Mailer, Truman Capote, Irwin Shaw, William Gardner Smith, John Cobb, Ross Lockridge Jr., Hollister Noble, Ruby Redinger and Merle Miller.

49.3 Untitled article by Associated Press writer. 1 May. In response to the condemnation of *The Naked and the Dead* (48.2) by the (London)*Sunday Times*, Mailer replies, "The *Sunday Times* is certainly entitled to its opinion—but I don't agree with it. I wrote the book in good faith and don't think it is obscene. I think as a matter of fact, that it's less obscene than some salacious books that have foul words only here and there. When you look at the book as a whole, I don't think you notice any obscenity in it. The obscenity—if you want to call it that—in *The Naked and the Dead* is like a bell ringing in the background while you work. Before long you don't

8

notice it any more." The possible banning of the book was discussed on the floor of the House of Commons, and widely in the British press. The British Attorney General, Sir Hartley Shawcross, while finding the novel to be "foul, lewd and revolting," ultimately decided not to initiate proceedings against it. See 65.21, 68.31, 92.12, 95.53.

49.4 Statement for class record. In *Harvard Class of 1943: Sexennial Report*, 208-9. Cambridge: Harvard University. In his 83-word statement, Mailer summarizes his activities from March 1944 through his participation in the Henry Wallace campaign in the fall of 1948. See 53.5, 58.6, 83.59.

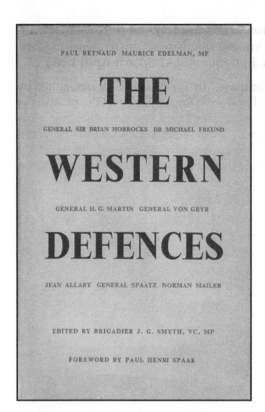

PAUL REYNAUD MAURICE EDELMAN, MP

THE

GENERAL SIR BRIAN HORROCKS DR MICHAEL FREUND

WESTERN

GENERAL H. G. MARTIN GENERAL VON GEYR

DEFENCES

JEAN ALLARY GENERAL SPAATZ NORMAN MAILER

EDITED BY BRIGADIER J. G. SMYTH, VC, MP

FOREWORD BY PAUL HENRI SPAAK

51.4

51.1 *Barbary Shore*. New York: Rinehart, 24 May; London: Cape, 21 January 1952. Novel, 312 pp., $3. The 1971 Cape hardcover edition and the 1973 softcover Panther edition (a Cape imprint) contains a "Note from the Author," which consists of "Second Advertisement for Myself: Barbary Shore" (minus final sentence, with one other small change) from 59.13. Dedication: "To Jean Malaquais." A dramatic version was presented at the New York Shakespeare Festival Public Theater, 10-27 January 1974. Jack Gelber wrote and directed the adaptation, which has never been published. Rpt: 59.13 (eight brief excerpts from novel, nine pp. total); 98.7 (partial).

Mailer: "I started *Barbary Shore* as some sort of fellow-traveler, and finished with a political position which was a far-flung mutation of Trotskyism. And the drafts of the book reflected these ideological changes so drastically that the last draft of *Barbary Shore* is a different novel altogether and has almost nothing in common with the first draft but the names" (64.1).

51.2 "Talk with Norman Mailer." Interview by Harvey Breit. *New York Times*, 3 June, Sec. 7, p. 3. Important comment on the influence of *Moby-Dick* on *The Naked and the* Dead (48.2). Mailer says of 48.2: "I had Ahab in it, and I suppose the mountain was Moby Dick. Of course, I also think the book will stand or fall as a realistic novel." Rpt: *The Writer Observed*, by Harvey Breit. Cleveland: World, 1956; 88.6. See Bernard Horn's article, "Ahab and Ishmael at War: The Presence of *Moby-Dick* in *The Naked and the Dead*," *American Quarterly* 34 (fall 1982), 379-95.

51.3 "Authors and Humanism." *Humanist* 11 (October- November), 201. Mailer answers the question "Are you a humanist?" by reference to Marx, Freud and his current atheism. Rpt: *Humanist* 41 (March-April 1981), 23.

51.4 "The Defence of the Compass." In *The Western Defences*, edited by Sir John George Smyth, 134-44. London: Wingate. Essay on the prospect of a military collision between the state capitalism of Russia and the monopoly capitalism of the U.S., "the Colossi." This version strongly echoes the arguments of *Barbary Shore* (51.1) and was obviously written shortly before or after the novel appeared. Rpt: Mailer's extended comments on the Korean War were cut out of the greatly revised version which appeared as "The Meaning of 'Western Defense'" in *Dissent* (54.1); 59.13.

51.5 "Norman Mailer." *American Novelists of Today*, by Harry R. Warfel, 276. New York: American Book Co. Biographical entry containing Mailer's 102-word statement on his plans for future work. He says, "I have no concerted program. I would like to experiment and to grow, but I pursue this aim through no particular standards. Technique must always be secondary to the world one constructs in a novel." Rpt: Westport, Conn.: Greenwood Press, 1972.

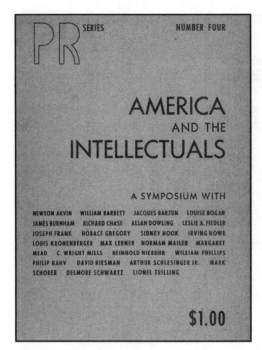

SERIES   NUMBER FOUR

AMERICA
AND THE
INTELLECTUALS

A SYMPOSIUM WITH

NEWTON ARVIN   WILLIAM BARRETT   JACQUES BARZUN   LOUISE BOGAN
JAMES BURNHAM   RICHARD CHASE   ALLAN DOWLING   LESLIE A. FIEDLER
JOSEPH FRANK   HORACE GREGORY   SIDNEY HOOK   IRVING HOWE
LOUIS KRONENBERGER   MAX LERNER   NORMAN MAILER   MARGARET
MEAD   C. WRIGHT MILLS   REINHOLD NIEBUHR   WILLIAM PHILLIPS
PHILIP RAHV   DAVID RIESMAN   ARTHUR SCHLESINGER JR.   MARK
SCHORER   DELMORE SCHWARTZ   LIONEL TRILLING

$1.00

1952

See 52.1

52.1 "Our Country and Our Culture: A Symposium." *Partisan Review* 19 (May-June), 298-301. Symposium contribution. Twenty-five American writers wrestle with four questions on the "new" and more positive relationship between American writers and intellectuals and mass democratic culture. Mailer declares straightaway that he is "in almost total disagreement with the assumptions of this symposium," and goes on to argue for the efficacy of alienation and opposition to current society, rather than "a strapping participation in the vigors of American life." Among those joining Mailer in his (first) contribution to *Partisan Review* are : Louise Bogan, Leslie Fiedler, Irving Howe, Margaret Mead, C. Wright Mills, William Phillips, Philip Rahv, David Riesman and Lionel Trilling. Rpt: *America and the Intellectuals: A Symposium* (*PR* Series, Number Four). New York: Partisan Review, May 1953, softcover; 59.13.

52.2 "The Paper House." In *New World Writing: Second Mentor Collection*, 58-69. New York: New American Library, November, softcover. Story set in occupied Japan. Dedicated to Vance Bourjaily, "who told me the anecdote on which the story is based." Rpt: *Lilliput's Extra Holiday Reading (London), August 1953;* 59.13, 67.11, 68.32, 82.19.

52.3 "The Dead Gook." In *Discovery, No. 1*, edited by John W. Aldridge and Vance Bourjaily, 56-76. New York: Pocket Books, December, softcover. Story about a jungle patrol with partisans in the Philippines. In his prefatory "advertisement" to this story, 52.2 and 53.2 in *Advertisements for Myself* (59.13), Mailer notes that he has "no great pride in them, because they are respectable. They make no attempt to raise the house an inch or two." Rpt: 59.13, 67.11, 68.32, 82.19.

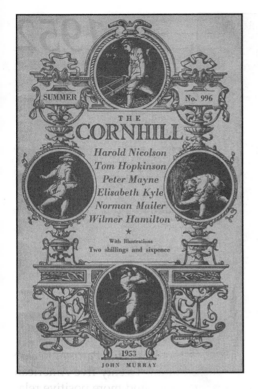

1953

53.4

53.1 "Backstage with Esky." Interview by *Esquire* editor. *Esquire*, April, 15-16. Comment on *Barbary Shore* (51.1), 53.2 and Mailer's stint in Hollywood, 1949-50. Rpt: 88.6.

53.2 "The Language of Men." *Esquire*, April, 61, 115-17. Story, based on Mailer's experience as an Army cook in occupied Japan. First of more than 40 contributions to the magazine with which Mailer has been most closely identified. Rpt: *Various Temptations*. New York: Avon, 1955, softcover; *The Armchair Esquire*, edited by Arnold Gingrich and L. Rust Hills. New York: Putnam's, 1958; 59.13, 67.11, 68.32, 82.19.

53.3 "Pierrot." *World Review* (London), New Series 50 (April-May), 44-50. Story about a prototype Greenwich Village Beatnik. Rpt: With many small changes in 59.13 as "The Patron Saint of MacDougal Alley." Mailer notes in 59.13 that he wrote it about the same time as his war stories (52.2, 52.3, 53.2) and "The Notebook" (53.4).

53.4 "The Notebook." *Cornhill Magazine*, no. 996 (summer), 481-84. Story, "written in an hour," as Mailer reports in the "advertisement" prefacing it in *Advertisement for Myself* (59.13), about writers as perpetual observers. Rpt: *The Berkley Book of Modern Writing, No. 3*, edited by William Phillips and Philip Rahv. New York: Berkley, 1956, softcover; 59.13, 67.11, 82.19. Although *Cornhill* is not listed on the acknowledgments page in 59.13, and *The Berkley Book Modern Writing* is, Mailer says in the prefatory "advertisement" to the story that *Cornhill* has precedence.

53.5 Statement for class record. In *Harvard College, Class of 1943: Tenth Anniversary Report*, 262. Cambridge, Harvard University. In his 214-word statement, Mailer reprises his activities from induction into the Army in March 1944 to work on an unnamed novel [*The Deer Park* (55.4)]. See 49.4, 58.6, 83.59.

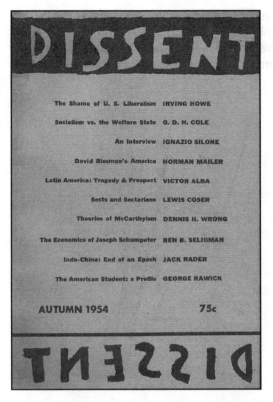

1954

54.3

54.1 "The Meaning of 'Western Defense.'" *Dissent* 1 (spring), 157-65. Essay. Greatly revised version of "The Defence of the Compass" (51.4). Mailer's first appearance came in the second number of *Dissent*, issued on 1 April. He was a member of the editorial board of *Dissent* from 1954 until the mid-80s. Rpt: 59.13.

54.2 "In Re: Sidney Hook." Letter to the editor. *Dissent* 1 (summer), 303. Mailer refuses to recant his "facetious" description of Sidney Hook in 54.1 as a "liberal-with-muscles." He ends by saying that if Hook is "an almost lone philosophical defender of democratic socialist and humanist values, it makes me Leo Tolstoy."

54.3 "David Riesman Reconsidered." *Dissent* 1 (autumn), 349-59. Review essay of David Riesman's *Individualism Reconsidered*. Rpt: 59.13.

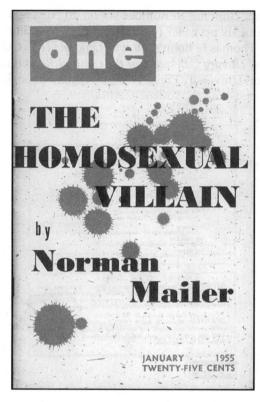

55.1

55.1 "The Homosexual Villain." *One: The Homosexual Magazine*, January, 8-12. Essay. In 61.3, Mailer says this piece "was the bravest thing I ever did, because it was done out of a dim, dull sense of duty." Rpt: 59.13.

55.2 "What I Think of Artistic Freedom." *Dissent* 2 (spring), 98, 192-93. Essay. Mailer's accompanying note says this essay, dated February, was written for "those German Stalinists whose faith might be fluttering." He further states that "Bert Brecht might answer it in the West Berlin periodical *Der Monat*," in which case Mailer's essay would be reprinted in some East German publication. Nothing came of the proposed exchange.

55.3 "Two Ex-GI's Write Revenge on Army." Article-interview by W.G. Rogers. *Battle Creek* (Mich.) *Enquirer-News*, 5 September. Mailer and Army friend Francis I. "Fig" Gwaltney comment briefly on the Army and writing.

55.4 *The Deer Park*. New York: Putnam's, 14 October; London: Wingate, 1957. Novel, 375 pp., $4. Republished with preface by Mailer and "Fourth Advertisement for Myself: The Last Draft of *The Deer Park*" from *Advertisements for Myself* (59.13). New York: Berkley, November 1976 (76.14). Dedication: "To Adele, my wife and to Daniel Wolf my friend." Discarded title: *The Idol and the Octopus*. The suppressed Rinehart version of this novel was to have been published 14 February. Six other publishers rejected it before Walter Minton of Putnam's accepted it. The novel spent 15 weeks on the

New York Times bestseller list, climbing to number six on 20 November. Rpt: 59.13 (three brief excerpts, six pp.); 98.7 (partial). See 55.5, 55.7, 56.17, 59.14, 67.13, 68.11, 89.6, and Thomas L. Bonn's, *Heavy Traffic and High Culture: New American Library as Literary Gatekeeper in the Cultural Revolution* (Carbondale: Southern Illinois University Press, 1989), for comment on the legal anxiety at NAL over publishing the softcover edition of 55.4.

Mailer: "...I had an idea of what I was going to do. I knew it was going to be a story about a most unhappy love. The problem was getting to the affair: I could hardly wait to reach it, especially because the early parts of the novel were so difficult to write. It is truly difficult to trap Hollywood in a novel. Only in the last draft did I finally get the setting the way I wanted it. I think now the setting is probably the best part. In fact I would judge that the first fifty pages of *The Deer Park* are the best writing I have ever done in fiction. But they were the hardest fifty pages of the book to write and certainly took the longest time" (64.1).

55.5 "All over America *The Deer Park* is Getting Nothing but Raves." *Village Voice*, 16 November, 8. Paid advertisement composed by Mailer consisting of negative appraisals from 16 reviewers. Mailer used this technique many times before and after 55.4, for example, 73.45. Rpt. 59.13, 59.14, 76.14.

55.6 "An Intimate Interview with Norman Mailer." By Lyle Stuart. *Exposé*, no. 49 (December), 1, 4. Written answers to 69 submitted questions, many relating to 55.4. Mailer also comments on organized religion, Marilyn Monroe, Sigmund Freud, Feodor Dostoyevsky, Ernest Hemingway and William Faulkner. He ends by stating that the role of the artist "is to be as disturbing, as adventurous, as penetrating as his energy and courage make possible." Rpt: 59.13, 88.6.

55.7 Letter to Herman Kogan, Book Review Editor, *Chicago Sun-Times*, 18 December. Complaint about comments in reviews of *The Deer Park* (55.4) that Mailer had "'cleaned up' the book to satisfy the demands of G.P. Putnam's, my publisher." He explains that the book was not bowdlerized and is actually 50 pages longer than the Rinehart version. In *Advertisements for Myself* (59.13), Mailer recalls that this letter was sent to "twenty-odd newspapers."

55.8 "Mailer, Norman." In *Twentieth Century Authors*, edited by Stanley J. Kunitz, 628-29. New York: H.W. Wilson. Autobiographical entry.

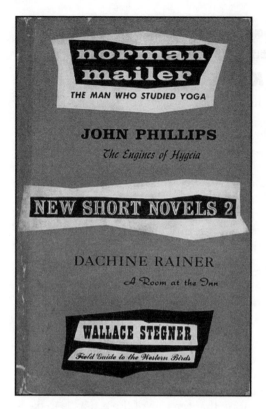

56.25

56.1-56.17 Quickly: A Column for Slow Readers (originally "Thinkers"). *Village Voice* (11 January-2 May). Last three columns are titled "The Hip and the Square." Mailer's column (accompanied by a photograph), his first appearance in the *Voice*, is introduced by Edwin Fancher, publisher, 4 January, 1-2. Mailer co-founded and named this weekly newspaper *The Village Voice*; first issue, 26 October 1955. Rpt: Six of the columns below (11 and 25 January, 28 March, 18 and 25 April and, in part, 2 May) in *The Village Voice Reader: A Mixed Bag from the Greenwich Village Newspaper*, edited by Daniel Wolf and Edwin Fancher. Garden City, N.Y.: Doubleday, 1962. The 25 April column is reprinted nowhere else; the 28 March column is reprinted in its entirety only in this collection. Kenneth Tynan's hard-to-find review of *Advertisements for Myself* (59.13) is also reprinted in this collection. See 78.7.

56.1 11 January, 5. Introduction and *raison d'etre* for the column. Rpt: 59.13, 98.7.

56.2 18 January, 5, 11. On lies, power, obscenity. Rpt: 59.13.

56.3 25 January, 5. Parodies of gossip columnists. Rpt: 59.13.

56.4 1 February, 5. Kenneth J. Schmidt's parody of 18 January column, and a dialogue with his daughter Susan, age six. Rpt: 59.13.

56.5 8 February, 5. On the distortions of the media. Rpt: 59.13.

QUICKLY #1

a column for slow thinkers
by Norman Mailer

Many years ago I remember reading a piece in the newspapers by Ernest Hemingway and thinking: "What windy writing." That is the penalty for having a reputation as a writer. Any signed paragraph which appears in print is examined by the usual sadistic literary standards, rather than with the easy tolerance of a newspaper reader pleased to get an added fillip for his nickel.

But this is a fact of life which any professional writer soon learns to put up with, and I know that I will have to put up with it since I doubt very much if this column is going to be particularly well-written. That would take too much time, and it would be time spent in what is certainly a losing cause. Greenwich Village is one of the better provinces—it abounds in snobs and critics. That many of you are frustrated in your ambitions, and undernourished in your pleasures, only makes you more venomous. Quite rightly. If I found myself in your position, I would not be charitable either. Nevertheless, given your general animus to those more talented than yourselves, the only way I see myself becoming one of the cherished traditions of the Village is to be actively disliked each week.

At this point it can fairly be asked: "Is this your only reason for writing a column?" And the next best answer I suppose its: "Egotism. My search to discover in public how much of me is sheer egotism." I find a desire to inflict my casual opinions on a half-captive audience. If I did not,

there would always be the danger of putting these casual opinions into a new novel, and we know what a terrible thing that it to do.

I also feel tempted to say that novelists are the only group of people who should write a column. Their interests are large, if shallow, their habits are sufficiently unreliable for them to find something to say quite often, and in most other respects they are more columnistic than the columnists. Most of us novelists who are any good are invariably half-educated, inaccurate, albeit brilliant upon occasion; insufferably vain of course; and—the indispensable requirement for a good newspaperman—as eager to tell a lie as the truth. (Saying the truth makes us burn with the desire to convince our audience, whereas telling a lie affords ample leisure to study the result.)

We good novelists also have the most unnewspaperly virtue of never praising fatherland and flag unless we are sick, tired, generally defeated, and want to turn a quick dishonest buck. Nobody but novelists would be asked to write columns if it were not for the sad fact that newspaper editors are professionally and obligatorily patriotic, and so never care to meet us. Indeed, even *The Village Voice*, which is remarkably conservative for so young a paper, and deeply patriotic about all community affairs, etc., etc., would not want me either if they were not so financially eager for free writing, and a successful name to go along with it, that they are ready to put up with almost anything. And I, as a minority stockholder in the Voice corporation, must agree that this paper does need something added to its general languor and whimsy.

56.1. Paste-up of first Quickly column (first part), January 11, 1956

19

56.6 15 February, 5, 10. Begins with a parody supplied "by my good friend and competitor, Sergius O'Shaugnessy," but ends with reflections on human virtue, liberty and action. Rpt: 59.13 (partial).

56.7 22 February, 5, 14. Appreciations of Steve Allen, George Gobel and Ernie Kovacs, with "odd thoughts" on narcissism and other matters.

56.8 29 February, 5, 9. Invitation to debate him on psychoanalysis. Rpt: 59.13 (partial).

56.9 7 March, 5. Eulogy for Robert Lindner, friend and psychoanalyst, with quotes from his book, *The Fifty-Minute Hour* (New York: Rinehart, 1955). Rpt: 59.13.

56.10 14 March, 5, 9. Debate with Dr. Y, a Greenwich Village psychoanalyst. Rpt: 59.13 (partial).

56.11 21 March, 5, 11. More on psychoanalysis, and the qualifications of Mailer's unnamed nominee for Democratic nominee for President. Rpt: 59.13 (partial).

56.12 28 March, 5, 11. Nomination of Ernest Hemingway for President, accompanied by photograph of Hemingway. Rpt: 59.13 (partial).

56.13 4 April, 5. Letters to the columnist and his responses. Karl L. Ekstand complains about Mailer's egotism, to which Mailer replies: "Let others profit by my unseemly self-absorption, and so look to improve their own characters." Rpt: 59.13 (partial).

56.14 11 April, 5. Letter from Joe Jensen, Mailer's reply; letter from J.V.W. on his debate with Dr. Y, and a reply.

56.15 18 April, 5. Discussion on the death of six U.S. Marines at Parris Island. Rpt: As "The Tragedy at Parris Island," *Dissent* 3 (fall), 435-37.

56.16 25 April, 5. Letter from Barnard Zemble on the definition of "Hip," and Mailer's reply, which foreshadows "The White Negro" (57.1).

56.17 2 May, 5. Comment on Samuel Beckett's "Waiting for Godot." Includes Sergius O'Shaughnessy's poem, "The Drunk's Bebob and Chowder," from *The Deer Park* (55.4). Rpt: 59.13. See 56.26.

56.18 Reply to letter to the editor of *Village Voice* from Joe Jensen about Quickly column, an exchange that continues irregularly until final column, 18 January, 4.

56.19 Reply to letters to the editor of *Village Voice* concerning Quickly column, 25 January, 5.

56.20 Reply to letters to the editor of *Village Voice* concerning Quickly column, 1 February, 11.

56.21 Reply to letter to the editor of *Village Voice* from Kenneth J. Schmidt about Quickly column, 8 February, 4.

56.22 Reply to letters to the editor of *Village Voice* concerning Quickly column, 22 February, 4.

56.23 Reply to letter to the editor of *Village Voice* from Kenneth J. Schmidt concerning Quickly column, 14 March, 4.

56.24 Reply to letters to the editor of *Village Voice* concerning Quickly column, 25 April, 4. Mailer notes that favorable letters outnumbered unfavorable ones after his 15 April column.

56.25 "The Man Who Studied Yoga." In *New Short Novels 2*, 1-29. New York: Ballantine, early May, simultaneously as a softcover. Novella (with brief prefatory comment on unnumbered page facing p. 1) intended as preface to a cycle of eight interlocking novels (*The Deer Park* [55.4] was the only novel of the cycle to be published). Mailer's penultimate extended use of an omniscient narrator in fiction. Rpt: 59.13 (with revised and expanded preface), 67.11, 82.19, 98.7. See 58.4.

56.26 "A Public Notice by Norman Mailer." *Village Voice*, 9 May, 12. A paid statement on Samuel Beckett's "Waiting for Godot" in which Mailer reverses his negative comments on the play given in his 2 May column (56.17). The statement contains Mailer's first published statement of his personal belief in a limited God. Herbert Gold claimed in a 10 November article in the *Nation* that Mailer was "fired" from the *Voice* for what he wrote about "Godot." Daniel Wolf, editor of the *Voice*, denied this in an 8 December letter to the *Nation*. Rpt: 59.13 (minus prefatory "Advertiser's Note" in which Mailer explains that he has paid for this notice "rather than embarrass editorial caution by asking it to be printed otherwise."

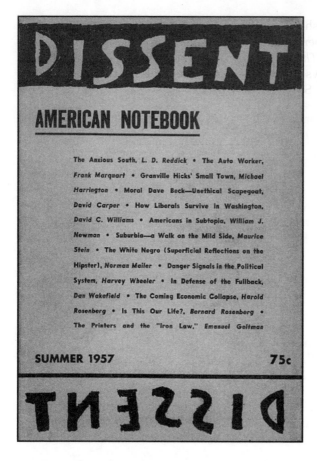

57.1

57.1 "The White Negro (Superficial Reflections on the Hipster)." *Dissent* 4 (summer), 276-93. Essay. Mailer's most celebrated and castigated essay is also one of the most anthologized since World War II. It is usually reprinted with "Reflections on Hipsterism" (58.1), a follow-up discussion of the original essay. Rpt: *The Beat Generation and the Angry Young Men*, edited by Gene Feldman and Max Gartenberg. New York: Citadel Press, May 1958; *Voices of Dissent: A Collection of Articles from "Dissent" Magazine*. New York: Grove Press, after 15 October, 1958; 58.8, 59.13, 98.7 (partial). See 56.16, 83.12, and James Baldwin's response, "The Black Boy Looks at the White Boy," *Nobody Knows My Name: More Notes of a Native Son* (New York: Dial, 1961).

Mailer: "What makes a novelist great is that he illumines each line of his work with the greatest intensity of experience. One thing about Hip you have to admit is that the Hipster lives in a state of extreme awareness, and so, objects and relations that most people take for granted become terribly charged for him; and, living in a state of self-awareness his time slows up. His page becomes more filled. The quality of his experience becomes more intense. That doesn't make for less expression; it makes for greater difficulty of expression" (59.2).

22

57.2 "Mailer Finishes First Stage Work." Article by Louis Calta. *New York Times*, 5 December 47. Mailer tells Calta that he has finished a stage version of his novel, *The Deer Park* (55.4), and it is being read by a Broadway producer. He says the play is in four acts, calls for twelve characters and runs three hours. See 59.11, 60.4, 67.13.

the
white
negro

norman
mailer

35¢

Photograph by Harry Redl
58.8

58.1 "Reflections on Hipsterism." *Dissent* 5 (winter), 73-81. Response to "The White Negro" (57.1) by Jean Malaquais and Ned Polsky with Mailer's counterpoint. Rpt: As "Reflections on Hip" in 58.8, 59.13.

58.2 "Mike Wallace Asks: Norman Mailer." *New York Post*, 24 and 25 July. Excerpts from a longer interview done in May or June, focusing on sex, morality and *The Deer Park* (55.4). The first of several antagonistic interviews with Wallace. See 58.7, 77.7.

58.3 "Norman Mailer Answers Gregory." Letter to the editor. *New York Post*, 25 August. Denial of accusations about Mailer's conduct in a restaurant made by Paul Gregory, producer of film version of *The Naked and the Dead* (48.2), in Archer Winsten's 11 August *Post* column. Rpt: 59.13. See 58.5.

58.4 "Advertisements for Myself on the Way Out." *Partisan Review* 25 (fall), 519-40. Story. From omniscient perspective, about Marion Faye of *The Deer Park* (55.4) in Provincetown. Rpt: 59.13 (with subtitle, "Prologue to a Long Novel"), 67.11, 82.19. See 56.25.

58.5 Letter to the editor, *Contact* (San Francisco) 1, pp. 97-98. Mailer responds to a request for a review of the film version of *The Naked and the Dead* (48.2) by noting that he doesn't have time. He offers instead his letter to the *New York Post* (58.3) about his disagreements with the film's director. *Contact* publishes Mailer's note and the *New York Post* letter.

58.6 Statement for class record. In *Harvard College, Class of 1943: Fifteenth Anniversary Report*, 148. Cambridge: Harvard University. Mailer's 157-word statement summarizes his publishing activities from 1953 to 1958. In the first half of the statement, Mailer speaks of his ambition and "the slapping [sic] of one's creative rage by our most subtle and clear totalitarian time, politely called the time of conformity." In the "First Advertisement for Myself," the opening essay of *Advertisements for Myself* (59.13), Mailer notes that "slapping" should have been "sapping" and concludes that "what I was trying to say was simply, 'The shits are killing us.'" See 49.4, 53.5, 83.59.

58.7 "Norman Mailer." Interview by Mike Wallace. In *Mike Wallace Asks*, edited by Charles Preston and Edward A. Hamilton, 26-27. New York: Simon and Schuster. Excerpts from Wallace's 5 March 1957 "Night Beat" television program; mainly concerned with Mailer's views on sex and censorship. See 58.2, 73.19, 77.7.

58.8 *The White Negro.* San Francisco: City Lights Books. Essay, 27 pp., 35¢, softcover. This often-reprinted pamphlet is almost always given a 1957 date in bibliographies, an unlikely date in that the essay is followed in the pamphlet by the 1958 piece, "Reflections on Hipsterism" (58.1). A 23 August 1959 *Chicago Sun-Times* review of the second (50¢) City Lights edition supports, but does not absolutely confirm, a 1958 publication date. In addition, the list of available City Lights publications in the 50¢ edition contains only 1958 publications. Rpt: 57.1, 59.13, 98.7 (partial), and *Voices of Dissent: A Collection of Articles from Dissent.* New York: Grove (without 58.1).

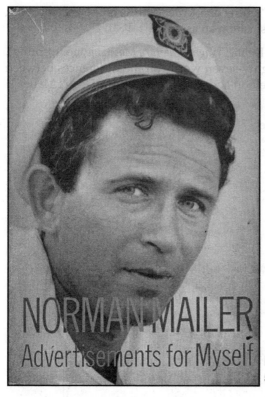

NORMAN MAILER
Advertisements for Myself

Photograph by Judy Scheftel
59.13

59.1 "Comment." *Dissent* 6 (winter), 9-10. Response to "A New Political Atmosphere in America" by Irving Howe. Mailer's perspective on the 1958 congressional elections.

59.2 "Hip, Hell, and the Navigator: An Interview with Norman Mailer." By Richard G. Stern and Robert F. Lucid. *Western Review* 23 (winter), 101-9. Mailer's first extended comment on his belief in an embattled God in one of his most important interviews. Rpt: 59.13, 82.16 (partial), 88.6, 98.7 (partial). See "The Psychology of Machines" in *Of a Fire on the Moon* (71.1) for a continuation of Mailer's discussion in this interview of the "Navigator," the ego's agent in the unconscious. See also 75.2, 75.11, 82.15, 83.45, 89.11.

59.3 "Capote, Mailer and Miss Parker." Article by Janet Winn. *New Republic*, 9 February, 27-28. Summarizes David Susskind's 18 January "Open End" television program on which Mailer, Truman Capote and Dorothy Parker discussed Jack Kerouac, the Beats and writing in general. See 59.4, 73.22, 77.7.

59.4 "Who Said What?" Letter to the editor. *New Republic*, 9 March, 3, 23. Mailer corrects Janet Winn's report (59.3) on his comments about Truman Capote and E.M. Forster.

59.5 "Ingenue." Letter to the editor. *Village Voice*, 11 March, 4. Mailer criticizes Marta Curro's 7 March *Village Voice* review of Millicent Brower's novel, *Ingenue*. He says that "letting one writer-actress revise [sic] the work of another is like leaving hashish on an assassin."

59.6 "Ten Words from the Dean." *Wagner Literary Magazine*, no. 1 (spring), 26-27. One hundred and eighty-seven words on the differences between Beat and Hip, "between rebellion and revolution," from "Dean" Mailer.

59.7 "From Surplus Value to the Mass-Media." *Dissent* 6 (summer), 254-57. Essay on Marxist and capitalist philosophies. Rpt: 59.13.

59.8 "An Eye on Picasso." *Provincetown Annual*, August, 27-28. Essay. Rpt: 59.13 (with one small change), and in *Beat Coast East: An Anthology of Rebellion*, edited by Stanley Fisher. New York: Excelsior, 1960. See 61.10, 95.37, 95.38.

59.9 "Buddies, or the Hole in the Summit: An Apocryphal and Interrupted Transcript." *Village Voice*, 16 September, 1, 4-5. One-act play, a conversation between President Dwight D. Eisenhower and Premier Nikita Khrushchev. Rpt: 59.13 (without subtitle and with a slightly different accompanying note). See 92.8.

59.10 "Quick and Expensive Comments on the Talent in the Room." *Big Table 3* (autumn-winter), 88-100. Essay in which Mailer appraises the writing of James Jones, William Styron, Truman Capote, Jack Kerouac, Saul Bellow, Nelson Algren, J.D. Salinger, Paul Bowles, Vance Bourjaily, Chandler Brossard, Gore Vidal, Anatole Broyard, Myron Kaufmann, Calder Willingham, Ralph Ellison, James Baldwin and Herbert Gold. Rpt: It is difficult to say if this essay appeared in *Big Table* before *Advertisements for Myself* (59.13) appeared. The former references the latter, but not vice versa. See 63.8, 63.40.

59.11 "Scenes from 'The Deer Park'" [scenes 7 and 10]. *Partisan Review* 26 (fall), 527-34. Dramatic fragment. Rpt: 60.4, and in a greatly revised form in 67.13. Other scenes appear in 59.13. See 57.2.

59.12 "Sentiments Larger than Work." *Saturday Review*, 10 October, 21. Advance excerpt of 200 words from essay, "Last Advertisement for Myself Before the Way Out," from forthcoming *Advertisements for Myself* (59.13).

59.13 *Advertisements for Myself*. New York: Putnam's, 6 November; London: Deutsch, October 1961 (see 61.15 for note on British edition). Miscellany, 532 pp., $5. Republished with preface by Mailer. New York: Berkley, December 1976 (76.15). Preface reprinted (minus first paragraph) as "An Advertisement Advertised" in 82.16. Dedication: "I dedicate this book to the memory of Anne Mailer Kessler (1889-1958) and to David Kessler and to my father Isaac Barnett ("Barney") Mailer." Portions of this miscellany appeared in periodicals at approximately the same time the book was published, a tactic that Mailer used to herald most of his major books from 1959 on. Rpt: 59.12; all of the short stories appear in 67.11 and 82.19; several selections appear, usually in truncated form, in 98.7. See 59.10, 59.14.

Mailer: "So *Advertisements* became the book in which I tried to separate my legitimate spiritual bile from my self-pity and maybe it was the hardest continuing task I had yet set myself. What aggravated every problem was that I was also trying to give up smoking, and the advertisements in this book, printed in italics, are testimony to the different way I was now obliged to use language" (76.14).

59.14 "The Mind of an Outlaw." *Esquire*, November, 87-90, 92, 94. Watershed essay on the struggle to publish *The Deer Park* (55.4). The November *Esquire* appeared earlier or at about the same time as *Advertisements for Myself* (59.13). Rpt: 55.5; as "Fourth Advertisement for Myself: The Last Draft of *The Deer Park*" in 59.13; 76.14.

59.15 "2 Symposium Authors Say Write for Elite, Not Masses." Article-interview by Dorthy Collin. *The Daily Iowan*, 5 December, 1. Report on the first day of a symposium co-sponsored by *Esquire* magazine and the University of Iowa's Writers' Workshop, 4-5 December. Mailer is quoted on the corruption of American writers by the mass media. See 59.16-59.18, 83.10.

59.16 "Interest in Books Flowers Where the Tall Corn Grows." Article-interview by Van Allen Bradley. *Chicago News*, 7 December. Another report on the 4-5 December University of Iowa symposium titled "The Writer in a Mass Culture." Mailer says the writer's task is to "build a bridge across the no man's land of the mass media and reach the serious reader who cannot stand bad books." See 59.15, 59.17, 59.18, 83.10.

59.17 "Critic At-Large: Mailer's Apology." Article-interview by Hoke Norris. *Chicago Sun-Times*, 10 December, Sec. 2, p. 26. Discussion of the University of Iowa symposium at which the film version of *The Naked and the Dead* (48.2) was shown. See 59.15, 59.16, 59.18, 83.10.

59.18 "Eggheads in the Tall Corn." Article by unidentified writer. *Newsweek*, 28 December, 65. Final report on the 4-5 December symposium at the State University of Iowa at which Mailer, Dwight Macdonald, Mark Harris and Ralph Ellison discussed literature and culture. The symposium sessions were moderated by Paul Engle of the university and Arnold Gingrich, editor-publisher of *Esquire*. Mailer said that the totalitarian threats of the 1930s were less terrifying than the current "conformity, monotony and boredom." See 59.15-59.17, 83.10.

59.19 "Is Modern Man Meaningless." Article by Mary Perot Nichols. *Village Voice*, 30 December, 1, 3. Report on an 18 December symposium at Judson Memorial Church, New York City, sponsored by *Dissent*, titled "Happy Critics and a Rigged Society." Joining Mailer on the panel were Judson pastor Rev. Howard R. Moody, Rev. Stephen Chinlund, Irving Howe and Harold Rosenberg, all of whom are quoted.

60.1 "A Program for the Nation." *Dissent* 7 (winter), 67-70. Symposium contribution. Consists of five suggestions for debate in the 1960 presidential campaign, written "at the very beginning of 1960" in response to an *Esquire* questionnaire, but sent instead to *Dissent*. Rpt: 63.37 in a slightly abridged form. Mailer says in "Appendix B—Projects and Places" that it was "written at two or three in the morning in February 1959."

60.2 "'Angry Americans' Air Dissent on British TV." Article by William Harcourt, Reuters News Service correspondent. *Washington Post*, 28 January. Report on British television program produced by Kenneth Tynan and featuring the following American "dissenters": C. Wright Mills, John Kenneth Galbraith, Robert Hutchins, Mailer, Mort Sahl, Jules Feiffer, Allen Ginsberg, Alger Hiss, Alexander King and Norman Thomas. Mailer derided the "boring, cancerous state of American life."

60.3 "The Shiny Enemies." Letter to the editor. *Nation*, 30 January, inside front cover. Friendly response, with one sharp correction, to Gore Vidal's 2 January review of *Advertisements for Myself* (59.13). Vidal's review is reprinted in his collection, *United States: Essays, 1952-1992* (New York: Random House, 1993).

60.4 "Excerpts from 'The Deer Park'" [scene 2, extracts from scenes 3 and 4, scenes 7, 10, 11]. In *The Beats*, edited by Seymour Krim, 169-201. Greenwich, Conn.: Fawcett, March. Mailer restructured the play for its off-Broadway production in 1967. The script was published that year as *The Deer Park: A Play* (67.13). Rpt: Scenes 2, 3, 4 in 59.13; scenes 7 and 10 in 59.11. See 57.2.

60.5 "Brooklyn Minority Report: 'She Thought the Russians Was Coming.'" *Esquire*, June, 129, 137. Essay on juvenile delinquency. Rpt: *Dissent* 8 (summer 1961), 408-12; 63.37 (without first half of title, which was *Esquire's*, not Mailer's).

60.6 "Norman Mailer Cleared: Not Drunk." Article by J.H. Cummings. *New York Post*, 23 June. Mailer is quoted in this report on his court appearance and exoneration on a drunk charge. See 60.7, 60.8.

60.7 "A Letter from Provincetown." *New York Post Magazine*, 3 July, 5. Letter of approximately 1,000 words correcting and commenting on J.H. Cummings's 23 June *Post* story (see 60.6) concerning Mailer's arrest, trial and acquittal for drunkenness in Provincetown. See 60.8.

60.8 "Massachusetts vs. Mailer." Article by Dwight Macdonald. *New Yorker*, 8 October, 154, 156, 158, 160-66. Another account of Mailer's brush with the Provincetown police. Rpt: *Norman Mailer: The Man and His Work,* edited by Robert F. Lucid. Boston: Little, Brown, 1971; and Macdonald's collection, *Discriminations: Essays and Afterthoughts.* Introduction by Norman Mailer. New York: Grossman, 1985. Macdonald restored the original conclusion excised by the *New Yorker* in the first, 1974 edition of *Discriminations.* See 60.6, 60.7, 83.57.

60.9 "Superman Comes to the Supermart." *Esquire,* November, 119-27. Nonfiction narrative on the 1960 Democratic Convention and presidential candidate John F. Kennedy. This narrative, which was written in July-August 1960 in Provincetown and appeared just before the 1960 election, is the first of Mailer's reports on American political conventions and an early, important precursor to the New Journalism. Mailer's portrait of J.F.K. was his first and one of the first of his series of profiles of American politicians, athletes, movie stars, and writers. He has also written about the conventions of 1964 (64.20), 1968 (68.25), 1972 (72.17), 1992 (92.9) and 1996 (96.8). Rpt: As "Superman Comes to the Supermarket" (Mailer's original title) in 63.37, 68.11, 76.5, with some trimming of the brief, italic headlines preceding each section of the narrative. These were written by an *Esquire* editor. Mailer complained of the title change in a letter to the editor (61.1). *Esquire* used "supermarket" when it reprinted the piece in *Smiling though the Apocalypse: Esquire's History of the Sixties,* edited by Harold Hayes. New York: McCall, 1970. But when an excerpt was reprinted in the "Fiftieth Anniversary Collector's Issue," *Esquire: How We Lived, 1933-1983* (June 1983), it was titled "Enter Prince Jack"; 98.7 (partial). See 65.3.

60.10 "Norman Mailer in Tiff." Article by unidentified writer. *New York Times,* 15 November, 28. Report on Mailer's arrest at a New York night club, Birdland, after the manager refused to accept his credit card. See 60.12.

60.11 "Norman Mailer Sent to Bellevue over His Protest in Wife Knifing." Article by Jack Roth. *New York Times,* 23 November, 26. Committed to Bellevue Hospital on 22 November after being charged with the 20 November stabbing of his wife, Adele, Mailer protested, and is quoted on why he should not be sent there. He was released on 9 December. See 61.20, 91.38 and "The Shadow of the Crime: A Word from the Author" in 98.7.

60.12 "Birdland Head Drops Charge against Mailer." Article by unidentified writer. *New York Post,* 20 December, 9. Mailer is quoted briefly in this account over a bar tab dispute. See 60.10.

SEX
SUICIDE
HOMOSEXUALITY
SPORTSWRITING
JEWS
NEGROES
JAZZ
GENIUS
INSANITY
NEW YORK:
  THE LITER
  LOWER DE

by
Seymour
Krim

VIEWS OF A NEARSIGHTED CANNONEER

Foreword by Norman Mailer $1.45

1961

Photograph by Fred W.
McDarrah
61.23

61.1 "A Farewell to His Honor." Letter to the editor. *Esquire*, January, 15. Complaint about *Esquire* editors changing the title of 60.9, the use of an old, unflattering, photograph of Mailer, and the "intercalated small headlines" in 60.9.

61.2 "Objectivity." Letter to the editor. *Time*, 20 January, 6. Mailer responds to *Time*'s comment (2 January) that he is a "cop hater" by noting it is "too small a role," but that being a cop lover is "cancer gulch."

61.3 "An Interview with Norman Mailer." By Eve Auchincloss and Nancy Lynch. *Mademoiselle*, February, 76, 160-63. Discussion of existentialism and "The White Negro" (57.1), with short comments on Presidents Dwight D. Eisenhower and John F. Kennedy, Jean-Paul Sartre, and William Burroughs. Mailer says: "If you believe that people in their natural state are more beautiful than in their conditioned state, you are optimistic, and you do believe in moral and sexual revolutions." Rpt: 88.6. See 55.1.

61.4 "Angry Young Rebel with a Cause: An Interview with Norman Mailer." By Bruce Cook. *Rogue*, April, 16-18, 76. Comment on various topics, including sex, totalitarianism, writing and his works. Rpt: *The Beat Generation* by Bruce Cook. New York: Scribner's, 1971 (partial).

61.5 "An Open Letter to JFK and Fidel Castro." *Village Voice*, 27 April, 1, 14-15. Rpt: 63.37, where Mailer notes in "Appendix B—Projects and Places"

31

that the letter was submitted to and rejected by *New York Times*, *New York Herald Tribune* and *New York Post*. He also notes that the Castro letter was finished in November 1960 and the J.F.K. letter in April 1961; *Journal for the Protection of All Beings*, no. 1, the "Love-Shot Issue." Published "irregularly" by City Lights Books, San Francisco. The editors, Michael McClure, Lawrence Ferlinghetti and David Meltzer, acknowledge that the letter originally appeared in *Village Voice*; 98.7 (partial, but including comment on the timing of the letter's appearance).

61.6 "The Blacks." Parts 1 and 2. *Village Voice*, 11 May, 11, 14; 18 May, 11, 14-15. Review of Jean Genet's play. Rpt: 63.37 (partial). See 61.7.

61.7 "Mailer to [Lorraine] Hansberry." *Village Voice*, 8 June, 11-12. Reply to Hansberry's 1 June essay in the *Voice* attacking Mailer's review of "The Blacks" (61.6) and his views on blacks.

61.8 "Sex and Censorship in Literature and the Arts." *Playboy*, July, 27-28, 72, 74, 76, 88, 92, 95-99. Symposium contribution. First of many contributions. Rpt: As part of "Petty Notes on Some Sex in America" (66.11, 68.11, partial). See 62.11.

61.9 Letter to the editor. *Village Voice*, 27 July, 4. Reply to 20 July letter of Richard Grossman, who complains of seeing too much in the *Voice* on Mailer, James Baldwin and Seymour Krim.

61.10 "The First Day's Interview." *Paris Review*, no. 26 (summer-fall), 140-53. Self-interview. Mailer followed this piece, his first in *Paris Review*, with two vastly more ambitious self-interviews, "The Metaphysics of the Belly" (63.37 and 66.11) and "The Political Economy of Time" (66.11), and a briefer one, "Mr. Mailer Interviews Himself" (67.16). The first three of these self-interviews were prompted by his interest in the life and work of Pablo Picasso. Rpt: 66.11 (partial), 88.6. See 95.37, 95.38.

61.11 "Gourmandise." *New Yorker*, 16 September, 107. Poem. Mailer's first appearance here. Rpt: 62.3.

61.12 "The Pursuit of Experience: W.J. Weatherby Talks to Norman Mailer." Interview. *Manchester Guardian Weekly*, 28 September, 14. Mailer comments on his war experience, influences on his first three books, and literary style.

61.13 "Living Like Heroes." Interview by Richard Wollheim. *New Statesman*, 29 September, 443-45. Philosophic interview on the morality of violence, Sartre, socialism and Hip. Accompanied by 61.14. Rpt: 88.6 (interview only).

61.14 "To the Lower Classes." *New Statesman*, 29 September, 445. Poem. Accompanied by 61.13. Rpt: 62.3, 63.37 (poem only).

61.15 Untitled postscript to "The Time of Her Time." *Advertisements for Myself*, 418-19. London: Deutsch, October. When Deutsch published the British edition of *Advertisements for Myself* (59.13), the second part of "The

Time of Her Time" (20 of 26 pages) was dropped because, as Mailer notes in his 400-word postscript, it "is the considered opinion of some of the best legal and literary names of the Realm" that "this piece cannot be printed in Britain" without holding up the book's publication. Mailer goes on to challenge British writers to fight against the censorship which hides behind "good taste, caution and the public trust." The full text of the story was restored in Britain in the 1968 Panther softcover edition. See 61.16, 74.19, 98.7.

61.16 "Peter Underwood Meets Norman Mailer." Article-interview. *British Books*, November, 12-13, 15. Account of Mailer's press conference at the offices of his British publisher, André Deutsch, on the occasion of the British publication of *Advertisements for Myself* (59.13). Mailer's comments (mainly paraphrased) deal with American notions of success and the British censorship of a portion of 59.13. See 61.15, 61.17.

61.17 "Young American Rebel: An Interview with Norman Mailer." Article-interview by W.G. Smith. *Books and Bookmen*, November, 28. Another interview derived from Mailer's press conference at the offices of his British publisher, André Deutsch, on the occasion of the British publication of *Advertisements for Myself* (59.13). Comment on British authors Kingsley Amis, Evelyn Waugh, Graham Greene and Joyce Cary, and American authors John O'Hara, James Gould Cozzens, Robert Penn Warren and Allen Drury; the American temper; and 59.13. See 61.16.

61.18 "TV Violence? It's a Sedative, Says Norman Mailer." Interview by David Griffiths. *TV Times* (London), 3 November, 18. Consists of Mailer's answers linked together in short paragraphs, without Griffiths's questions. Mailer assails television for being too "sober" and "serious."

61.19 "Eternities." *New Yorker*, 11 November, 200. Poem. Rpt: 62.3.

61.20 "Mailer's Sentence: Good Behavior." Article by Judy Michaelson. *New York Post*, 13 November, 5. Report on suspended sentence received by Mailer for stabbing his wife Adele with a penknife on 20 November 1960. Asked to comment on the court's action, Mailer said, "I feel singularly inarticulate today." See 60.11.

61.21 "Open Poem to John Fitzgerald Kennedy." *Village Voice*, 23 November, 4. Rpt: *Dissent* 9 (winter 1962), 33-34; 63.37, 68.11.

61.22 "Norman Mailer in Austin." Article-interview by Winston Bode. *Texas Observer*, 15 December, 1, 6. Account of Mailer's visit to University of Texas interspersed with questions and answers concerning politics, civil rights and poetry. Rpt: 88.6.

61.23 Foreword to *Views of a Nearsighted Cannoneer*, by Seymour Krim, 6. New York: Excelsior, softcover. Mailer's first foreword, preface or introduction to a book by another writer. Rpt: New York: E.P. Dutton, 1968 (revised, expanded edition).

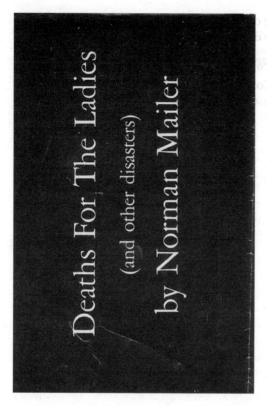

62.3

62.1 "Poems." *Atlantic*, January, 62. Five poems, one titled "Testaments"; the others (untitled) begin: "Men who are not married"; "I know the belly of Mexico"; "Promise? I won't make a promise"; and "Poems written by masochists." Rpt: 62.3.

62.2 "Norman Mailer Speaks His Mind." Interview by Redford MacDougall. *McGill Daily Panorama* (Montreal), 19 January. Brief interview focusing on the hipster, but also containing a long list of writers who have influenced Mailer, and comment on the trial of Adolf Eichmann.

62.3 *Deaths for the Ladies (and Other Disasters).* New York: Putnam's, 30 January; simultaneously as a softcover; London: Deutsch, softcover only. Poems, 252 unnumbered pp., $4. Republished with preface by Mailer. New York: New American Library, December 1971 (71.31). Dedication: "To Jean Campbell." Rpt: In 72.7 and 82.19 (preface only). A number of these poems are reprinted in *The Presidential Papers* (63.37) and *Cannibals and Christians* (66.11); of particular interest is the reprinting of "The Harbors of the Moon" in 63.37, 84.17 and 98.7; and "Togetherness" in 98.7. See 62.5, 62.7, 64.2.

Mailer: "I felt that all of *Deaths for the Ladies* made up one poem, not at all a great poem, never in any way, but still a most modern poem about a man loose in our city, for one cannot talk of New York without saying *our* city, there, majestic, choking in its own passions, New York, the true capital of the Twentieth Century. And *Deaths for the Ladies* was like a small sea breeze running through some of those electronic canyons where a myriad of fine moments were forever dying in the iridescence of foam" (71.31).

62.4 "A Glass of Milk." *Village Voice*, 1 February, 4. Poem. Rpt: 63.37, 68.11.

62.5 The Week in Books. Column by Martha MacGregor. *New York Post Magazine*, 4 March, 11. At the Algonquin Hotel in New York, Mailer discusses his new book of poetry, *Deaths for the Ladies* (62.3). His explanation for the fact that the pages of 62.3 are unnumbered: "I want it to be a bit of a physical experience to read this book. You'll have to do a lot of thumbing to find things. The book will be dog-eared, what every author wants." Only known interview devoted to 62.3.

62.6 "Last Word on Love: Ode to Lady J." *Queen Magazine* (London), April. Poem. According to two gossip columnists, Cholly Knickerbocker in *New York Journal-American* (29 April), and Suzy in *New York Mirror* (30 April), "Lady J" is Lady Jean Campbell, whom Mailer had secretly married shortly before. Rpt: As "Ode to a Lady" in 66.11. See 62.9, 62.10.

62.7 The Man's World. Column by Seymour Krim. *Nugget*, April, 3. In Editorial Director Seymour Krim's column previewing the April issue, Mailer is quoted (92 words) on his recent trip to England and British interest in "hip." He says, "London is now like New York was in 1948." Six of Mailer's poems from 62.3 are reprinted in this issue under the title "Art of the Short Hair: Poetry by Norman Mailer."

62.8 "Poem to the Book Review at *Time*." *Time*, 6 April, 12. Poem-letter written in response to Charles Simmons's 30 March poem-review of 62.3. Rpt: 63.37, 71.31, 72.7, 82.19.

62.9 "Wed to Lady Jean? A Mystery, by Norman Mailer." Article-interview by Fern Marja Eckman and Alfred G. Aronowitz. *New York Post*, 26 April, 4. Mailer confirms reports that he has divorced his second wife, Adele Morales, in Juarez, Mexico, but won't confirm (accurate) reports that he had wed Lady Jean Campbell, daughter of the Earl of Argyll and granddaughter of Lord Beaverbrook. "There's a theory that Jeannie and I both love a mystery," Mailer says, "and that's why we're keeping a firm secret on the little matter—whether we're married or not." See 62.6, 62.10.

62.10 "Norman Mailer Confirms Marriage to Lady Jean." Article by unidentified writer. *New York Times*, 18 May, 62. Mailer says he has been married to Lady Jean Campbell "for some time." See 62.6. 62.9.

62.11 "The Womanization of America." *Playboy*, June, 43-50, 133-34, 136, 139-44. Symposium contribution. Rpt: As part of "Petty Notes on Some Sex in America" in 66.11 and 68.11 (partial). See 61.8.

62.12 "An Evening with Jackie Kennedy: Being an Essay in Three Acts." *Esquire*, July, 56-61. Essay. Rpt: As "The Existential Heroine: An Evening with Jackie Kennedy, or, The Wild West of the East" in 63.37 and (without subtitle) in 68.11; 98.7 (partial). See 83.54.

62.13 "Truth and Being; Nothing and Time: A Broken Fragment from a Long Novel." *Evergreen Review*, no. 26 (September-October), 68-74. Story. Rpt: 63.37, 67.11, 82.19; *Evergreen Review Reader: A Ten Year Anthology, 1962-1967*, Vol. II, edited by Barney Rosset. New York: Grove Press, 1980.

62.14 "The Literate at the Fight." Column by Leonard Shecter. *New York Post*, 25 September, 83. Quotes Mailer's prediction on the first Floyd Patterson-Sonny Liston fight on 25 September: Patterson will "end it with one punch in the sixth." See 62.15-62.17, 63.3.

62.15 "The Big Fight." Column by Red Smith. *New York Herald Tribune*, 27 September. Account of Mailer's exchange with Sonny Liston at Liston's press conference after his knockout victory over Floyd Patterson. See 62.14, 62.16, 62.17, 63.3.

62.16 "Liston and the Author: 'I Can Call You a Bum.'" Article by Stan Isaacs. *Newsday*, 27 September. Another account of Liston's press conference. See 62.14, 62.15, 62.17, 63.3.

62.17 "The Prizefighter and the Author." Article by Leonard Shecter. *New York Post*, 27 September. Still another account of Mailer at Sonny Liston's press conference. See 62.14-62.16, 63.3.

62.18 The Big Bite. *Esquire*, November, 134. First of a series of 14 monthly columns (November 1962-December 1963). Comment on the passing of Marilyn Monroe and Ernest Hemingway. Rpt: 63.37 (partial). See 62.19, 63.2-63.13.

62.19 The Big Bite. *Esquire*, December, 168. Column, second in a series. Comment on the suicides of the spy, Henry Soblen, and Ernest Hemingway, and on American heroism as manifested by John Glenn. Accompanied by 62.20. Rpt: 63.37 (partial, and without 62.20). See 62.18, 63.2-63.13.

62.20 "Sing the Ballad of the Sad Saint." *Esquire*, December, 169. Poem. Accompanied by 62.19. Rpt: As "The Ride of the Sad Saint" in 66.11 (without 62.19).

62.21 "An Impolite Interview with Norman Mailer." By Paul Krassner. *The Realist*, no. 40 (December), 1, 13-16, 18-23, 10. Rpt: Partial in 63.37, 68.11, 82.16; complete in *Best of "The Realist,"* edited by Paul Krassner. Philadelphia: Running Press, 1984.

62.22 Responses and Reactions I. *Commentary*, December, 504-6. First of a series of six bi-monthly columns (December 1962-October 1963) devoted mainly to commentary on Martin Buber's *Tales of the Hasidim*. Mailer's first appearance in *Commentary*. Rpt: Partial in 63.37, 98.7. See 63.16-63.20.

62.23 "An Open Letter to JFK from Norman Mailer." *Village Voice*, 20 December, 1, 7. Rpt: As "A Second Open Letter to JFK" in 63.37; 68.11.

62.24 Conference Remarks. In Transcript of Proceedings of the 20-24 August International Writers' Conference: "The Novel Today," Edinburgh,

138 pp. Never published, this court stenographer's mimeographed transcript (replete with egregious, humorous, errors) is a fascinating document. Mailer speaks several times, and co-chairs the final day's session, "The Novel and the Future." His interaction with Mary McCarthy, Lawrence Durrell, William Burroughs, and his comments on *Das Kapital* as a novel, deserve to be rescued. See 65.1, 65.13, 81.21, 92.12, 96.7.

1963

Dustwrapper photograph
by Lester L. Krauss
63.37

63.1 "Punching Papa." *New York Review of Books* (special issue, winter), 13. Review of *That Summer in Paris*, by Morley Callaghan. This inaugural issue, containing the first of many contributions by Mailer, probably appeared in February. Rpt: 66.11, 98.7 (partial), and in *Selections from the First Two Issues of The New York Review of Books* (Winter, Spring 1963), edited by Robert B. Silvers and Barbara Epstein. New York: New York Review of Books, 1988.

63.2-63.13 The Big Bite. Monthly column. *Esquire* (November 1962-December 1963). In February and July, Mailer wrote much longer pieces and dropped the column title. See 62.18, 62.19.

63.2 January, 65. Comment on television, the astronauts and totalitarianism. Rpt: 63.37 (partial).

63.3 February, 109-20. "Ten Thousand Words a Minute." Account of the first Floyd Patterson-Sonny Liston fight. Mailer also comments on his 22 October 1962 debate with William F. Buckley Jr. One of Mailer's most anthologized essays. Rpt: 63.37, 98.7 (partial). See 62.14-62.17, 63.15.

63.4 March, 98, 139. Comment on American journalism, the Kennedys and U.S. policy toward Cuba. Rpt: partial in 63.37 and 68.11.

63.5 April, 74, 138. Meditation on the coming of spring, fear, apathy and the possibility of war with Russia. Rpt: partial in 63.37 and 68.11.

63.6 May, 37, 40. Comment on the coming "architectural plague." Rpt: 63.37 (partial).

63.7 June, 23-24, 28, 32. Important remarks on the decline of the novel, including specific comment on Gore Vidal, Vance Bourjaily, Ernest Hemingway, William Faulkner and Feodor Dostoyevsky. Rpt: As the first part of "Some Children of the Goddess" (with a few minor changes) in 66.11.

63.8 "Some Children of the Goddess: Further Evaluations of the Talent in the Room." July, 63-69, 105. This long essay of literary criticism is titled "Norman Mailer versus Nine Writers" on the table of contents page. The nine, in order of Mailer's consideration, are William Styron, James Jones, James Baldwin, William Burroughs, Joseph Heller, John Updike, Philip Roth, J.D. Salinger and Saul Bellow. Mailer also comments on Vance Bourjaily. The essay's subtitle links it with his 1959 essay (59.10) on 17 writers, including Jones, Styron, Bellow and Baldwin. One of Mailer's finest critical pieces. Calder Willingham responded in "The Way It Isn't Done: Notes on the Distress of Norman Mailer, *Esquire*, December. Rpt: *Contemporary American Novelists*, edited by Harry T. Moore. Carbondale: Southern Illinois University Press, October; as the second part of "Some Children of the Goddess" (preceded by 63.7) in 66.11.

63.9 August, 16, 18, 21, 24. An essay on American totalitarianism. Rpt: 63.37, 64.10.

63.10 September, 16, 18, 20. Comment on Nelson Algren, and violence in America. Rpt: First two-thirds as "A Television Show with Nelson Algren" in 66.11; second two-thirds (minus final two paragraphs) as "Postscript to the Second Presidential Paper" in 63.37 (with a number of small changes). See also 64.11.

63.11 October, 50, 52. Rpt: First third as an untitled introduction to "The Seventh Presidential Paper: On Dread" in 63.37. Mailer fails to note this reprinting in his otherwise careful list of acknowledgments in 63.37, titled "Appendix B—Projects and Places." The remainder of the column, with the exception of the first sentence, is reprinted in 72.7 and 82.19 as "Two Oddments from *Esquire*." In addition, approximately 250 words from the first third are reprinted in the November Big Bite (63.12) as an excerpt from 63.37, which was published on 8 November. It is uncertain whether Mailer was reprinting portions of "Big Bite" in 63.37, or publishing advance excerpts from his miscellany in the column, or both. Whatever the case, the same 250 words on dread, politics and journalism appeared in print three times during October and November. See 90.2.

63.12 November, 26, 28, 30, 32. Comment on J.F.K., Cuba, Jacqueline Kennedy, politics and death. Rpt: First 500 words comment on October column and note that the remainder (approximately 2,500 words) is reprinted from 63.37. This remainder, divided into eight sections, comes from the following pages, in this order, of 63.37: 26-27, 60-61, 64-65, 81-82, 161, 151-52, 214-15, 214.

63.13 December, 22, 24, 26. Comment on the September civil rights march on Washington followed by Mailer's announcement that he will attempt to write a serial novel for *Esquire* over the next eight months. He ends the column: "One is tempted to call this novel *An American Dream*." See 64.2-64.9, 65.7.

63.14 Untitled poem beginning: "One never hears the words intended." *Way Out* (School of Living, Brookville, Ohio) 19 (January), 20.

63.15 "The Real Meaning of the Right Wing in America: Opposing Statements on the Role of the Right Wing in America Today: A Conservative's View by William F. Buckley Jr.; A Liberal's View by Norman Mailer." *Playboy*, January, 110-12, 165-70, 172-74. Statements written for *Playboy* and read as part of a 22 September 1962 public debate in Chicago. Rpt: 63.37, 65.14 (partial), 68.11, 98.7 (partial). See 63.3, 63.22, 63.27.

63.16-63.20 Responses and Reactions I-VI. Bi-monthly column. *Commentary* (December 1962-October 1963). Commentary in first five columns on Martin Buber's *Tales of the Hasidim*. See 62.22.

63.16 February, 146-48. Rpt: 63.37, 67.11 (as "The Locust Cry"), 82.19.

63.17 April, 335-37. Rpt: 63.37, partial in 98.7.

63.18 June, 517-18. Rpt: 63.37, partial in 98.7.

63.19 August, 164-65. Rpt: 66.11, 98.7.

63.20 October, 320-21. Mailer departs from Buber in his final column for *Commentary* and discusses the minority status of Jews and Negroes. Rpt: Except for introductory paragraph, this column comprises the bulk of the untitled preface to "The Tenth Presidential Paper— Minorities" in 63.37; and in *The Idol and the Octopus* (68.11), where it is partially reprinted in two sub-chapters, "On Minorities" and "Action for Minorities."

63.21 "Smog Doggerel for the Haze"; "Static." *Way Out* (School of Living, Brookville, Ohio) 19 (February), 49-50. Poems. This issue also contains "An Open Letter to Norman Mailer" by Robert Anton Wilson, 51-57, in which Wilson quotes from an earlier letter from Mailer asking Wilson to "expand your remarks on entropy." Rpt: 66.11 ("Static" only).

63.22 "The Role of the Right Wing: A Debate." *Playboy*, February, 115-16, 119-22. Transcript of a debate with William F. Buckley Jr. in Chicago on 22 September 1962, moderated by Irv Kupcinet. Debate opened with Mailer and Buckley reading statements. See 63.15.

63.23 "Classes." *New Statesman*, 8 February, 207. Poem. Rpt: 63.37.

63.24 "The Hipster and the American Right." Interview by unidentified interviewer. *Phoenix* (University of Chicago), spring, 4-5. Focuses on alienation with long answer on the distinction between the psychopath and the psychotic.

63.25 Untitled poem beginning: "The most eligible bachelor in London." *Harvard Advocate* 97 (spring), 47. Rpt: 66.11.

63.26 "Norman Mailer Returns to Read, Philosophize on Existential Life." Article by Paul S. Cowan. *Harvard Crimson*, 25 March, 1. Account of Mailer's 24 March appearance at Harvard at which he discussed existentialism and psychoanalysis: "I am profoundly cynical about psychoanalysis."

63.27 "Reading from Left to Right." Letter to the editor. *Playboy*, April, 8. Complaint about being labeled a liberal in his January debate with William F. Buckley Jr. in *Playboy* (63.15). Mailer's letter is notable for his description of himself, perhaps for the first time, as a "left conservative."

63.28 "Norman Mailer: The Conservative Leftist." Interview by Jan Henry. *Brooklyn Heights Press*, 30 May, 1, 3. Mailer describes himself as a "Left Existential Conservative" and discusses *Deaths for the Ladies* (62.3) and the book he is working on: "Frankie and Johnny: The Presidential Papers of Norman Mailer" (63.37).

63.29 "The Novelist Comes to Carnegie Hall." Article-interview by Millicent Brower. *Village Voice*, 30 May, 1, 6-7, 18. On the eve of his reading at Carnegie Hall, Mailer discusses his desire to deliver "an existential evening."

63.30 "Carnegie Hall Audience Listens to Norman Mailer's Thoughts." Article by Brian O'Doherty. *New York Times*, 1 June, 15. Account of Mailer's reading at Carnegie Hall on 31 May, with quotes dealing with the FBI, Communism and J.F.K. See 63.31.

63.31 "Existential Leader or Just Another Reader?" Article by Darryl Henriques. *Brooklyn Heights Press*, 6 June, 1, 2. A more extensive account of Mailer's 31 May reading at Carnegie Hall than 63.30.

63.32 "The First Presidential Paper." *Dissent* 10 (summer), 249-54. Rpt: As the introduction to *The Presidential Papers* (63.37), titled "A Prefatory Paper—Heroes and Leaders," with several minor changes including the addition of a list of 34 of the miscellany's topics.

63.33 "Antidote." No Author. *Harper's Bazaar*, July, 74-75. Questionnaire seeking the negative opinions, or "anathemas of five noted Americans," on 13 various artistic categories and activities: play, book, painter, food, film, musical work, celebrity, activity, virtue, place, mental attitude, type of humor and "Anti-dote in a category of my own." Participating are Theodore Roethke, Mailer, Marianne Moore, Orson Bean and Jules Feiffer. Mailer says: "The worst celebrity in America is of course J. Edgar Hoover," a comment that caused this article to be placed in his FBI file.

63.34 "The Talent and the Torment." Article-interview by Frederick Christian. *Cosmopolitan*, August, 63-67. Sketchy and sensationalized overview of Mailer's personal and literary life; contains accounts of several meetings with Mailer during the period he lived in Connecticut, and a 1963 interview in which Mailer discusses his involvement with the Actors' Studio in New York. A letter to Christian from Mailer's Harvard professor, Theodore Morrison, is quoted.

63.35 "The Leading Man, or the Dark Ambiguities within Us All." *Book Week* (*New York Herald Tribune*), 29 September, 1, 16- 17. Review of *J.F.K.:*

The Man and the Myth, by Victor Lasky. Rpt: 66.11, 68.11.

63.36 "The Mary McCarthy Case." *New York Review of Books*, 17 October, 1-3. Review of *The Group*, by Mary McCarthy. Perhaps Mailer's finest book review. Rpt: As "The Case Against McCarthy" in 66.11.

63.37 *The Presidential Papers.* New York: Putnam's, 8 November. London: Deutsch, late April or early May 1964, with new preface (same as Bantam edition). Miscellany, 310 pp. Republished with "Special Preface" by Mailer. New York: Bantam, May 1964 (64.15); republished with new preface by Mailer. New York: Berkley, October 1976 (76.13). Dedication: "This book is dedicated to some ladies who have aided and impeded the author in his composition. They are: Beverly Rentz Sugarfoot Bentley; Jean Louise Slugger Campbell; my daughters: Susan, Dandy, Betsy, Kate; my adopted daughter: Jeanne H.W. the Invaluable Johnson; my secretary: Anne Morse Towel-Boy Barry; my sister: Barbara Jane Alson; and Sadie, and Hetty Diggs, and Every-Mae." Discarded titles: *The Devil Revisited, Frankie and Johnny.* Mailer gives dates and details of composition for the volume's contents in "Appendix B—Projects and Places." Rpt: Several selections appear in truncated form in 98.7. See 1963 entries.

Mailer: "Its anxiety is its anxiety, and its half-satisfied ambition is very much its throttled ambition, but for anyone who would like a clue to the mood of the country in the summer of 1963 just before that autumn of assassination which would change the psychic history of America forever, the book is a document. Besides—I whisper it—*The Presidential Papers* does have a couple of the better pieces I've written" (76.13).

63.38 "The Fate of the Union: Kennedy and After." *New York Review of Books*, 26 December, 6. Symposium contribution. This 175-word tribute is echoed, in part, by Mailer's "Special Preface to Bantam Edition" of *The Presidential Papers*, May 1964 (64.15). Rpt: *A Tribute to John F. Kennedy*, edited by Pierre Salinger and Sander Vanocur. Chicago: Encyclopedia Britannica, 1964. See 76.13.

63.39 "The Last Night." *Esquire*, December, 151, 274-80. Story. The concluding piece in *Cannibals and Christians* (66.11), Mailer's nuclear fantasy has been reworked into an unpublished screenplay by Mailer and his wife Norris Church. Rpt: 67.11, 82.19, 84.35.

63.40 Letters to Myrick Land. In "Mr. Norman Mailer Challenges All the Talent in the Room," *The Fine Art of Literary Mayhem: A Lively Account of Famous Writers and Their Feuds*, by Myrick Land, 216-38. New York: Holt, Rinehart and Winston. Chapter recapitulating "Quick and Expensive Comments on the Talent in the Room" (59.10), followed by rejoinders from Mailer and some of those he appraised in the original essay: Chandler Brossard, Herbert Gold, William Styron, Gore Vidal and Vance Bourjaily. The revised second edition (San Francisco: Lexikos, 1983) contains a 1982 postscript with valedictory comments from Mailer, Bourjaily and Gold, 228-44. See also "Appendix A—Professional Mendacity" in 63.37 where Mailer criticizes the 18 January *Time* review of Land's book.

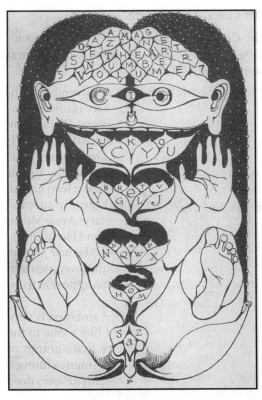

Drawing by Robert LaVigne
64.18

64.1 "Norman Mailer: The Art of Fiction XXXII." Interview by Steven Marcus. *Paris Review*, no. 31 (winter-spring), 28-58. Omnibus interview, one of Mailer's most important, conducted 6 July 1963. Rpt: *Writers at Work: The "Paris Review" Interviews*, edited by Alfred Kazin. 3rd ser. New York: Viking, 1967; *Norman Mailer: A Collection of Critical Essays*, edited by Leo Braudy. Englewood Cliffs, N.J.: Prentice-Hall, 1972; partial in 66.11, 82.16 (where it appears as "Craft and Consciousness"); complete in 88.6.

64.2-64.9 *An American Dream*. Eight-part serialization. *Esquire* (January-August). Rpt: 65.7 (revised). See 65.3, 63.13, 83.6, 88.5.

64.2 "An American Dream: A New Novel Serialized Exclusively in *Esquire* by Norman Mailer; Installment One: The Harbors of the Moon." *Esquire*, January, 77-81, 131-32. Mailer took the title of this chapter from a poem about Provincetown in 62.3; he then reprinted the poem after his preface to the Franklin Library edition of *Tough Guys Don't Dance* (84.17); and again as the final selection of *Time of Our Time* (98.7). See 64.9.

64.3 "Installment Two: A Messenger from the Casino." *Esquire*, February, 107, 109, 111-12, 114. Title changed to "A Runner from the Gaming Room" in 65.7. A summary by *Esquire* editors of the first installment is found on 125.

64.4 "Installment Three: A Messenger from the Maniac." *Esquire*, March,

89-92, 144-50. A summary by *Esquire* editors of the first two installments is found on 143.

64.5 "Installment Four: Green Circles of Exhaustion." *Esquire*, April, 97-100, 146-48. A summary by *Esquire* editors of the first three installments is found on 154. Rpt: *Dial Souvenir Sampler, 1964*. New York: Dial (mistitled as chapter 2).

64.6 "Installment Five: A Catenary of Manners." *Esquire*, May, 124-27, 143-44, 146-52. A summary by *Esquire* editors of the first four installments is found on 158. The summary concludes with the line, "The Dial Press will publish *An American Dream* in August." Dial did publish the novel, but not until the following March. The 12 October *Publishers' Weekly* contains an advertisement for the novel and gives a January publication date.

64.7 "Installment Six: A Vision in the Desert." *Esquire*, June, 114-16, 148-49. The installment is followed by a note which ends, "The Dial Press will publish *An American Dream* in the fall."

64.8 "Installment Seven: A Votive is Prepared." *Esquire*, July, 41-42, 44, 105-8. The installment is followed by the same line as in 64.7.

64.9 "Installment VIII: At the Lion and the Serpent." *Esquire*, August, 41-43, 94, 96, 98, 100-108. The installment is followed by this note: "This concludes *An American Dream*. Dial Press will publish it in hardcover form this fall." In the novel's final version, the concluding (and revised) portion of 64.9 is broken off as "Epilogue: The Harbors of the Moon Again." See 64.2, 65.7.

64.10 "Mailer vs. Scully." *Architectural Forum*, April, 96-97. Debate on modern architecture with Vincent J. Scully Jr., Professor of Art History at Yale, in three parts: 1) excerpts from Mailer's August 1963 "Big Bite" column (63.9); 2) Scully's response, which appeared almost simultaneously in the *Village Voice* on 16 April; 3) Mailer's rebuttal, which appears here for the first time. The editors of *Architectural Forum* state that the first part of Mailer's contribution is a condensation of two of Mailer's *Esquire* columns. This is not the case; all of the first part is from the August 1963 column. A final note: Mailer has published one section of this column five times. It represents his polemical style at its best: "The essence of totalitarianism is that it beheads. It beheads individuality, variety, dissent, extreme possibility, romantic faith; it blinds vision, deadens instinct; it obliterates the past." Rpt: Rebuttal only, slightly revised in 64.16 and 64.17; partial in 66.11 and 68.11.

64.11 Untitled announcement. In "Backstage with Esquire," *Esquire*, April, 40. Mailer announces the five winners ($5 apiece) of his essay contest, announced in his September 1963 Big Bite column (63.10): "Why I am not now and never have been a member of the Federal Bureau of Investigation."

64.12 "The Killer." *Evergreen Review*, no. 32 (April-May), 26-27, 86. Story. Rpt: 66.11 (mistitled "The Killing" in acknowledgments), 67.11, 82.19.

64.13 "A Conversation with Mailer." Article-interview by Gavin Young. *Observer Weekly*, 26 April, 26. In the midst of writing installments of *An American Dream* for *Esquire* (64.2-64.9), Mailer meets with an English journalist to discuss the project.

64.14 "Greasing the Radar"; "A Study of Cancer in English Grammar." *Cleft* (Edinburgh) 2 (May), 8-9. Poems. Mailer may have published one or more poems in an earlier issue of *Cleft*.

64.15 "Special Preface to the Bantam Edition." *The Presidential Papers.* New York: Bantam, May, softcover, v-vii. Foreshadowed by Mailer's contribution to "The Fate of the Union: Kennedy and After" (63.38). Same preface appears in the first British edition (63.37). The first American edition of 63.37 has a jacket photograph of Mailer in a J.F.K.-style rocker. The same picture is used on the cover of the Bantam edition, but the photograph has been altered to remove the rockers. Rpt: 76.13.

64.16 "Architects: Blindness Is the Fruit of Your Design." *Village Voice*, 18 June, 5. Essay consisting of part three of 64.10, slightly revised. The *Village Voice* editors note that when Vincent Scully was offered the last word in this debate on modern architecture, he said, "I feel that I have had the last word already." Rpt: 64.17; and partial in 66.11 and 68.11.

64.17 "Gargoyle, Guignol, False Closet." Dublin: Dolmen Press, July, 2 pp. pamphlet. Limited edition of 100. Essay, consisting of the rebuttal portion (part three) of 64.10, slightly revised. Rpt: 64.16, partial in 66.11 and 68.11.

64.18 "The Executioner's Song." *Fuck You/A Magazine of the Arts* 7 (no. 5), September [23-25]. Poem. The magazine, 83 pages, is reproduced typescript on sheets of various colors, unbound, stapled. Edited by Ed Sanders (founder of "The Fugs," described in 68.8), it contains poems by Allen Ginsberg, Robert Creely, William Burroughs, Charles Olson, Michael McClure, Judith Malina, Gary Snyder and several others. Mailer later used the poem's title for chapter 15 of *The Fight* (75.12), and for *The Executioner's Song* (79.14). Rpt: 66.11 (with slight changes and mistitled "The Executioners" in acknowledgments).

64.19 "A Vote for Bobby K.—Possibility of a Hero." *Village Voice*, 29 October, 4, 10. Essay. Rpt: 66.11, 68.11.

64.20 "In the Red Light: A History of the Republican Convention in 1964." *Esquire*, November, 83-89, 167-72, 174-77, 179. Nonfiction narrative. Rpt: 65.14 (partial), 66.11, 68.11, 76.5.

64.21 "The Best Man, 1964: To Pick Him, We Must Choose between Nostalgic Extremism and Overwhelming Moderation." *Book Week* (*New York Herald Tribune*), 1 November, 1, 7-8. Review of *My Hope for America*, by Lyndon B. Johnson. The second half of the review's title is most likely the work of the editors of *Book Week*, according to Mailer. Rpt: 65.14 (partial), 66.11, 68.11, 98.7.

64.22 "Talking of Violence." Interview by W.J. Weatherby. *Twentieth Century* 173 (winter 1964-65), 109-14. Rpt: 82.16 (partial).

64.23 Letter to Pierre Brodin. In *Présences: Contemporaines Écrivains Américains D'Aujourd'hui*, by Pierre Brodin, 205. Paris: Les Nouvelles Éditions Debresse. Mailer answers Brodin's query about his favorite French novels by saying that "the French novel has always been more congenial to me than the English, and much of what I learned as a young novelist came from Stendhal, from [Marcel] Proust, and from [André] Malraux." He goes on to mention others: Gustave Flaubert, Emile Zola, André Gide, J.K. Huysmans, Charles Baudelaire, Jean-Paul Sartre and Georges Simenon, and "the largest single personal influence on my intellectual life has been my dear and old friend, Jean Malaquais." Mailer's letter is included in an appendix to this study of American writers.

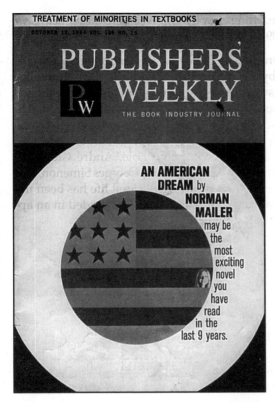

TREATMENT OF MINORITIES IN TEXTBOOKS

OCTOBER 12, 1964 VOL. 186 NO. 15

PUBLISHERS'
P̲ᵂ WEEKLY
THE BOOK INDUSTRY JOURNAL

AN AMERICAN
DREAM by
NORMAN
MAILER
may be
the
most
exciting
novel
you
have
read
in the
last 9 years.

See 65.7

65.1 "Defenders of 'Naked Lunch' Compare Burroughs to Authors of Classics." Article by Joseph M. Harvey. *Boston Globe*, 13 January, 14. Report on the obscenity trial of William Burroughs in Suffolk County Superior Court, Boston. Beside Mailer, John Ciardi, Paul Hollander, Gabrielle Bernhard, Norman H. Holland, Dr. Stanley Eldred and Dr. John Barry Sturrock testified. Mailer extolled the novel as "marvelously well-written" and Burroughs as "possibly the most talented writer in America." See 62.24, 65.13, 81.21, 92.12, 96.7.

65.2 "Cities Higher than Mountains." *New York Times Magazine*, 31 January, 16-17, 30, 32-33, 40. Essay, the first of several in the *Times*. Accompanied by a photograph of Mailer's seven-foot high "Vertical City," which he and two friends assembled with Lego Blocks. Rpt: In a revised form in *Cannibals and Christians* (66.11), the dustwrapper of which depicts "Vertical City"; same color photograph is tipped in opposite title page of first edition, first issue only. A photograph is printed in later issues and editions. See 98.5.

65.3 "Norman Mailer's 'American Dream': Superman Returns." Interview by Nancy Weber. *Books*, March, 14-16. Comment on the forthcoming *An American Dream* (65.7), including preliminary remarks from Mann Rubin, who wrote the screenplay for the movie version. Mailer speculates on whether Frank Sinatra could play Stephen Rojack; discusses the possibility of writing sequels to the novel in the manner of Lawrence Durrell's *Alexandria Quartet*; discusses the *Esquire* and book versions; comments on J.F.K. and the roots of the novel in "Superman Comes to the Supermarket" (60.9); makes passing reference to a number of writers—Saul Bellow, Michael McClure, Claude Brown, LeRoi Jones, Edward Albee, Nelson Algren, William Styron, James Jones and Marcel Proust; and recites a poem on Rojack: "He's a pretty good man/with fairly good guts/reasonably decent/not at all unintelligent/and sensitive/and kind of nice/and very aware/who finally discovers with it all/that it's just not enough/there must be bravery or will or/genius." The interview also includes two excerpts from the novel, the first to be published. See 83.6.

65.4 "Authors Discuss Sick Book Trend." Article by Harry Gilroy. *New York Times*, 11 March, 30. Mailer, attending a National Book Awards news conference, is quoted on obscenity and morality in the novel, with comments on Saul Bellow. See 65.6, 65.8, 65.10.

65.5 In and out of Books. Column by Lewis Nichols. *New York Times Book Review*, 14 March, 8. Mailer is quoted on why Dial Press published *An American Dream* (65.7) instead of his regular publisher, Putnam's. Concerned that the pressure of writing the novel for monthly serialization in *Esquire* (see 64.2-64.9) might affect its quality, Mailer concluded that it could "be very good, good, bad or very bad indeed, and there would be a lot more pressure on me if I were doing it for a pal [Walter Minton, Putnam's president]. Let a stranger [Richard Baron of Dial] take a bath."

65.6 The Week in Books. Column by Martha MacGregor. *New York Post*, 14 March, 47. Includes quotes from Mailer's question-and-answer session with reporters at the National Book Awards ceremony, including comment on the winning novel, Saul Bellow's *Herzog* : "There is something Russian about *Herzog* in its depth of feeling. There are plenty of faults, but my heart was literally burning as I read." See 65.4, 65.8, 65.10.

65.7 *An American Dream*. New York: Dial, 15 March. London: Deutsch, 26 April. Novel, 270 pp., $4.95. Dedication and acknowledgment: "To Beverly and to Michael Burks; an appreciation to Anne Barry, Richard Baron, Walter Minton, Harold Hayes, Donald Fine *and not least*, Scott Meredith." Mailer's fourth wife, Beverly Bentley, is the woman pictured on the dustwrapper of the first edition. Rpt: First appeared, in a different form, in *Esquire*, January-August 1964 (64.2-64.9); partial in 98.7. See 63.13, 65.3, 65.5, 65.9, 65.11, 70.4, 70.14, 83.6.

Mailer: "It's a novel of suspense, not of intellectual action. I wanted an intellectual for a hero who was engaged in 32 hours of continuous action and so did not have time to cerebrate. But the only idea in *An American Dream* (it is the idea which I think makes the book so repellent to some reviewers) is that love is the one human condition we never capture without paying an extraordinary and continuing price. This is certainly not a new idea. But it is desperately out of fashion now, and besides—I did my best to pose this lone idea in as vivid and unendurable a manner as possible" (65.11).

48

65.8 "'Four Years Ago My Life Went Out of Control.'" Article by George Troy. *Providence Journal*, 21 March. Another account of Mailer's session with reporters at the National Book Awards ceremony. See 65.4, 65.6, 65.10.

65.9 "A Small Public Notice by Norman Mailer." *Partisan Review* 32 (spring), 180-81. Paid advertisement consisting of a brief statement by Mailer prefacing a reprinting of the heart of John W. Aldridge's 19 March *Life* review of 65.7, to "accompany" Elizabeth Hardwick's negative review in the same number of *Partisan Review*.

65.10 "PPA Press Conference." *Publishers' Weekly*, 22 March, 41-45. Account of a series of press conferences with authors of new books during National Book Awards Week. Mailer's comments deal with the "moral nihilists' wing" of current writers, including himself, William Burroughs, Allen Ginsberg and Terry Southern. He also comments on his new novel, 65.7. Another comment from Mailer, on Saul Bellow's *Herzog*, is quoted on 30-31. See 65.4, 65.6, 65.8.

65.11 "Norman Mailer on *An American Dream*." Interview by unidentified interviewer. *New York Post*, 25 March, 38. Comment on the novel (65.7) and its reviews. Rpt: 88.6.

65.12 "'Viet Nam Day'—Few Surprises: The Theme Was 'Hate America.'" Article by unidentified writer. *Tocsin: The West's Leading Anti-Communist Weekly* (Oakland, Cal.), 6 (no. 20) 27 May, 1, 3. Report on the May 21-22 Vietnam protest meetings at the University of California, Berkeley, including quotes from the speeches of Dick Gregory, I.F. Stone and Mailer, who says, "We are a property-loving nation, obsessed with the desire to destroy other people's property." See 65.14, 65.18.

65.13 "The Boston Trial of *Naked Lunch*." *Evergreen Review*, no. 36 (June), 40-44, 46-49, 86-88. Court testimony of Mailer and Allen Ginsberg opposing the suppression of William Burroughs's novel. Rpt: As "Excerpts from the Boston Trial of *Naked Lunch*" in *Naked Lunch*. New York: Grove Press, 1966 (softcover edition). See 62.24, 65.1, 81.21, 92.12, 96.7.

65.14 "Norman Mailer on LBJ." *Realist*, no. 60 (June), 1, 10-15. Transcription of speech given on 21 May (Vietnam Day) on the Berkeley campus of the University of California. In an accompanying "Author's Note," Mailer states that portions of the speech were taken from "my article on the Republican Convention printed in *Esquire* in November 1964 [64.20]...from a review I did in the *New York Herald Tribune* on Lyndon Johnson's book *My Hope for America* [64.21]....[and] a fragment from a debate in Chicago with William Buckley [63.15]." The final line of *Why Are We in Vietnam?* (67.15)—"Vietnam. Hot dam [sic]"—is used in the essay as a way of describing L.B.J.'s relief and excitement at finding an issue to shift the country's attention from the civil rights movement, except that Mailer reverses the order: "Hot Damn. Viet Nam." Rpt: *Peace News* (London) no. 1522 (27 August), 5-8; with an additional introductory paragraph (in which he refers to himself as a "left conservative") in *We Accuse*, edited by James

Petras. Berkeley: Diablo Press, September; as "A Speech at Berkeley on Vietnam Day" in 66.11 and 68.11; partial in 98.7. See 65.12, 65.18.

65.15 "2,000 Hear 'Teachers-In' Demand LBJ Resignations." Article by W.J. McCarthy. *Boston Herald*, 15 July, Sec. C, p. 44. Report on a Harvard teach-in organized by Martin Peretz, Harvard instructor, at which Mailer, Staughton Lynd and others spoke against U.S. policy in South Vietnam. Mailer: "A future death of the spirit lies close and heavy upon American life." See 65.16.

65.16 "President Assailed by Norman Mailer." Article by unidentified writer. *New York Times*, 16 July, 17. Another report on the Harvard teach-in at which Mailer said that L.B.J. "is the expression of the near-insanity of most of us, and his need for action is America's need for action." See 65.15.

65.17 "Clay, Mailer in 'Draw.'" Article-interview by Robert Friedman. *Sunday San Juan Star*, 1 August, 1, 12. Mailer arm wrestles Muhammad Ali and comments on the "vitality" of Puerto Rican culture and the Spanish "tragic view of life" during a visit to San Juan to attend a José Torres-Tom Mc Neeley boxing match.

65.18 "Distorted Vision of Mailer." Article by unidentified writer. *Tocsin: The Weekly Intelligence Report* 6 (25 or 26 August), 2. A second report (see 65.12; note change in publication's name) on Mailer's 21 May speech at the University of California, Berkeley, including Mailer's call to publish upside-down photographs of President Johnson in protest against the Vietnam War. See 65.14.

65.19 "On Vietnam." *Partisan Review* 32 (fall), 638-39, 641-43, 645-46. Essay written in response to "Statement by the Editors of *Partisan Review*" on Vietnam and the Dominican Republic in the summer number. Mailer is one of 14 to respond. Rpt: As "A Happy Solution to Vietnam: From a *Partisan Review* Symposium" in 66.11 and 68.11. "Mailer's Reply," which follows a reprinting of the editor's statement, prefigures his argument against the war in *The Armies of the Night* (68.8).

65.20 "In This Corner, Norman Mailer: Never the Champion, Always the Challenger." Article by Brock Brower. *Life*, 24 September, 94-96, 98, 100, 102, 105-6, 109-12, 115, 117. First major biographical article on Mailer, who is quoted throughout, as are his family, friends and contemporaries. Rpt: As "Norman" in Brower's collection, *Other Loyalties: A Politics of Personality*. New York: Atheneum, 1968. Reprint concludes with "The Updating," which quotes from Mailer's telegrams of displeasure ("your piece...gelded the strongest remarks, and bypassed the work") about the article and Brower's subsequent reflections. See 65.21, 79.9.

65.21 "Always the Challenger." Letter to the editor. *Life*, 15 October, 34. Complaint about being misquoted in 65.20 concerning the purported excision of profanity in *The Naked and the Dead* (48.2). See 49.3, 68.31, 92.12, 95.53.

65.22 "Norman Mailer on Lindsay and the City." *Village Voice*, 28 October, 1, 10. Essay endorsing John Lindsay for Mayor of New York. Rpt: As "Lindsay and the City" in 66.11, 68.11, and in *The Village Voice Anthology, 1956-1980: Twenty-Five Years of Writing from the Village Voice*, edited by Geoffrey Stokes. New York: Quill, 1982. See 65.24.

65.23 "Mailer on Buckley: 'Tarnished Charm.'" Article-interview by Pete Hamill. *New York Post*, 2 November, 6. Comment by Mailer on William F. Buckley Jr. as a spoiler in the New York mayoral election.

65.24 Letter to the editor. *Village Voice*, 11 November, 4. One-line retort to accompanying letter from William F. Buckley Jr. that complains about Mailer's comments about Buckley's interpretation of John Lindsay's support for Adam Clayton Powell in 65.22. Mailer says, "Dear Bill, Be a swell, don't sue."

Photograph by Simeon C. Marshall
66.11

66.1 "3 Poems." *East Side Review* 1 (January-February), 43. First and only issue. First poem titled "Epitaph of a Rail"; the others (untitled) begin: "Your idea of sucking cock" and "Mr. Answer Man what is a weapon." Rpt: 66.11.

66.2 "A Band of New York Intellectuals Meets with Prof. Schlesinger for a Talk-In on Vietnam." *New York Times Magazine*, 6 February, 12, 72, 74-80. Partial transcript of a meeting of a Theatre for Ideas panel consisting of Irving Kristol, Staughton Lynd, Arthur Schlesinger Jr., Michael Walzer and moderator Elizabeth Hardwick. Mailer, in the audience, comments on communism's self-destructive tendencies on 78. See 66.4.

66.3 "What Norman Means...." Article by James Yuenger. *Chicago Tribune Magazine*, 6 February, 50, 52. Account of presentations by Mailer, Ralph Ellison and John Cheever at the 1965 Modern Language Association meeting in Chicago. Mailer's presentation consisted largely of 66.5. See 66.7.

66.4 "What about Immolation?" Letter to the editor. *New York Times Magazine*, 20 February, 21. Complaint that his comments about a man burning himself in protest of the Vietnam War were cut out of the magazine's report on the meeting of the Theatre of Ideas. See 66.2.

66.5 "Modes and Mutations: Quick Comments on the Modern American Novel." *Commentary*, March, 37-40. Essay containing his most considered overview of American literature. First presented at the 1965 Modern Language Association meeting in Chicago. Rpt: Slightly revised in 66.11 and *The American Novel Since World War II*, edited by Marcus Klein. Greenwich, Conn.: Fawcett, 1969. See 66.3, 66.7.

66.6 "Will Success Spoil the 'Village Voice.'" Article by Mel Gussow. *New York [Herald Tribune] Magazine*, 10 April, 12-13, 20. Gussow quotes Mailer briefly in this article, which chronicles the rise to prominence and respectability of the *Village Voice*.

66.7 "Pearl or Jew?" Letter to the editor. *New York Review of Books*, 28 April, 26-27. Response to Richard G. Stern's description in the *New York Review of Books*, 17 February, titled "Report from the MLA." Stern reports what Mailer said and did in an elevator in the Palmer House in Chicago in December 1965, and also gives an account of Mailer's "corrosive, brilliant" MLA talk (66.5). Mailer cites 66.3 in his letter, which is followed by Stern's friendly disagreement with Mailer's version. Rpt: As "To the *New York Review of Books*" in 72.7, 82.19.

66.8 "On Cannibals and Christians." *Dissent* 13 (May-June), 304-6. Essay. Rpt: As "Introducing Our Argument" in 66.11.

66.9 "In and Out of Books: Mailer." Article-interview by Christopher Lehmann-Haupt. *New York Times Book Review*, 21 August, 8. Brief comment on the theatrical version of *The Deer Park: A Play* (67.13), and his novel-in-progress, *Why Are We in Vietnam?* (67.15).

66.10 "The Great American Mystery: A New Dissent on the Methods and Findings of the Warren Commission." *(Washington Post) Book Week*, 28 August, 1, 11-13. Review of *Rush to Judgment*, by Mark Lane. According to Mailer, the editors at *Book Week* probably supplied the second half of this review's title. Rpt: 72.7, 82.19 and *Village Voice* (1 September), where the acknowledgments of 72.7 say, erroneously, that this review first appeared.

66.11 *Cannibals and Christians*. New York: Dial, 29 August; London: Deutsch, 1967 (minus all but one of the 54 poems in the American edition, which were restored in later editions, those lacking an "A" on the inside back flap of the dustwrapper and the truncated introduction of the first state). Miscellany, 400 pp., $5.95. Dedication: "To Lyndon B. Johnson, whose name inspired young men to cheer for me in public." The acknowledgments note that "Ministers of Taste," letters to Robert B. Silvers, editor of the *New York Review of Books*, appeared in *Partisan Review*. An extensive search has failed to turn them up. They are reprinted, however, in 67.11 and 82.19. Rpt: "The Metaphysics of the Belly" is reprinted from 63.37; several selections from 66.11 appear, usually in a truncated form, in 98.7. See 65.2.

Mailer: "Apocalypse or debauch is upon us. And we are close to dead. There are faces and bodies like gorged maggots on the dance floor, on the highway, in the city, in the stadium; they are a host of chemical machines who swallow the product of chemical factories, aspirin, preservatives, stimulant, relaxant, and breathe out their chemical wastes into a polluted air. The sense of a long last night over civilization is back again; it has perhaps not been here so intensely in thirty years, not since the Nazis were prospering, but it is coming back" (66.11).

66.12 "Mail from Mailer." Letter to the editor. *Newsweek*, 12 September, 2. Complaint about being misquoted in the 29 August review of 66.11.

66.13 "The Writer and Hollywood: Norman Mailer." *Film Heritage* 2 (fall), 23. Mailer answers two editors' questions: "(1) Has Hollywood treated your work justly? (2) Can the serious writer's work survive in Hollywood?" In 125 words apiece, Mailer answers "no" to each, adding to his second answer that complaining about the results after an author has sold work for money is "belly-aching" and "smacks too much of sniffing the armpit and wrestler's moans."

66.14 "Henry Miller." In *Double Exposure: A Gallery of the Celebrated with Commentary by the Equally Celebrated*, compiled and photographed by Roddy McDowall, 168-69. New York: Delacorte. Essay. Rpt: As "An Appreciation of Henry Miller" in 72.7, 82.19 and in the premier issue of *Black Messiah* (1981), published by Vagabond Press, Ellensburg, Wash., where Mailer adds a footnote noting that he saw Miller in 1975 or 1976 "out in Pacific Palisades. We did a TV show together, and he was blind in one eye, had to use a walker to move about and was still sensational." See 76.12, 77.11.

66.15 "His Childhood Was a Happy Time: Norman Mailer Remembers Long Branch." Interview by Edward Pell. *Daily Register* (Red Bank, New Jersey), 12 December, Sec. 2, p. 13. Memories of the resort town where Mailer was born and spent his summers until 1941.

Evergreen Program
MAY 1967
Volume 1, Number 6

NORMAN MAILER'S
"THE DEER PARK"

Drawing by Tom Morrow
See 67.13

67.1 "Norman Mailer's 'Deer Park': Countdown Drama." Article-interview by Stephanie Harrington. *Village Voice*, 5 January, 1, 23. Quotes Mailer on Hollywood, the nature of theater, the cast and staging of "The Deer Park: A Play" (67.13), which opened in New York on 31 January and ran for 127 performances.

67.2 "A Requiem for the Rube." *Village Voice*, 5 January, 4, 16. Essay on Jack Ruby, written in the style of *Why Are We in Vietnam?* (67.15). See 95.15.

67.3 "A Statement of Aims by the Playwright." *Village Voice*, 5 January, 16. Paid advertisement of 161 words on the meaning of the "The Deer Park: A Play" (67.13). Mailer says, it is "a play about sex...Hollywood and hypocrisy and artistic integrity, about memory and reality, love, snobbery, sorrow, manic will, farce and tragedy...." The version of this statement prefacing the working scripts of the play reads: "a play about fucking."

67.4 "Mr. Mailer Passes Out the Cigars." *New York Times*, 22 January, Sec. 2, pp. 1, 3. Essay on theater, reviewers and the meaning of "The Deer Park: A Play." Rpt: The essay was incorporated into the introduction to *The Deer Park: A Play* (67.13); the introduction was reprinted in *Existential Errands* (72.7) and *The Essential Mailer* (82.19) as "The Playwright as Critic."

67.5 "Norman Mailer, Playwright." Article-interview by Jerry Tallmer. *New York Post Magazine*, 11 February, 2. Quotes Mailer on the genesis of "The Deer Park: A Play" (67.13), and gives a capsule biography, including

Mailer's statement on his refusal to get into a shelter during a New York City air raid drill.

67.6 "Norman Mailer Has Calmed Quite a Bit." Article- interview by William A. Raidy. *Long Island Press*, 12 February. Quotes Mailer on "The Deer Park: A Play" (67.13), and mentions his forthcoming novel, *Why Are We in Vietnam?* (67.15).

67.7 "Joe Shaw and the Hip Boxing Syndicate." Article by Leroy F. Aarons. *Washington Post*, 26 March, Sec. B, p. 5. Chronicles involvement of Mailer, George Plimpton, Roger Donoghue, Harvey Breit, Charles Addams, Tom Quinn and Pete Hamill in career of welterweight contender Joe Shaw. Mailer is quoted briefly.

67.8 "Mailer Says U.S. Dangerously Split." Article by Carolyn Barta. *Dallas Morning News*, 29 March, Sec. D, p. 4. Quotes from Mailer's Southern Methodist University speech against the Vietnam War.

67.9 "Mailer—Man of Fevered Words." Article by Lee Coppola. *Buffalo Evening News*, 1 April. Quotes from Mailer's comments after a reading from *Why Are We in Vietnam?* (67.15) at State University of New York at Buffalo.

67.10 "Mailer's Street Scene: Renewal on Sunday." Article by Stephanie Harrington. *Village Voice*, 4 May, 1, 21. Quotes Mailer at block party given in honor of the 100th performance of "The Deer Park" (67.13).

67.11 *The Short Fiction of Norman Mailer*. New York: Dell, 11 May, softcover; Sevenoaks, Kent: New English Library, August 1982. Short stories, 285 pp., 95¢. The British edition combines 67.11 with *Existential Errands* (72.7) under the title *The Essential Mailer* (82.19). Nineteen previously published stories with an original introduction (later reprinted in 72.7 and 82.19). No dedication. Rpt: Accompanied by separate editions of *Barbary Shore* (51.1) and *The Deer Park* (55.4), *The Short Fiction of Norman Mailer* (80.23) appeared in a hardcover edition (the first) in 1980. New York: Howard Fertig. All 19 stories appeared previously in one or another of Mailer's miscellanies (59.13, 63.37, 66.11); 13 of the stories appeared in periodicals or other collections prior to being reprinted in one of the miscellanies. "The Man Who Studied Yoga" and "The Time of Her Time" were reprinted in 98.7. Shohakusha (Tokyo) published *A Selection from the Short Fiction of Norman Mailer* (68.32). See 74.19.

Mailer: "It has been remarked that the short fiction of this author is neither splendid, unforgettable, nor distinguished, and I hasten hereby to join such consensus.... He does not have the gift to write great short stories, or perhaps even very good ones. In fact, he will confess he does not have the interest, the respect, or the proper awe. The short story bores him a little. He will admit he rarely reads them. He is, in secret, not fond of writers who work at short stories. Nor are they often, he suspects, fond of him. He has a private sneer for the reputations they have amassed. There is a terrible confession to make: he thinks the short story is relatively easy to write" (67.11).

67.12 "In Clay's Corner." *Partisan Review* 34 (summer), 458-62. Symposium contribution. Mailer, Frank Conroy, Nat Hentoff, John Hollander, Robert Lowell and Richard Poirier comment on the refusal of Cassius Clay (Muhammad Ali) to be drafted into the U.S. Army. Mailer's statement is 240 words in length. Rpt: As "An Appreciation of Cassius Clay" in 72.7, 82.19. See 75.12.

67.13 *The Deer Park: A Play.* New York: Dial, 7 August; simultaneously as a softcover; New York: Dell; London: Weidenfeld and Nicolson, 1970. 192 pp., $4.50. Dedication: "To Leo Garen and James F. Walsh, Director and Producer of "The Deer Park," and to Paul John Austin—Stage Manager, and the brave players in the first New York company: Rip Torn, Rosemary Tory and Hugh Marlowe, Will Lee, Beverly Bentley and Mickey Knox, Gene Lindsey and Margaret Fairchild, Mara Lynn and Joe McWherter, Marsha Mason and Gary Campbell, Bernard Farbar; and to the fine work of the technical crew and the box office, and the standbys. And to Elizabeth Farley, Richard Shepard, Dan Durning and Tom Baker for the first production of "The Deer Park" at Act IV in Provincetown." This published version of the play follows the stage version which ran from 31 January through 21 May at the Theatre de Lys in New York; it is markedly different in form, but consistent in spirit with the fragments published in 1959 and 1960. See 57.2, 59.11, 59.13, 60.4, other 1967 entries, 72.7 and the novel on which the play is based: 55.4.

Mailer: "There were times when I thought I even cared more for it than the novel from which it was delivered; it was certainly different from the novel, narrower, more harrowing, funnier I hoped, sadder, certainly more tragic. It was also more multi-layered. If I was a novelist trying to write plays, I was also trying to put more into this play than I had put into the novel. If the compass was obligatorily more narrow, the well was being dug to a deeper water...." (67.3).

67.14 "Uncle Norman Makes the Ob-scene." Article-interview by Nancy Weber. *Books* (September), 8. Focuses mainly on forthcoming *Why Are We in Vietnam?* (67.15) with asides on the war in Vietnam, Ronald Reagan, *An American Dream* (65.7) and *The Deer Park: A Play* (67.13). Mailer says that *Why Are We in Vietnam?* "took five months, June to November 1966, with a month and a half out to do 'The Deer Park' in Provincetown." He says, "It's a book to be read out loud; it uses language more for its sound than for what it means."

67.15 *Why Are We in Vietnam?* New York: Putnam's, 15 September; London: Weidenfeld and Nicolson, March or April 1969. Novel, 208 pp., $4.95. Republished with preface by Mailer. New York: Berkley, January 1977 (77.1). Preface reprinted as "Are We in Vietnam?" in 82.16. Dedication (Putnam's only): "To My Friends: Roger Donoghue, Buzz Farber [sic], Mickey Knox, Norman Podhoretz, Cy Rembar and José Torres." Two states of the Putnam's "first impression" exist. One contains a tipped-in dedication page with Buzz Farbar's name misspelled Farber; the other has no dedication page. It seems likely that the dedication page was an afterthought, added just before publication and then excised when the spelling error was found. This interpretation is supported by two facts: first, the great majority of examined copies do not have the dedication page; and second, the British first edition also lacks one. The dedication, with correct spelling of Farbar's name, appears in three subsequent softcover editions. *Why Are We in Vietnam?* is one of the few Mailer books not preceded by pre-publication excerpts in periodicals. Mailer adapted the novel into a one-act sketch, "Why Are We in Vietnam," before it was published. It was staged at least twice: on 19 August at Act IV in Provincetown, and on 6 December 1971 at an anti-war rally at the Cathedral of St. John the Divine in New York. Under the title "A Fragment from *Vietnam*: A One-Act Play," the 13-page sketch was included in *Existential Errands* (72.7) and *The Essential Mailer* (82.19). Finally, Eurographica (Helsinki) published it, along with 67.16, in a separate volume under the title *A Fragment From Vietnam* (85.11). Rpt: Four chapters of the novel in 98.7. See 65.14, 72.18.

Mailer: "You see, there are times when I read *Why Are We in Vietnam?* and it displeases me too, but there are times when I decide it's one of the 10 funniest books written since *Huckleberry Finn*" (67.16).

67.16 "Mr. Mailer Interviews Himself." *New York Times Book Review*, 17 September, 4-5, 40. Catechetical comment on 67.15. Rpt: As "An Imaginary Interview" in 72.7, 82.19, *A Fragment From Vietnam* (85.11), 88.6.

67.17 "The Crazy One." *Playboy*, October, 91-92, 112, 211- 14. Portrait of the Mexican bullfighter, Amado Ramirez, a.k.a. El Loco. Rpt: As "Footnote to 'Death in the Afternoon'" in 67.20; "Homage to El Loco" in 72.7 and 82.19. It is likely that 67.20, while published later than 67.17, was written earlier. These two versions are not significantly different from each other or from the final version in 72.7 and 82.19. This version also appeared in *The Twentieth Anniversary Playboy Reader*, edited by Hugh M. Hefner. Chicago: Playboy Press, 1974; complete in 98.7.

67.18 "Why We Are Interviewing Norman Mailer." By Mike McGrady. *Newsday*, 7 October, 3, 20, 30. Comment on violence and Vietnam, L.B.J., book reviews and his influence: "You know, I realize that my style of article writing has influenced more people than my fiction style. When I started doing articles, I didn't see why I couldn't use my equipment as a novelist." Rpt: 88.6.

67.19 "Following the Bouncing Talk of Norman Mailer." Article-interview by Phyllis Meras. *Providence Journal*, 8 October, Sec. W, p. 20. Report of a conversation in a New York bar with Mailer and Edward White of G.P. Putnam's, publishers of *Why Are We in Vietnam?* (67.15). Mailer says 67.15 "has its roots in *Cannibals and Christians*" (66.11), and goes on to link the total warfare practiced by Ulysses S. Grant with modern science's "gross methods of experimentation." He continues, noting that he abandoned a formal style in 67.15 for one that has been described as "Joyce gone hip," a "pure American" style.

67.20 *The Bullfight: A Photographic Narrative with Text by Norman Mailer.* New York: CBS Legacy Collection Book, distributed by Macmillan, mid-November. Essay, 112 unnumbered pp., $7.95. Mailer's essay, titled "Footnote to 'Death in the Afternoon,'" a portrait of the Mexican bullfighter Amando Ramirez (El Loco) is 23 pp.; it is accompanied by a fragment from Federico García Lorca's "Lament for Sánchez Mejías," and 91 photographs, comprising a complete depiction of a *corrida de toros,* but using a series of bullfighters, including Luis Miguel Dominguin and Antonio Ordónez (the rivals in Ernest Hemingway's *The Dangerous Summer*), and El Cordobes. The volume is accompanied by a 33 1/3, 60-minute, monaural record on which Mailer reads selections from his essay; Hugh Marlowe and Rosemary Tory read "Lament For Sánchez Mejías," translated by Mailer and his daughter Susan (see 67.22); traditional Spanish music is performed on five cuts by the Bullring Band of Madrid, Pedro Cortes, flamenco guitarist and Paco Ortiz, flamenco singer. The record is produced by Bernard "Buzz" Farbar. Rpt: As "The Crazy One" in 67.17; "Homage to El Loco" in 72.7, 82.19. See 67.17 for explanation of differences among the three versions; 84.2.

67.21 "Some Dirt in the Talk: A Candid History of an Existential Movie Called *Wild 90.*" *Esquire,* December, 190-94, 261, 264-69. Essay. Rpt: As "Some Dirt in the Talk" in 72.7, 82.19.

67.22 Translation (with Susan Mailer) of "Lament for Ignacio Sánchez Mejías," by Federico García Lorca. *The Poetry Bag* 1 (winter 1967-68), 5-10. Rpt: 67.20, where a fragment first appears. The entire poem is read on the recording accompanying 67.20; 72.7, 82.19. See 84.2.

67.23 Foreword to *The Beard,* by Michael McClure. N.p.: Coyote; distributed by City Lights Books, San Francisco. Rpt: New York: Grove, 1985. One hundred eighty-two words on the merits of McClure's play about a meeting in eternity of Jean Harlow and Billy the Kid. The first edition (Berkely: Oyez, 1965) did not include Mailer's foreword.

67.24 Two untitled excerpts (168 words) from speech at Fifth Avenue Vietnam Peace Parade. In *In the Teeth of War: Photographic Documentary of the March 26th, 1966, New York City Demonstration Against the War in Vietnam,* edited by Donna Gould and Dave Dellinger, 34, 59; Introduction by Dave Dellinger. Additional excerpts from speeches of Juan Mari Bras, Donald Duncan, Rev. Howard Moody, A.J. Muste, Cleveland Robinson, Jerry Rubin, Gilberto Gerena Valentin. New York: Fifth Avenue Vietnam Peace Parade Committee; Selling Agent: OAK Publications, New York.

THE ARMIES OF THE NIGHT

History as a Novel
The Novel as History

NORMAN MAILER

68.8

68.1 "Playboy Interview: Norman Mailer." By Paul Carroll. *Playboy,* January, 69-72, 74, 76, 78, 80, 82-84. One of Mailer's most important interviews, with extended discussion of drugs, sex, fame, politics and Vietnam; less on purely literary matters. Rpt: *Norman Mailer: The Man and His Work,* edited by Robert F. Lucid. Boston: Little, Brown, 1971; as "Excerpts from *Playboy*" (partial) in 72.7 and 82.19; as "Vices" in 82.16 (partial).

68.2 "The Steps of the Pentagon." *Harper's,* March, 47-78, 83-98, 101-30, 136, 138, 140, 142; cover story. Nonfiction narrative on the anti-war March on the Pentagon, 19-21 October 1967. Mailer's first appearance in *Harper's* was also the longest article in the history of the magazine and U.S. journalism, to that date. See Henry Raymont's article, *"Harper's* and *Atlantic* Put Out 'Vietnam' Issues," *New York Times,* 19 February, 14. Rpt: In a revised form as "History as a Novel: The Steps of the Pentagon," book 1 of *The Armies of the Night* (68.8). See 68.6.

68.3 "Black Power: A Discussion." *Partisan Review* 35 (spring), 218-21. Symposium contribution written in response to Martin Duberman's piece on Black Power in the previous number of *Partisan Review*. Other contributors are Robert Coles, Ivanhoe Donaldson, Paul Feldman, Charles V. Hamilton, Abbie Hoffman, Tom Kahn, William Melvin Kelley, Jack Newfield, Fred Powledge, Stephen Thernstrom and Dr. Nathan Wright Jr. Rpt: As "Contribution to a Partisan Review Symposium" in 72.7, 82.19. See 68.13, 68.19.

68.4 "Up the Family Tree." *Partisan Review* 35 (spring), 234-52. Review of *Making It*, by Norman Podhoretz, that foreshadows his use of the third person personal in 68.2 and subsequent nonfiction narratives. Mailer's most extensive comment on the *Partisan Review* and "the Family" that wrote for it. Rpt: With the additional title, "One Literary Critique," in 72.7, 82.19.

68.5 "Beyond the Law." *Scholastic* (student weekly, University of Notre Dame), 29 March, 24-25. Transcript of Mailer's remarks before the world premiere of his cinéma vérité film, "Beyond the Law," at Notre Dame on 2 April. This issue of *Scholastic* obviously appeared late.

68.6 "The Battle of the Pentagon." *Commentary* 45 (April), 33-57. Nonfiction narrative on the anti-war March on the Pentagon. See Alden Whitmen article, "*Commentary* Gets Mailer 'Epilogue,'" *New York Times*, 11 March, 48. Rpt: In a revised form as "The Novel as History: The Battle of the Pentagon," book 2 of *The Armies of the Night* (68.8). See 68.2.

68.7 "Direct." Interview by Ellen Kaye. *Women's Wear Daily*, 1 May, 4. Comment on the Vietnam War, the blurring of the sexes, and racial politics.

68.8 *The Armies of the Night: History as a Novel, The Novel as History.* New York: New American Library, 6 May; London: Weidenfeld and Nicolson, October. Nonfiction narrative on the anti-war March on the Pentagon, 317 pp., $5.95. Dedication and acknowledgment: "To Beverly; An acknowledgment to Sandy Charlebois for work beyond the call of duty." Published 20 years to the day after *The Naked and the Dead* (48.2). Winner of the Pulitzer Prize for general nonfiction and the National Book Award for arts and letters. In 1999, it was ranked nineteenth on a list of the top 100 works of journalism of the twentieth century by 36 judges under the aegis of New York University's journalism department. See "Journalism's Greatest Hits: Two Lists of a Century's Top Stories," *New York Times*, 1 March 1999, Business Section, pp.1, 13. Discarded title: *The Armies of the Dead*. For an account of the work's genesis and reception written by the editor of *Harper's*, see *New York Days* by Willie Morris. (New York: Little, Brown, 1993), 213-22. Rpt: Entire narrative appeared earlier in two parts, in *Harper's* (68.2), and *Commentary* (68.8), respectively and was then revised for book publication; 98.7 (partial). See 68.26, 69.3, 69.4, 69.25, 69.26, 70.8-70.11, 72.7, 74.20, 79.14, 96.5.

Mailer: "There is no sex [in *The Armies of the Night*]. In that sense, it's a nineteenth-century novel. It's courtly, it's deliberate, it's amused with its time and place. It's taken for granted that its characters are all very fine and substantial people. We know it's going to turn out well in the end. I suppose it has the restrained merriment of the early nineteenth-century picaresque novel" (82.16).

68.9 "Democracy Has / Hasn't a Future...a Present." *New York Times Magazine*, 26 May, 30-31, 98-104. Abridged transcript of Theatre for Ideas panel discussion on "the nature and future of democracy" on 3 May at the Friends Meeting House, Gramercy Park, New York City. Besides Mailer, the panelists were Nat Hentoff (moderator), Herbert Marcuse and Arthur Schlesinger

Jr. Questions from the floor came from Elizabeth Hardwick and Robert Lowell. Rpt: As "Democracy: Does It Have a Future?" in *Dissent, Power, and Confrontation,* edited by Alexander Klein. New York: McGraw Hill, 1971.

68.10 "On the Steps of a Zeitgeist." Article-interview by Jack Newfield. *Village Voice,* 30 May, 1, 26-27. Day-in-the-life article; a record of Mailer's words and moods while visiting with, among others, José Torres, Pete Hamill, Tom Hayden, Dwight Macdonald, Mark Rudd, George Plimpton, Robert Silvers, Frances FitzGerald, Merv Griffin, Morey Amsterdam and Jake LaMotta. Rpt: In Newfield's *Bread and Roses Too: Reporting about America.* New York: E.P. Dutton, 1971; *Critical Essays on Norman Mailer,* edited by J. Michael Lennon. Boston: G.K. Hall, December 1986.

68.11 *The Idol and the Octopus: Political Writings by Norman Mailer on the Kennedy and Johnson Administrations.* New York: Dell, 6 June, softcover. Miscellany, 284 pp., 95¢. No dedication. In a note appended to the foreword, Mailer explains that the title "was once to be used for *The Deer Park* [55.4]. The Idol was to represent Charles Francis Eitel, the artist; the Octopus was Herman Teppis, the producer, the man of power. Here I use it to characterize two administrations, The Idol and The Octopus," or J.F.K. and L.B.J. Rpt: Except for the foreword and some brief introductory and transition material, the bulk of this collection consists of selections from *The Presidential Papers* (63.37) and *Cannibals and Christians* (66.11). The most notable exception is "On *Lady Chatterley* and *Tropic of Cancer*" (168-70), which gives hints of his later comments on D.H. Lawrence in 71.20 and Henry Miller in 71.20 and 76.12.

68.12 "Pick of the Paperbacks." Interview by Rollene W. Saal. *Saturday Review,* 8 June, 50. Brief and sympathetic comment on the Columbia students who took over the university.

68.13 "Doctoring the Evidence." Letter to the editor. *Partisan Review* 35 (summer), 489-90. Mailer's response to a letter from Irving Howe who commented on Mailer's views on the health of American Negroes in the spring issue (68.3). Rpt: 72.7, 82.19. See 68.19.

68.14 "Norman Mailer Enlists His Private Army to Act in Film." Article by J. Anthony Lukas. *New York Times,* 23 July, Sec. M, p. 35. First of several accounts of the filming of Mailer's movie, "Maidstone," in the Hamptons on Long Island, New York. Mailer is quoted at length: "We hope to prove that one can make a beautiful, tasteful, resonant, touching, evocative picture with cinéma vérité methods in four days. If we can do it, a lot of people out in Hollywood are going to commit suicide." Rpt: Mailer included an excerpt in *Maidstone: A Mystery* (71.28). See 68.15-68.17, 68.28, 71.30.

68.15 "Produced by Norman Mailer, Directed by Norman Mailer, Written by Norman Mailer, Starring Norman Mailer, and Introducing Norman Mailer's Friends." Article by Harvey Aronson. *Weekend with Newsday,* 27 July, 10-13, 38. Account, with 12 photographs, of the filming of "Maidstone." See 68.14, 68.16, 68.17, 68.28, 71.28, 71.30.

68.16 "Mailer Film Party a Real Bash: 1 Broken Jaw, 2 Bloody Heads." Article by J. Anthony Lukas. *New York Times*, 31 July, 29. Account of a fight between Mailer and a member of the cast of "Maidstone." See 68.14, 68.15, 68.17, 68.28, 71.28, 71.30.

68.17 "Norman Mailer, Movie Maker." Article by Sally Beauman. *New York*, 19 August, 50-57. Another long account of the making of Mailer's experimental movie, "Maidstone." Rpt: Mailer included excerpts in *Maidstone: A Mystery* (71.28). See 68.14-68.16, 68.28, 71.30.

68.18 "Hundred Injured: 178 Are Arrested as Guardsmen Join in Using Tear Gas." Article by J. Anthony Lukas. *New York Times*, 28 August, Sec L. pp. 1, 23. Report on the riots at the Democratic National Convention in Chicago, including a description of the Grant Park Rally where Mailer, Allen Ginsberg, Jean Genet, William Burroughs and Dick Gregory spoke. Mailer said: "I'm a little sick about all this and also a little mad, but I've got a deadline on a long piece and I'm not going to go out and march and get arrested. I just came here to salute all of you." The piece referred to is *Miami and the Siege of Chicago* (68.25).

68.19 Letter to the editor. *Partisan Review* 35 (fall), 647- 50. Continuation of the exchange with Irving Howe cited in 68.13, with an additional letter by Dr. H. Jack Geiger of Tufts School of Medicine. Rpt: 72.7, 82.19. See 68.3.

68.20 "Pooter: Vidal on Mailer on Vidal." Interview by unidentified interviewer. *London Times*, 21 September. Linked interviews with Gore Vidal and Mailer on politics. Mailer says, "I don't agree with Gore much about anything, but if you smelted us together we'd make one great politician."

68.21 "Norman Mailer: Why Do People Dislike America?" Profile-interview by Oriana Fallaci. *The Egotists: Sixteen Surprising Interviews.* Chicago: Regnery, October, 1-18. Conducted in April 1967, this unusual interview focuses on the American character, America and Europe, and violence. Rpt: As "Interview with Norman Mailer" (minus the prefatory five-page profile) in *Writer's Digest*, December 1969, 40-47, 81; cover photograph of Mailer. Mailer complained about Fallaci's inaccuracy in 70.5.

68.22 "Mailer, McLuhan and Muggeridge: On Obscenity." Transcript of a television program, "The Way It Is," on CBLT (Toronto) moderated by Robert Fulford. The panel consisted of Mailer, Marshall McLuhan and Malcolm Muggeridge. *Realist*, October, 5-12. Rpt: 88.6 and (in a truncated form) in *Montrealer*, May 1968.

68.23 "Mailer's Musings." Interview by Harvey Matusow. *International Times* (London), 4-17 October, 5. Comment on demonstrations at the Pentagon and Democratic Convention in Chicago, Robert Kennedy, Hubert Humphrey, George Wallace, Eugene McCarthy and the Vietnam War.

68.24 "Norman Mailer in Focus." Article-interview by William Foster. *Week-End Scotsman*, 19 October, 1. In London to promote *The Armies of the Night* (68.8), Mailer comments on the influence of Leo Tolstoy, William Faulkner and Ernest Hemingway, his films, and race relations in the U.S.

68.25 *Miami and the Siege of Chicago: An Informal History of the Republican and Democratic Conventions of 1968.* New York: World, 24 October; simultaneously as a softcover: New York: New American Library; London: Weidenfeld and Nicolson, November or December, with different subtitle: *An Informal History of the American Political Conventions of 1968.* Nonfiction narrative, 223 pp., $5.95. Dedication: "To my Father." Nominated for the National Book Award in the history and biography category. Rpt: 68.27, 76.5, 98.7 (partial). See 68.18, 69.3, 72.7.

Mailer: "...you end up writing best about those historic events which have a magnetic relation to your own ideas and tend to write less well about situations where that doesn't occur. I think, for example, *Miami and the Siege of Chicago* is probably a better book than *St. George and the Godfather* [72.17]. For a number of reasons including the fact that the conventions themselves were more exciting, but also because there was a polarity in '68 more congenial to me than in '72" (75.11).

68.26 "When Irish Eyes Are Smiling, It's Norman Mailer." Article-interview by Vincent Canby. *New York Times,* 27 October, Sec. 2, p. 15. Brief profile followed by a lively discussion of moviemaking, Mailer's movie, "Beyond the Law," *The Armies of the Night* (68.8), the Irish and the Jews. Rpt: 88.6. See 84.18.

68.27 "Miami Beach and Chicago." *Harper's,* November, 41-52, 55-66, 69-84, 89-104, 107-30; cover story. Nonfiction narrative. Appeared at virtually the same time as the American book versions (68.25). The only difference between the versions is that the title of the first chapter in 68.25 is "Miami Beach, August 3-9." In 68.27, it is "Miami Beach, August 5-9." The correct dates for Mailer's coverage of the Republican convention are 2-8 August, as noted in the partial reprint in *The Time of Our Time* (98.7). Rpt: 76.5.

68.28 "At Play in the Fields of the Bored." Article by James Toback. *Esquire,* December, 150-55, 22, 24, 26, 28, 30, 32, 34, 36. The most extended account of the filming of "Maidstone," prefaced by Toback's memories of his earlier contacts with Mailer. Rpt: Mailer included excerpts in *Maidstone: A Mystery* (71.28). See 68.14-68.17, 71.30.

68.29 "Flying High with Mailer." Article-interview by Raymond A. Sokolov. *Newsweek,* 9 December, 84, 86-88; cover photograph of Mailer. Profile with brief Mailer comments sprinkled throughout, mainly from earlier writing and interviews. Accompanied by 68.30. See 68.31.

68.30 "Norman Mailer's Open Letter to Richard Nixon." *Newsweek,* 9 December, 85. Accompanies 68.29. Rpt: 72.7, 82.19.

68.31 Letter to the editor. *Newsweek,* 23 December, 7. Mailer corrects four errors in 68.29, the most important of which is: "No publisher ever forced me to censor *The Naked and the Dead* [48.2]. I decided to use the word fug before the book was even begun. In those days the big brother of fug was simply not ready for public hire." See 49.3, 65.21, 92.12, 95.53.

68.32 *A Selection from the Short Fiction of Norman Mailer,* edited with notes by Iwao Iwamoto. Tokyo: Shohakusha, softcover, 88 pp. Unusual English language edition containing three stories set in Japan and the Philippines during and after WWII: "The Paper House," "The Language of Men" and "The Dead Gook." Rpt: 52.2, 52.3, 53.2, 59.13, 67.11, 82.19. See 74.19.

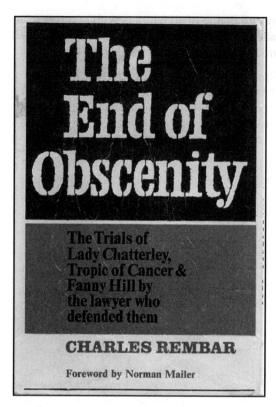

The
End of
Obscenity

The Trials of
Lady Chatterley,
Tropic of Cancer &
Fanny Hill by
the lawyer who
defended them

CHARLES REMBAR

Foreword by Norman Mailer

69.82

69.1 "Looking for the Meat and Potatoes—Thoughts on Black Power." *Look*, 7 January, 57-58, 60. Essay, Mailer's lengthiest comment on blacks in the U.S. Rpt: 72.7, 82.19; partial in *The Look Book*, edited by Leo Rosten. New York: Harry N. Abrams, 1975.

69.2 "Scholars Debate Whether 'Feel' Has Killed Rationalists' 'Think.'" Article by Israel Shenker. *New York Times*, 4 March, 52. Account of Theatre of Ideas debate on "The End of the Rationalist Tradition?" Moderated by Conor Cruise O'Brien with Robert Lowell as timekeeper; the debaters were Mailer, Leslie Fiedler, Peter Gay and Jean Malaquais, all of whom are quoted.

69.3 "Norman Mailer Wins an Award." Article-interview by Jerry Tallmer. *New York Post Magazine*, 15 March, 2. Account of Mailer at the 12 March National Book Awards ceremony at Philharmonic Hall in New York, with excerpts from his speech. Nominated for two awards—for *The Armies of the Night* (68.8) in the arts and letters category and *Miami and the Siege of Chicago* (68.25) in history and biography—Mailer won the former. The second half of the article-interview reports Tallmer's conversation with Mailer the next day on Nixon's victory, Hubert Humphrey, and movie-making. The full text of Mailer's speech is in *Existential Errands* (72.7) and *The Essential Mailer* (82.19). See 69.4, 74.20, 86.34.

69.4 "The Book Industry Presents the 20th National Book Awards." Article by unidentified writer. *Publishers' Weekly*, 24 March, 26-32. Full account of the award ceremony and listing of all winners with excerpts from their remarks, including Mailer. The full text of his speech is in *Existential Errands* (72.7) and *The Essential Mailer* (82.19). See 68.8, 69.3, 74.20, 86.34.

69.5 "Norman Mailer, Film Maker." Interview by Joseph Morgenstern. *Channel 13* [New York City] *Program Guide*, April, 8-9. Transcript of "Critique" television program explaining Mailer's views on making movies without scripts: "A sort of river of activity gets started, and we have cameramen who are picking up large parts of that river."

69.6 "Norman Mailer for Mayor?" Article by unidentified writer. *Village Voice*, 3 April, 1. Short piece suggesting that Mailer might run for mayor of New York in the 17 June Democratic primary by forging, in his words, a "hip coalition of the right and the left."

69.7 "The City Politic: Can Mailer and Breslin Put This City Back on Its Feet?" Article by Peter Maas. *New York*, 14 April, 8-9. Maas, one of Mailer's campaign advisors, recounts the origins of Mailer's campaign for the Democratic nomination for mayor of New York and Jimmy Breslin's for president of the City Council, with brief quotes from both. To a skeptical Jerry Rubin, Mailer says, "Jerry, why not make the machine spiritual...make *it* hum?" Rpt: 69.80 (partial). See 69.10, 69.24.

69.8 "Mailer Aims to Be Everyman's Mayor." Article-interview by Bernard Weinraub. *New York Times*, 17 April, 50. Mailer announces his intention to run in the Democratic mayoral primary "assuming there's support among students." He goes on to say "There's a terrible sense of isolation and impotence. We have a miserable environment, and we can't affect it. That inspires a demonic bitterness."

69.9 "Mailer and a Member of S.D.S. Seeking Posts on Harvard's Board of Overseers in a Poll of Alumni." Article by Robert M. Smith. *New York Times*, 21 April, 37. Mailer was not elected.

69.10 "Private Opinion: The Mailer-Breslin Ticket: Vote the Rascals In." Article by Joe Flaherty. *Village Voice*, 24 April, 1, 59. Flaherty, Mailer's campaign manager, tells the same story as Maas does in 69.7, and Jimmy Breslin does in 69.24. Rpt: In a greatly revised form in *Managing Mailer* (70.7).

69.11 "Norman Mailer on the Campaign Trail." Article by Timothy Lee. *New York Post*, 25 April, 14. Report on Mailer's campaign appearance at Wagner College on Staten Island, New York.

69.12 "Mailer-Breslin: Give City to People." Article by Don Holloschutz. *Washington Square Journal* (New York University), 29 April, 1, 3. Account of an appearance by Mailer and Breslin at New York University. Mailer tells the audience that "we are running as amateurs with no resources and no authorization from the party."

69.13 "Hibernian Amateur Hour: The Dems Are Doubtful." Article by Nick Browne. *Village Voice*, 1 May, 8. Mailer tells a meeting of Park Slope

Independent Democrats in an old Irish neighborhood that he stands for "everything from black power to Irish self-righteousness."

69.14 "Mailer-Breslin Typewriters in the Ring Officially Now." Article by Judy Michaelson and Edward Katcher. *New York Post*, 1 May, 5. Account of the official 1 May announcement of the candidacies of Mailer and Breslin at the Overseas Press Club in New York. See 69.17, 69.20.

69.15 "Norman Mailer—the Candidate." Article by Steve Abel. *Brooklyn Heights Press and Cobble Hill News*, 1 May, 1, 6. Account of Mailer at Brooklyn College and Long Island University where he discussed the "complete decentralization of the city according to the wishes of the people." See 69.18.

69.16 "Eye Too." Article by unidentified writer. *Women's Wear Daily*, 2 May, 12. Mailer is described as having "the grace of the Doge and the depth of Dante" at a campaign outing in an East 79th St. penthouse.

69.17 "Mailer and Breslin Enter Race." Article by Richard Reeves, *New York Times*, 2 May, 24. A second account of the 1 May announcement at the Overseas Press Club. See 69.14, 69.20.

69.18 "Mailer: 'City Must Get Shit Together.'" Article by D.M. *Seawanhanka* (Long Island University), 2 May, 3. A second account of Mailer and Breslin at Long Island University. See 69.15.

69.19 "Mailer For Mayor? The Novelist Insists Campaign Is No Joke." Article by Alan Adelson. *Wall Street Journal*, 2 May, 1, 25. This basically unfriendly article concludes with Mailer's comment on the departed Brooklyn Dodgers: "When they went to Los Angeles I knew things had gotten bad. To leave this great city for that Queen City of Plastic."

69.20 "Official! Odd Couple Running." Article by Joseph Modzelewski. (New York) *Daily News*, 2 May, 18. Another account of the 1 May announcement at the Overseas Press Club, with additional quotes. See 69.14, 69.17.

69.21 "Mayoralty: Mailer Insists It's Not Just for Kicks." Article by Sidney E. Zion. *New York Times*, 4 May, 53. Humorous account, in the "News of the Week in Review" section of the Sunday *Times*, of the beginning of the Mailer-Breslin campaign.

69.22 "Who Is to Declare that the Minority Do Not Deserve to Determine the Schools' History?" *New York Times Magazine*, 4 May, 35, 134. In approximately 750 words, Mailer answers the question, "When, If Ever, Do You Call in the Cops?" The question was asked of several scholars, social critics, students and an ex-police official in the wake of uprisings at several campuses. The other respondents are: Andrew Schlesinger, Erich Wise, Arthur Schlesinger Jr., Robert Ross, Francis T.P. Plimpton, Christopher Lasch, Sanford D. Garelik, Herbert Marcuse, David Riesman and Charles V. Hamilton.

69.23 "The Campaign Slogan Is 'Vote the Rascals In.'" Article-interview by James R. Dickenson. *National Observer*, 5 May, 1, 16. Longest account of the campaign to date, with generous quotations from both Mailer and Breslin. Mailer says a victory "would be a piece of political magic."

69.24 "I Run to Win." Article by Jimmy Breslin. *New York*, 5 May, 40-44; cover photograph of Mailer and Breslin. The most humorous of the accounts of how the Mailer-Breslin ticket was created, with brief quotes from all the principals. Rpt: 69.80. See 69.7, 69.10.

69.25 "Mailer the Author Will Donate Prize to Mailer the Politician." Article-interview by Bernard Weinraub. *New York Times*, 6 May, 35. Comment on winning the Pulitzer Prize for *The Armies of the Night* (68.8) and his point of view in it: "Good journalism is acquainting the reader with your idiosyncrasies as a reporter. You're the instrument through which they view the event so they ought to know what corrections to make for the inevitable large or small bias of your personality." See 69.26, 74.20.

69.26 "On Accepting the Pulitzer Prize." *Village Voice*, 6 May, 5. Transcript of Mailer's speech, including questions from the media about the mayoral campaign and his replies. Rpt: 69.80. See 69.25, 74.20.

69.27 "Ex-Cop Hater Mailer Talks to Cops." Article by Paul Meskil. (New York) *Daily News*, 7 May, 5. Account of Mailer and Breslin campaigning before 200 police officers and trainees at John Jay College of Criminal Justice in New York. Mailer says he had "the reputation of being a cop-hater," but said he had changed: "A cop-hater cannot be mayor." See 69.28, 69.29.

69.28 "Mailer Campaigns among Police with Good Word for 'Good Cop.'" Article by Francis X. Clines. *New York Times*, 7 May, 43. A fuller report of the Mailer-Breslin visit to John Jay College which leads with Mailer's tribute to the good cop: "a fantastically complicated guy." See 69.27, 69.29.

69.29 "Mailer Hits Press Coverage." Article by Joe Pilati, *Village Voice*, 8 May, 1, 60. Report of Mailer's complaints about poor press coverage, made immediately after a speech at John Jay College. See 69.27, 69.28.

69.30 "Mailer Pulls Throng in Village." Article by Associated Press writer, *New York Post*, 8 May, 18. Brief account of Mailer's speech at the Village Gate, a New York night club, the previous evening. "I'm running on a platform of Free Huey Newton and fluoridation." See 69.31.

69.31 "Mailer Plays a Nightclub Date in Mayoral Quest." Article by Sidney E. Zion. *New York Times*, 9 May, 24. Longer account of Mailer's appearance at the Village Gate, three days after winning the Pulitzer Prize for *The Armies of the Night* (68.8). Rpt: 69.80. See 69.30.

69.32 "Mailer Says That Alienation Is Major Problem in City." Article-interview by Bernard Weinraub. *New York Times*, 12 May, 26. Summary of candidate Mailer's positions on pollution, crime, welfare, housing, taxes, school violence, and the most important problem, alienation.

69.33 "Politics? The Odd Couple." Article by unidentified writer.

Newsweek, 12 May, 37-38. Account of Mailer and Breslin campaigning, with brief quotes from both.

69.34 "Million Advance for Mailer Seen." Article by Henry Raymont. *New York Times*, 13 May, 44. Overview of publishing plans for the then-untitled *Of a Fire on the Moon* (71.1), with quotes from Mailer and his agent, Scott Meredith, who calls Mailer "the most sought-after author in America today."

69.35 "Wagner Petition Leads Democrats." Article by Peter Kihss. *New York Times*, 14 May, 28. Account of the filing of petitions by seven candidates for the Democratic nomination for mayor of New York in the 17 June primary: Mario A. Procaccino, Herman Badillo, James H. Scheuer, Mailer, Adam Clayton Powell and John W. Seder. Mailer is quoted as pledging "not to use four-letter obscenities 'in public' for the duration of the campaign."

69.36 "'Crazies' Break Up Mailer Rally." Article by unidentified writer. *New York Post*, 15 May, 65. Account of the disruption of a Mailer rally at P.S. 41 in Manhattan by "Crazies," who waved Viet Cong flags and fought with the audience. Mailer left after saying "If you don't get that North Vietnam flag out of here in five minutes, I'm leaving."

69.37 "Mayor Mailer: The Writer as Politician." Article-interview by Dan O. Kent. *Pousto* (spring-summer), 14-18; cover photograph of Mailer. *Pousto*, a publication of the United States Student Association, reprinted articles from various college publications, without exact attribution. From internal references, a 15 May date for this number of *Pousto* is assumed. The article is built around a 24 April appearance by Mailer and Breslin at Yeshiva University. Alice Krakauer, Mailer's press aide, is also quoted in the piece.

69.38 "Vote for Yourself, Vote for Anarchy, Vote for Mailer-Breslin." Article-interview by David Herres. *Win* (War Resisters League, New York), 15 May, 6-9. Herres questions Mailer on the relationship of literature and politics in an omnibus article which also includes reflections on the campaign, a full transcript of Mailer's speech of 22 April at his campaign headquarters and an interview with Breslin.

69.39 "The Mayoral Debate: Who Lost?" Article by Paul Hoffman. *New York Post*, 16 May, 7. Summary of the comments made by six of the candidates for mayor on a 15 May Channel 11 debate. Mailer tangled with ex-mayor Robert F. Wagner noting that he "was so out of touch that the first thing he did when he returned from his term as Ambassador to Spain 'was call up Cardinal Spellman.'" See 69.40.

69.40 "Six Democratic Candidates for Mayor Tangle in First TV Debate." Article by Richard Reeves. *New York Times*, 16 May, 32. A longer account of the Channel 11 debate. See 69.39.

69.41 "Why Are We in New York?" *New York Times Magazine*, 18 May, 30-31, 96, 98, 101, 103, 106, 108-9, 111, 113. Essay. Mailer's most considered statement on why he should be mayor of New York. Rpt: 69.80 and as "An

Instrument for the City" (original title) in 72.7, 82.19.

69.42 "Sutton's Tip-of-Manhattan Highway Plan Is Called Infeasible." Article by Edward C. Burks. *New York Times*, 21 May, 35. Mailer is quoted in opposition to a new Manhattan expressway.

69.43 "The Latest Model Mailer." Article-interview by Joseph Roddy. *Look*, 27 May, 22-28. Collage of snippets and scenes from other Mailer interviews and books, interspersed with conversation with Roddy. Rpt: 88.6.

69.44 "On Wall St. with Mailer, Breslin and George Washington." Article by Kenneth Gross. *New York Post*, 28 May, 73. Report of an appearance by Mailer and Breslin before George Washington's statue on Wall Street. Mailer tells the crowd of "a few thousand" that "New York has the best people and the worst administration in the world." See 69.45.

69.45 "Wall St. Takes Stock of Mailer-Breslin Campaign." Article by Gene Spagnoli. (New York) *Daily News*, 28 or 29 May. Second report, with quotes from both candidates, of the appearance of Mailer and Breslin on Wall Street. See 69.44.

69.46 "Citizen Mailer Sees No Point in Losing." Article by Nick Browne. *Village Voice*, 29 May, 3, 54. Portrait of candidate Mailer, with brief quotes, at various campaign stops.

69.47 "No Missiles, More for Cities Is Anti-A.B.M. Rally Theme." Article by unidentified writer. *Brooklyn Heights Press and Cobble Hill News*, 29 May, 1, 4. Report on a 24 May anti-A.B.M. rally on Montague Street, Brooklyn. Mailer and Congressman Edward Koch were among the speakers.

69.48 "Mailer Defends Dual-Admission Plan." Article-interview by Bill Kovach. *New York Times*, 30 May, 25. Mailer defends his endorsement of the projected dual-admission policy at City College because "it may be the price we have to pay for our complacency through the years."

69.49 "Life Style of a 'Left Conservative.'" Article- interview by Raymond J. Tuers. *Asbury Park Evening Press*, 31 May, 3A; cover photograph of Mailer. A day in the life of candidate Mailer, with brief quotes and a profile highlighting his Jersey Shore roots.

69.50 "Long Shot Is Best Bet: Mailer Picks Winner in Mayoral Handicap." Article by unidentified writer. *Long Island Press*, 31 May. Speaking at Temple Menorah in Little Neck, New York, Mailer handicapped himself and others in the Democratic mayoral primary. Robert Wagner, for example, was cited as "Wagner (12-year-old gelding by Meade Esposito—Out of Machine): Knows the track, 8-5." Of himself he said, "First time starter, good barn, 20-1. ***Best bet***"

69.51 "The Bore Busters." Article by William Reel. *Sunday News* (New York), *Daily News*, 1 June, pp. 1, 35. Portrait of Mailer campaigning in Red Hook and elsewhere, with brief quotes. Rpt: 69.80.

69.52 "The Norman Conquest." Article-interview by Betsy Dirnberger. *Other Voices* (Elmira College), June, 36-47. With alternating humor and earnestness, Mailer discusses his campaign with a deputation from an upstate New York college. Includes statements from Jimmy Breslin, press coordinator Alice Krakauer and campaign workers Roger Kirby and Paul Tully.

69.53 "What City Candidates Say." Brief quotes from seven political candidates, including Mailer. *New York Times*, 3 June, 37. Mailer gives his views on legalized gambling.

69.54 "What City Candidates Say." Brief quotes from seven political candidates, including Mailer. *New York Times*, 4 June, 33. Mailer comments on education, which he likens to crime: "The solutions to the problems are spiritual."

69.55 "Understanding Mailer." Column by Murray Kempton. *New York Post*, 4 June. Reflections on Mailer's campaign in the Democratic primary. Mailer is quoted on the dangers in his various proposals: "Hundreds of dangers. People who have vitality and energy are dangerous."

69.56 "Mailer Brings the Word to B'klyn." Article by Ron Hollander. *New York Post*, 5 June, 18. Report on an earlier campaign stop in Bedford-Stuyvesant where both Mailer and Breslin spoke.

69.57 "The Candidates: Norman Mailer." Article-interview by Helen Dudar. *New York Post*, 6 June, 49 (first page of the *Post Daily Magazine*, an insert). Mailer is quoted at length in this piece, one of a series on the mayoral primary candidates.

69.58 "Norman Mailer's Dream...It Could Be a Nightmare." Article by James Garrett. *Showtime: A Magazine of the Lively Arts (Cleveland Press)*, 6 June, 1-3; cover photograph of Mailer. Unexceptional profile memorable only for its quotes from and brief profiles of Mailer campaign workers, including Alice Krakauer and Peter Manso.

69.59 "What the City Candidates Are Saying." Brief quotes from nine political candidates, including Mailer. *New York Times*, 7 June, 25. Mailer's quote: "No campaign today. It is the first anniversary of Robert Kennedy's death, and there is no desire to look for votes on this June 6."

69.60 "Mailer's Style: An Orthodox Campaign Waged with Some Unorthodox Ideas." Article-interview by Bernard Weinraub. *New York Times*, 8 June, 73. A day in the life of candidate Mailer with quotes from him and advance man Jack Banning.

69.61 "Candidate Mailer: Savior or Spoiler?" Article- interview by Alan M. Adelson. *New Leader*, 9 June, 14-16. Skeptical report, with substantial quotes from Mailer, by a reporter "for a national financial newspaper which does not wish to be identified."

69.62 "The Primary: Mailer Says He'll 'Probably' Stay in Politics; Marchi Tours Bronx." Article-interview by unidentified writer. *New York Times*, 10

June, 38. Mailer says, "I will probably be in politics for the rest of my life. I mean it."

69.63 "What the Candidates Say." Brief quotes from seven political candidates, including Mailer. *New York Times*, 10 June, 38.

69.64 "The Primary: Procaccino Urges Democratic Candidates to Speak on the Issues." Article by unidentified writer. *New York Times*, 11 June, 50. Mailer is quoted in this roundup article on the primary. He proposes that the city dispense legal heroin to certain types of addicts and that local neighborhoods have local police forces.

69.65 "In the Nation: Mailer with His Hair Combed." Article by Tom Wicker. *New York Times*, 12 June, 46. Column favorable to the Mailer-Breslin ticket with brief quotes from Mailer. Rpt: 69.80.

69.66 "Mailer and Marchi: Pick the 'Conservative.'" Article by unidentified writer. *Brooklyn Heights Press and Cobble Hills News*, 12 June, 1, 3. Brief report on Mailer's earlier campaign appearance at Spencer Memorial Church in Brooklyn, juxtaposed with an appearance with Mailer's state senator, John J. Marchi, a candidate for mayor in the Republican primary.

69.67 "New York: Mailer for Mayor." Article by unidentified writer. *Time*, 13 June, 21-22. Summary article with Mailer quotes, some from earlier articles.

69.68 "Mayoral Candidates Reply to 7 Questions from the Times on Governing the City." Interview by unidentified interviewer. *New York Times*, 14 June, 14. Herman Badillo, Mayor John V. Lindsay, Mailer, John J. Marchi, Mario A. Procaccino, James H. Scheuer and Robert F. Wagner answer questions on city services, crime, finances, race relations. Mailer stresses neighborhood control and his idea of the 51st state. Excellent summaries of the candidates' positions.

69.69 "Democrats Trade Charges of Bigotry." Article by unidentified writer. *New York Times*, 15 June, 1, 56. Omnibus article on the mayoral primaries in New York. Mailer is quoted during his visit to Macy's with his fourth wife, Beverly Bentley.

69.70 "A Letter from Norman Mailer to the Voting Democrats of New York." *New York Times*, 15 June, Sec. E, p. 7. Signed "Norman and Jimmy," this 2,000-word paid advertisement-letter attacks the New York media for making the Mailer-Breslin campaign "look like clowns," and outlines the team's platform. Mailer's long letter is followed by excerpts from position papers on revenue, law and order, transportation, housing authorities and banks, schools and "Sweet Sunday," a proposed once-a-month cessation of all motorized traffic entering or leaving New York City. Rpt: Mailer's position papers, including much of the language in these excerpts, are collected in *Running against the Machine* (69.80). See Joe Flaherty's op-ed piece on "Sweet Sunday," "I Hate to Say I told You So, But...," *New York Times*, 8 February 1974, 31.

69.71 "Mayoral Candidates Vie in Two TV Debates: Democrats Get 10 Questions." Article by Clayton Knowles. *New York Times*, 16 June, 1, 50. Report on a television question-and-answer session for mayoral candidates the day before the primary election.

69.72 "Five Democratic Mayoral Candidates in Primary Today Trade Last-Minute Gibes: Badillo, Mailer, Wagner Hold News Conferences." Article by William E. Farrell. *New York Times*, 17 June, 32. Summary of last-minute statements, including Mailer's attack on Robert F. Wagner.

69.73 "From Norman Mailer, a Word of Caution for the Winners." Article by Timothy Lee. *New York Post*, 18 June, 70. Report on the post-election party at Mailer-Breslin headquarters at Columbus Circle. Mailer said, "If I'm right about this city being on the edge of doom, then heaven help this city because there's not much to look forward to with the men elected today." Breslin said, "I am mortified to take part in a process that requires the bars to be closed."

69.74 "Mailer to Back Lindsay, If..." Article by Pamela Howard. *New York Post*, 19 June, 39. Report that Mailer might back John V. Lindsay if he promises to do more for low-income people in New York.

69.75 "A Candid Talk with Mailer (Who Wants to Be Mayor of New York)." Article-interview by Joe Walker. *Muhammad Speaks* (New York), 20 June, 11-12. Focuses on minority rights and educational access. Concludes: "To be continued," but part two has not been located.

69.76 "A Literary Ticket for the 51st State." Article by Richard Woodley. *Life*, 30 June, 71-72. New and old quotes stitched into an overview of the campaign, appearing after Mailer and Breslin lost on 17 June.

69.77 "Be My Guest, Norman Mailer." *New York Post*, 1 July, 57. James A. Wechsler turns his column over to Mailer for a post-mortem. Mailer counters the "liberal canon, cemented in concrete, that we ruined Herman Badillo's chance of winning the mayoralty primary." Rpt: 69.80.

69.78 "Dear Norman Mailer." Article-interview by Irma Kurtz. *Sunday Express* (Johannesburg), 6 July, 1, 4. A 2,500-word portrait of Mailer buttressed by engaging quotes from an interview at Mailer's Brooklyn Heights apartment: "I'm in a pleasant position right now because I don't know what I'm up to. I'm not burning with a mission. I'm free to move." Rpt: A slightly truncated version appeared earlier in *Nova* (London), March, 106-7, 109.

69.79 "Shoot-for-the-Moon Mailer: An Interview with Norman Mailer on the Literary Life and Practical Politics." By Leticia Kent. *Vogue*, 15 August, 86-89, 139. Conducted in May before the primary election for mayor, Kent's interview focuses on the tension between literature and politics, writing and action. Rpt: 69.80.

69.80 *Running against the Machine: A Grass Roots Race for the New York Mayoralty* by Norman Mailer, Jimmy Breslin, Peter Maas, Gloria Steinem and others. Edited by Peter Manso. Garden City, New York: Doubleday, late August; simultaneously as a softcover. Miscellany, 313 pp., $6.95. Articles, debates, interviews, position papers, speeches and columns concerning the campaign of Mailer and Breslin for the Democratic nomination for mayor and City Council president of New York, respectively. One-paragraph preface, dated 22 July, from Mailer ending with a dedication "to the hard-working staff and the enthusiastic volunteers of the Mailer-Breslin Campaign."

69.81 "A Fire on the Moon." *Life*, 29 August, 24-41; cover photograph of Mailer. Nonfiction narrative, the first of five by Mailer in *Life*. First of a three-part series on the 1969 moon shot, later incorporated with much re-ordering into *Of a Fire on the Moon* (71.1). According to the "Editor's Note: Norman Mailer at the Typewriter" by Ralph Graves (p.1), this first installment of 26,000 words is "the longest non-fiction piece *Life* has ever published in one issue." Graves quotes Mailer on the length: "I can't write anything in 5,000 words, and 10,000 words is just for poker money." See 69.83, 70.1.

69.82 Foreword to *The End of Obscenity: The Trials of "Lady Chatterley," "Tropic of Cancer" and "Fanny Hill,"* by Charles Rembar, vii-xi. London: Deutsch, September. The 1968 American edition (New York: Random House) does not contain Mailer's foreword or introduction. It does carry a jacket blurb from Mailer taken from the first sentence of the foreword: "The book in your hand is a quiet and essentially modest account of a legal revolution." Presumably, the foreword was written too late to be included in the American first edition, and so appeared only in subsequent editions. Rembar is Mailer's first cousin, and the foreword is an admiring sketch of "Cy," who, as a student, preceded Mailer at Harvard. Rpt: As Introduction to the Bantam softcover edition, New York, September; 72.7, 82.19. See 92.12.

69.83 "The Psychology of Astronauts." *Life*, 14 November, 50-60, 62-63. Nonfiction narrative. Second of a three-part series on the 1969 moon shot, later incorporated with much reordering into *Of a Fire on the Moon* (71.1). See 69.81, 70.1.

Managing Mailer

A Saga of Mailer and Breslin's Siege of City Hall by Norman Mailer's Campaign Manager

JOE FLAHERTY

1970

Photograph by Richard Frank
70.7

70.1 "A Dream of the Future's Face." *Life*, 9 January, 56-57, 60, 62, 62B, 64, 66, 68, 70, 72, 74. Nonfiction narrative. Third of a three-part series on the 1969 moon shot, later incorporated with much reordering into *Of a Fire on the Moon* (71.1). See 69.81, 69.83.

70.2 "Mailer on Chi 7 Judge: 'A Fast Featherweight.'" Article by Doug Ireland. *New York Post*, 28 January. Report on Mailer's press conference where he commented on his testimony at the trial of the Chicago Seven for conspiracy to incite a riot at the 1968 Democratic National Convention in Chicago. The presiding judge, Julius J. Hoffman, chided Mailer for loquacity. Rpt: Part of Mailer's testimony in 70.6. See 70.3.

70.3 "'68 Yippie Plans Stunned Mailer." Article by J. Anthony Lukas. *New York Times*, 28 January, 20. Another account of Mailer's press conference on the trial of the Chicago Seven, more comprehensive than 70.2. Also included is an account of Mailer, Jerry Rubin and Abbie Hoffman eating lunch at Chicago's Standard Club, with Judge Hoffman present. Rpt: Part of Mailer's trial testimony in 70.6.

70.4 "Mailer's Opera." Article by Charles Matz. *Opera News*, 21 February, 14-16; cover photograph of Mailer. Account of the genesis of Matz's libretto for *An American Dream* (65.7) and its first reading at Mailer's home, with quotes from Mailer. No composer was found and the opera remains incomplete.

70.5 Letter to the editor. *Writer's Digest,* March, 10. Complaint about accuracy of Oriana Fallaci's interview with Mailer in *Writer's Digest* (68.21). Mailer says, "My words, my style, my very clumsiness of speech" were converted via translation from English to Italian back to English "into the spoiled and petulant tones of an Italian intellectual loved somewhat too much by his mother."

70.6 Testimony at the trial of the Chicago Seven. *The Tales of Hoffman,* edited from the official transcript by Mark L. Levine, George C. McNamee and Daniel Greenberg, 204-7. Introduction by Dwight Macdonald. New York: Bantam, March, softcover. Mailer explains his involvement with Jerry Rubin, one of those indicted, and summarizes his speech given at Grant Park in Chicago during the 1968 Democratic Convention. Mailer's speech is given in *Miami and the Siege of Chicago* (68.25). See 70.2, 70.3.

70.7 Untitled prefatory statement to *Managing Mailer,* by Joe Flaherty. New York: Coward-McCann, 1 May; London: Michael Joseph. This account of Mailer's campaign for the Democratic nomination for mayor of New York by his campaign manager quotes Mailer extensively. Mailer says in the untitled prefatory statement or blurb that "Flaherty treats a dozen delicate egos like golf balls and then proceeds to see how far he can whap them." Rpt: Flaherty's earlier account of the campaign's origins (69.10) was later incorporated into *Managing Mailer.* See numerous other 1969 entries on the mayoral campaign.

70.8 "Mailer Starts Term in Jail, Labels Nixon 'Uriah Heep.'" Article by unidentified writer. *Evening Star* (Washington, D.C.), 5 May. As he turns himself in to begin serving three days for his conviction for disorderly conduct at the Pentagon anti-war protest in October 1967, Mailer called President Nixon "the living embodiment of Uriah Heep," and implicates him in the death of four students at Kent State University. See 68.8, 70.9-70.11.

70.9 "Mailer Calls Nixon a Dickens 'Heep' Creep." Article by Betty Jones. *Washington Daily News,* 6 May. Repeats Mailer's comments about Nixon and Uriah Heep from 70.8, and adds, "It is routine for anyone in the peace movement to spend time in prison. I am hardly one of the martyrs of the movement." See 68.8, 70.10, 70.11.

70.10 "Norman Mailer to Serve Sentence in Alexandria." Article by Nancy Scannell. *Washington Post,* 6 May. Another report on Mailer beginning his sentence for crossing a police line at the Pentagon. Included is Mailer's characterization of Nixon as Uriah Heep, "the veritable cathedral of hypocrisy." See 68.8, 70.8, 70.9, 70.11.

70.11 "The Nonviolent Norman Mailer." Article-interview by Myra MacPherson. *Washington Post,* 8 May, Sec. B, pp. 1, 2. Recounts Mailer's final hours in prison serving a 30-day sentence (25 days suspended) for crossing a police line at the 22 October 1967 demonstration at the Pentagon, and a conversation in the offices of his lawyer, Phil Hirschkop. Mailer counsels the anti-war movement to be nonviolent, because "to be violent is to strengthen Nixon's hand." He characterizes Nixon's fears of losing the war as "the babblings of a Chekovian character." See 68.8, 70.8-70.10.

70.12 "Mailer at Venice with Film Aiming to Be Memorable." Article by Associated Press writer. *New York Times*, 31 August, 21. Account of Mailer's comments at Venice Film Festival where he hoped "to pick up the marbles" with his film, "Maidstone" (71.28). See 70.13.

70.13 "Mailer, in London, Trades Jabs with Audience over New Film." Article by John M. Lee. *New York Times*, 17 October, 21. Account of Mailer's interaction with audience after a showing of his film, "Maidstone" (71.28), at Cinema City, London. See 70.12.

70.14 "Deborah—from *An American Dream.*" In *This Is My Best: In the Third Quarter of the Century*, edited by Whit Burnett, 99-110. New York: Doubleday. The selection chosen—the murder of Deborah from chapter 1 of *An American Dream* (65.7)— is prefaced by a 313-word letter in which Mailer characterizes his novel as "a tea ceremony on the edge of a cliff," and calls it "my best book."

70.15 "Norman Mailer." Interview by Joseph Gelmis. In *The Film Director as Superstar*, by Joseph Gelmis, 42-63. New York: Doubleday. One of 16 interviews in this collection. Rpt: *Cavalier*, July 1970; excerpts from the interview appeared in Gelmis's "Mailer Reviews a Chaotic Year," *Newsday*, 10 January 1971, 39A; 88.6.

71.29

71.1 *Of a Fire on the Moon.* Boston: Little, Brown, 11 January; London: Weidenfeld and Nicolson, 3 September, with a different title: *A Fire on the Moon.* Nonfiction narrative, 472 pp., $7.95. Dedication: "For Susan, for Dandy, for Betsey [sic] and Kate, for Michael and Stephen Mailer." Because both the American and British editions carry a 1970 copyright date, and advance excerpts appeared in 1969 and 1970, there has been confusion about the precedence of these editions, and the actual dates of publication, which are as stated above. Nominated for the National Book Award in the sciences category. Rpt: Mailer's three-part series in *Life* on the 1969 moon shot (69.81, 69.83, 70.1) was incorporated, with major revisions, into *Of a Fire on the Moon*; 98.7 (partial). See 69.34, 72.7.

Mailer: "Nonetheless, he might be in superb shape to study the flight of Apollo 11 to the moon. For he was detached this season from the imperial demands of his ego; he could think about astronauts, space, space programs, and the moon, quite free of the fact that none of these heroes, presences, and forces were by any necessity friendly to him. No, he felt like a spirit of some just-consumed essence of the past, and so finally took the liberty to christen himself Aquarius" (71.1).

71.2 "The Siege of Mailer: Hero to Historian." Article- interview by Ron Rosenbaum. *Village Voice,* 21 January, 1, 38, 40-42, 48. Contains Mailer's most extensive comment on 71.1, drawn from Rosenbaum's report of Mailer's appearance on the David Frost Show, and his subsequent conversation with Mailer. Rpt: 88.6.

71.3 "Authors and Editors: Norman Mailer." Article- interview by Barbara A. Bannon. *Publishers' Weekly*, 25 January, 177-79. Comment on 71.1.

71.4 "The Rape of the Moon: Norman Mailer Talks about Sexual Lunacy and the WASP." Article-interview by Leticia Kent. *Vogue*, 1 February, 134-35. Extended comment on the WASP: "disciplined, stoical, able to become the instrument of his own will, has extraordinary boldness and daring together with a resolute lack of imagination."

71.5 "Light on Orwell." Article by unidentified writer. *Listener*, 4 February, 144-45. Summary of an "Omnibus" (BBC 1) program titled "The Road to the Left," which consists of a portrait of George Orwell. In 413 words, Mailer analyzes Orwell's narrative power in *1984* and praises his "profoundly prophetic" vision of a future filled with "dull, awful, obscene, miserable, picayune little wars...that would...kill the world slowly."

71.6 "Norman Mailer Crosses Swords with Women's Lib." Article-interview (part 1) by Digby Diehl. *Los Angeles Times Calendar*, 14 February, 1, 56. Mailer discusses his essay in the March *Harper's*, "The Prisoner of Sex" (71.10), with asides on his narrative persona, "Aquarius." A brief excerpt from "The Prisoner of Sex" is included. See 71.7.

71.7 "Norman Mailer—Ego, Movies and the Moon." Article- interview (part 2) by Digby Diehl. *Los Angeles Times Calendar*, 21 February, 12. Contains Mailer's explanation of the epistemological problems of using his own persona as a narrative lens: "In the most ghastly terms possible: how much of yourself should 'go public,' like a stock?" Also includes comment on 71.1 and moviemaking. See 71.6.

71.8 "Unseemly Scourged Bystander." Letter to the editor. *Saturday Review*, 27 February, 25. Mailer complains about the treatment of his friend Eddie Bonetti in Benjamin DeMott's 16 January review of *Of a Fire on the Moon* (71.1).

71.9 "The Mailer Plan to Save Los Angeles." Article- interview by unidentified writer. *Los Angeles Magazine*, March, 18-19. Mailer contrasts Los Angeles and New York and suggests how both might be improved.

71.10 "The Prisoner of Sex." *Harper's*, March, 41-46, 48, 50, 52-60, 62-66, 68-72, 77-92; cover story. Essay. This 50,000 word analysis of the Women's Liberation movement, which occupies almost the entire issue and sold out in nine days, was contributory to the resignation of *Harper's* editor Willie Morris and Mailer's separation from the magazine. Rpt: In a revised book form under the same title (71.20). See 71.11-71.13, 71.21 for contemporaneous comment, and Willie Morris's *New York Days* (New York: Little Brown, 1993) for a retrospective discussion.

71.11 "Morris Resigns in *Harper's* Dispute." Article by Alden Whitmen. *New York Times*, 5 March, 37, 71. Full report, including the text of Morris's resignation letter and an excerpt from Mailer's response to the events leading to Morris's departure shortly after the publication of "The Prisoner of Sex" (71.10). See 71.12, 71.13, 71.21.

71.12 "Mailer Tells Harper's—Me, Too." Article by Barbara Trecker. *New York Post*, 6 March, 3. In the wake of Willie Morris's resignation triggered by the publication of "The Prisoner of Sex" (71.10), Mailer says he won't write for *Harper's* in the future (which he hasn't). He praises Morris's "extraordinary courage." See 71.11, 71.13, 71.21.

71.13 "Hang-Up at *Harper's*." Article by unidentified writer. *Time*, 15 March, 41. Another article summarizing the circumstances surrounding the resignation of *Harper's* editor Willie Morris, "precipitated in large degree by a prominently displayed, controversial article [71.10] by Norman Mailer." *Time* provides a longer excerpt from Mailer's statement on Morris's resignation, which he calls "the most depressing event in American letters in many a year." See 71.11, 71.12, 71.21.

71.14 "Ego." *Life*, 19 March, 18F, 19-30, 32-36. Nonfiction narrative on the first Muhammad Ali-Joe Frazier fight. Some of the accompanying photographs were taken by Frank Sinatra. Rpt: As *King of the Hill* in 71.15, 72.7, 82.19. See 83.46.

71.15 *King of the Hill: Norman Mailer on the Fight of the Century.* New York: New American Library, April, softcover. Nonfiction narrative, 93 pp., $1. Dedication: "For Muhammad Ali and Joe Frazier." Report on the first Muhammad Ali-Joe Frazier fight. Includes "over 50 action photographs" of the fight and previous heavyweight matches back to Jack Johnson. Rpt: 71.14, 72.7, 82.19. See 75.12, 83.46.

71.16 "Norman Mailer vs. Women's Lib." Article by Israel Shenker. *New York Times*, 1 May, 19. Report on a 30 April meeting sponsored by New York University and the Theatre for Ideas titled "A Dialogue on Women's Liberation" at Town Hall in New York. Joining Mailer, the moderator, on the panel were Jacqueline Ceballos, President of the New York City chapter of the National Organization for Women, and three writers: Germaine Greer, Jill Johnston and Diana Trilling. All are quoted and/or paraphrased. A documentary film, "Town Bloody Hall," was later made about the evening by Donn Pennebaker. Mailer said later that his hair began to turn white on this night. See 71.17-71.20, 71.23, 71.27, 77.14.

71.17 "Sexism—A Better Show than Sex." Article by Frederic Morton. *Village Voice*, 6 May, 28, 70, 75. One of two *Village Voice* articles on "A Dialogue on Women's Liberation." Longer report than 71.16 with more quotes. See 71.16, 71.18-71.20, 71.23, 71.27, 77.14.

71.18 "Theatre for Ideas: Mailer and the Women." Article by Helen Kruger. *Chelsea Clinton News*, 6 May, 10. Another report on "A Dialogue on Women's Liberation," with many short quotes. See 71.16, 71.17, 71.19, 71.20, 71.23, 71.27, 77.14.

71.19 "What Happened to Mozart's Sister?" Article by Rosalyn Drexler. *Village Voice*, 6 May, 28, 70, 72. Second of two *Village Voice* articles on "A Dialogue on Women's Liberation." Contains fewer direct quotes than in 71.17. See 71.16, 71.18, 71.20, 71.23, 71.27, 77.14.

81

71.20 *The Prisoner of Sex*. Boston: Little, Brown, 27 May; London: Weidenfeld and Nicolson, August. Essay, 240 pp., $5.95. Only the first U.S. edition carries the price on the inside front dustwrapper flap. Dedication: "To Carol Stevens." Nominated for the National Book Award in the arts and letters category. Contains Mailer's most thoughtful literary criticism, an exploration of the writing of D.H. Lawrence. Rpt: Entire essay first appeared in *Harper's* (71.10), and was revised for book publication; 98.7 (partial). See 68.11, 71.16-71.19, 71.23, 71.27, 77.14.

Mailer: "Since PW [prizewinner] could also stand for Prisoner of War (which he could amend to Prisoner of Wedlock, for he had never been able to live without a woman) he had another name for himself, the PW, Prisoner or Prizewinner? They were polar concepts to be regarded at opposite ends of his ego—so they provided a base for his reactions whenever that equivalent of a phallus, that ghost-phallus of the mentality, firm strong-tongued ego, had wandered into unfamiliar scenes. After a time he thought of himself as the Prisoner" (71.20).

71.21 "Norman Mailer's Side on 'Harper's.'" Letter to the editor. *Saturday Review*, 12 June, 56. Mailer corrects a number of errors in Stuart W. Little's 10 April *Saturday Review* article about the resignation of *Harper's* editor Willie Morris following the publication of "The Prisoner of Sex" (71.10). One of the errors concerns the amount that *Life* paid Mailer for *Of a Fire on the Moon* (71.1). He received $450,000 from all sources for the book: for hardcover, softcover, serial and foreign rights. Rpt: As "To the *Saturday Review*" in 72.7, 82.19. An incorrect publication date in *Harper's* of 20 April is given in both of these reprintings.

71.22 Letter to the editor. *New York Times Book Review*, 13 June, 2. Mailer takes issue with Brigid Brophy, who questioned his use of the word "rendered" in the phrase "politics rendered every pride" in her 23 May review of *The Prisoner of Sex* (71.20). Brophy concludes that it is a malapropism and that he meant to use "surrendered" or "rent." Mailer correctly defines the word as "that process where fat heated upon a fire is returned to oil and clarified of its impurities." Rpt: As "To the *New York Times Book Review*" in 72.7, 82.19. In both reprintings an incorrect publication date in the *Book Review* of 20 June is given in the acknowledgments.

71.23 "Norman Mailer: Devil in the Fire." Article-interview by Natalie Gittelson. *Harper's Bazaar*, July, 14, 16. Another article on "A Dialogue on Women's Liberation"; a report on a later brief conversation with Mailer is appended. See 71.16-71.20, 71.27, 77.14.

71.24 "Portrait of a Man Reading." Interview by Charles Monaghan. *Book World* (*Washington Post*), 11 July, 2. Summary of Mailer's reading from boyhood to present, Edgar Rice Burroughs to Jimmy Breslin. Rpt: 88.6.

71.25 "A Course in Film-Making." *New American Review*, no. 12 [August], 200-241. Essay, containing Mailer's most extensive insights on the nature of film. This number was advertised in the 16 August *New York Times*. Rpt: 71.28, 72.7, 82.19.

71.26 Preface to...*Sting Like a Bee: The Muhammad Ali Story*, by José Torres, ix-xiv. Epilogue by Budd Schulberg. Sketches by LeRoy Neiman. New York: Abelard-Schuman, late August or early September. See 75.12.

71.27 "My Mailer Problem." Article by Germaine Greer. *Esquire*, September, 90-93, 214, 216. Still another account of "A Dialogue on Women's Liberation" from the perspective of one of the participants. Many quotes from Mailer and a good deal of context from Greer. Mailer is parodied on the cover as King Kong holding Greer as Fay Wray in his hands, and inside as a vampirish boxer. *Esquire* later apologized for its treatment of Mailer. See 71.16-71.20, 71.23, 77.14 and *Covering the Sixties: George Lois, The Esquire Era*, by George Lois. New York: Monacelli Press, 1996. Lois created the cover and reports the responses of Mailer and *Esquire* editor, Harold Hayes. Rpt: In *Norman Mailer: Modern Critical Views*, edited by Harold Bloom. New York: Chelsea House, 1986; and in Greer's collection, *The Madwoman's Underclothes: Essays and Occasional Writings*. New York: Atlantic Monthly Press, September 1987.

71.28 *Maidstone: A Mystery*. New York: New American Library, October, softcover. Screenplay, 189 pp., $1.50. Dedication: "To Ricky Leacock, Donn Pennebaker, Nick Proferes, Jim Desmond, To Jan Welt *and* Lana Jokel *and to* Buzz Farbar." Includes "A Combined Account of the Filming of *Maidstone*" drawn from accounts by Sally Beauman (68.17), J. Anthony Lukas (68.14) and James Toback (68.28); "A Course in Film-Making" (71.25); 12 pages of color photographs; a cast list and various notes on the film. The only differences between 71.25 and 71.28 is that "Film-Making" becomes "FilmMaking" in 71.28; and "I: On the Theory" is reordered in 71.28. Rpt: 71.25, 72.7, 82.19. See 68.16, 81.19, 84.1. See also *Filmmakers Newsletter* 4 (no. 11) which contains an account of the piece by Jan Welt and an interview with Rip Torn that comments on his famous fight with Norman T. Kingsley that concludes "Maidstone."

71.29 *The Long Patrol: 25 Years of Writing from the Work of Norman Mailer*, edited with an introduction by Robert F. Lucid. New York: World, 25 October, 739 pp., $15. Selections from all of Mailer's major books through *Of a Fire on the Moon* (71.1), with an important critical introduction and short introductions (containing publication details) to each selection. Lucid (and Mailer's mother) created Mailer's literary archive in the late 1960s. He is one of Mailer's literary executors, and the authorized biographer.

71.30 "Norman's Phantasmagoria." Review-interview by Jay Cocks. *Time*, 15 November, 97-98. Review of "Maidstone" (71.28) with interspersed comment from Mailer on its production and significance. See 68.14-68.18, 68.28.

71.31 Introduction to *Deaths for the Ladies (and Other Disasters)*. 5 pp., unnumbered. New York: New American Library, December, softcover. Mailer ends his introduction with a reprinting of the 30 March 1962 *Time* review of the first edition of *Deaths for the Ladies* (62.3), and his poetic response to it (62.8), followed by this concluding sentence: "Instead, the review in *Time* put iron into my heart again, and rage, and the feeling that the enemy was more alive than ever, and dirtier in the alley, and so one had to mend, and put on the armor, and go to war, go out to war again, and try to hew huge strokes with the only broadsword God ever gave you, a glimpse of something like Almighty prose."

71.32 Untitled comment. In *Attacks of Taste*, edited by Evelyn B. Byrne and Otto M. Penzler, 29. New York: Gotham Book Mart. Limited edition of 500 copies. In response to the editors' question about his adolescent reading, Mailer responded: "I'm afraid my favorite novels in high school were The *Amateur Gentleman* by Jeffrey Farnol and Rafael Sabatini's *Captain Blood*." This volume consists of the answers of writers to this question. See 79.30.

72.7

1972

72.1 "Mailer's on Tour, Recouping." Article by Janet Chusmir. *Miami Herald*, 7 February, 16A. Speaking at Temple Israel, Mailer discusses his debate with the Women's Liberation movement.

72.2 "Mailer Discusses His Film." Article by Marta Justak. *Chronicle* (Duke University), 9 February, 1-2. After a showing of "Maidstone" (71.28), Mailer responds to comments and criticism from a student audience, one of many such encounters during this year on the road. See 72.3.

72.3 "Mailer Hails Cinéma Vérité of His Film 'Maidstone.'" Article by David Arneke. *Chronicle* (Duke University), 11 February, 2. Another article on the showing of "Maidstone" (71.28) at Duke University and Mailer's subsequent dialogue with the audience. He said, "...it's too tricky to have to be in the center of the film as an actor and also be the director." See 72.2.

72.4 "Getting at the Truth about Norman Mailer." Article by Bob Schwaback. *Evening Journal* (Wilmington, Del.), 22 February, Sec. 2, pp. 1-2. One of two articles on Mailer's meeting with students at the University of Delaware, which followed a showing of "Maidstone" (71.28). See 72.5.

72.5 "Mailer Offers Views on 'Amateur' Movie." Article by Janet Piorko and Mimi Boudart. *Review* (University of Delaware), 22 February, 1, 10. A second article on Mailer's appearance at the University of Delaware, where he showed "Maidstone" (71.28) and spoke to the audience. Mailer said that the film's impetus came from the assassination of Robert Kennedy. The event "hit deep....in a way which is almost impossible to describe now."

72.6 "Drunken Mailer Amuses Full House." Article by David G. Hoffman. *Harvard Crimson*, 15 April, pp. 1, 7. Brief report on Mailer's appearance at a *Harvard Advocate* benefit which included a showing of excerpts from his films. According to Hoffman, Mailer displayed "magnetic charisma" during his talk, which included this comment: "I don't know what I'm going to say next, but whatever I say, it will have my full heart behind it." See 72.8.

72.7 *Existential Errands.* Boston: Little, Brown, 17 April; Sevenoaks, Kent: New English Library, August 1982. The British edition combines 72.7 with *The Short Fiction of Norman Mailer* (67.11) under the title *The Essential Mailer* (82.19). Miscellany, 365 pp., $7.95. Dedication: "To Barbara, to Susan, to Adeline, and to Al." Rpt: 98.7 (partial).

Mailer: "This collection covers pieces written almost entirely in the last five years, a period in which *The Deer Park* as a play [67.13] was given its last draft and then produced, *Why Are We in Vietnam?* [67.15] was written and then *The Armies of the Night* [68.8], *Miami and the Siege of Chicago* [68.25], *Of a Fire on the Moon* [71.1] and *The Prisoner of Sex* [71.20]. Three movies ["Wild 90," "Beyond the Law" and "Maidstone"] were also made. So it is a period when, with every thought of beginning a certain big novel which had been promised for a long time, the moot desire to have one's immediate say on contemporary matters kept diverting the novelistic impulse into journalism" (72.7). Of the six books named above all but *The Deer Park: A Play* were nominated for a National Book Award in four different categories. *The Armies of the Night* won for arts and letters, and a Pulitzer Prize in general nonfiction as well.

72.8 "God Bless Drinking in Public." Article by Bill Beckett. *Harvard Crimson*, 20 April, 2. Longer (than 72.6), wittier report on Mailer's appearance at a *Harvard Advocate* benefit, from the cocktail hour to the wee hours.

72.9 "Why Is the Moon So Boring." Panel Discussion. *National Observer*, May, 22. Excerpts from a transcript of an NBC panel moderated by John Chancellor and Edwin Newman. Besides Mailer, the other panelists were Arthur C. Clarke, James Dickey and Rear Admiral Alan B. Shepard Jr. Mailer dominates the discussion of why the Apollo 11 mission failed to excite public imagination: "One of the reasons it didn't is there was no attempt made to explore the sensuous properties of the moon." See 71.1, 72.24, 73.1.

72.10 "The Evil in the Room." *Life*, 28 July, 26-28, 30. Nonfiction narrative on the Republican convention in Miami. Rpt: In a slightly revised form as "Portraits and Powers," part 1 of *St. George and the Godfather* (72.17).

72.11 "Norman Mailer Speaks: Films vs. Plays." Interview by Leticia Kent. *Vogue*, 1 September, 200, 202, 204. Mailer contrasts film and literature, reprising " A Course in Film-Making" (71.25), with additional comment on Andy Warhol as a filmmaker.

72.12 "Norman Mailer Talks Politics at Towson." Article by Randi Henderson. (Baltimore) *Sun*, 9 October, Sec. B, p. 1. Report on Mailer's appearance at Towson State University where he discussed the Women's Liberation movement and *St. George and the Godfather* (72.17), which he said had not yet been released because "book publishers are all Democrats and distributors all Republicans." See 72.19.

72.13 "Mailer Finds Book Is No Advertisement for Himself." Article by Eric Pace. *New York Times*, 18 October, 49, 93. Report on a meeting between Mailer and Alan Lelchuk at which Mailer complained about Lelchuk's forthcoming novel, *American Mischief*, in which Norman Mailer is shot dead. See 72.15.

72.14 "Mailer Criticizes American Politics." Article by Jeanne Janes and Tom Richards. *Daily Texan* (University of Texas), 19 October, 1. Report on Mailer's appearance at the University of Texas where he discussed the 1972 conventions and the Vietnam War.

72.15 "Norman Mailer Asks Correction of Quote." Article by unidentified writer. *New York Times*, 19 October, 49. Mailer corrects the report of what he said to Alan Lelchuk in 72.13.

72.16 "Norman Mailer in Full Cry." Article by William Moore. *San Francisco Chronicle*, 26 October, 7. Report on an impromptu discussion with students after Mailer's speech at University of California, Berkeley on October 25. Mailer comments on the Women's Liberation movement, Gore Vidal, Dick Cavett, Johnny Carson and Richard Nixon.

72.17 *St. George and the Godfather*. New York: New American Library, late October, softcover. Nonfiction narrative on the 1972 political conventions, 229 pp., $1.50. Dedication: "To dad (alias Isaac Barnett Mailer)." A September publication date is given on the copyright page; it is incorrect, as explained in 72.12, 72.19. Rpt: Advance excerpts appeared in *Life* (72.10) and *New York Review of Books* (72.20); 76.5; with an introduction by John Leonard in the first hardcover and (simultaneous) softcover editions. New York: Arbor House (83.49); 98.7 (partial).

Mailer: "So Norman Mailer, who looked to rule himself by Voltaire's catch-all precept, 'Once a philosopher, twice a pervert' and preferred therefore never to repeat a technique, was still obliged to call himself Aquarius again for he had not been in Miami two days before he knew he would not write objectively about the Convention of '72" (72.17).

72.18 "The Day the Movement Died." Article by Dotson Rader. *Esquire*, November, 130-35, 194, 196-98, 200, 202, 204. Mailer is quoted several times in this long article on the decline and fall of various protest movements. Rpt: In a revised form as "With Mailer at the Senator's" in *Blood Dues*. New York: Knopf, 1973. Rader's book also includes an account of the anti-war rally at the Cathedral of St. John the Divine in New York in December 1971 at which a dramatic fragment from *Why Are We in Vietnam?* (67.15) was read. Also reprinted in the "Fiftieth Anniversary Collector's Issue," *Esquire: How We Lived, 1933-1983* (June 1983). See 67.15, 85.11.

72.19 "Norman Mailer in Illinois." Article-interview by Mike Lennon. *Sunrise* (Macomb, Ill.), no. 4 (November), 24-26. Report on a late October appearance at Western Illinois University where Mailer showed his second film, "Beyond the Law," and read from the still-unreleased *St. George and the Godfather* (72.17). Interview questions center on narrative perspective in Mailer's nonfiction. Mailer also mentions "a very long novel" he is working on with "60,000 words or six chapters completed." The novel is *Ancient Evenings* (83.18). See 72.12.

72.20 "The Genius." *New York Review of Books*, 2 November, 16-20. Election issue, lead story. Nonfiction narrative. Advance excerpts from part 3, "Program," of *St. George and the Godfather* (72.17) focusing on Richard Nixon. This issue appeared on newsstands at approximately the same time as 72.17, in late October.

72.21 "Mailer: A Maverick Who Became...Aquarius Rex." Article-interview by Bruce Cook. *National Observer*, 4 November, 1, 15. Report on Mailer's late October appearance at State University of New York at Stony Brook where he read from 72.17, and then answered Cook's questions on the 60s, film, and the future of American society. Asked what shape radical movements should take in the 70s, he said: "And if I have a fundamental notion it's that people have to do their own work. I'm not prescribing." Rpt: As "Aquarius Rex" in *Will the Real Norman Mailer Please Stand Up*, edited by Laura Adams. Port Washington, N.Y.: Kennikat, 1974.

72.22 "TV Review: Mailer and Laing Seen in Channel 13 Talk." Article by John J. O'Conner. *New York Times*, 10 November, 72. Review of a program hosted by Patrick Watson, on which Mailer and R.D. Laing discussed schizophrenia and other matters. O'Conner found the show to be a "disaster," but the Mailer quotes he gives suggest otherwise. Mailer says that if he could be born again, he would choose to spend nine months in the womb of "a black woman of marvelous grace and strength."

72.23 "Moral Superiority." Letter to the editor. *Time*, 11 December, 9. Complaint about being quoted out of context in the "People" section, 6 November, regarding the moral superiority of George McGovern.

72.24 "Caribbean Cruise Attempts to Seek Meaning of Apollo." Article by Tim Buckley. *New York Times*, 12 December, 49, 53. Report on a cruise aboard the S.S. Statendam organized to observe the launch of the Apollo 17 mission and give seminars on space and humanity's future. Mailer was joined by the following at panel discussions: Hugh Downs, narrator, Dr. Robert D. Enzmann, Isaac Asimov, Ben Bova and Robert Heinlein. Katherine Anne Porter, covering the event for *Playboy*, was in the audience. Mailer criticized N.A.S.A. for having "taken the most exciting event of the 20th century [Apollo 11, the moon shot] and succeeded in making it monumentally boring and profoundly depressing." See 71.1, 72.9, 73.1.

You are invited to attend the party in celebration of

NORMAN MAILER'S FIFTIETH BIRTHDAY

On which occasion he will make an announcement of national importance (major)

Monday, February 5, 1973 from 10 p.m.

Four Seasons Restaurant
Park Avenue & 52nd Street

Music, Food & Beverage

Dress: Finery

Proceeds for the benefit of THE FIFTH ESTATE
$50 per couple (2 tickets)
$30 individual (1 ticket)
Make checks payable to: The Fifth Estate
For Information: MU 7-4400

See 73.2

73.1 "What Apollo Has Meant to Mankind." Interview by Diana Loercher. *Christian Science Monitor*, 3 January, 13. Aboard the S.S. Statendam as a participant in a symposium on space and humanity's future, and to observe the launch of Apollo 17, Mailer made extended remarks which were edited into a 1,000 word statement centering on the possibility that moon and space colonies might address "the fundamental impasse of 20th-century man and woman...they cannot find communities which express their philosophical ideas, their social ideas, and their private ideas." The comments of Katherine Anne Porter, who also made the voyage, are juxtaposed to Mailer's on the same page. See 71.1, 72.9, 72.24.

73.2 "Mailer's Guests ($50 a Couple) Hear His Plan on 'Secret Police.'" Article by Mel Gussow. *New York Times*, 6 February, 23. Report on Mailer's 5 February 50th birthday party at the Four Seasons restaurant in New York at which he announced "The Fifth Estate," a "democratic secret police" to keep tabs on the FBI and the CIA. Five hundred people attended, including many members of Mailer's family. The magazine *Counter-Spy* (see 75.4) was one of the fruits of the effort. See 73.3-73.8, 73.10, 73.11, 73.18, 74.6, 75.6.

73.3 "A Party Scripted by Norman Mailer, Age 50." Article by Jan Hodenfield. *New York Post*, 6 February, 2, 74. Report on Mailer's 50th birthday party, with quotes from Mailer and a number of guests. See 73.2, 73.4-73.8, 73.10, 73.11, 73.18.

73.4 "Mailer Clarifies His 'Fifth Estate.'" Article by unidentified writer. *New York Times*, 7 February, 45. On 6 February, the day after he had proposed "The Fifth Estate," Mailer called a news conference to say that he regretted calling his proposed organization "a people's police." He went on to compare "The Fifth Estate" with the American Civil Liberties Union, Common Cause and Nader's Raiders. He said it would be a "kind of ombudsman" that would perform "objective, scholarly work," and he would like to have "an umbilical relationship" to it. See 73.2-73.4, 73.6-73.8, 73.10, 73.11, 73.18.

73.5 "Norman Mailer Turns 50: The Rise and Fall of the 'Fifth Estate.'" Article by Sally Quinn. *Washington Post*, 7 February, Sec. B ("Style"), pp. 1, 7. An unfriendly report on Mailer's birthday party and his 6 February news conference. See 73.2-73.4, 73.6-73.8, 73.10, 73.11, 73.18.

73.6 "Mailer's Birthday: 'People's CIA?'" Article by Lucian K. Truscott IV. *Village Voice*, 8 February, 1, 24-25. Contains the most complete account of Mailer's comments at his 50th birthday party, including his opening dirty joke. See 73.2-73.5, 73.7, 73.8, 73.10, 73.11, 73.18.

73.7 "A Half Century of Mailer." Article by Linda Francke. *Newsweek*, 19 February, 78. Later report on Mailer's 50th birthday party. See 73.2-73.6, 73.8, 73.10, 73.11, 73.18.

73.8 "Fifth Estate at the Four Seasons." Article by Patricia Bosworth. *Saturday Review*, March, 5, 7. Another later report on Mailer's birthday party; contains additional Mailer quotes. See 73.2-73.7, 73.10, 73.11, 73.18.

73.9 "Writer as Something Else." Article by Wilfred Sheed. *New York Times Book Review*, 4 March, 2. Six writers—Mailer, Philip Roth, Jean Stafford, John Updike, Kurt Vonnegut and Murray Kempton—respond to Sheed's inquiry as to their profession had they not chosen writing. Mailer says he can't think of what he might have been except "a lazy lover with women working for me." Rpt: In Sheed's *The Good Word and Other Words*. New York: E.P. Dutton, 1978.

73.10 "The Morning After." *New York Times Book Review*, 11 March, 55, 46. Essay. Responding, in part, to John Leonard's 18 February *Book Review* essay, "Happy Birthday, Norman Mailer!" Mailer ruminates on "a fundamental question of government: Is our history developing into a string of connected conspiracies?" He also admits that he failed to properly introduce his idea of "The Fifth Estate" at his 50th birthday party. See 73.2-73.8, 73.11, 73.18, 74.6, 75.4, 75.6.

73.11 "Reliable Source: Norman Mailer's Sex Change Operation." Article by Timothy Ferris. *Rolling Stone*, 15 March, 24. Still another report on Mailer's 50th birthday party. See 73.2-73.8, 73.10, 73.18.

73.12 "A Transit to Narcissus." *New York Review of Books*, 17 May, 3-10. Review of "Last Tango in Paris," directed by Bernardo Bertolucci. One of two movie reviews by Mailer. Mailer's review appeared at almost the same time in *Evergreen Review*, no. 97 (summer), 19-22. Rpt: *Bernardo Bertolucci's "Last Tango in Paris."* New York: Delacorte; 82.16. See 73.40, 74.2, 78.2, 92.4.

73.13 "Class of '43—Waiting for Mailer." Article by Bill Fripp. *Boston Globe*, 15 June. Report on Mailer at his Harvard 30th class reunion and his speech at the occasion. Mailer is quoted on his forthcoming book, *Marilyn: A Biography* (73.30), *Of a Fire on the Moon* (71.1) and Watergate. See 73.15.

73.14 "Mailer on Mailer: An Interview." By Matthew Grace and Steve Roday. *New Orleans Review* 3 (no. 3), 229-34. Important interview in which Mailer discusses several of his books, narrative technique and the novel. He gave the interview just before "The Prisoner of Sex" (71.10) appeared in the March 1971 *Harper's*. The interview was held back so as to be included with three essays on Mailer in this number of the *Review*.

73.15 "Mailer 'Misquoted' Self." Letter to the editor. *Boston Globe*, 21 June. Mailer restates his comments on Marilyn Monroe made to Bill Fripp at his Harvard reunion. See 73.13.

73.16 "Mailer Denies He Plagiarized." Article by Eric Pace. *New York Times*, 27 June, 68. Report on statements by Mailer and his lawyer, Charles Rembar, denying the unauthorized use of the work of Marilyn Monroe biographers, Fred Lawrence Guiles and Maurice Zolotow, in *Marilyn: A Biography* (73.30). Accompanied by an article from the *Times'* London correspondent reporting that Mark Goulden, publisher of the biographies by Guiles and Zolotow, stood by the plagiarism charge. The parties later settled the matter out of court. See 73.19 and following entries; "The Mailer Case: Authors and Law," article by Lesley Oelsner, *New York Times*, 19 July, 30; also the huge advertisement for 73.30 in *New York Times Book Review*, 9 December, 14-15, in which Zolotow retracts his charge of plagiarism and Guiles says he never made a charge.

73.17 "Marilyn." *Ladies' Home Journal*, July, 79-83, 106, 108, 110-11; cover story. Biography. Rpt: Appearing one month before the biography, this advance excerpt appeared with numerous changes and additions as chapter 1 of *Marilyn: A Biography* (73.30).

73.18 "Mailer's 5th Estate: Who's Paranoid Now?" Article by Frank Crowther. *Village Voice*, 12 July, 1, 10-13. A reconsideration of Mailer's 5 February birthday party at the Four Seasons restaurant in New York by its organizer. Crowther summarizes the media's initial conclusions about the event and then polls a number of the same reporters and some of the other guests about their estimates of Mailer's ideas about governmental conspiracy in light of recent Watergate revelations. Most argue that Mailer was prophetic. Crowther also quotes from a then-unpublished interview with Mailer (74.3) and from a 30 June conversation with him in which Mailer characterizes his 5 February speech: "I knew the height of the hurdle, and I missed. I gave them [the media] a free ride." See 73.2-73.8, 73.10, 73.11, 73.18, 76.10.

73.19 "TV: Mailer Discusses Death of Marilyn Monroe." Article by John J. O'Conner. *New York Times*, 13 July, 71. Report on Mailer's interview with Mike Wallace on "60 Minutes" in which he discussed the possibility of Monroe being murdered, her relationship with Robert Kennedy and the reasons why the final chapter of 73.30 was incomplete. Rpt: A small portion of the interview appears in *Minute by Minute...*, by Don Hewitt, 69. New York: Random House, 1985. A longer excerpt is found in *Close Encounters: Mike Wallace's Own Story*, by Mike Wallace and Gary Paul Gates, 366-67. New York: William Morrow, 1984. Neither book gives the full interview; both quote Mailer disadvantageously. See other 1973 entries, 75.3, 74.12, 77.7.

73.20 "Two Myths Converge: NM Discovers MM." Article-interview by Marsh Clark. *Time*, 16 July, 60-64, 69-70; cover photograph of Mailer and Marilyn Monroe. Mailer makes brief comments about 73.30 in this cover story, which is also a book review and a profile of Mailer. See other 1973 entries.

73.21 "Wallace vs. Mailer: Guess Who Won?" Column by Clarence Petersen. *Chicago Tribune*, 18 July. Mailer is quoted to the same effect as in 73.19. See other 1973 entries, 74.12, 77.7.

73.22 "The Capote Perplex: An Open Letter from Norman Mailer." *Rolling Stone*, 19 July, 8. Mailer reprises a 1958 "Open End" television program with David Susskind (host), Truman Capote and Dorothy Parker, and his later conversations about the show with Capote, recalled to counter Capote's memories of the show given in a 12 April *Rolling Stone* interview. See 59.3, 77.7.

73.23 "Mailer Meets the Press and Issues a Challenge." Article by unidentified writer. *New York Times*, 19 July, 30. Brief report (one of four) on an 18 July press conference at which Mailer invited the press to investigate the possibility that Marilyn Monroe was murdered. He also noted that he would probably rewrite the final chapter of 73.30 for its softcover edition (75.3). The article is accompanied by another analyzing the charges of plagiarism against Mailer (later dropped): "The Mailer Case: Authors and Law" by Lesley Oelsner. See other 1973 entries, 74.12, 77.7.

73.24 "Mailer Takes the Spotlight for 'Marilyn.'" Article by John DeCanio. *The Record* (Bergen County, N.J.), 19 July, Sec. B, pp. 1-2. One of several articles, with many quotes, on Mailer's 18 July press conference at the Algonquin Hotel in New York, called to present his theory that Marilyn Monroe may have been murdered, and to complain about his treatment by Mike Wallace on "60 Minutes." See other 1973 entries, 74.12, 75.3, 77.7.

73.25 "Mailer Urges Probe of Marilyn's Death." Article by Carol Kramer. *Chicago Tribune*, 19 July, Sec. 3, p. 16. Another article on Mailer's press conference at which he urged that the death of Marilyn Monroe be investigated as a possible murder. See other 1973 entries, 74.12, 75.3, 77.7.

73.26 "Problems of Writing 'Marilyn.'" Article by Stephen Isaacs. *New York Post*, 19 July, Sec. B, pp. 1, 13. The longest and most sympathetic of several articles on Mailer's press conference called to urge a fuller investigation of Marilyn Monroe's death. Mailer also defended his methods of researching *Marilyn* (73.30), calling it "one of my best books," and criticized Mike Wallace for the editing of Mailer's appearance on "60 Minutes." In response to Wallace's comment that he had undertaken the book only for money, Mailer noted that he was paid a royalty of four percent for 73.30, as opposed to his customary fifteen percent. See other 1973 entries, 74.12, 75.3, 77.7.

73.27 "A Conversation with Norman Mailer." Interview by James Whitfield Ellison. *Book-of-the-Month-Club News*, August, 4, 24; cover story. Mailer explains his motives and methods (he saw 18 of Monroe's 23 movies) for 73.30. It was a main B-O-M-C selection with a press run of 240,000.

73.28 "The Jewish Princess." *Atlantic*, August, 33-53; cover story. Biography. Rpt: Appearing at about the same time as the biography, this excerpt, with small changes at the beginning and end, appears as chapter 7 of 73.30.

73.29 "Marilyn." *Ladies' Home Journal*, August, 79, 126-28, 130-34. Biography. Rpt: Appearing at about the same time as the biography, this excerpt, with several small changes, appears as "Lonely Lady," the eighth and final chapter of 73.30.

73.30 *Marilyn: A Biography; Pictures by the World's Foremost Photographers.* Produced by Lawrence Schiller; Designed by Allen Hurlburt. New York: Grosset and Dunlap, 1 August; London: Hodder and Stoughton, 8 October. 111 photographs, 271 pp., $19.95. No dedication. Mailer's contribution was originally to have been a 25,000-word preface to a selection of Monroe photographs, but it grew into a 95,000 word biography. Rpt: Advance excerpts appeared in *Ladies' Home Journal* (73.17, 73.29), *Atlantic* (73.28) and *New York Review of Books* (73.34). A three-hour adaptation by Dalene Young, "Marilyn: The Untold Story," appeared on ABC-TV on 28 September 1980. The 1988 reprint edition (New York: Galahad) carries the title, *Marilyn: The Classic*. Two excerpts also appeared in *The Time of Our Time* (98.7). See other 1973 entries, 75.1, 75.3, 80.14, 80.15, 81.4, 82.9, 86.23, 86.25, 94.5.

Mailer: "...the next question is whether a life like hers is not apathetic to biographical tools. Certainly the two guides already published show the limitations of a conventional approach. The first, by Maurice Zolotow, *Marilyn Monroe*, written while she was still alive, is filled with interesting psychoanalytical insights of the sort one can hear at a New York coffee table when two intelligent people are analyzing a third, but his material is reamed with overstressed and hollow anecdotes untrustworthy by the very style of their prose, a feature writer heating up the old dishes of other feature writers, and so a book which has fewer facts than factoids (to join the hungry ranks of those who coin a word), that is, facts which have no existence before appearing in a magazine or newspaper..." (73.30).

73.31 "The Author on Norman Mailer: Style Is As Good As It Ever Was." Article-interview by Tom Fitzpatrick. *Chicago Sun-Times*, 5 August, 66. More comment on 73.30 including the fact (revealed by Fitzpatrick) that it "is already near the top of the best-seller list."

73.32 "Mailer Threatens 'Marilyn' Suit: Calls for Apology from Zolotow." Article by Eric Pace. *New York Times*, 7 August, 28. Report on a statement from Mailer deriding a complaint by Maurice Zolotow that Mailer had violated an agreement on the use of materials from Zolotow's biography of Marilyn Monroe. See other 1973 entries and earlier article on Zolotow's charges in the *Times*, 4 August, 19.

73.33 "Marilyn Monroe's Sudden Death." *Village Voice*, 9 August, 4, 60. Consists of Mailer's press release, distributed at an 18 July press conference, with a brief introductory statement by him questioning why Ron Rosenbaum did not make much of the release in his 2 August *Village Voice* article, "Mailer on Monroe: Through a Gloss, Darkly." Rpt: With additional prefatory and concluding comments as "The Murder File" in the softcover edition of *Marilyn: A Biography* (75.3); and without any contextual comments in 75.1. See other 1973 entries.

73.34 "Married to Marilyn." *New York Review of Books*, 9 August, 11-14. Biography. Rpt: Appearing at about the same time as the biography, this excerpt, with a number of small changes appears as part of "Marilyn," chapter 5 of 73.30.

73.35 "Mailer Enjoys a Day in the Sun at MacDowell Colony." Article by unidentified writer. *New York Times*, 20 August, 20. Report on the 18 August awarding of the MacDowell Medal "in recognition of the tremendous body and wide variety of work he has published to date." Mailer "delivered an acceptance speech that obviously captivated" the audience, including comments about an idea for a novel about Watergate, his 50th birthday party, and the individual who presented the medal, John Leonard. Rpt: Mailer's speech appears, in part, in 74.7, the preface to 76.5 and the foreword to 98.7.

73.36 "The Masquerader in a Male Chauvinist Wig." Article-interview by Joyce Haber. *Los Angeles Times Calendar*, 2 September, 11, 59. Essentially a long review of *Marilyn* (73.30), this piece includes a few quotes from Mailer, including his comment that the first draft was 105,000 words in length.

73.37 "Marilyn, Mailer's *Marilyn*." Article-interview by Jim Wood. *California Living* (*San Francisco Chronicle*), 9 September, 22-24. Report on Mailer's visit to San Francisco on the occasion of the publication of 73.30.

73.38 "Mailer Says His Perception of Marilyn Important." Article-interview by Roger Ebert. *Mobile, Alabama Press-Register*, 23 September. Rpt: From *Chicago Sun-Times*. See other 1973 entries.

73.39 "Mailer and the Siege of Chicago." Article-interview by Clifford Terry. *Chicago Tribune Magazine*, 30 September, 32, 34, 37, 39-41, 42. One of the best reports of Mailer-on-the-book-tour, including Mailer's interaction with Irv Kupcinet, Bob Cromie, Lee Phillip and other Chicago journalists. Focus is on 73.30. See 73.42.

73.40 "Mailer on Marriage and Women." Interview by Buzz Farbar. *Viva*, October, 74-76, 144, 146, 148, 150, 152. Mailer's lengthiest interview on women, sex and marriage, with comment on his review of "Last Tango in Paris" (73.12) and 73.30. Mailer comments on this interview in 75.1. Rpt: As "Marriage" in 82.16 (partial). See 81.23, 90.3.

73.41 "Norman Mailer: Narcissus and an Untold Joke." Article by Judy Flander. *Washington Star-News*, 2 October, Sec. C, p. 3. Report of Mailer's appearance before the Woman's National Democratic Club in Washington, where he commented on 73.30, his 50th birthday party, and the profession of journalism. See other 1973 entries.

73.42 "'Marilyn Would Have Eaten Me Alive.'" Article by Jane Shapiro. *Village Voice*, 11 October, 87-88. Report on Mailer's appearance on Bob Cromie's television show, "Book Beat," where he discusses Marilyn Monroe and his biography (73.30) of her: "You know, you always live on the edge of mystery when you're dealing with a beautiful woman." See 73.39.

73.43 Untitled interview. By William Baises, Robert Harvey, Robert Merrill, Henry Nuwer and William Wilborn. *Brushfire* (University of Nevada at Reno) 23 (no. 1), November or December, 7-20. Wide-ranging interview with faculty and students of the Department of English conducted after his 4 October reading at the University. Mailer comments on several of his books, the writers of the 1930s, John Updike, Stephen Crane, and James Agee, whom Mailer knew slightly.

73.44 "Norman Mailer at the Tufts Gym." Article by Martin F. Kohn. *Providence Sunday Journal Leisure Weekly*, 2 December, Sec. H, p. 23. Report of Mailer's appearance at Tufts University where he spoke on journalism and the novel: "It is my profoundest idea, at least my profoundest idea tonight, that if we cannot perceive an idea for ourselves, we should know the observer through whom we perceive it secondhand." See 81.2.

73.45 Advertisement for *Marilyn: A Biography*. *New York Times*, 9 December, 13-15. Mailer composed this advertisement, which consists of both positive and negative quotes from reviews of 73.30 (similar to 55.5), a response to Mike Wallace's editing of his interview with Mailer on "60 Minutes," and publication figures: 400,000 copies in print. See earlier 1973 entries, 74.12, 77.7.

73.46 "Norman Mailer Talks to Melvyn Bragg about the Bizarre Business of Writing a Hypothetical Life of Marilyn Monroe." Interview. *Listener*, 20 December, 847-50. Transcript of a "Second House" (BBC 2) television interview. Conducted during his British promotional tour for the book, this is Mailer's longest and best interview on 73.30. Rpt: 88.6. See other 1973 entries.

73.47 "A Mystery," chapter 11 of *The Martian Invasion*. In *As They Were*, edited by Tuli Kupferberg and Sylvia Topp, no pagination. New York: Links, softcover. One page, one chapter, excerpt from space adventure written by Mailer at age 10, or perhaps earlier. Volume consists of childhood photos of famous people and some juvenilia. Rpt: *First Glance: Childhood Creations of the Famous*, edited by Tuli Kupferberg and Sylvia Topp. New York: Hammond, 1978.

MAY 1974
PRICE $1

THE MAGAZINE FOR MEN

The great art of the 70's
Norman Mailer reports on graffiti

Dwight Macdonald's
plan to save the
U.S. Constitution

The return of the
sexy nightgown

The roughest,
toughest men in
the U.S.A.

Photograph by Jean-
Paul Goude
74.8

74.1 "The Rich, Famous, Talented and Powerful Resolve...." Article-interview by Deirdre Carmody. *New York Times*, 1 January, Sec. C, p. 21. A number of notables, including Mailer, Senator Sam J. Ervin Jr., David Rockefeller, Ralph Nader, Julia Child, Alice Roosevelt Longworth and a dozen others, were asked to give their objectives for the coming year. Mailer's full reply: "To work on a novel....Just those five words, to work on a novel."

74.2 "Some Notables Name Their Bests." Questionnaire by unidentified writer. *New York Times*, 6 January, Sec. II, p. 9. Mailer and 14 others, including Joyce Carol Oates, Joan Crawford, Billie Jean King, Beverly Sills and Wilt Chamberlain, name their favorite movies of 1973. Mailer's choices: "Spider's Strategem," "The Conformist," "Last Tango in Paris" (see 73.12), "Cries and Whispers," "Save the Tiger," "Paper Moon," "The Life and Times of Judge Roy Bean," "The Heartbreak Kid," "The Way We Were," "The Devil in Miss Jones," "Hex."

74.3 "Frank Crowther: Norman Mailer, Part II." Interview by Frank Crowther. *Changes*, no. 86 (mid-January), 25-26. The first part of this interview, still unlocated, apparently appeared in an earlier issue of this New York-based cultural tabloid. Crowther, whom Mailer later eulogized (see 76.10), was one of the organizers of Mailer's 50th birthday party (see 73.18). In this interview conducted in fall 1971, Mailer responds to quotations served up by Crowther from E.B. White, Konrad Lorenz, Georges Simenon, William Burroughs, Alberto Giacometti and two Nobel laureates in science, Sir John Eccles and Peyton Rous.

74.4 "A Section of an Interview between Norman Mailer and David Young." *Scholastic: Notre Dame Review* (special issue), 1 March, 5-9. Consists of half of a long, important interview on art, science, magic, religion and technology conducted in 1970. The other half appeared in 74.5.

74.5 "Norman Mailer on Science and Art." Interview by David Young. *Antaeus*, nos. 13/14 (spring/summer), 334-45. Other half of Mailer's best interview on these topics; the first half appeared in 74.4. Rpt: 82.16.

74.6 "Mailer Headlines Counter-Spy Pitch." Article by Louise Lague. *Washington Star-News*, 25 March, Sec. D, pp. 1 and one additional page. Report on a reception to celebrate the merger of the organization Mailer launched at his 50th birthday party, "The Fifth Estate" (see 73.10), and CARIC, the Committee for Actions/Research on the Intelligence Community, into one organization, which would in turn publish *Counter-Spy* magazine (see 75.4). Mailer said he wanted "to be remembered as old Uncle Norman who had something to do with it." See also 73.2, 75.6 and "Follow-Up on the News," *New York Times*, 17 March, 33.

74.7 Excerpts from acceptance speech. *The MacDowell Colony: Report for 1973.* Mrs. David F. Putnam, Secretary. Published after the 23 January annual meeting, in April or May. A report on the awarding of the Edward MacDowell Medal to Mailer on 19 August 1973 is given on pp. 12-13, including excerpts from Mailer's acceptance speech: "...So the novelist...is out there...to deal with life as something that God did not give us as eternal and immutable, but rather gave us [as] something half-worked...." Rpt: Mailer gives a slightly longer and somewhat different excerpt from the speech in the preface to *Some Honorable Men: Political Conventions, 1960-1972* (76.5). A 120-word excerpt from Mailer's speech and the bulk of John Leonard's introduction are reprinted in *Medal Day at the Colony*, a 1994 booklet published by the Colony. A quarter of a century later, Mailer again drew on his speech for the foreword to *The Time of Our Time* (98.7). See 73.35.

74.8 "The Faith of Graffiti." *Esquire*, May, 77-79, 88, 154, 157-58. Essay on New York City's graffiti artists. Rpt: In an expanded form in 74.9.

74.9 *The Faith of Graffiti.* Documented by Mervyn Kurlansky and Jon Naar. Prepared by Lawrence Schiller. Text by Norman Mailer. An Alskog Book, New York: Praeger, 7 May; simultaneously as a softcover; London: Mathews, Miller Dunbar, with a different title: *Watching My Name Go By.* Essay on New York City's graffiti artists, 96 pp. (15 of text, 81 of photographs of graffiti art), $14.95. No dedication. Rpt: In a shorter form, as 74.8; complete in 82.16, 98.7. See 74.12.

74.10 "Is He Writing the Big One?" Article-interview by Roger Ebert. *Journal-Star* (Peoria), 18 May, Sec. C, p. 10. *Chicago Daily News-Sun Times* wire story. Ebert discusses Mailer's plans for a long new novel (*Ancient Evenings*, 83.18), and quotes Mailer on journalism and deadlines. Mailer is not quoted in an earlier article, "Mailer Getting $1-Million for Rights to Next Novel" by Eric Pace (*New York Times*, 21 February, Sec. C, p. 24), but both his agent, Scott Meredith, and his Little, Brown editor, Larned G. Bradford, are quoted. Unnamed sources are also quoted and provide the erroneous information that the novel will trace "a family from ancient history to future history" and end aboard a spaceship. Mailer corrected this story several times before 83.18 was published.

74.11 "The Talk of the Town: Notes and Comments." *New Yorker*, 20 May, 29-34. Symposium contribution. Thirty-four individuals comment on the tape recordings made by President Nixon, including Mailer, William Scranton, Joseph A. Califano, Arthur Schleslinger Jr., William Westmoreland, George Reedy and John Kenneth Galbraith. Mailer's comment is the longest. He calls Nixon "the stubbornest man in America," a man "obliged to drink the cup of his own excretions." Rpt: 98.7. See 74.13.

74.12 "Mailer: I'm Sorry about the 'Marilyn' Book." Article-interview by Sandra Pesman. *Chicago Daily News*, 21 May, 13. Report on a Chicago press conference promoting 74.9, at which Mailer also answered questions about *Marilyn: A Biography* (73.30), and lamented that he had "jumped into the ending without enough research." See 1973 entries.

74.13 "Expletive Restored." *Village Voice*, 13 June, 4. With great *bravura*, Mailer imagines what the unedited transcripts of the frank talk of three presidents—Lyndon B. Johnson, John F. Kennedy, Harry S. Truman— would sound like. See 74.11.

74.14 Preface to *The Joker*, by Jean Malaquais, 11-24. New York: Warner, September, softcover. Malaquais's novel, originally published in the U.S. in 1954 by Doubleday, was reissued with Mailer's preface as part of Warner's "Rediscovery Series." Malaquais, one of Mailer's closest friends and his mentor in the 40s and 50s, translated *The Naked and the Dead* (48.2) into French, and is the dedicatee of *Barbary Shore* (51.1). Rpt: 75.5; without the third of its three parts as "My Friend, Jean Malaquais" in *Pieces and Pontifications* (82.16); and complete in *Rediscoveries II: Important Writers Select Their Favorite Works of Neglected Fiction*, edited by David Madden and Peggy Bach. New York: Carroll and Graf, 1988.

74.15 "Norman on Senator [Jacob] Javits." *Village Voice*, 31 October, 22. Two hundred-word political endorsement of Javits, "the personification of a great legislator," for a fourth term as Senator from New York.

74.16 "Gladiators: For Hemingway." *New Republic*, 30 November, 22. Poem. One of two contributions to *New Republic*. See 92.10.

74.17 Letter to Warren Farrell. In *The Liberated Man*, 66- 67. New York: Random House. Mailer explains to Farrell that he is not interested in joining a men's consciousness-raising group because "it's a way of digging too close to the source of one's work."

74.18 "Norman Mailer." Article-interview by Selden Rodman. In *Tongues of Fallen Angels*, by Selden Rodman, 162-81. New York: New Directions. Rodman links a few conversations with Mailer from 1948 to 1971 together with his insights and impressions. Other writers interviewed include Jorge Borges, Robert Frost, Ernest Hemingway, Pablo Neruda, Gabriel García Márquez, Allen Ginsberg, Octavio Paz and Derek Walcott. Rodman included an excerpt from *The Naked and the Dead* (48.2), the storm sequence (part 2, chapter 4), in *One Hundred Modern Poems* (New York: New American Library, 1951).

74.19 "Norman Mailer: 'The Time of Her Time.'" In *Writer's Choice: Each of Twenty American Authors Introduces His Own Best Story*, edited by Rust Hills, 251-77. New York: David McKay. In a 271-word preface to the story, Mailer says that his "credentials as a writer of short stories are, say the word, compact," and therefore choosing "The Time of Her Time" was not hard. He goes on to say that Walter Minton of G.P. Putnam's confided in him that publishing the story in 59.13 made Minton realize that *Lolita* could be published in the U.S. Rpt: Mailer shortens this preface when he reprints it and the story in *The Time of Our Time* (98.7). See 61.15, 67.11, 68.32.

74.20 Letter to John Hohenberg (28 December 1972). In *The Pulitzer Prizes: A History of the Awards in Books, Drama, Music, and Journalism, Based on the Private Files over Six Decades*, by John Hohenberg, 202, 339. New York: Columbia University Press. Mailer comments on why *The Naked and the Dead* (48.2) did not receive the Pulitzer Prize: "I had come out all ten thumbs and ten big toes for Henry Wallace, and for all I know may have been considered a fellow-traveler or a Communist dupe." Mailer also comments on the effect the Pulitzer he received for *The Armies of the Night* (68.8) had on his campaign for mayor of New York.

Fiction
Writer's
Handbook
by Hallie & Whit Burnett

PREFACE BY Norman Mailer

Practical advice on every aspect
of writing novels and short stories
with illustrations from modern
and past fiction writers

75.14

75.1 "The Rolling Stone Interview, Part I: Aquarius Hustling." By Richard Stratton. Photographs by Annie Leibovitz. *Rolling Stone*, 2 January, 41-47, 71. Extended discussion of *Marilyn: A Biography* (73.30), which includes the full text of Mailer's press release on Monroe's death (see 73.33, 75.3), followed by comment on Truman Capote and Charles Manson. Mailer refers to an earlier interview with Buzz Farbar (73.40) at the beginning of the interview. Rpt: As the first part of "In Search of the Devil" in 82.16 (partial). See 75.2.

75.2 "The Rolling Stone Interview, Part II: Sympathy for the Devil." By Richard Stratton. Photographs by Annie Leibovitz. *Rolling Stone*, 16 January, 42-43, 45-47, 54, 56-57. Contains Mailer's longest interview discussion of God and the Devil since 59.2 (see 75.11, 82.15, 83.45, 89.11), and comment on a variety of other topics: Women's Liberation, Ken Kesey, Thomas Pynchon, his novel-in-progress (*Ancient Evenings*, 83.18), the Rolling Stones and rock and roll, Patti Hearst, LSD, Ulysses S. Grant and literary deadlines: "Literature is not a temple. Literature is an act. If you're a working literary man, it's obviously analogous to a sexual act. You're better on some days than on others." Rpt: As the second part of "In Search of the Devil" in 82.16 (partial). See 75.1.

75.3 "The Murder File." In *Marilyn: A Biography*. New York: Warner, March, softcover, 340-51, $2.50. Consists of Mailer's 18 July 1973 press release on Monroe's sudden death (see 73.19, 73.33, 75.1) with new prefatory and concluding comments, as the final chapter of this reprint edition of 73.30.

75.4 "The CIA vs. Democracy." *Counter-Spy* 2 (spring/summer), 40. Essay. Dated 24 January, Mailer's contribution to the magazine he helped found focuses on the sins of the CIA and the role of "The Fifth Estate" as "homeopathic medicine—one small drop for a large disease." See 73.2, 73.10, 74.6, 75.6.

75.5 "A Preface to *The Joker.*" *Partisan Review* 42 (spring), 9-22. Rpt: 74.14, 82.16 (partial).

75.6 "CIA, FBI 'Threaten Nation.'" Article by unidentified writer. *Kansas City Times*, 22 April. Report of Mailer's 21 April speech at Wichita State University on the need to create intelligence agencies to counter the CIA and FBI. "What we are speaking about here," he said, "is an invisible government that has powers that are huge, undefined and uncertain even to themselves." See 73.2, 73.10, 74.6, 75.4.

75.7 "Norman Mailer: Humor Saves Day for the Man of LaMancha." Article-interview by Bill Bryan. *St. Louis Globe-Democrat*, 23 April, Sec. C, p. 11. Report on Mailer's appearance at St. Louis University, where he presented a lecture, "From Poetry to Espionage."

75.8 "The Dead Are Dying of Thirst: *The Fight*, Part I." *Playboy*, May, 78-82, 104, 146, 192, 196, 198-200, 202, 204, 206, 208, 210, 212-14, 216, 218, 220-22. Nonfiction narrative on the Muhammad Ali-George Foreman 30 October 1974 boxing match in Zaire. Rpt: With many changes as part I of *The Fight* (75.12).

75.9 "All Night Long: *The Fight*, Part II." *Playboy*, June, 124-26, 130, 172-84, 186-88, 192-93, 196. Nonfiction narrative on the Muhammad Ali-George Foreman 30 October 1974 boxing match in Zaire. *Playboy* awarded this excerpt and 75.8 its annual award for best nonfiction of 1975. Rpt: With many changes as part II of *The Fight* (75.12).

75.10 "The Meaning of Vietnam." *New York Review of Books*, 12 June, 23-33. Fifteen individuals "were asked to consider the questions of the responsibility for the war; its effects on American life, politics, and culture, and the U.S. position in the world; and the prospects of recovery from it—or any other questions they felt to be important." Besides Mailer, the contributors include Noam Chomsky, Elizabeth Hardwick, Christopher Lasch, Robert Lowell, Mary McCarthy, Susan Sontag and Gore Vidal.

75.11 "Existential Aesthetics: An Interview with Norman Mailer." By Laura Adams. *Partisan Review* 42 (summer), 197-214. Omnibus interview notable for Mailer's comments on karma and the role of James Jones in convincing him of its justice. Rpt: Partial in 82.16, 98.7; complete in 88.6. See 59.2, 75.2, 82.15, 83.45, 89.11.

75.12 *The Fight*. Boston: Little, Brown, 21 July; London: Hart-Davis, 1976. Nonfiction narrative on the Muhammad Ali-George Foreman 30 October 1974 boxing match in Zaire, 239 pp., $7.95. No dedication. Rpt: An earlier, shorter version of the narrative appeared in two parts in *Playboy* (75.8, 75.9). Mailer includes excerpts from eight chapters in *The Time of Our Time* (98.7). See 64.18, 67.12, 71.15, 71.26, 75.13, 77.13.

Mailer: "Now our Man of wisdom had a vice. He wrote about himself. Not only would he describe the events he saw, but his own small effect on events. This irritated critics. They spoke of ego trips and the unattractive dimensions of his narcissism. Such criticism did not hurt too much. He had already had a love affair with himself, and it used up a good deal of love. He was no longer pleased with his presence. His daily reactions bored him. They were becoming like everyone else's. His mind, he noticed, was beginning to spin its wheels..." (75.12).

75.13 "Norman Mailer: I'm Like a Minor Champ." Interview by Stan Isaacs. LI: *Newsday's Magazine*, 21 September, 10-13, 22-26. Mailer's longest interview on boxing, with additional comment on his books, Ernest Hemingway, John Updike, J.F.K., President Harry S. Truman and Feodor Dostoyevsky. See 75.12, 77.13.

75.14 Preface to *Fiction Writer's Handbook*, by Hallie and Whit Burnett, xvii-xxi. New York: Harper and Row, prior to 9 November. Copy examined has date stamped "November 9 1975." Mailer discusses the beginning of his writing career at Harvard under Theodore Morrison, Mark Schorer, Albert Guerard, Robert Gorham Davis and Murray Kempton. Mailer later explained that this Kempton was "not *our* Murray." See 41.1, 77.2, 83.10.

75.15 "Before He's Naked or Dead, Norman Mailer Goes for Broke: The Biggest Novel of All." Article-interview by Mark Goodman. *People Weekly*, 10 November, 47-50. Profile with a few comments on *The Fight* (75.12) and his work-in-progress, *Ancient Evenings* (83.18). See 75.16.

75.16 Letter to the editor. *People Weekly*, 24 November, 10. Mailer complains that Mark Goodman's article-interview (75.15) was inaccurate and broke an agreement that no mention would be made of Mailer's private life.

Genius and Lust *1976*

A journey through the major writings of **Henry Miller** By **Norman Mailer**

Drawing by Norris
Church Mailer
76.12

76.1 "Book Ends." Article by unidentified writer. *New York Times Book Review*, 14 March, 37. Report on a National Arts Club banquet in New York at which Mailer was awarded the club's Medal of Honor for Literature. Mailer is quoted on the difficulty of writing during this period: "The nature of existence cannot be felt anymore. As novelists, we cannot locate our center of values."

76.2 "Set Theory." *New York Review of Books*, 18 March, 42. Poem.

76.3 "Henry Miller: Celebrating a Cause Celebre." *Los Angeles Times Book Review*, 28 March, 1, 3. Essay. Rpt: Consists of the bulk of the first eight pages of 76.4, which itself was excerpted from the manuscript of 76.12; 82.16 (partial).

76.4 "Henry Miller: Genius and Lust, Narcissism." *American Review: The Magazine of New Writing* (formerly *New American Review*), no. 24 (April), 1-40; cover portrait of Mailer. Essay. Rpt: 76.3 (opening eight pages of 76.4); sections 2, 3 and 4 of *Genius and Lust* (76.12) correspond roughly to sections 1, 2 and 3 of 76.4; 82.16 contains a new, compressed, version of the opening chapters of 76.12.

76.5 *Some Honorable Men: Political Conventions, 1960-1972.* Boston: Little, Brown, 1 April. Nonfiction narrative, 499 pp., $12.50. Dedication and acknowledgment: "To the memory of my father; In particular appreciation—

104

Willie Morris, Midge Decter, Tom Griffith, Ralph Graves, Jack Newcombe, Molly Malone Cook, Mary Oliver, Suzanne Nye." Opening with an original preface, this collection contains four previously published narratives on political conventions: "Superman Comes to the Supermarket" (60.9); "In the Red Light" (64.20); *Miami and the Siege of Chicago* (68.25); and *St. George and the Godfather* (72.17). Mailer uses a portion of the preface to 76.5 in the foreword to 98.7. See 73.35, 74.7, 92.10, 96.8, 97.1.

Mailer: "...in the years from 1960 to 1972 there was some easy marriage between my literary desires and my ability to perceive a fair amount of what was happening in those clouds of moral ambiguity where politics itself existed. So it may be right to put these four pieces together now into a book. They may even justify my confidence that the world (not the techniques but the *world*) of fiction can be brought to the facts of journalism" (76.5).

76.6 "The State of the Art of Alger Hiss." Article by Philip Nobile. *Harper's*, April, 67-68, 73-74. Mailer voted "undecided" when polled, along with 103 others, on the guilt or innocence of Alger Hiss.

76.7 "Norman Mailer on Women, Love, Sex, Politics, and All That!" *Cosmopolitan*, May, 182-85, 235. Self-interview. Mailer wrote the questions, which focus on non-literary matters: marriage, sex, Women's Liberation, drinking and marijuana, television and his novel-in-progress, *Ancient Evenings* (83.18).

76.8 "Do Writers Ride in Cadillacs?" Article by Eliot Fremont-Smith. *Village Voice*, 3 May, 47. Report on the 1976 National Book Awards ceremony in New York. Mailer, the featured speaker, is quoted on the psychological struggles of writers.

76.9 "A Harlot High and Low: Reconnoitering through the Secret Government." *New York*, 16 August, 22-32, 35-38, 43-46; cover photograph of Mailer. Essay on the CIA, Watergate, the assassination of J.F.K., and other mysteries. The essay's subtitle, according to Mailer, is the work of the editors of *New York*. *Harlot's Ghost* (91.26) has its origin here. Rpt: 82.16, 98.7 (partial). Subtitle dropped in reprints.

76.10 "Two Letters from Frank Crowther." *Paris Review*, no. 67 (fall), 195-98. Essay of eulogy for Crowther, who managed Mailer's 50th birthday party and later committed suicide. Rpt: 82.16. See 73.2, 74.3, 73.18.

76.11 "The Search for Carter." *New York Times Magazine*, 26 September, 19-21, 69-85, 88-92; cover story. Essay-interview. Mailer traveled to Plains, Georgia, to interview Jimmy Carter for this piece. Rpt: Partial in both *New York Times Magazine*, 14 April 1996, 132, and 98.7.

76.12 *Genius and Lust: A Journey through the Major Writings of Henry Miller*. New York: Grove, October. Anthology with critical commentary, 576 pp., $12.50. Dedication: "to Henry Miller." Contains excerpts from 10 of Miller's books—*Black Spring, Tropic of Cancer, Tropic of Capricorn, Sexus, Nexus* and *Plexus, Sunday after the War, The Colossus of Maroussi, Big Sur and the Or-*

anges of Hieronymus Bosch and *The Air-Conditioned Nightmare*—and 88 pages, in a foreword and nine sections, of commentary by Mailer, comprising his lengthiest piece of literary criticism. The book jacket drawing of Miller is by Norris Church Mailer, his sixth wife. Discarded titles: *Mailer on Miller*; *The Cosmic Demon*. Rpt: Part of section 2 of Mailer's commentary appeared in 76.3; all of sections 2, 3 and 4, with a few changes, appeared in 76.4. *Pieces and Pontifications* (82.16) contains two excerpts: parts of the foreword and sections 1 and 2 appear as "Miller and Hemingway"; the last two-thirds of section 4, "Narcissism," appears under the same title. Two excerpts, pp. 3-10 and 173-94, appear as "Status" and "Narcissism," respectively, in *Critical Essays on Henry Miller*, edited by Ronald Gottesman. New York: G.K. Hall, 1992. See 66.14, 68.11, 77.11.

Mailer: "One had to go back to Melville to find a rhetoric which could prove as noble under full sail. Indeed one has to ask oneself if Miller could not out-write Melville if it came to describing a tempest at sea. Miller at his best wrote a prose grander than Faulkner's and wilder—the good reader is revolved in a farrago of light with words heavy as velvet, brilliant as gems, eruptions of thought cover the page. You could be in the vortex of one of [Joseph] Turner's oceanic holocausts when the sun shines in the very center of the storm. No, there is nothing like Henry Miller when he gets rolling" (76.12).

76.13 Preface to *The Presidential Papers*. New York: Berkley, October, softcover, v-vi. This new preface is followed by a piece titled "Special Preface to the First Berkley Edition," which is in fact the "Special Preface to the Bantam Edition" (64.15). The 1970 Berkley softcover edition also contains and mistitles the Bantam preface. The first edition of *The Presidential Papers* (63.37) has no preface.

76.14 Preface to *The Deer Park*. New York: Berkley, November, softcover, v. This preface is only 250 words in length because Mailer had his say in "Fourth Advertisement for Myself: The Last Draft of *The Deer Park*," which he reprints from *Advertisements for Myself* (59.13) after the text in this edition. Mailer does add in the preface that the novel "is I think of all my novels the one which shows the fewest signs of the work which went into it, and I like it that way." The first edition of *The Deer Park* (55.4) has no preface.

76.15 "A Conversation between Norman Mailer and John Ehrlichman: The CIA and Watergate." *Chic* 2, December, 16-21, 32, 34, 40, 70, 88, 90, 92. Mailer's three-page introduction is followed by a transcript of his conversation with Ehrlichman. Rpt: The (blue cover) bound, uncorrected, advance proof of *Pieces and Pontifications* (82.16) reprinted this dialogue as "Rounding Watergate." It was dropped from the first and subsequent printings and has been reprinted only in *Best of Chic 1* (1978) and *The Time of Our Time* (98.7, partial).

76.16 Preface to *Advertisements for Myself*. New York: Berkley, December, softcover, v-vii. The first edition of *Advertisements for Myself* (59.13) contains no preface. Rpt: As "An Advertisement Advertised" in 82.16.

76.17 "Trial of the Warlock." *Playboy*, December, 121-24, 126, 132, 232, 235-36, 240, 243-44, 246, 249-52, 254, 256. Screenplay adaptation of J.K. Huysmans's 1891 novel, *Lá-Bas*. *Playboy* gave "Warlock" its annual award for best major work in fiction; it tied with an excerpt from Kurt Vonnegut's *Slapstick*. Rpt: *Playboy Stories: The Best of Forty Years of Short Fiction*, edited by Alice K. Turner. New York: E.P. Dutton, 1993.

76.18 "Mailer Takes on the Heavyweight Novel." Article- interview by Herbert Mitgang. *New York Times*, 10 December, Sec. C, p. 24. Mailer discusses his novel-in-progress, *Ancient Evenings* (83.18), with additional comment on Henry Miller and Saul Bellow, who received the Nobel Prize in Literature the same day: "To my surprise, I felt good about Saul getting it, because he deserved it. I sent him a telegram of congratulations."

76.19 "Mailer's Poetry Reading at the Y Rated A for Effort, X for Content." Article by Israel Shenker. *New York Times*, 14 December, 24. Report, with brief quotations, of a Mailer reading at New York's 92nd Street Y.M.-Y.W.H.A., where he read from *Deaths for the Ladies (and Other Disasters)* (62.3) and other works, including his novel-in-progress (83.18).

76.20 "New Yorkers, etc." Article by Charlotte Curtis. *New York Times*, 20 December, Sec. C, p. 14. Mailer is quoted briefly in a report on a party for Richard and Doris Kearns Goodwin at his Brooklyn Heights apartment.

76.21 Letter to Elsa Lanchester. In *Charles Laughton: An Intimate Biography*, by Charles Higham, 197-98. Mailer wrote to Laughton's widow detailing the five days he had spent with him discussing a screenplay for *The Naked and the Dead* (48.2). Laughton finished a draft of the screenplay, but because of financial problems he never completed a final version and the film was produced by Paul Gregory for Warner Brothers, "with very inferior results," according to Higham. See 87.3.

76.22 Preface to *Papa: A Personal Memoir*, by Gregory H. Hemingway, M.D., xi-xiii. Boston: Houghton Mifflin. Rpt: As "Papa and Son" in 82.16.

76.23 Foreword to *St. Patrick's Day with Mayor Daley, and Other Things Too Good to Miss*, by Eugene Kennedy, ix-xiii. New York: Seabury.

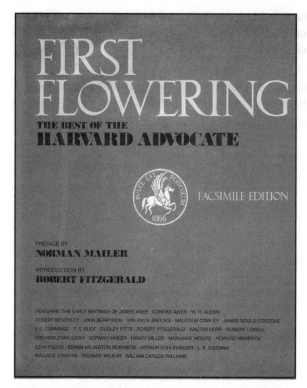

FIRST FLOWERING

THE BEST OF THE
HARVARD ADVOCATE

FACSIMILE EDITION

PREFACE BY
NORMAN MAILER

INTRODUCTION BY
ROBERT FITZGERALD

FEATURING THE EARLY WRITINGS OF JAMES AGEE · CONRAD AIKEN · W. H. AUDEN
ROBERT BENCHLEY · JOHN BERRYMAN · VAN WYCK BROOKS · MALCOLM COWLEY · JAMES GOULD COZZENS
E.E. CUMMINGS · T. S. ELIOT · DUDLEY FITTS · ROBERT FITZGERALD · WALTER KERR · ROBERT LOWELL
ARCHIBALD MACLEISH · NORMAN MAILER · HENRY MILLER · MARIANNE MOORE · HOWARD NEMEROV
EZRA POUND · EDWIN ARLINGTON ROBINSON · ARTHUR SCHLESINGER · L. E. SISSMAN
WALLACE STEVENS · RICHARD WILBUR · WILLIAM CARLOS WILLIAMS

1977

See 77.2

77.1 Preface to *Why Are We in Vietnam?* New York: Berkley, January, softcover, vii-x. The first edition of this novel (67.15) contains no preface. Rpt: As "Are We in Vietnam?" in 82.16.

77.2 "Our Man at Harvard." *Esquire,* April, 110-12. Memoir of the *Harvard Advocate* in the spring of 1942. Rpt: As Preface to *First Flowering: The Best of the "Harvard Advocate."* Reading, Mass.: Addison-Wesley; 82.16 (where the acknowledgments incorrectly note that the piece appeared in the 22 March *Esquire*), 98.7 (partial). See 41.1, 75.14, 83.10.

77.3 "Johnny Reeferseed." Article by Barbara Amiel. *Maclean's,* 13 June, 26, 29-30, 32, 34, 37-38, 40. Report on the Robert Rowbotham's trial in Canada for smuggling hashish, with Mailer as a witness for the defense. Rowbotham was convicted and given a 14-year sentence. Complete transcript of Mailer's testimony is given in 78.1.

77.4 "Vidal Plus Mailer: Pow." Column by Liz Smith. *Daily News* (New York), 26 October. Report on Mailer's 24 October fight with Gore Vidal at Lally Weymouth's New York party, precipitated by Vidal's 22 July 1971 *New York Review of Books* review of *Patriarchal Attitudes* by Eva Figes. See 77.5-77.9, 85.6, 91.3.

77.5 "There's Always a Morning After." Column by Liz Smith. *Daily News* (New York), 27 October, 6. Mailer corrects errors in Smith's 26 October column (77.4). See 77.6-77.9, 85.6, 91.3.

77.6 "'The Fight,' Starring Mailer and Vidal." Article by Nancy Collins. *Boston Globe*, 28 October, 24-25. Another report on the Mailer-Vidal fight, with quotes from participants and observers. See 77.4, 77.5, 77.7-77.9, 85.6, 91.3.

77.7 "Of a Small and Modest Malignancy, Wicked and Bristling with Dots." *Esquire*, November, 125-48. Listed on the table of contents page under the heading "The Big Bite" (see 62.18). Essay-memoir in which Mailer recalls his appearances on television programs with Mike Wallace (see 58.2, 58.7, 73.19, 73.23), Truman Capote and Dorothy Parker (see 59.3, 73.22), Gore Vidal, Dick Cavett and a half-dozen others while advancing his ideas of television's deadening effects. Mailer quotes in full on 139 a letter he wrote to *Women's Wear Daily* in 1970 or early 1971 about Vidal. Rpt: In a limited hardcover edition of 400 copies. Northridge, Calif.: Lord John Press, 1980 (80.25); 82.16 (where the acknowledgments give an incorrect original publication date of 20 October); six separate excerpts from this piece are scattered throughout *The Time of Our Time* (98.7). See 77.4-77.6, 77.8, 77.9, 85.6, 91.3.

77.8 "Newsmakers." Article by unidentified writer. *Newsweek*, 7 November, 67, 69. Mailer and Vidal add final words on their fight in this summary. See 77.4-77.7, 77.9, 85.6, 91.3.

77.9 "Still Feuding after All These Years, Gore and Norman Stage Fight Night at Lally's." Article by unidentified writer. *People Weekly*, 14 November, 42-43. More comment on the Mailer-Vidal fight. See 77.4-77.8, 85.6, 91.3.

77.10 "A Transit to Narcissus." *New York Times Book Review*, 4 December, 9, 94. Advance publication of Mailer's introduction to his novel of the same title, written in 1942-43 and published in 1978. See 78.2.

77.11 "Writers' Writers." *New York Times Book Review*, 4 December, 3, 58, 62, 66, 70, 74. Mailer and 20 other writers respond to the question: "Who is the living writer you most admire?" Mailer says, "Good lord, I think it's Henry Miller. Among writers nearer to my own age, I confess to a vast admiration for Gabriel García Márquez." See 66.14, 76.12.

77.12 "Norman Mailer: Writer." Interview by Francesco Scavullo. In *Scavullo on Men*, by Francesco Scavullo, with Bob Colacello and Sean Byrnes, 126-29. New York: Random House. Focus on personal issues: marriage, divorce, children, drugs, clothes, health and aging.

77.13 Comments. In *Shadow Box*, by George Plimpton, passim. New York: Putnam's. Mailer is quoted at length in Plimpton's book on boxing. Both of them covered the 1974 Muhammad Ali-George Foreman boxing match in Zaire. Rpt: As "Hunter Thompson and Norman Mailer" in *The Best of Plimpton*, edited by George Plimpton. New York: Atlantic Monthly Press, 1980. See 75.12, 75.13. See also "When We Were Kings," the 1997 Academy Award-winning documentary on the fight. Both Mailer and Plimpton comment in the film on the fight of a quarter-century earlier.

77.14 Comments. In "The Prisoner of Sex." In *We Must March My Darlings: A Critical Decade,* by Diana Trilling, passim. New York: Harcourt Brace Jovanovich. The best report on "A Dialogue on Women's Liberation" at Town Hall in New York, 30 April 1971. Rpt: *Critical Essays on Norman Mailer,* edited by J. Michael Lennon. Boston: G.K. Hall, December 1986. See 71.16-71.20, 71.23, 71.27.

A Transit
to Narcissus
A FACSIMILE OF THE ORIGINAL TYPESCRIPT

Norman
Mailer

78.2

78.1 "On Weed and Karma." Transcript of Mailer's testimony at trial of Robert Rowbotham in Ontario for drug smuggling. *Stone Age*, no. 1 (winter), 28-29. See 77.3.

78.2 *A Transit to Narcissus*. New York: Howard Fertig, 29 March. Facsimile of typescript of previously unpublished novel, written in 1942-43, 820 pp., $100. Includes Appendices A-G containing later revisions. No dedication. Limited edition of 1,000. See 73.12, 77.10.

78.3 "Mom Mailer's Advice, and Other Things." Article by William Hamilton. *Boston Globe*, 8 June, 1, 19. Report on Mailer's 35th Harvard reunion, at which he spoke after being introduced as "the folk hero of our class and the nation."

78.4 "Mailer's Real-Life Escapades Outdo Fiction." Article-interview by Tom Sullivan and Harold Banks. *Boston Herald-American*, 10 December, Sec. A, p. 3. Summary article on Mailer's divorce from Beverly Bentley drawn from trial testimony and an interview. Mailer also discusses his forthcoming book, *The Executioner's Song* (79.14): "It's as long as Dostoyevsky's *The Brothers Karamazov*, and about a quarter as good. If it's a quarter as good, it's good enough." See 78.5, 79.2, 79.3, 79.5, 79.8, 80.13.

78.5 "The Many Marriages of Norman Mailer." Article-interview by Kay Longcope. *Boston Globe*, 11 December, 1, 16. Alternating comment on their failed marriage from Beverly Bentley and Mailer, who summed up:

"If I am a prisoner of wedlock, I'm a recidivist. Some people are criminals, some are criminal conformists. I'm in the second category." See 78.4, 79.2, 79.3, 79.5, 79.8, 80.13.

78.6 "Notes on People." Article by unidentified writer. *New York Times,* 12 December, Sec. C, p. 6. Report on an exchange between Mailer and Susan Brownmiller at a New York Public Library event.

78.7 Comments. In *The Great American Newspaper: The Rise and Fall of the "Village Voice,"* by Kevin Michael McAuliffe, passim. New York: Scribner's. The most extensive treatment of Mailer's association with the *Village Voice.* See 56.1-56.24.

1979

79.1 "Norman Mailer: Gary Gilmore and Cornish Game Hens Are on His Mind These Days." Article-interview by James Brady. *Miami News*, 16 January, Sec. B, p. 1. At a small dinner with his wife, Norris, John W. Aldridge and John Simon, Mailer spoke of his experience as a cook in the army and compared *The Executioner's Song* (79.14) to Truman Capote's *In Cold Blood*: "Truman became emotionally involved. He took no notes. He claimed to have total recall. I took notes; I was not emotionally involved." See 80.1, 80.10.

79.2 "Mailer: Poor Manager." Article by Tom Sullivan and Harold Banks. *Boston Herald-American*, 25 January, 1, 5. Report on Mailer's appearance in Probate Court, Barnstable, Mass., in connection with his divorce from Beverly Bentley, focusing on his financial affairs: "My talent is to make money, not manage it." See 78.4, 78.5, 79.3, 79.5, 79.8, 80.13.

79.3 "Battling Mailers Agree Norman's a Genius." Article-interview by Harold Banks. *Boston Herald-American*, 28 January. Mailer is quoted briefly in another piece on his divorce from Beverly Bentley, who is quoted at length. See 78.4, 78.5, 79.2, 79.5, 79.8, 80.13.

79.4 "Life with Mailer: After Four Years, So Far, So Good." Article-interview by Judy Klemesrud. *New York Times*, 16 April, Sec. B ("Style"), p. 13. Focuses on Norris Church, Mailer's sixth wife, and her life with Mailer, with brief quotes from him. First major interview with Church. See 80.13.

79.5 "Norman Mailer: Warrior in the Battle of the Sexes." Article-interview by Spencer Vibbert. *New England (Boston Sunday Globe)*, 24 June, 9, 27-29. Quote-laden report on Mailer's 2 May court appearance in Barnstable, Mass., accompanied by Norris Church and his lawyer, Monroe Inker, in connection with his divorce from fourth wife Beverly Bentley. Includes a flashback to his February court appearance; comment from his publisher's publicity director, William Guthrie, and his editor, Larned Bradford, on his forthcoming narrative, *The Executioner's Song* (79.14); and an account of his 6 May benefit reading for Harvard's literary magazine *The Advocate*, at which he first read from 79.14. See 78.4, 78.5, 79.2, 79.3, 79.8, 80.13.

79.6 "Where Nothing Is Felt." Article by Stewart Weiner. *Writers Digest*, August, 15. Consists of a few short quotations written down "a few seasons back by Weiner from Mailer's talk about the writing life at a benefit for the Museum of Art in Provincetown."

79.7 "Norman Mailer: The Champ of American Letters Takes All the Tough Questions on Art, Life, Death, Love, Hate, War, Drugs, Etc., from

Punk Contender Legs McNeil." Interview. *High Times*, September, 43-47, 49, 51-53, 55, 107-9, 111, 113, 115, 117. Omnibus interview including discussion of the stabbing of his second wife, Adele, but scant comment on drugs for a magazine devoted to the topic. Mailer is only slightly avuncular with the 16-year old McNeil.

79.8 "Novelist Shelved." *Boston*, September, 91. Comic auto-obituary. Accompanied by four other auto-obituaries by Thomas P. "Tip" O'Neill, Elaine Noble, Alfred Fiandaca and Darrell Martine described collectively in a headnote as "five of Boston's favorite people." The five short pieces are pendants to Joel Rosen's article about obituary writers, "The Bad News Bearers," 91-93, 130. Mailer says of himself, "He was renowned in publishing circles for his blend of fictional journalism and factual fiction." He also notes that he had been married 16 times and had twenty-four children and seven grandchildren, "of whom four are older than six of their uncles and aunts." When asked why he married so often, he replied, "To get divorced. You don't know anything about a woman until you meet her in court." This issue of *Boston* also contains a profile of Mailer's lawyer for his divorce from Beverly Bentley, Monroe Inker, who comments on the case on 116. See 78.4, 78.5, 79.2, 79.3, 79.5, 80.13.

79.9 "Life with Mailer." Biographical article by James Atlas. *New York Times Magazine*, 9 September, 52-55, 86, 88, 90, 92, 94, 96, 98, 102, 104, 107; cover photograph of Mailer. Longest biographical essay on Mailer since Brock Brower's piece in *Life* (65.20). Like Brower, Atlas concentrates on whether Mailer will make good on his early promise to write the great American novel. Mailer's family and friends are also quoted in this well-illustrated piece.

79.10 "The Executioner's Song." *Playboy*, October, 96-100, 102, 110, 228-32, 237-38, 241-42, 244-46, 248-50, 252-54, 256-58, 260. Nonfiction narrative on Gary Gilmore. Illustrated by Marshall Arisman. Rpt: With many changes, as the first eight-and-a half chapters of *The Executioner's Song* (79.14). First of three installments.

79.11 "Talking with Mailer." Interview by Paul A. Attanasio. *Harvard Crimson* (Fall Book Supplement), October, 1, 8, 22-23. Excellent interview on 79.14; Mailer comments on the problem "of getting myself out of the book," and the two halves of 79.14: "the real meaning is in the second half, which is not as well-ordered and not as amenable to a simple narrative line."

79.12 "PW Interviews: Norman Mailer." Interview by Kenneth C. Davis. *Publishers' Weekly*, 8 October, 8-9. Mailer discusses his collaboration with Lawrence Schiller on 79.14, and his view of Gary Gilmore as "another major American protagonist," a man "malignant at his worst and heroic at his best."

79.13 "Norman Mailer Meets Middle Age and Wins with a Knockout Book." Article-interview by Jan Herman. *Show, Sunday Chicago Sun-Times*,

14 October, 1, 14. More interview than article, Herman's piece quotes Mailer at length on his ambitions, work schedule and the style employed in *The Executioner's Song* (79.14): "This book was a reaction against my last books. I felt I was getting into filigree much too much. I'm not turning on the old style. It's just that it's a very dangerous style because you have to have an awful lot to say and you have to be centrally located." Rpt: As "Up Off the Canvas, with a Troubled Look Ahead," *Philadelphia Inquirer*, 25 October, Sec. D, pp. 1, 4.

79.14 *The Executioner's Song*. Boston: Little, Brown, 15 October; London: Hutchinson, 5 November. Nonfiction narrative on Gary Gilmore, 1056 pp., $16.95. Dedication: "To Norris, to John Buffalo, and to Scott Meredith." Discarded titles: *Violence in America, The Saint and the Psychopath, American Virtue*. Mailer's title is taken from his poem of the same title published in 1964 (see 64.18), and then used as the title of chapter 15 of *The Fight* (75.12). In 80.1 Mailer explains this borrowing and also notes that the "old prison rhyme" that prefaces *The Executioner's Song* "is an old diddy [sic] from my movie 'Maidstone' [71.28] which was just perfect for the book." Although scrupulously factual, the book is described on its jacket, and the cover of the later softcover edition, as a "true life novel." Validating this subtitle, it won the *Playboy* Writing Award for fiction in 1979 and the Pulitzer Prize for fiction in 1980. Mailer is the only writer to win Pulitzers for fiction and nonfiction, the latter for *The Armies of the Night* (68.8). *The Executioner's Song* was also nominated for the American Book Award for fiction (1980 as a hardcover, 1981 as a softcover) and the National Book Critics Circle Award for fiction in 1979. Mailer, Philip Roth, William Styron and many other writers withdrew their books from the American Book Award competitions. See article by Michiko Kakutani, "Mailer, Styron and Roth Shun American Book Awards," *New York Times*, 21 March, Sec. C, p. 28. In 1999, it was ranked number 72 on a list of the top 100 works of journalism of the twentieth century by 36 judges under the aegis of New York University's journalism department. See "Journalism's Greatest Hits: Two Lists of a Century's Top Stories," *New York Times*, 1 March 1999, Business Section, pp. 1, 13. Mailer later wrote the screenplay for the film version of 79.14, which was nominated for an Emmy. The four-hour adaptation, staring Tommy Lee Jones and Eli Wallach, appeared on NBC-TV on 28 and 29 November 1982. Rpt: Three sections of the narrative appeared in a different form in *Playboy* (79.10, 79.19, 79.33). Excerpts from five chapters are reprinted in *The Time of Our Time* (98.7). See 68.8, 78.4, 1979 entries, 81.5, 82.22, 94.3.

Mailer: "You know, a painter may find something on the street that he thinks is incredible. Sometimes he'll glue it right into the painting. It becomes part of the work. In *The Executioner's Song*, newspaper stories became part of the painting and part of the transcript of the trial—a lot of found objects. I felt acted upon, in a funny way, while doing this book, by painting terms. It was as if I'd shifted from being an expressionist, not an abstract expressionist, but an expressionist—like [Charles] Munch, or Max

Beckmann...those kinds of painters who worked with large exaggeration and murkiness and passionate power—into now being a photographic realist, even a photographic realist with found objects. The reason, I think, is that a painter like a writer sometimes gets to a point where he can no longer interpret what he sees. Then the act of painting what he literally sees becomes the aesthetic act" (80.10).

79.15 "Taking the Measure of Mailer." Article-interview by Wayne Warga. *Los Angeles Times*, 25 October, Sec. 4, pp. 30, 33. On the book tour for 79.14, Mailer tells Warga, "I realized that it was what I'd been looking to do ever since I wrote *The Naked and the Dead* [48.2]. I wanted to do an immense panoramic novel with a strong narrative thread to it, a sort of collective novel of America."

79.16 "Author Calls Biography a 'Risk.'" Article by Associated Press writer. (Albany, Ore.) *Democrat-Herald*, 26 October. Report on Mailer's 25 October speech at the University of Utah in Salt Lake City on 79.14. Mailer said his intention was not to glorify Gilmore but to inspire "a sense of awe about the complexity of human nature." Longer versions of this AP story appeared in the following newspapers: (Greeley, Colo.) *Tribune* (27 October); (Billings, Mont.) *Gazette* (28 October); (Provo, Utah) *Herald* (28 October); (Watertown, S.D.) *Public Opinion* (29 October). See 79.18.

79.17 "Is New Mailer Book Fiction, in Fact?" Article-interview by Tony Schwartz. *New York Times*, 26 October, Sec. C, p. 24. Mailer, Bill Guthrie of Little, Brown, Jason Epstein of Random House, Townsend Hoopes of the Association of American Publishers and John W. Aldridge of the University of Michigan discuss the merits of calling 79.14 a "true life novel." Mailer says, "To me, nonfiction provides answers and novels illumine questions. I think my book does the latter." One of Mailer's many reflections on fiction/nonfiction. See 80.4.

79.18 "Mailer Speaks on Moral Nature." Article by Heather Sprake. *Daily Utah Chronicle*, 26 October, 1. Another report on Mailer's speech at the University of Utah. He says that he drew 79.14 from "15,000 pages of interview transcripts and court records." See 79.16.

79.19 "The Executioner's Song." *Playboy*, November, 136-39, 170, 193-94, 264, 266-70, 272, 274, 276-78, 280, 282, 284, 288. Nonfiction narrative on Gary Gilmore. Illustrated by Marshall Arisman. Rpt: Appearing at the same time or shortly after the first edition of *The Executioner's Song* (79.14), this excerpt is a compressed version of chapters 9-18. Second of three installments.

79.20 Letter to the editor. *The Harvard Advocate* 103, nos. 1 and 2), November. Robert Lowell commemorative issue. Mailer's letter, which precedes his portrait of Lowell from *The Armies of the Night* (68.8), notes that he wrote about him in that book "out of a superficial knowledge and from a tangent, and so was seeing facets of him they [close friends] had long forgotten about."

79.21 "Private Lives." Article by John Leonard. *New York Times*, 7 November, Sec. C, p. 14. Humorous article chronicling Leonard's relations with Mailer including Mailer's comments on Leonard's review of his book of poems, *Deaths for the Ladies (and Other Disasters)* (62.3).

79.22 "Intimations of Violence." Article-interview by Tom Davies. (London) *Observer*, 11 November, 51. Mailer is interviewed in New York just prior to his promotional trip to England for 79.14. He talks about 79.14, and comments on Ernest Hemingway: "I really hated him when he killed himself. It was like your own father killing himself."

79.23 "Mailer Sings of a Killer." Article-interview by David Spark. (Darlington, Durham) *Northern Echo*, 13 November. On the book tour in England for 79.14, Mailer tells Spark in this brief piece that "ideas are in the book only as people embody them. There are no ideas of my own in the book."

79.24 "Prisons of Wedlock!" Article-interview by Diana Hutchinson. (London) *Daily Mail*, 13 November, 7. Mailer talks as much about his financial problems as 79.14 in this piece, another interview on the book tour in England.

79.25 "Tamed—by Four Wives and Two Lovers." Article-interview by Peter Grosvenor. (London) *Daily Express*, 13 November, 9. Focus of this piece is Gilmore's character as presented in 79.14. Mailer says, "He could be mean, nasty, selfish and violent. And yet he also proved he could truly love a woman, and not every man can say that."

79.26 "A Murderer's Tale: Norman Mailer Talking to Melvyn Bragg." Interview. *Listener*, 15 November, 660-62; cover photograph of Mailer. Conducted in early 1979 at Mailer's Brooklyn Heights apartment, this important interview was broadcast in a greatly truncated form on BBC's "The South Bank Show" before appearing in the same form in *Listener*. Contains extended discussion of 79.14, including Gilmore's suicide attempt, his relations with the media, fan mail, and Mailer's views on the documentary novel. Rpt: 88.6.

79.27 "Dick Cavett Looks behind Norman Mailer's New Face." Article by Craig Wyatt, Gannett News Service. *Tucson Daily Gazette*, 16 November. Provides a few quotes from Mailer's two-part interview with Dick Cavett on PBS, broadcast on 20 and 21 November on 79.14. See 79.29.

79.28 "Mailer and a Monument to Death." Article-interview by Philippa Toomey. (London) *Times*, 17 November, 14. On the book tour for 79.14, Mailer discusses Lawrence Schiller, his working schedule and American politics.

79.29 "Mailer Elated after 'Song.'" Article by unidentified writer for Newspaper Enterprise Association. (Council Bluffs, Iowa) *Nonpareil*, 22 November. Another report on Mailer's two-part interview with Dick Cavett, 20 and 21 November, on 79.14. See 79.27.

79.30 "The Books That Made Writers." Symposium contribution. *New York Times*, 25 November, 7, 80-82. Twenty-two writers, including Mailer, Gabriel García Márquez, Joyce Carol Oates, Dr. Suess, Tom Wolfe, Malcolm Cowley and P.D. James, answer the question: "What book made you decide to become a writer and why?" Mailer names *Studs Lonigan* by James T. Farrell, Rafael Sabatini's *Captain Blood*, Jeffrey Farnol's *The Amateur Gentleman* and the novels of Sir Walter Scott and Thomas Hardy. See 71.32.

· 79.31 "Mailer on Gilmore's Obsession with Life and Death." Interview by Will Hearst. *Los Angeles Herald Examiner*, 25 November, Sec. A, p. 1, Sec. B, p. 8. Mailer reflects on 79.14 in this interview.

79.32 "Crime and Punishment: Gary Gilmore." Interview by William F. Buckley Jr. and Jeff Greenfield. *Firing Line*, no. 390, December, 19 pp. Pamphlet consisting of a transcript of this interview, which took place in New York City on 11 October and was broadcast on PBS on 4 November. Publication date determined by postmark on pamphlet. Mailer's longest published interview on 79.14 touches on all the major issues surrounding it. Rpt: 88.6.

79.33 "The Executioner's Song." *Playboy*, December, 176-77, 192, 196, 386, 370, 372, 374, 376, 382, 384, 386, 388, 390. Nonfiction narrative on Gary Gilmore. Illustrated by Marshall Arisman. Rpt: This third and final installment from *The Executioner's Song* (79.14) is a much-compressed and edited version of Gilmore's execution (chapters 30-40), appearing after 79.14 was published. *Playboy* gave this and the earlier two excerpts from 79.14 (79.10, 79.19) its annual award for best major work.

79.34 "Death, Taxes and Norman Mailer." Article-interview by Adrianne Blue. *Time Out* (London), 7-13 December, 14-16; cover photograph of Mailer. Notable mainly for Mailer's comment on 79.14 that "If I had it to do over again, I'd call it a true crime novel."

79.35 "Mailer on the '70s—Decade of 'Image, Skin Flicks and Porn.'" *U.S. News and World Report*, 10 December, 57-58. Essay. Summary of Mailer's views on several topics: the 70s, journalism, technology, literary perspective and the blockbuster novel.

79.36 "A Special Message to Subscribers from Norman Mailer." One-page preface to limited, leather-bound edition of *The Naked and the Dead*. Franklin Center, Pa.: Franklin Library, $75. Signed by Mailer on the 30th anniversary of *The Naked and the Dead* (48.2). Illustrated by Alan E. Cober. In this 306-word preface, dated 1978, Mailer ponders the confidence of the 25-year old who wrote 48.2. See 98.6.

Of a Small and
Modest Malignancy,
Wicked and Bristling
with Dots

NORMAN MAILER

1980: LORD JOHN PRESS
NORTHRIDGE, CALIFORNIA

80.25

80.1 "Mailer on Gilmore." Interview by Kevin Bezner. *Washington Book Review*, January-February, 2-8. Excellent interview on *The Executioner's Song* (79.14), in which Mailer discusses his narrative stance; Gilmore's character and appeal; the source for his title and the "old prison rhyme" prefacing the book; Joan Didion's review in the *New York Times Book Review* (7 November 1979); and Truman Capote's *In Cold Blood*, which Mailer calls "beautifully written. It had to be because I don't think that the two guys that Truman had in the book were terribly interesting." Capote commented on Mailer and the "nonfiction novel" in the preface to *Music for Chameleons* (New York: Random House). Rpt: *San Francisco Review of Books*, February, 6-9, 26-27, 31. See 79.1, 80.10.

80.2 Letter to the editor. *Hollywood Reporter*, 3 January, 3. Mailer responds to comments made by Germaine Greer in her 7 December review of 79.14. He stresses that her implication that the book was "spliced" together largely through the efforts of others is false, and that Larry Schiller, far from being a "super ghoul," was "a powerful asset" who did half the interviews for the book.

80.3 Letter to the editor. *New York Times Book Review*, 6 January, 27. Complaint about being quoted out of context in James Atlas's 2 December article, "The Case for Thomas Wolfe." Mailer adds that "Wolfe is a hero of mine," and that he is unhappy about being counted as one of his detrac-

119

tors. Atlas responds on the same page by saying that Mailer is angry at not being quoted at greater length in his article.

80.4 "Do Facts and Fiction Mix?" Article-interview by Michiko Kakutani. *New York Times Book Review*, 27 January, 3, 28-29. Mailer, along with Irving Howe, Michael Wood, William Styron, John Hersey, E.L. Doctorow, William Shawn and Michael Korda are quoted in a round-up article on the issue of how fact and fiction are and should be mixed in narrative. Mailer defends *The Executioner's Song* (79.14) as a novel, saying "God was at least as good a novelist as I am." See 79.17.

80.5 "Mailer Singing Pulitzer 'Song.'" Article-interview by Herbert Mitgang. *Chicago Tribune*, 17 April, Sec. 2, p. 14. Mailer comments briefly on his pleasure at being awarded the Pulitzer Prize for fiction for 79.14. Mitgang is a *Times* reporter and the article is attributed to the New York Times News Service, but a search has failed to discover it in the *Times*.

80.6 "An Appeal to Lillian Hellman and Mary McCarthy." *New York Times Book Review*, 11 May, 1, 33. In a open letter, Mailer appeals to his two friends to end their quarrel, which culminated with Hellman's defamation suit against McCarthy for saying of Hellman, on the Dick Cavett show, "every word she writes is a lie."

80.7 "Findings Hardly Startling to Oft-Married Mailer." Article-interview by Harold Banks. *Boston Herald-American*, 25 May, Sec. A, pp. 1, 4. Mailer says he is not surprised in the projected increase in single-parent households: "I have only one friend with three kids who has been married to the same woman."

80.8 "To Mailer, Joyce Was 'a Wild Sound Track.'" Article-interview by Robert Taylor. *Boston-Globe*, 14 June. Speaking at a Joyce program at the Universalist Church in Provincetown, Mailer remembered catching "some of Harry Levin's Joyce lectures" at Harvard, and that James Joyce, Marcel Proust and Thomas Mann were the three great writers during his college years. Mailer also read from his novel-in-progress, *Ancient Evenings* (83.18).

80.9 "In Prison." *New York Review of Books*, 26 June, 34. In this 389-word note prefacing Jack Henry Abbott's firsthand account of the violence in America's prisons, Mailer says that Abbott's "writing impressed me as being as good as any convict's prose I had read since Eldridge Cleaver." Abbott's essay was later revised for his book, *In the Belly of the Beast: Letters from Prison*, for which Mailer wrote an introduction (81.10). Along with several others in the literary world, Mailer later helped Abbott gain parole, and hired him after his release. Abbott was convicted of murder in 1982. Mailer regularly attended his trial. See 1981 and 1982 entries.

80.10 "An Interview with Norman Mailer." By John W. Aldridge. *Partisan Review* 47 (July), 174-82. Focuses on the narrative opportunities and challenges Mailer faced in writing *The Executioner's Song* (79.14). Mailer again compares it with Capote's *In Cold Blood* and notes that Gilmore was an appealing character "because he embodied many of the themes I've been living with all my life." Rpt: 88.6. See 79.1, 80.1, 85.15.

80.11 "A Librarian Interviews Norman Mailer." By Ophelia Georgiev Roop. *American Libraries*, July-August, 412-13. Consists of notes of Roop's conversation with Mailer before he gave the third annual Marian McFadden Memorial Lecture at the Indianapolis-Marion County Public Library, where he also read from his novel-in-progress, *Ancient Evenings* (83.18). His comments focus on television and libraries and the magazines he likes: *Scientific American*, *Adventure Travel*, *Mariah*, *Nation*, and *New Republic*. Rpt: Roop's interview originally appeared in the June issue of *Reading in Indianapolis*.

80.12 "Norman Mailer Writes a New 'Fantasy Autobiography' of Marilyn Monroe: *Of Women and Their Elegance.*" *Ladies' Home Journal*, September, 93-95, 154, 156, 159-60, 162, 164. Advance excerpt from 80.15 dealing with Monroe's marriage to Arthur Miller. Except for the addition of several paragraph breaks, the excerpt is identical to the following pages of the first edition: 143-49, 172-80, 227-28. It is followed by a "Publisher's Note": "While based on Marilyn Monroe's life and the reminiscences of Amy and Milton Greene, the episodes depicted here are not intended to be wholly factual representations of the life of Marilyn Monroe and in no way pretend to offer the actual thoughts of Marilyn Monroe or anyone else named in this book." This disclaimer appears in a slightly different form on the copyright page of 80.15. Lenore Hershey's "Editor's Diary: Mailer and Marilyn" on p. 2 of this issue quotes Mailer on his reason for writing a "fantasy autobiography" of Monroe: "I felt an obvious identity with her because she came out of nothing and achieved such notoriety. In a less embattled way, the same is true of me." See 73.30, 80.14, 86.24, 86.25.

80.13 "In a Merry Marriage-Go-Round, Norman Mailer Plans a Double Wedding, to Wives Five and Six." Article by unidentified writer. *People Weekly*, 3 November, 34-35. Sketchy report garnered from Liz Smith's column on Mailer's divorce from wife number four, Beverly Bentley, followed by marriage to Carol Stevens, with whom he lived from 1969 to 1975, then immediate divorce from her and immediate marriage (on 11 November) to Norris Church, with whom he has lived since 1975. Mailer described the marriage to and divorce from Stevens as "civilized," undertaken to "honor" his years with her and their child, Maggie. The article is accompanied by photographs of all six of his wives, and quotes from Church and Bentley. An editorial in *New York Times*, 19 October, Sec. 4, p. 30, subtitled "Mailer's Ring Cycle," lauds Mailer for these marriages: "In a time when the very idea of matrimony is in question, when parents are becoming an endangered species...Norman Mailer comes along and reminds us of the verities....Call the novelist a matrimaniac, or call him a *mensch*. We call Norman Mailer a still point in a turning world." See also "The Amours of Norman, Chapters 5 and 6," *New York Times*, 14 October, Sec. B, p.12; 78.4, 78.5, 79.2-79.5, 79.8.

80.14 "Before the Literary Bar." *New York*, 10 November, 27-31, 33-36,

121

38, 40, 43-46; cover photograph of Mailer. Self-interview in the form of a courtroom proceeding in defense of 80.15, which Mailer describes as "a false autobiography" and "an imaginary memoir." Illustrated with Milton Greene's photographs of Marilyn Monroe from 80.15. Rpt: 88.6. See 73.30, 80.12, 86.22, 86.25.

80.15 *Of Women and Their Elegance.* Photographs by Milton Greene. New York: Simon and Schuster, 26 November; London: Hodder and Stoughton. Novel, 288 pp., $29.95. No dedication. In a concluding "Author's Note," Mailer calls the book "an imaginary memoir." Discarded title: *Of Women and Their Elegance: by Marilyn Monroe as Told to Norman Mailer.* Of the 124 photographs, 34 are of Marilyn Monroe and illustrate, in part, Mailer's text. The remainder are of other show business and/or fashion figures, including Marlene Dietrich, Audrey Hepburn, Amy Greene, Suzy Parker, Judy Garland, Gene Kelly and many others. The individuals or scenes in 23 of the photographs are unidentified. The softcover edition (New York: Tom Doherty; distributed by Pinnacle, November 1981) contains 93 of these photographs; most of them are poorly reproduced. In both editions, a few photographs are misidentified or given incorrect page numbers on the "Identifications" page. For example, the second photograph of Tedi Thurman is not on 17, as listed in the first edition, but on 18-19. Mailer drew heavily on *Of Women and Their Elegance* for his later play "Strawhead" (86.25). Rpt: 80.12, 80.14 (partial). See 73.30, 80.17-80.19, 82.9, 86.22.

Mailer: "I wanted the reader to be jarred into a comprehension of the size and spectrum of a movie star's soul. There is more to a movie star than we think, not less. I wanted to deepen the legend of Marilyn Monroe, not sweeten it" (80.14).

80.16 "Norman Mailer on Love, Sex, God, and the Devil." Interview by Cathleen Medwick. *Vogue*, December, 268-69, 322. Comment on the matters cited in the title; Marilyn Monroe; his novel-in-progress, *Ancient Evenings* (83.18); his recent reviews; and his potential as an actor. Rpt: As "One-Night Stands" in 82.16 (partial).

80.17 "Norman Mailer on Wives, Women, Books." Article-interview by Marian Christy. *Boston Sunday Globe*, 7 December, Sec. A, pp. 8, 16. Mailer talks about elegance, his ex-wives and children, the discipline of writing and his talent: "What I'm concerned about is my talent becoming larger or smaller. I'm as obsessed with that as a fashion model is about the dimensions of her waist."

80.18 "Mailer on Mailer." Article-interview by Beverly Beyette. *Style, Sunday Pantagraph* (Bloomington, Ill.), 14 December, Sec. C, p. 1. Beyette is identified as a *Los Angeles Times* writer and this piece presumably appeared there when Mailer was on a book tour for 80.15. The questions are hackneyed: "Is Marilyn Monroe some sort of obsession?" and "Are you in some way obsessed with violence?" Mailer's replies reveal his irritation. He mentions this interview in 81.8.

80.19 "Mailer Writes Another Monroe Doctrine." Article-interview by Rick Kogan. *Chicago Sun-Times*, 15 December, 49, 69. On the book tour for 80.15 (four cities: Chicago, Houston, Los Angeles and New York), Mailer notes that he "was never altogether happy" with his first book on Monroe (73.30), because "I was never inside her head."

80.20 "Mailer, Dying for a Part in 'Ragtime.'" Article by William Borders. *New York Times*, 17 December, Sec. C, p. 25. Report on the London filming of Milos Forman's "Ragtime," based on E.L. Doctorow's 1975 novel of the same name, in which Mailer plays the role of architect Stanford White, who is murdered in the film. Mailer is quoted briefly on his role and the richness of the film. Norris Church, his sixth wife, had a small role in the film. See 80.21, 81.18-81.20.

80.21 "Mailer on 'Ragtime.'" Letter to the editor. *New York Times*, 24 December, Sec. C, p. 6. Mailer explains that William Borders was in error in his 17 December article in saying that Mailer had asked that his wife replace the extra who was playing his date in the film. See 80.20.

80.22 "Cousins." In *Wonders: Writings and Drawings for the Child in Us All*, edited by Jonathan Cott and Mary Gimbel, 390. New York: Rolling Stone Press. Poem. Illustrated by Norris Church.

80.23 *The Short Fiction of Norman Mailer*. New York: Howard Fertig. Short stories, 285 pp., $18.50. First hardcover edition of this collection, which previously appeared in a softcover edition (67.11), and earlier as part of *The Essential Mailer* (82.19). See 68.32, 72.7, 74.19.

80.24 Sworn Affidavit of Norman Mailer, 7 January 1953. In *The Law of the Land: The Evolution of Our Legal System*, by Charles Rembar, 370-75. New York: Simon and Schuster. Mailer's deposition concerns the loyalty of his father, Isaac Barnett Mailer, an accountant with the War Department, whose job was under the Civil Service Commission. Despite Norman Mailer's own leftist sympathies, his testimony convinced the Commission to clear his father without even holding a hearing. Mailer says he himself is not a "concealed Communist," as charged, but "admittedly and openly a dissident from the conventional and generally accepted attitudes about America and its position in the world today."

80.25 *Of a Small and Modest Malignancy, Wicked and Bristling with Dots*. Northridge, Cal.: Lord John Press. Essay, 103 pp., $75. Limited, signed edition of 400 hardcover copies. Rpt: 77.7, 82.16, 98.7 (partial).

80.26 Introduction to *Soon to Be a Major Motion Picture*, by Abbie Hoffman, xii-xv. New York: Perigee Books, G.P. Putnam's. Rpt: With slight changes (made after Hoffman's 1989 suicide) as Foreword to *The Best of Abbie Hoffman*, edited by Daniel Simon and Hoffman. New York: Four Walls Eight Windows, 1989; 98.7 (partial).

81.1 "A Bad Uncle's News: Correspondence and Cheers with Norman Mailer." Article by Richard Lee-Fulgham. *Writer's Digest*, January, 72, 54. Includes quotations from Mailer's letters to Lee-Fulgham on writing and life, e.g.: "Never duck an experience if you feel your fundamental motivation is fear."

81.2 "Creators on Creating: Norman Mailer." Interview by Hilary Mills. *Saturday Review*, January, 46-49, 52-53. Major interview focusing on Mailer's development as a writer by the author of *Mailer: A Biography* (82.23). A good deal of the interview is devoted to Mailer's shifts between the novel and journalism: "But I think if I started any aspect of that New Journalism—and I did—it was an enormously personalized journalism where the character of the narrator was one of the elements not only in telling the story but in the way the reader would assess the experience." Rpt: Partial in both 82.16 (as "The Mad Butler") and 82.23. See 73.44.

81.3 "The Literary Life: Thoughts on Buying a Silver BMW." Article-interview by Scott Parkin. *Esquire*, January, 103. While buying a car, Mailer discusses the writing life, with asides on John Cheever and Saul Bellow.

81.4 "Broadway." Interview by Carol Lawson. *New York Times*, 30 January, Sec. C, p. 2. Brief interview concerning Mailer's adaptation of *Of Women and Their Elegance* (80.15) into a play, "Strawhead" (86.25). Mailer's comments are sandwiched in with other notes and quotes about the New York theater scene. See 86.22, 86.25.

81.5 "Until Dead: Thoughts on Capital Punishment." *Parade*, 8 February, 6-9, 11; cover photograph of Mailer. Essay of approximately 5,000 words prompted by the experience of writing *The Executioner's Song* (79.14). Mailer's first appearance in *Parade*.

81.6 "Prisoner of Success." Interview by Paul Attanasio. *Boston Phoenix*, 24 February, 1-2, 11. Conducted in late December 1980, Attanasio's interview elicits insights on other writers: Ernest Hemingway, William Faulkner, Leo Tolstoy, E.L. Doctorow; his pessimistic response to Ronald Reagan's election; comment on the fact/fiction debate and on two of his own works, *The Executioner's Song* (79.14) and *Of Women and Their Elegance* (80.15). Speaking of his depiction of Marilyn in 80.15, he says: "I invented an episode for her that was quite possibly more extreme than anything she ever did herself in her life. And that gave me pause....but I wrote it with the idea that Marilyn, wherever she is, would accept this treatment of her." Rpt: 82.16.

81.7 "Norman Mailer at Columbia." Interview at a 17 February Columbia University seminar moderated by Joseph McElroy; edited by Paul Hoagland and Kurt Duecker. *Columbia: A Magazine of Poetry and Prose*, no. 6 (spring-summer), 103-15. Rpt: As "A Little on Novel-Writing" in 82.16.

81.8 "An Evening with Norman Mailer." Interview by William McDonald. *Lone Star Review, Dallas Times Herald*, April, 1, 3, 13. Mainly comments on the genesis of *Of Women and Their Elegance* (80.15), with two humorous stories as bookends: one about Mailer's first days in the 112th Cavalry and another about going to a Brooklyn bar with Truman Capote. See 80.18.

81.9 "A Sinister Occupation." *Book Digest Magazine*, April, 20, 22-24, 27-29. Essay on the "spooky" psychology of writing; includes comment on reviews, royalties, ego, early success and fear of failure. He concludes: "I am still getting up my nerve at the age of fifty-seven to take a deep breath and tell the only personal story that any of us ever have, the true story of my own life and its curious turns, and all its private parts, yes, to look into the mirror and begin to write. Oh, what a fear is that." This little-known essay, with many changes (including the excision of the sentence quoted), is the foundation of a longer essay, "The Hazards and Sources of Writing" (85.4).

81.10 "Discovering Jack H. Abbott." *New York Review of Books*, 11 June, 15-16. Titled "A Vision of Hell" on the cover, Mailer's essay accompanies two notes by Abbott, "On Women" and "On Nature." In it, Mailer explains how he met Abbott during the time he was writing *The Executioner's Song* (79.14). Rpt: With a few very minor changes, as Introduction to *In the Belly of the Beast: Letters from Prison*, by Jack Henry Abbott. New York: Random House, late June. See 80.9, other 1981 and 1982 entries.

81.11 "Convict-Author Free at Last with New Book—Thanks to Mailer, *NYRB* and Random Editor." Article-interview by Stella Dong. *Publishers' Weekly*, 12 June, 39-40. Quotes Mailer, Robert Silvers of the *New York Review of Books*, Erroll McDonald of Random House and Jack Abbott on Abbott's release from prison and his forthcoming book. See 80.9, other 1981 and 1982 entries.

81.12 "A Lifelong Con Springs Himself with a Book." Article by Mary Vespa. *People Weekly*, 7 July, 62, 67. Quotes Mailer on the progress of Jack Henry Abbott, whom Mailer helped obtain parole. See 80.9, other 1981 and 1982 entries.

81.13 "Freedom for Convict-Author: Complex and Conflicting Tale." Article by M. A. Farber. *New York Times*, 17 August, Sec. A, p. 1, Sec. B, p. 4. Report on Jack H. Abbott, his prison life, literary prospects and flight from New York City authorities who sought him for murder. Excerpts from Mailer's 15 April 1980 letter to Utah authorities on Abbott's behalf are quoted. See earlier *Times* articles by Farber on 20 and 26 July; 80.9, other 1981 and 1982 entries.

81.14 Letter to the editor. *Soho News*, 19-25 August, 24. Writing in response to a comment in John Lombardi's article, "Norman Mailer's White Negro: Jack Henry Abbott and the End of Hip," in the 5-11 August issue, Mailer says, "You wrote a factoid. I keep no bodyguard. Never have" [full text]. See 80.9, other 1981 and 1982 entries.

81.15 "The Famous Writers' Cooking School." Favorite recipes of 16 writers, including Mailer, who provides one for stuffed mushrooms. *Playboy*, October, 163-64, 188, 190-91. This piece is an advance excerpt from *The Great American Writers' Cookbook*, edited by Dean Faulkner Wells. Introduction by Craig Claiborne. Oxford, Miss.: Yoknapatawpha Press. Mailer's recipe leads off the appetizers and beverages section in this collection of 200 recipes by 175 American writers. Willie Morris's recipe for John Birch Society Beans (in *Playboy*) has literary as well as gustatory merit.

81.16 "Una Conversacion con Norman Mailer." Interview with Barbara Probst Solomon. *El País* (Madrid), 4 October, 10-15. Comment on his forthcoming novel, *Ancient Evenings* (83.18), and a number of writers: Jean Malaquais, Jorge Borges, Gabriel García Márquez, Saul Bellow and, at some length, Henry Adams and his influence on *The Armies of the Night* (68.8). Rpt: Conducted in Provincetown, on 16 July 1981, and translated into Spanish for *El País*, this interview was then published as "From NASA to the Nile: A Conversation with Norman Mailer" in *New Boston Review*, March/April 1982, and subsequently, edited and cut to one-third its length, as "To Pontificate on Europe and America" in *Pieces and Pontifications* (82.16). Solomon reprinted the full interview in her collection, *Horse-Trading and Ecstasy*. San Francisco: North Point Press, 1989.

81.17 "A Rally of Literary Lions for Public Library." Article by Judy Klemesrud. *New York Times*, 23 October, Sec. B ("Style"), p. 8. Report on a fundraiser for the New York Public Library on 22 October. Mailer's humorous exchange with Barbara Bush is quoted.

81.18 "'Ragtime': Dreaming America." Article-interview by Joan Juliet Buck. *Vogue*, November, 440-43, 492-93. Mailer discusses playing the role of Stanford White in "Ragtime," directed by Milos Forman. See 80.20, 81.19, 81.20.

81.19 "Mailer Writes Off Acting...Too Hard." Article-interview by Roderick Mann. *Boston Globe*, December. Mailer discusses his role as Stanford White in Milos Forman's newly released film, "Ragtime," and comments on the money he lost making his own films: "Wild 90" (1967), "Beyond the Law" (1968), "Maidstone" (1971): "I could just as easily have bought a yacht, taken it out into the harbor and sunk it." See 71.28, 80.20, 81.18, 81.20, 84.1.

81.20 "Milos Forman Searches for the Right Key." Article by Harlan Kennedy. *American Film*, December, 38-43. Mailer is quoted on the large number of rehearsals required in professional filmmaking. See 80.20, 81.18, 81.19.

81.21 Conference remarks and court testimony related to William Burroughs's *Naked Lunch*. In *Contemporary Literary Censorship: The Case History of Burroughs's "Naked Lunch,"* by Michael Barry Goodman. Metuchen, N.J.: Scarecrow Press. Mailer's comments on *Naked Lunch*, given as a participant in the International Writers' Conference, Edinburgh International Festival, 20-24 August 1962, are quoted by Goodman, 153-55. Mailer's later testimony in support of *Naked Lunch* at its June 1965 censorship trial in Boston is also quoted, 195-200. The entire story is told again by the chief lawyer for the defense: Edward de Grazia, *Girls Lean Back Everywhere: The Law of Obscenity and the Assault on Genius*, with new material, including quotes from Mailer (92.12). See 62.24, 65.1, 65.13, 96.7.

81.22 "Game Cooking with Alfredo Foffé." In *Shooter's Bible* (no. 72), 113-14. Mailer's introduction to Foffé's game cookbook (which has not been located) was "excerpted" in this gun catalog and trade journal. Mailer praises Foffé's Montague Street restaurant where he ate regularly.

81.23 "Norman Mailer: The Interview." By Jeffrey Michaelson and Sarah Stone. *Puritan Quarterly Journal Number 7*, 26-32, 44-47, 72, 107. Mailer's most extensive interview on sex and pornography. The interview was conducted at Mailer's Brooklyn Heights apartment on 28 January. Rpt: In an abridged form as "Ethics and Pornography" in 82.16. See 73.40, 90.3.

Norman Mailer

1982

Pieces and
Pontifications

82.16

82.1 "Abbott Tells Trial of His Life in Foster Homes and Prisons." Article by Paul L. Montgomery. *New York Times*, 15 January, Sec. B, p. 3. Account of the trial of Jack Henry Abbott for murder. Mailer, who helped him gain parole, is quoted: "As I said in the beginning, it's a tragedy all around and I don't see any reason to change that remark." See 80.9, 1981 and other 1982 entries.

82.2 "Abbott Rejects Account of Him as Violent Man: Mailer Testifies on Ties to the Accused Slayer." Article by Paul L. Montgomery. *New York Times*, 19 January, Sec. B, p. 3. Continuing account of Jack Henry Abbott's murder trial, at which Mailer testified. At a press conference after his testimony, Mailer said when asked if he felt remorse, "I can't give you my blood, but you can have my psychic blood. It's something Abbott's friends are going to have to live with for the rest of their lives." See 80.9, 1981 and other 1982 entries.

82.3 "Author Mailer Accepts 'Blame' in Fatal Stabbing." Article by United Press International writer. *Chicago Tribune*, 19 January, Sec. 1, p. 5. Another in a series of accounts of Mailer's press conference after his testimony at Jack Henry Abbott's murder trial. Mailer called the murder of Richard Adan "an absolute tragedy, a hideous waste and horror." See 80.9, 1981 and other 1982 entries.

82.4 "Mailer Feels 'Responsibility' for Parolee's Killing of Actor." Article by Doyle McManus of the *Los Angeles Times*, reprinted in *Chicago Sun-*

Times, 19 January. Another report on Mailer's press conference called in the wake of his testimony at the trial of Jack Henry Abbott for murder. See 80.9, 1981 and other 1982 entries.

82.5 "Mailer: I Would Risk Freeing Killer." Article by Mike Pearl and Cynthia R. Fagen. *New York Post,* 19 January, 3. Sensationalized article that selectively quotes Mailer's comments at a press conference and leaves out his statement taking partial responsibility for the death of Richard Adan at the hands of Jack Henry Abbott. See 80.9, 1981 and other 1982 entries.

82.6 "Abbott Convicted of Manslaughter in Stabbing of East Village Waiter." Article by Paul L. Montgomery. *New York Times,* 22 January, Sec. A, p. 1, Sec. B, p. 5. Mailer says, "It's a fair verdict" in this report on Jack Henry Abbott's conviction for first-degree manslaughter. See 80.9, 1981 and other 1982 entries. See also Abbott's response to his conviction, a book (with Naomi West) titled *My Return* (Buffalo, N.Y.: Prometheus, 1987), which consists of a play about the killing of Richard Adan, several appendices of self-justification and letters to Mailer, Lionel Abel, Robert B. Silvers, William Styron, Jerzy Kosinski and others.

82.7 "Mailer Says He Shares Abbott's Guilt." Article by United Press International writer. *Boston Herald-American,* 23 January. Following the conviction of Jack Henry Abbott for manslaughter, Mailer said the victim's family had "an absolute right to hate and revile me." See 80.9, 1981 and other 1982 entries.

82.8 "Reporter's Notebook: Cinéma Vérité of Abbott Trial." Article by Paul L. Montgomery. *New York Times,* 23 January, 27. Mailer is quoted briefly on the reaction of Jack Henry Abbott to his conviction for manslaughter. See 80.9, 1981 and other 1982 entries.

82.9 "Marilyn Monroe's Sexiest Tapes and Discs." *Video Review,* February, 70-74. Critiques of 11 of Monroe's films, with brief comment on 11 more, drawn from Mailer's research for *Marilyn: A Biography* (73.30).

82.10 "Mailer Feels 'Responsibility' for Slaying." Article by Albin Krebs and Robert McG. Thomas Jr. *New York Times,* 22 February, Sec. B, p. 4. Advance report on Mailer's appearance on the Dick Cavett Show, telecast in two parts on PBS, 24 and 25 February. Mailer said, "I have a very large responsibility for the death of Richard Adan." He also said that he "never thought Abbott was close to killing, and that's why I have to sit in judgment on myself." See 80.9, 1981 and other 1982 entries.

82.11 "Convict Author Given Term of 15 Years to Life." Article by Reuters News Service correspondent. *Boston Globe,* 16 April, 4. Report on the sentencing of Jack Henry Abbott for the killing of Richard Adan; Mailer is quoted: "The real question is when does a man expiate his crime." See 80.9, 1981 and other 1982 entries.

82.12 "Mailer's Protege Draws 15 Years to Life in Slaying." Article by United Press International writer. *Chicago Sun-Times,* 16 April, 26. Another report on the sentencing of Jack Henry Abbott; Mailer is quoted briefly. See 80.9, 1981 and other 1982 entries.

82.13 Letter to the editor. *New York Times Magazine*, 18 April, 30. Mailer responds to Rebecca West's comments about him in a 4 April article.

82.14 "Mailer Talking." Interview by Michiko Kakutani. *New York Times Book Review*, 6 June, 3, 38-41. On the occasion of the publication of *Pieces and Pontifications* (82.16), Mailer discusses the trajectory of his own career, the transition from "embattled artist" to "alchemical artist," and comments on the power of Ernest Hemingway's style. Rpt: 88.6; Kakutani's *The Poet at the Piano: Portraits of Writers, Filmmakers, Playwrights and Other Artists at Work*. New York: Times Books, 1988.

82.15 Letters to Mike Lennon (30 January 1972, 7 October 1974). Excerpts reprinted in J. Michael Lennon's essay, "Mailer's Cosmology," *Modern Language Studies*, 12 (summer), 18-29. Mailer's comments deal with his cosmology, "obviously the most ticklish, dense, incomprehensible and for most readers perverted part of my thicket," and "the difficulty in comprehending the authority of the senses," respectively. Rpt: *Critical Essays on Norman Mailer*, edited by J. Michael Lennon. Boston: G.K. Hall, December 1986. See 59.2, 75.2, 75.11, 83.45, 89.11.

82.16 *Pieces and Pontifications* (*Pontifications* edited with introduction by Michael Lennon). Boston: Little, Brown, 21 June; simultaneously as two softcovers, *Pieces* and *Pontifications*; Sevenoaks, Kent: New English Library, July 1983. Essays (208 pp.) and Interviews (192 pp.), respectively, $20. Dedication: "For my sister, Barbara." Discarded titles: *After "The White Negro"*; *Sinking in the Seventies* (subtitle for *Pieces*). Rpt: A number of essays and interviews are in *The Time of Our Time* (98.7). See 76.15.

Mailer: "Here, then, are two sides of myself as I survived the Seventies—my literary ghost looking for that little refinement of one's art which becomes essential as one grows older, and the cry of the street debater, front and center, who always speaks in the loudest voice" (82.16).

82.17 Interview by Jean Stein. In *Edie: An American Biography*, by Jean Stein; edited with George Plimpton, 234, 315. New York: Alfred A. Knopf, 28 June. Mailer's comments deal with Edie Sedgwick's acting in Andy Warhol's film, "Kitchen," and her tryout for a part in his play "The Deer Park" (67.13). See 97.24.

82.18 "Artful Subtleties." Letter to the editor. *Time*, 19 July, 5-6. Mailer complains about being quoted out of context by Stefan Kanter in his 28 July review of 82.16.

82.19 *The Essential Mailer*. Sevenoaks, Kent: New English Library, 1 August. Miscellany, 586 pp. Combines *The Short Fiction of Norman Mailer* (67.11) and *Existential Errands* (72.7), with two excisions: the introduction to 67.11, which was reprinted in 72.7, appears only once in 82.19: at the beginning of the short fiction; original dedication to 72.7 was dropped.

82.20 "Cinema's Wild Man: Mailer Movies at Coolidge Corner." Article-interview by Paul Restuccia. *Boston Herald American*, 5 November, Sec. B, p. 6. Mailer comments on his films after a showing of "Maidstone" (71.28) by the Institute of Contemporary Art at Coolidge Corner Theater in Brookline, Mass., and later at a bar. He says: "One reason I started making films was that I was upset about the movies made from my books....I knew 'An American Dream' wasn't going to be very good because the novel [65.7] took place in New York and they filmed it in L.A. Anybody who could do that doesn't know lox from tuna salad." See 82.21.

82.21 "A Vintage Mailer Performance." Article by Mark Muro. *Boston Globe*, 5 November, 21-22. Account of Mailer's exchanges with the audience after a showing of "Maidstone" (71.28). See 82.20.

82.22 "How Novels Get Titles." Article by Robert F. Moss. *New York Times Book Review*, 7 November, 13, 18. Mailer explains that Stanley Rinehart, his publisher, thought that *The Naked and the Dead* (48.2) was "a dreadful title," in an article for which a dozen contemporary writers, including Eudora Welty, Joyce Carol Oates, Anne Tyler, Walker Percy, Robert Penn Warren and William Styron, were canvassed. Mailer also reveals that his working title for *The Executioner's Song* (79.14) was "The Saint and the Psychopath."

82.23 Interview by Hilary Mills. In *Mailer: A Biography*, by Hilary Mills, passim. New York: Empire Books, mid-November. First book-length biography of Mailer. Valuable for its interviews with several of his wives, including his first, Beatrice Silverman, and a number of his friends and acquaintances including Jean Malaquais, Scott Meredith, George Plimpton, Dwight Macdonald, Mickey Knox, Vance and Tina Bourjaily, John W. Aldridge, Gore Vidal, Joe Flaherty, Walter Minton, James Baldwin, Seymour Krim, Jason Epstein, Arthur Schlesinger Jr., Roger Donald, Gloria Jones, Pete Hamill, Milton Greene, Jimmy Breslin, Larry Alson, Daniel Wolf, William and Rose Styron, Adeline Lubell, Harold Hayes, Rust Hills, Midge Decter, Norman Podhoretz, Willie Morris, Abbie Hoffman, Dotson Rader, Buzz Farbar, and José Torres. Mills's biography contains little new material from Mailer himself, but many important perspectives from family and friends. Mills is fair, but not always accurate or alive to nuance. Her method of documentation is sketchy and difficult to follow. See 81.2, 83.32, 83.50, 84.5.

82.24 "From 'A Work in Progress.'" *Paris Review*, no. 86 (winter), 10-14. First advance excerpt from *Ancient Evenings* (83.18), taken, according to a note, from the installment forthcoming in *Playboy* , although the selection does not appear in either *Playboy* excerpt (83.17 and 83.28). An "Author's Note" explains the seven parts of the soul delineated by the ancient Egyptians, an explanation necessary to follow the description of the embalming process (from the point of view of the embalmee). Rpt: Appearing several months before the novel, this excerpt is taken from chapter 5 of book 1, "The Book of One Man Dead."

82.25 Contribution to *Happy Birthday, Kurt Vonnegut: A Festchrift for Kurt Vonnegut on His Sixtieth Birthday*, compiled by Jill Krementz, 99. New York: Delacorte. Five hundred numbered copies. In 147 words, Mailer talks of his pleasure in dining with Vonnegut, who "is almost a dead ringer in physical appearance for Mark Twain."

82.26 Foreword to *Dear Muffo* [Bob Musel]: *35 Years in the Fast Lane*, by Harold Conrad, xix-xxii. Introduction by Budd Schulberg. New York: Stein and Day.

The War on Wall Street's Inside Dopesters
Men's Spring Fashion: The International Style

MAILER GOES EGYPTIAN

By Marie Brenner

Illustration by
Eraldo Carugati
83.13

83.1 "Mailer's Nativity." Letter to the editor. *Time*, 10 January, 5. Correction to a 20 December 1982 article on Norris Church Mailer's paintings in which his age was misstated.

83.2 "Mailer, at 60, Unveils Novel of Escapism." Article-interview by Nicholas A. Basbanes. (Worcester) *Evening Gazette*, 2 February. The first of several reports on Mailer's 28 January luncheon with out-of-town newspaper book editors at New York's Lotos Club to discuss the forthcoming *Ancient Evenings* (83.18). Basbanes appears to have greatly truncated the conversations he reports. See 83.3-83.5, 83.7.

83.3 "Mailer Hits 60." Article-interview by William Robertson. *Miami Herald*, 6 February, Sec. G, pp. 1-2. Longest report on the Lotos Club luncheon. Robertson quotes Mailer verbatim on his reasons for writing the novel (to explore the death customs of the Egyptians, and the immortality of the soul, and to write about a culture "before the Judeo-Christian begins"); and on why he hasn't read Gore Vidal's novel set in ancient times, *Creation* ("Gore is not the worst writer in the world....I don't want to go off in directions that have nothing to do with what I'm doing"). See 83.2, 83.4, 83.5, 83.7.

83.4 "New Perspectives on [Stanley] Elkin and Mailer." Article-interview by Clarence E. Olson. *St. Louis Post-Dispatch*, 6 February. Briefest report on the Lotos Club luncheon. Mailer tells Olson that "on a good day he produces 1,000 words, in longhand." See 83.2, 83.3, 83.5, 83.7.

83.5 "Norman Mailer: 60 and Still Challenging for the Championship." Article-interview by Robert Taylor. *Boston Globe*, 6 February, Sec. B, pp. 10-11. Another perspective on the discussion of *Ancient Evenings* (83.18) at the Lotos Club. Taylor is the only one of the editors present to quote Mailer's comment on William Faulkner: "I'm as good a hardworking pro as anyone around. When I work I don't like to know where I'm going. After I get there, out on the rockface, I look back at how far I've come—and then I look up and see Mt. Faulkner towering above me." See 83.2-83.4, 83.7.

83.6 "On the Scholarly Trail of the New Revisionists." Article-interview by Herbert Mitgang. *New York Times*, 10 February, Sec. C, p. 22. Explanation of how the work of several authors—Ignazio Silone, Mailer, Mark Twain, Henry James and Anthony Trollope—was revised in one way or another. Mitgang reports on Hershel Parker's comparison of the *Esquire* version of *An American Dream* (64.2-64.9) with the Dial Press book version (65.7), including the original manuscripts. Parker concluded that the magazine version was superior. Mailer said, "I think the Dial version is better. The publisher preferred to print the *Esquire* serial, but I devoted four months to revising it for the book." Parker's essay was collected in his volume *Flawed Texts and Verbal Icons* (Evanston, Ill.: Northwestern University Press). See 65.3.

83.7 "Norman Mailer Finally Delivers the 'Big One.'" Article-interview by Digby Diehl. *Los Angeles Herald Examiner*, 23 February, Sec. C, pp. 1, 6. The last and best article on the Lotos Club luncheon. Diehl covers most of the same ground as the others, but also includes Mailer's comments on the complexity of the ancient Egyptian language, his effort to remove anachronisms, and his plan, later dropped, to use *Ancient Evenings* (83.18) as the first volume in a trilogy: "After this novel, the next one will be set in the future, although not conventional science fiction, I hope. And the third one will take place in the contemporary era." When asked how this novel, 11 years in the writing, ranks with his others, he says, "This is my best book, or I've been married to the wrong woman for 11 years." See 83.2-83.5, 83.22.

83.8 "The World's Greatest Minds Convene, and Agree: Paris Is Better than Dallas." Article by Pamela Andriotakis and Joel Stratte-McClure. *People Weekly*, 28 February, 32-33. Frothy piece on some of the 300 intellectuals invited to Paris by Culture Minister Jack Lang 12-13 February to attend "The Cultural Congress of Paris: Creation and Development." Mailer is quoted briefly.

83.9 "A Room in the Mind's Eye." *House and Garden*, March, 100-103. Advance excerpt from *Ancient Evenings* (83.18). Rpt: Appearing about a month before the novel, this excerpt is taken from the opening of chapter 4, book 3, "The Book of the Child."

83.10 "Twelfth Round: An Interview with Norman Mailer." By Robert

Begiebing. *Harvard Magazine*, 85 (March-April), 40-50; cover photograph of Mailer. One of the three or four most important interviews Mailer has given; on the subject of his Harvard experience, it is the best, with especially interesting remarks on the *Harvard Advocate* (see 41.1, 75.14, 77.2). He comments on all aspects of his career, and at length on the forthcoming *Ancient Evenings* (83.18). He ends the interview with an anecdote about Ralph Ellison, with whom he attended a 1959 conference in Iowa. Rpt: 88.6. See 59.15-59.18.

83.11 "Norman Wasn't Stormin.'" Article by John Engstrom. *Boston Globe*, 8 March, 57, 62. Report on the first staged reading of "Strawhead" (86.25) at Loeb Drama Center in Boston. This two-act play, written in collaboration with Richard Hannum, is based on *Of Women and Their Elegance* (80.15). It has never been commercially produced, but has been staged at Actors' Studio in New York and in Provincetown, with Mailer's daughter Kate portraying Marilyn Monroe. Mailer answered questions after the reading and said, "Women never dismiss the notion of being 'elegant' without a slight doubt in their hearts."

83.12 "Mailer at Penn." Article by Carlin Romano. *Philadelphia Inquirer*, 24 March, Sec. C, pp. 1, 5. Detailed report with long quotes on Mailer's week-long appointment as a Pappas Fellow at the University of Pennsylvania where he lectured and met with a variety of classes. The centerpiece of the week was a lecture titled "The White Negro Reconsidered," which was followed by a pointed exchange with black students about Mailer's "antique view of blacks," as one student put it. Mailer "neither completely endorsed nor disavowed what he had once felt" about blacks, but as he explained, he had wished to compliment blacks by "celebrating their ability to live in the present." Mailer's friend and English Department Chairman, Robert F. Lucid, organized the visit. Of the Penn students who met Mailer, Lucid said, "These are the sons and daughters of the generation that *knew* Mailer. So they know that he's important from an authoritative source, but they're not sure why." See 83.14-83.16, 83.21, 83.35.

83.13 "Mailer Goes Egyptian." Article-interview by Marie Brenner. *New York*, 28 March, 28-38. Long, sympathetic portrait of Mailer replete with revealing comments garnered during visits to his Brooklyn Heights apartment. His wife, Norris Church Mailer, is also quoted. Topics covered at length: *Ancient Evenings* (83.18); his parents ("my father was an elegant, impoverished figure out of Chekov"); his Jewishness; an extended description of how he met Norris; other writers, including Lillian Ross, William Styron, John Updike and Ernest Hemingway; the 1981-1982 Jack Abbott affair; and many remarks on the challenges of being a professional writer. "I never take Tom Wolfe seriously when he talks about the New Journalism as a higher form than the novel, because finally in the New Journalism your plot is handed to you, and once it is, you can concentrate on the writing. Plot is what drives me up the wall. The choices your characters have, the wrong choices they can make. I've had that experience in *The Deer Park* [55.4] and in *Barbary Shore* [51.1], and it frightened me for life."

135

83.14 "Mailer Leads with His Chin Again." Article by unidentified writer. *Boston Herald*, 28 March. Brief, derivative, report on Mailer's visit to University of Pennsylvania, with a few new quotes. See 83.12, 83.15, 83.16, 83.21, 83.35.

83.15 "For My Small Share, Norman Mailer." Article by Susan Schaefer Ingram. *South St. Star* (Philadelphia), 31 March, 1, 16, 17. Ingram's title is what Mailer signed in her copy of a history of the *Village Voice* during his visit to University of Pennsylvania. Mailer's comments on journalism in one of his public lectures at Penn, and at an ensuing press conference are quoted. Accompanied by 83.16. See 83.12, 83.14, 83.21, 83.35.

83.16 "Mailer on Nuclear War." Article by Maura Boland. *South St. Star* (Philadelphia), 31 March, 17. Accompanying 83.15, this piece quotes from another Mailer lecture at Penn, this one dealing with nuclear war. He proposes that "nations rent the Falkland Islands and have serious but small-scale wars there." See 83.12, 83.14, 83.15, 83.21, 83.35.

83.17 "Ancient Evenings." *Playboy*, April, 78-82, 118, 124, 162, 164, 166, 168, 170, 172, 174. Excerpt from novel of same name (83.18); titled "A Soldier in the Harem" on the cover. Illustrated by Ivan Punchatz. Rpt: Appearing just before the novel, this excerpt is a very compressed version of chapters 1-7 of book 5, "The Book of Queens," which deals with Menenhetet's tenure as harem master to Ramses II. First of two installments.

83.18 *Ancient Evenings*. Boston: Little, Brown, 4 April; London: Macmillan, 26 May. Novel, 709 pp., $19.95. Dedication: "To my daughters, to my sons, and to Norris." The copyright page carries this note: "I would like to express my appreciation to Ned Bradford, Roger Donald, Arthur Thornhill, Scott Meredith, and Judith McNally for their assistance and encouragement on this work." Discarded title: *Master of the Secret*. The novel's dates of composition, 1972-1982, are given on its last page. Rpt: Advance excerpts appeared in *Paris Review* (82.24), *House and Garden* (83.9), and *Playboy* (83.17), and, shortly after publication, in *Vogue* (83.30), again in *Playboy* (83.28), and in the (London) *Sunday Times* (83.42); excerpts from three chapters are reprinted in 98.7. See 72.19, 74.10, other 1983 entries.

Mailer: "This isn't the big book I promised [in *Advertisements for Myself*, 59.13], but it is a big book. I think in a literary sense it's the most innovative. I think this is far and away the most ambitious novel I've ever written" (83.13).

83.19 "The Bad Boy of Letters Grows Up: At 60, Norman Mailer Claims He Has Mellowed." Article-interview by Blake Green. *San Francisco Chronicle*, 8 April. Report on Mailer's reading from 83.18 in San Francisco at a program sponsored by City Arts and Lectures, Inc., and his later conversation with Michael McClure and others. He comments on the Abbott affair, Henry Miller, his reputation, and finances.

83.20 "Mailer: 'It's Easier to Talk of Sex than Death.'" Article-interview by Eugene Kennedy. *Chicago Tribune Bookworld*, 10 April, Sec. 7, pp. 1, 7.

136

Mailer is at ease with Kennedy, an old friend, and speaks reflectively about 83.18. "It may be," he concludes, "that this book will be approachable to the degree that Americans are ready to contemplate and live with people profoundly oriented toward death."

83.21 "The Impish Iconoclast at 60." Article-interview by Paul Gray and Janice C. Simpson. *Time*, 18 April, 82-84; cover photograph of Mailer (inset). *Time* has only rarely had a good word to say about Mailer; the string continues here in a long (for *Time*) piece centering on 83.18. Includes quotes from Mailer friends Buzz Farbar, José Torres, Scott Meredith and E.L. Doctorow, and from his comments at the University of Pennsylvania in March. Also includes Mailer's warm appreciation of John Updike: "He has great wisdom as a writer." Accompanied by Gray's negative review of the novel. See 83.12, 83.14-83.16, 83.35.

83.22 "Mailer Between Lives." Article-interview by Curt Suplee. *Washington Post Style*, 20 April, Sec. B, pp. 1, 11. Report on a meeting in the offices of Little, Brown in New York at which Mailer talks at length about sex, magic, excrement, and the probable responses to 83.18. He reveals the title of the third novel in the planned trilogy: "Of Modern Times." See 83.7, 83.29.

83.23 "Mailer: New Book Gets Shock Reactions." Article-interview by Sandy Hoefler. *State Journal-Register* (Springfield, Ill.), 23 April. Report on a press conference at Sangamon State University (now University of Illinois, Springfield). Mailer noted that *Ancient Evenings* (83.18) "received my best and worst reviews....It helps to have a firm ego in such a situation."

83.24 "Mellowing?...Not Mailer." Article-interview by Marty Gervais. *Windsor* (Ontario) *Star*, 23 April, Sec. A, pp. 1, 16. Report of Mailer's meeting with Canadian book editors in New York to discuss 83.18. Snide piece that repeats old stories, but does provide Mailer with the opportunity to explain that his contract with Little, Brown required him to submit installments of the novel, but forbade the editors from reading them, although Mailer did offer the opportunity to Larned G. Bradford, his chief editor.

83.25 "A Novel Mailer: Calm and Happy." Article-interview by Karen Heller. *USA Today*, 25 April. Mailer comments briefly on four previous books: *The Naked and the Dead* (48.2), *Barbary Shore* (51.1), *The Deer Park* (55.4), and *The Executioner's Song* (79.14).

83.26 "Outspoken in the '60s, Mailer Mellows in His 60s." Article-interview by Raymond G. Cushing. *Minneapolis Star and Tribune*, 25 April, Sec. C, pp. 1, 4. One more piece that attempts to contrast a young, fiery man with an older, mellow one. Cushing's by-line says *Los Angeles Times* and this piece apparently appeared there first. Reflecting on his age, Mailer says that being "fifty caused a long, continuous woe. Fifty had an awful sound to it. Worse that sixty. Sixty feels all right. Forty felt great. Thirty felt lousy. Maybe I've just got something against odd numbers."

83.27 "Mailer on Mummy: Novels with No End." Article-interview by William F. Ryan. *Washington Tribune*, 28 April, 3. A shorter version of 83.51, this piece contains Mailer's reflections on the endings of different kinds of narrative, and the information that *Ancient Evenings* (83.18) would be on the *New York Times* bestseller list the next week.

83.28 "Ancient Evenings." *Playboy*, May, 100-102, 188, 190-92, 194-96, 199-202, 203. Excerpt from the novel of same title (83.18). Illustrated by Ivan Punchatz. Rpt: Appearing just after the novel, this excerpt deals with Menenhetet's relationship with Nefertiri, and is taken from the second half of book 5, "The Book of Queens," beginning at the end of chapter 9, skipping 10, and running through chapter 14, with many excisions and small changes. It is the second of two *Playboy* installments which together cover most of book 5.

83.29 "Ancient Evenings." *Vogue*, May, 278-79, 342. Excerpt from the novel of same title (83.18). Accompanied by 83.30 and 83.34. Rpt: Appearing just after the novel, this excerpt is taken without change from the chapter 1 of book 3, "The Book of the Child."

83.30 "Mailer and Mailer." Article-interview by Cathleen Medwick. *Vogue*, May, 274, 277, 280, 343. Accompanied by 83.29 and 83.34. Description of the Mailers at home with a number of quotes from Norris Church Mailer on her life in Arkansas, and a few from Mailer on *Ancient Evenings* (83.18), and the writer's life. He explains that the second and third novels in the trilogy begun by 83.18 will be titled, respectively, "The Boat of Ra" (set in the future on a space ship), and "Modern Times" (set in the contemporary era). See 83.22.

83.31 "Mailer's Flight to Ancient Egypt." Article-interview by Bruce Weber. *Harper's Bazaar*, May, 160-61, 96, 104. Mailer tells Weber that "the one virtue I lay claim to for this book [83.18] is that I think I succeeded in creating a psychology that's comprehensive and owes nothing to Freud." He also discusses his 1969 mayoral campaign, possible feminist response to the novel, and his frustration in reading the biography of him by Hilary Mills (82.23). See 83.2, 83.50, 84.5.

83.32 "Norman Mailer: Love Him or Leave Him." Article-interview by James Paul. *San Francisco Review of Books*, May-June. Negative review of 83.18 containing a few of Mailer's remarks on 1 April at Herbst Theater in San Francisco. Accompanied by 83.33.

83.33 "One Woman's View." Article by Lorilee Howard. *San Francisco Review of Books*, May-June. Howard compares Mailer's boisterous presentation at the Herbst Theater on 1 April with the appearance of Joan Didion a few years earlier, and quotes him on several topics, including Jack Abbott, celebrity, Gore Vidal.

83.34 "Style Is Character: An Interview with Norman Mailer." By Cathleen Medwick. *Vogue*, May, 279, 343. Accompanied by 83.29 and 83.30.

Discussion of style, especially as related to 83.18. Mailer says he has seven styles in the novel because it is comprised of seven books, "built on the notion that the Egyptians had of the soul. They believed that when you died, you died with seven spirits, pieces of the soul, and they all went to different places."

83.35 "The Surreal Professor." Article-interview by Marshall Ledger. *Pennsylvania Gazette*, 87 (May), 14-22; cover photograph of Mailer. The longest report on Mailer's week-long stint as the University of Pennsylvania's first Pappas Fellow. Extended comments on the Abbott affair, his relationship to America, "The White Negro" (57.1), nuclear war, feminism, homosexuality, James T. Farrell, *Ancient Evenings* (83.18), and the writing life. Important article. Rpt: By the University of Pennsylvania in a booklet (hard and softcover) titled *Pappas Fellows: Norman Mailer*, with prefatory statements by T. Peter Pappas and President Sheldon Hackney, and Hackney's introduction of Mailer. See 83.12, 83.14-83.16, 83.21.

83.36 "Norman Mailer on 'Ancient Evenings' in Egypt." Article-interview by John Barkham. *Federal Times*, 2 May, 23. Brief interview in which Mailer says that he "hoped to attain a Proustian touch here and there" in 83.18.

83.37 "Brady: An Evening with Mailer." Article-interview by James Brady. *Advertising Age*, 9 May. Report on Brady's interview with Mailer on WCBS-TV in New York.

83.38 "Something Has Been Stolen from Us That We Can't Name." Interview by Alvin P. Sanoff. *U.S. News and World Report*, 23 May, 73. Sanoff's questions have been cut from this conversation, a classic Mailer fulmination against plastic, television, frozen food, drugs and "the culture of interruption."

83.39 "Norman's Conquests." Article-interview by Julia Braun Kessler. (Van Nuys, Cal.) *Daily News Magazine*, 29 May, 25-27. Significant interview for three reasons: 1) "Mailer's Law of Architectural Sequence on the American Campus": "the newer the building, the less attractive"; 2) "I have supposed that if there were one great Egyptian novelist, this is his novel. I was even tempted at one point to call it 'The Egyptian Novel'"; 3) on karma: "When you think of the incredible elaborations that go into any one human being, it does seem wasteful of the cosmos to send us out just once to learn all those things, and then to molder forever in the weeds."

83.40 "Unblooded by the Critical Pounding, Norman Mailer Defends the Egyptian Novel That Took a Decade to Write." Interview by George Plimpton. *People Weekly*, 30 May, 53-54, 59-60. Brief but penetrating interview in which Mailer discusses his research for 83.18, his fondness for describing odors, and his difficulties with plot. Rpt: 88.6.

83.41 "Behind the Lines." Article-interview by Julie Rubenstein and Greg Tobin. *Literary Guild Magazine*, June, 5. Brief piece with a few scattered quotes on *Ancient Evenings* (83.18): "The book feels much closer to me than *The Executioner's Song* (79.14), because finally it came out of my imagination, and I had to search for it all these years."

83.42 "Mailer Takes on the Pharaohs," Article-interview by Melvyn Bragg. (London) *Sunday Times Magazine*, 5 June, 18-19. Mailer tells Bragg about his motive and research for 83.18, including his belief in reincarnation: "For years I had been working on the theme that the only way to understand human behaviour was to see that it was not just working for one invested organisation—the present self." Accompanied by an excerpt from the novel, the embalming sequence, chapters 5, 6 and the beginning of 7 from book 1, "The Book of One Man Dead," encompassing the first excerpt published in the *Paris Review* (82.24).

83.43 "Macho Mailer Faces Up to Posterity's View." Article-interview by Adrianne Blue. (London) *Times*, 10 June, 12. Brief piece, published during Mailer's promotional tour in England for *Ancient Evenings* (83.18), with Mailer's comments on his public persona.

83.44 "Mailer on Moses." Article-interview by Clive Sinclair. *Jewish Chronicle*, 24 June, 23. Perhaps Mailer's longest utterance on his Jewishness. See 91.29, 97.3.

83.45 "God and Man and Norman Mailer." Article-interview by Eugene Kennedy. *Notre Dame Magazine*, 12 (July), 19-20. One of Mailer's most incisive explanations of his spiritual belief relayed and framed sympathetically by Kennedy, a former Catholic priest and good friend. For more on Mailer's theology, see 59.2, 75.2, 75.11, 82.15 and 89.11.

83.46 "Making Ends Meet: James Campbell Meets Norman Mailer." Article-interview by James Campbell. *Literary Review*, July, 28-31. On the English tour for 83.18, Mailer breakfasts with Campbell and discusses his new novel, irony in literature, the respective merits of journalism and the novel, and some of his contemporaries: James Baldwin, Saul Bellow and James Jones. He notes that his "toughest" journalistic assignment was his piece for *Life* (71.14) on the first Ali-Frazier fight. He had 32 hours to write 9,500 words.

83.47 "Norman Mailer: A Man, an Artist, a Cultural Phenomenon." Article-interview by Rick Soll. *Living, Chicago Sun-Times*, 7 August, 1, 6-7, 12; cover photograph of Mailer and Norris Church Mailer. In Chicago to promote *Ancient Evenings* (83.18), Mailer talks at length about the struggle to write the novel, and his image problems: "I never say exactly what I think—it's my style to circle around an issue," which causes problems for journalists, who "edit out the context." He also reveals that he and his wife, Norris Church, "were born within one minute of each other, 26 years apart." "Norris," he says, "has changed me enormously."

83.48 "Norman Mailer Moves to Random House." Article by unidentified writer. *Publishers' Weekly*, 12 August, 17. Mailer is quoted once in this brief article: "I have had a long relationship with Little, Brown, and for the most part an agreeable one." Also quoted are Scott Meredith, Mailer's agent, and his new editor, Jason Epstein, who reports that Mailer's first book for Random House will be "a major contemporary novel," perhaps the first mention of *Tough Guys Don't Dance* (84.17).

83.49 *St. George and the Godfather*. Introduction by John Leonard. New York: Arbor House, September; simultaneously as a softcover. Nonfiction narrative on the 1972 political conventions, 229 pp., $14.95. First hardcover version of the earlier softcover (72.17).

83.50 "Modern Evenings: An Interview with Norman Mailer." By Michael Schumacher. *Writer's Digest*, October, 30-34. The chief theme of this thoughtful interview is risk: the risk of being a working writer, the risk of reviews, of changing styles, fame, the tides of luck. Mailer says, "I'm almost more comfortable with a tough tide. I get nervous when I'm on a good tide, because I figure prosperity is something I've never steered too well." He also comments on Hilary Mills's biography (82.23), saying, "I think she stuck to every story at face value. None of them are adjusted or weighed." See 83.32, 84.5.

83.51 "Norman Mailer's Ancient Magic: Machismo, Elegance and Dogs That Don't Watch TV." Article-interview by William F. Ryan. *Virginia Country*, October, 34-39, 88. A longer version of 83.27, this is perhaps Mailer's most exhaustive conversation on *Ancient Evenings* (83.18), with long discussions of magic, technology, telepathy, reincarnation and erotic literature.

83.52 "The Poor American in London: The British Elections as Seen through the Trained Eye of an Innocent Abroad." *Esquire*, October, 49-50, 52, 54, 56, 58, 60, 62. Essay. Rpt: Divided into three parts, "The Left," "The Right," "The Outcome," Mailer's essay first appeared in three installments (29 May, 5 June, 12 June) in the English newspaper, *Mail on Sunday*.

83.53 "All the Pirates and People: Norman Mailer Discovers the Man Who Is Clint Eastwood." *Parade*, 23 October, 4-7. Portrait-interview.

83.54 "Jackie, the Prisoner of Celebrity." *Esquire*, "Golden Anniversary Collector's Issue: 50 Who Made a Difference." December, 185-89. Portrait of Jacqueline Kennedy. Rpt: The entire issue was republished with a preface by Lee Eisenberg and a foreword by Phillip Moffitt: New York: Villard Books, 1984. See 62.12.

83.55 "A Tamer Mailer Finds a Cause." Article-interview by Barbara Sullivan. *Chicago Tribune*, 5 December, Sec. 2, p. 8. In Chicago to speak at a fundraiser for cat agencies at the request of his friend Irma Robinson, Mailer talked about cats and other matters at a pre-fundraiser luncheon. He tells the reporter that his first murder mystery (84.17) will be published in 1984. See 83.56.

83.56 "Cat Lovers." Article-interview by Marcia Froelke Coburn. (Chicago) *Reader*, 16 December, 46-47. Reports on Mailer's talk at a Chicago fundraiser for cats. Mailer tells the story of two cats he knew in Paris in 1947-1948. See 83.55.

83.57 "Dwight Macdonald: 1906-1982." *Proceedings of the American Academy and Institute of Arts and Letters*, 2nd ser. (no. 34), 89-91. Portrait. Read at an Institute dinner meeting, 3 November. Rpt: As Preface to a new, posthumous, edition of Macdonald's collection, *Discriminations: Essays and Afterthoughts*. New York: Grossman, 1985. See 60.8.

83.58 Foreword to *Oswald's Game*, by Jean Davison, 7-10. New York: W.W. Norton. Written when Mailer had greater faith in the various conspiracy theories surrounding the Kennedy assassination, and thus worth comparing with *Oswald's Tale: An American Mystery* (95.16). Mailer discusses the coincidences of his life, including the fact that he worked in the same studio building in Brooklyn as Russian spymaster, Col. Rudolph Abel: "The net of conspiracy is always *more* or *less* finely woven than what we do perceive of it."

83.59 Statement for class record. *Harvard College, Class of 1943: Fortieth Anniversary Report*, 120-21. Cambridge: Harvard University. In his 95-word statement, Mailer notes his marriage to Norris Church, the births of his son John Buffalo and his granddaughter Valentina, the publication of *The Executioner's Song* (79.14) and finishing *Ancient Evenings* (83.18). See 49.4, 53.5, 58.6.

1984

84.1 "Mailer Will Star with His Movies." Article-interview by Nan Robertson. *New York Times*, 19 January, Sec. C, p. 17. Mailer discusses the making of "Maidstone" (71.28) on the occasion of its showing, along with his 1967 film, "Beyond the Law," and a documentary, "Norman Mailer: A Sanction to Write," produced by Jeffrey Van Davis, at the Thalia Theater in New York. Mailer tells Robertson his current opinion of "Maidstone": "Now I think it's a terribly flawed and imperfect movie that's really interesting for people who are obsessed by film. The production is an interesting idea, made by a man who didn't know how to make movies." See 81.19, 84.3.

84.2 *"Tough Guys Don't Dance*: An Exclusive Interview with Norman Mailer." Article-interview by Luke Breit. *Poet News: Sacramento's Literary Calendar and Review*, April, 1-3, 5, 7. Telephone interview. Mailer comments on a number of matters including feminism, architecture, how he came to translate (with his daughter Susan) Federico García Lorca's "Lament for Ignacio Sánchez Mejías" (67.22), President Reagan and Russia, and, at great length, the reviews of *Ancient Evenings* (83.18). His comments on Reagan and Russia lie at the heart of his motivation for several future projects: "I think when Reagan called Russia 'an evil force,' he did the worst possible single thing he could have done in terms of bringing our countries closer together. Nothing could have driven them further apart." Finally, Mailer describes the forthcoming *Tough Guys Don't Dance* (84.17), set in Provincetown, as a novel "written in an entirely American idiom." Lorca's translated poem accompanies the interview.

84.3 "Mailer Evening? Well, Maybe...One Hour Was Norman on Film." Article by Lee Dykas. *Providence Journal*, 16 April, Sec. A, p. 1. Report on Mailer's appearance at Sayles Hall, Brown University, where he answered questions after showing a documentary film about him made by Jeffrey Van Davis. He stated that *Ancient Evenings* (83.18) "may have to stand alone" because he might not write volumes two and three of the planned trilogy. See 84.1.

84.4 "Tough Guys Don't Dance." *Vanity Fair*, May, 74-90, 105-6. Advance excerpt from novel of same title (84.17). Accompanied by Irving Penn's photograph of Mailer. Rpt: Appearing six months before the novel, this excerpt consists of chapters 1 and 2 of the published novel, with only a few small changes.

84.5 "Mailer Muses on Marriage and Updike." Article by unidentified writer. *USA Today*, 31 May. Brief comments by Mailer on Hilary Mills's biography (82.23) and John Updike's style, which is mentioned in *Tough Guys*

Don't Dance (84.17). Mailer made his comments at a Washington D.C. party given by his publisher to launch 84.17. See 83.32, 83.50, 84.6, 84.8, 84.30.

84.6 "Mailer Presides over a Novel Launching." Article-interview by John Blades. *Chicago Tribune*, 31 May, Sec. 5, p. 9. Longer report on the Washington, D.C. dinner for book editors given by Random House to promote the forthcoming *Tough Guys Don't Dance* (84.17). Mailer reports that he was "shocked" that Little, Brown, to whom he owed a book under a previous contract, didn't like 84.17; Random House took it over as the first book under its new contract with Mailer. Mailer says he would like "to write a western as good as Ed Doctorow's *Welcome to Hard Times* and Walter Van Tilburg Clark's *The Ox-Bow Incident*," but not a romance, because "D.H. Lawrence did it all when it came to romance." See 84.5, 84.8, 84.30.

84.7 "Tough Guys Don't Dance." *Vanity Fair*, June, 74-90, 110. Advance excerpt from novel of same title (84.17). Accompanied by Irving Penn's photograph of Mailer. Rpt: Appearing five months before the novel, this excerpt covers pages 81-126, or most of chapters 4 and 5 of the novel as published, with eight excisions of a line or two.

84.8 "Publishing: Mailer Talks about His New Thriller." Article-interview by Edwin McDowell. *New York Times*, 8 June, Sec. C, p. 28. Another, and the most complete, account of the Random House dinner in Washington, D.C. given to promote the forthcoming 84.17. Mailer described the murder mystery as being "like an illegitimate baby—it was written in two months, therefore born out of wedlock, and I'm struck by the fact that the event took place." See 84.5, 84.6, 84.30.

84.9 "Norman Mailer Elected PEN President." *PEN American Center Newsletter*, no. 54 (summer), 1. One hundred and eighty-five-word excerpt from Mailer's statement on the importance of PEN given at the PEN annual meeting, 11 July. Mailer says that "writers can speak to one another across the world more quickly than can governments." His term ran 1984-86.

84.10 "An Excerpt [from *Tough Guys Don't Dance*]." *USA Today*, 27 July, Sec. D, p. 3. Accompanying John D. MacDonald's review is this brief excerpt from the last page of chapter 2 of 84.17, detailing Tim Madden's discovery of a severed blonde head in his marijuana hiding place in the Truro woods. MacDonald calls the passage "a good example of Mailer guile and versatility—Tim Madden finding a head, done in the formal archaic structures of Poe."

84.11 "Provincetown." *New York Times Book Review*, 29 July, 33. Accompanying Denis Donoghue's review is this brief excerpt from chapter 1 of *Tough Guys Don't Dance* (84.17), a description of the quality of light in Provincetown: "Perhaps this is why Provincetown is so beautiful. Conceived at night (for one would swear it was created in the course of one dark storm) its sand flats glistened in the dawn with the moist primeval innocence of land exposing itself to the sun for the first time. Decade after decade, artists came to paint the light of Provincetown...."

84.12 "Norman Mailer." Interview by Chuck Pfeifer. *Interview*, August, 58-60. Extended remarks on homosexuality, especially in *Ancient Evenings* (83.18) and *Tough Guys Don't Dance* (84.17), with briefer comment on the Italians of Brooklyn, Dotson Rader, Tennessee Williams, feminism, Russia, Marlon Brando, Jean-Paul Sartre, Ernest Hemingway, F. Scott Fitzgerald and William Faulkner. Rpt: In part in *Sunday, Boston Herald Magazine*, 21 October, 3-6; cover photograph of Mailer.

84.13 "Excerpt [from *Tough Guys Don't Dance*]." *Time*, 6 August, 66. Very brief excerpt from near the opening of chapter 3 of 84.17 dealing with the discovery of the severed head by Tim Madden. Accompanies negative review by Paul Gray.

84.14 "Mailer: Tough Guy at Ease in P'town." Article-interview by Peter E. Howard. *Cape Cod Times*, 12 August, 1, 12-13; front page photograph of Mailer. The conversation focuses mainly on 84.17, with a long aside on feminism. Mailer says, "I always wanted to write a book about Provincetown....It's full of mood. I think the mark of a good murder mystery is that it is full of mood."

84.15 "A 'Zen Koan' for a Title." *Los Angeles Herald Examiner*, 12 August, 10. Accompanying Digby Diehl's review of 84.17 is the anecdote from chapter 5 on which the title is based.

84.16 "A Country, Not a Scenario." *Parade*, 19 August, 4-9. Essay on Russia, based on Mailer's 15-day stay there in March.

84.17 *Tough Guys Don't Dance*. New York: Random House, 20 August; London: Michael Joseph, 15 October. Novel, 229 pp., $16.95. A signed, leather-bound edition appeared simultaneously carrying a one-page preface, "A Special Message for the First Edition by Norman Mailer," and accompanied by his poem about Provincetown, "The Harbors of the Moon," from *Deaths for the Ladies (and Other Disasters)* (62.3). Franklin Center, Pa.: Franklin Library, $75. Dedication: "To Scott Meredith." The dustwrapper photograph is by Mailer's Provincetown neighbor, Joel Meyerowitz. Rpt: Lengthy advance excerpts appeared in *Vanity Fair* (84.4, 84.7); brief ones in *USA Today* (84.10), *New York Times Book Review* (84.11), *Time* (84.13) and *Los Angeles Herald Examiner* (84.15); 98.7 (partial). The novel climbed to number four on the *New York Times Book Review* bestseller list on 30 September. See other 1984 entries and, for comment on the film version of the novel, see 1986 and 1987 entries.

Mailer: "After she left, there was a week when the weather never shifted. One chill morose November sky went into another. The place turned gray before one's eyes. Back in summer, the population had been thirty thousand and doubled on weekends. It seemed as if every vehicle on Cape Cod chose to drive down the four-land state highway that ended at our beach. Provincetown was as colorful then as St. Tropez, and as dirty by Sunday evening as Coney Island. In the fall, however, with everyone gone, the town revealed its other presence. Now the population did not boil up daily from thirty thousand to sixty, but settled down to its honest sediment, three thousand souls, and on empty weekday afternoons you might have said the true number of inhabitants must be thirty men and women, all hiding. There could be no other town like it. If you were sensitive to crowds, you might expire in summer from human propinquity. On the other hand, if you were unable to endure loneliness, the vessel of your person could fill with dread during the long winter" (87.17).

84.18 "The Essential Mailer: Author Norman Mailer Talks about His New Novel, the Irish, and His Love for Chicago." Article-interview by Eugene Kennedy. *Sunday, Chicago Tribune Magazine,* 9 September, 23-25, 28-29. Perhaps Mailer's longest utterance on the Irish, given in the midst of a discussion of 84.17. Rpt: 88.6. See 68.26.

84.19 "Inc.: Norman on Women." Column by Sneed and [Cheryl] Lavin. *Chicago Tribune,* 9 September, Sec. 1, p. 2. Brief comments on the Women's Liberation movement, Geraldine Ferraro, and President Reagan: "I think he has a brain that's never been violated by an intellectual concept."

84.20 "Crime and Puzzlement: The Real-Life Mystery behind Norman Mailer's New Thriller." Article-interview by Andrea Chambers. *People Weekly,* 10 September, 42-45. Discussion of the attempt by federal officials to entrap Mailer in the drug-dealing of his friend Buzz Farbar by recording a luncheon conversation. Mailer was not involved and the attempt failed. Farbar was convicted, went to prison for eight years, and later committed suicide. What is especially reprehensible, Mailer says, "is when the government tries to get a man to entrap his friend."

84.21 "Norman Mailer: Tough Writers Like Him Can Take a Little Heat When Moving in New Directions." Article-interview by Karen Heller. *USA Today,* 12 September, Sec. D, p. 1. Discussion of 84.17 with an aside on Truman Capote who died shortly before.

84.22 "Norman Mailer: Doing a Number on the American Dream." Article-interview by Jerry Bauer. *Midweek* (London), 20 September, 4-6. Despite several errors, Bauer's piece has some good exchanges with Mailer, whom he interviewed in his Brooklyn home over dinner. On *Tough Guys Don't Dance* (84.17): "From the title, you can tell I didn't take myself too seriously. I hope the reader won't either. I want him to have fun with the book."

84.23 "American Ego." Article-interview by Richard Rayner. *Time Out* (London), 27 September-3 October, 14-16. Based on an interview conducted in Brooklyn at the same time as 84.24, Rayner's article parallels Howard's closely.

84.24 "Thoughts of a Tough Guy." Article-interview by Richard Howard. *Mail On Sunday Magazine,* 14 October, 78. In this interview, conducted partly in Brooklyn and partly in London, where Mailer traveled for the 15 October publication of *Tough Guys Don't Dance* (84.17), Mailer explains how he came to write it: "I was truly in debt and I owed my publisher a great deal of money. And then the day of reckoning came and I realised I damn well had to write a book. It had been a book I had been trying to start all year and I hadn't been able to get near it. And it was if suddenly my mind cleared. It was one of those joke situations where they give Popeye the can of spinach. It took 61 days." See 84.23.

84.25 "Mixing It with Mailer." Article-interview by Martyn Harris. *New Society*, 18 October, 99-100. On the English promotional tour for 84.17, Mailer discusses theology with Harris.

84.26 "Television: Fisticuffs." Column by Hugo Williams. *New Statesman*, 19 October, 39-40. Report on a 14 October London television program, "Face the Press." Mailer is sharply questioned by journalists Germaine Greer, Christopher Hitchens and Anthony Howard on what they take to be his obsession with homoeroticism.

84.27 "Mailer and the Engines of Destruction." Article-interview by Terry Coleman. *Guardian*, 20 October. Rambling discussion at Brown's Hotel in London during Mailer's tour to promote 84.17. Politics—President Reagan, Geraldine Ferraro, Margaret Thatcher and Casper Weinberger— are discussed more than literature. Mailer says that Reagan "believes America's a magical place. And that everything will turn out all right. That's what they used to tell us in B-movies 50 years ago."

84.28 Letter to the editor. *Esquire*, November, 12. Letter of congratulation on the fiction in the August issue.

84.29 "Norman Mailer: Face to Face." Interview by Dan Treisman and Robin Davis. *Isis: Oxford University Magazine*, November or December, 8-9. Unremarkable interview in which Mailer touches several subjects lightly, including 84.17, Ernest Hemingway, his theology, his image and Margaret Thatcher: "She's probably the best politician I've ever seen at work anywhere."

84.30 "Norman Mailer: The Prisoner of Celebrity." Article-interview by Mark Bowden. *Philadelphia Inquirer Magazine*, 2 December, 40-44. Another report, presumably the last, based on the May dinner party thrown by Random House to promote 84.17, and a small news conference at Random House three months later when 84.17 had risen to the middle of most bestseller lists. The interview is valuable for Mailer's long statement about his unwillingness to plot his books out ahead of time: "Knowing what the plot of my book was going to be in detail would be like being married to someone whose every habit you knew." See 84.5, 84.6, 84.8.

84.31 "Mailer and [Erskine] Caldwell Join Academy's Select 50." Article by Herbert Mitgang. *New York Times*, 8 December, 13. Report on the 7 December induction into the American Academy of Arts and Letters of two new members to fill the chairs of departed members. Mailer inherited chair 19, last held by Tennessee Williams and before that by Alexander Calder. Mailer: "Maybe some of his [Williams's] talent will rub off on me. I'd like to do a good play before I die—before I give up the seat." In a citation by the Academy, Arthur M. Schlesinger Jr. said: "In a career of living dangerously, he has shown qualities of passion, imagination, literary power and psychological subtlety that will surely make posterity regard him as one of the giants—if at times a wounded giant—of our age." See 98.4.

84.32 "Huckleberry Finn, Alive at 100." *New York Times Book Review*, 9 December, 1, 36-37. Essay. Mailer's only extended comment on nineteenth-century American Literature, and one of his finest literary essays. Rpt: *Chicago Tribune Magazine*, 27 January 1985; 85.12, 98.7.

84.33 "Fast Track: Vital Statistics, Norman Mailer." Interview by Cheryl Lavin. *Parade*, 16 December, 7. Mailer fills in the blanks to a set of standard questions—age, birthplace, favorite foods and movie, etc.

84.34 "Norman Mailer: Fact and Fiction." Interview by Harvey Aronson. *PD: Sunday Magazine of the St. Louis Post-Dispatch*, 16 December, 4-6, 22-23. Solid interview that deals not with how Mailer lives, but how he writes. Asked if he outlined *Tough Guys Don't Dance* (84.17) in his head, Mailer said: "More or less. The nearer I'd come to the approaching chapter, the more outline I'd get in my head. But I never try to tap my head, so to speak...I respect my unconscious. I walk around it."

84.35 *The Last Night*. New York: Targ Editions. Story, 31 pp., $100. No dedication. Limited edition of 250 copies. Rpt: From the December 1963 *Esquire* (63.39), with the incorrect notation that it appeared there in December 1962; 66.11, 67.11, 82.19.

1985

Norman Mailer

A FRAGMENT FROM VIETNAM

A Play in one Act

[signature]

1985

Eurographica
Helsinki

85.11 (see 67.15, 72.7)

85.1 "1000 Writers to Meet in New York at PEN International Congress." Article-interview by Madalynne Reuter. *Publishers' Weekly*, 8 February, 23-24. Heralding the 12-18 January 1986 conference in New York, Mailer and PEN American Center executive director Karen Kennerly gave an overview on the event. Mailer came up with the idea of asking 16 American authors to speak two at time for eight evenings to raise money for the conference. They are: Mailer, William Styron, Kurt Vonnegut, Saul Bellow, Woody Allen, Eudora Welty, William F. Buckley Jr., Joan Didion, John Irving, James Michener, Arthur Miller, Isaac Bashevis Singer, Susan Sontag, John Updike, Gore Vidal and Tom Wolfe. Mailer explained the theme of the conference is the "imagination of the writer and the imagination of the state," but that there would be "no invidious comparisons of governments. Our purpose is to enhance relations rather than smash them." Asked if organizing a conference is harder than writing, Mailer said it was. "But after you turn 60, you have to take up church work." See 85.2, 85.6, 85.8, 85.9, winter and spring 1986 entries.

85.2 "International Writers' Congress Set." Article by unidentified writer. *New York Times*, 7 March, Sec. C, p. 14. Apparent summary of 85.1. See 85.6, 85.8, 85.9, winter and spring 1986 entries.

85.3 "Mailer Admits Someone's Better." Article by Brian Petersen. *Grand Forks* (North Dakota) *Herald*, 22 March, Sec. A, pp. 1, 8. Account of the 21 March University of North Dakota Writers Conference on narrative. Mailer,

Alex Haley, Amy Clampitt and Jorie Graham were the speakers. Mailer said his instincts told him to speed up the dialogue in *The Executioner's Song* (79.14) until he saw that it could not be improved. "I realized God is a better novelist than the novelist."

85.4 "The Hazards and Sources of Writing." *Michigan Quarterly Review* 24 (summer), 391-402. Expanded, revised version of "A Sinister Occupation" (81.9) given as a Hopwood Lecture at the University of Michigan, April 1984. Mailer's longest essay on his craft and his most important uncollected essay. Rpt: *Speaking of Writing: Selected Hopwood Lectures*, edited by Nicholas Delbanco. Ann Arbor: University of Michigan Press, 1990.

85.5 "Writers Assail FBI Seizures in Puerto Rico." Article by Edwin McDowell. *New York Times*, 2 October, Sec. B, p. 9. Account of press conference called by the American chapter of PEN to discuss what Mailer called the apparent "outrageous abuse" of Puerto Rican writer Coqui Santaliz's civil liberties. The apartment of Ms. Santaliz, former president of the Puerto Rican chapter of PEN, was searched, along with 37 others, in connection with the robbery of a Wells Fargo armored truck in 1983. "But what impressed me as singularly shocking," Mailer said, was that the novel Ms. Santaliz was writing "was taken from her and has not been returned." Mailer was joined at the conference by Rose Styron, Allen Ginsberg and Frances FitzGerald.

85.6 "Mailer and Vidal to Wield or Bury Hatchet for PEN." Article by Kenneth R. Clark. *Chicago Tribune*, 17 November, Sec. 14, p. 43. Summary of PEN event plans outlined in 85.1, with new quotes from Mailer on the event at which he would be paired with Vidal. "I think there are more important things in the world than a feud between Gore Vidal and myself." See 77.4-77.9, 85.1, 85.2, 85.8, 85.9, winter and spring 1986 entries, 91.3.

85.7 "Celebrating Norman Mailer." Article by Fred Ferretti. *New York Times*, 22 November, Sec. B, p. 12. Account of the 20 November dinner ceremony at which Mailer received Lord and Taylor's annual Rose Award for public accomplishment. Mailer is quoted as saying that he had been talking to his wife earlier and "said to her how nice it was that Lord & Taylor is honoring me on my 60th birthday. She smiled at me and said, 'You're 62, and it's not your birthday.'"

85.8 "Mailer Earns Praise for PEN Efforts." Article-interview by Edwin McDowell. *New York Times*, 23 December, Sec. C, p. 12. Comment on Mailer's role as organizer and fundraiser for the 12-18 January 1986 PEN Congress. Mailer also reveals that he is "working on a long novel [91.26] whose subject I would prefer to keep a secret." See 85.1, 85.2, 85.6, 85.9, winter and spring 1986 entries.

85.9 "Censorship to Be a Topic of PEN Congress Panel." Article by Edwin McDowell. *New York Times*, 24 December, Sec. C, p. 11. Overview of the program of the PEN Congress, with a quote from Mailer on the purpose of the event. See 85.1, 85.2, 85.6, 85.8, winter and spring 1986 entries.

85.10 "The Cathedral of St. Isaac in Leningrad." *Partisan Review* 51 (double issue: 51:4, 1984 and 52:1, 1985), 535. Poem. Rpt: *Partisan Review: The 50th Anniversary Edition*, edited by William Phillips. New York: Stein and Day.

85.11 *A Fragment From Vietnam: A Play in One Act*. Helsinki: Eurographica, softcover. One-act play with accompanying self-interview (67.16), 39 pp. Limited edition of 350, plus 12 author's copies. Adapted by Mailer from *Why Are We In Vietnam?* (67.15). Rpt: 72.7, 82.19. See 67.15 for context and description of this reprint; 72.18.

85.12 *Huckleberry Finn, Alive at 100*. Montclair, N.J.: Caliban Press. Essay, 9 pp., $18. Limited edition of 250, 200 softcover and 50 in boards. Rpt: 84.32, 98.7.

85.13 Interviews by Peter Manso. In *Mailer: His Life and Times*, by Peter Manso, passim. New York: Simon and Schuster. Second book-length (oral) biography of Mailer. Contains original interviews with Mailer, his family, friends and acquaintances; a total of 151 individuals are identified in the "Contributors" section, many of them never interviewed before or since. Includes a partial Mailer family tree, excerpts from reviews of many Mailer books and some of his letters to Francis Irby "Fig" Gwaltney, a detailed index and scores of photographs from all periods of Mailer's life. The brunt of the book is the wide range and number of utterances on Mailer's life; its weakness is the paucity of editorial synthesis and perspective. Mailer's work is scanted in favor of his life.

85.14 Introduction to new edition of *After the Lost Generation: A Critical Study of the Writers of Two Wars*, by John W. Aldridge, xvii-xxii. New York: Arbor House, softcover. Mailer received his first important critical notice in the first edition (New York: McGraw-Hill, 1951), and Aldridge became a good friend.

85.15 "Norman Mailer." Interview by Charles Ruas. In *Conversations with American Writers*, by Charles Ruas, 18-36. New York: Alfred A. Knopf. Thirteen other writers are included: Eudora Welty, Truman Capote, Gore Vidal, Tennessee Williams, Marguerite Young, William Burroughs, Joseph Heller, Susan Sontag, E.L. Doctorow, Toni Morrison, Paul Theroux, Robert Stone and Scott Spencer. Most of the interview, which took place in 1982, is given over to a discussion of Jack Abbott, violence, *The Executioner's Song* (79.14) and *Ancient Evenings* (83.18), of which Mailer says: "I just finished *Ancient Evenings* a couple of weeks ago, and it's 1,744 double-spaced pages." See 80.10.

85.16 Seminar Comments. In *From Fact to Fiction: Journalism and Imaginative Writing in America*, by Shelley Fisher Fishkin, 208-9. Baltimore: Johns Hopkins University Press. Speaking in Fishkin's 1982 journalism seminar at Yale, Mailer discusses the melding of journalism and fiction in *The Executioner's Song* (79.14).

86.1 "Norman Mailer." Interview by Carole Wagner Mallory. *Elle*, January, 36, 38-40. Brief interview notable for Mailer's explanation of PEN's opposition to the 1952 McCarran-Walter Act, which denies entry into the U.S. to people who have participated in subversive acts, or associated with those who have. He also states that he is "a northern spirit. My name's Norman, which means northman....Palm trees always leave my stomach feeling flat." See 85.1, 85.2, 85.6, 85.8, 85.9 and later 1986 entries.

86.2 "PEN Invitation to Shultz Criticized." Article by Herbert Mitgang. *New York Times*, 10 January, Sec. C, p. 24. Mailer responds to criticism for having invited Secretary of State George P. Shultz to be a welcoming speaker at the PEN conference without the approval of the Board of the American PEN Center. Mailer, president-elect of the center, said, "It seemed self-evident that the PEN Congress would be dignified by the presence of an American Secretary of State. We have also invited distinguished writers from all over the world, including Omar Cabezas of Nicaragua, and we're hoping the Russians will be there as observers." None of the Board members called for the invitation to be withdrawn. See 85.1, 85.2, 85.6, 85.8, 85.9 and 1986 entries.

86.3 Letter to the Guests of Honor and the PEN Delegates. Program of the 48th International PEN Congress, New York, 11-16 January, 32 pp. Mailer's 222-word letter of welcome is given in both English and French, as is the entire program. Conference theme: "The Writer's Imagination and the Imagination of the State." See 85.1, 85.2, 85.6, 85.8, 85.9 and 1986 entries.

86.4 "A Rampancy of Writers." *Time*, 13 January, 22. Article by unidentified writer. Overview of the PEN Congress with a brief quote by Mailer on his appearance with Gore Vidal at one of the PEN Celebrations (pre-conference fundraisers): "a meeting between two toothless tigers." See 85.1, 85.2, 85.6, 85.8, 85.9, 1986 entries, 91.3.

86.5 "Shultz Faces Critics in Speech Opening 48th PEN Assembly." Article by Walter Goodman. *New York Times*, 13 January, Sec. A, p. 1, Sec. C, p. 11. Mailer, who was elected American PEN president by acclamation on 12 January, defended the presence of Secretary of State Shultz on the opening day of the Congress. Shultz was greeted by a public letter signed by 65 of the 700 writers (from 40 countries) attending the conference, including E.L. Doctorow, Susan Sontag, Galway Kinnell, John Irving and Elizabeth Hardwick. A number of writers defended Mailer, including Gay Talese, John Kenneth Galbraith and Kurt Vonnegut. Mailer told the meeting that no applicant from overseas had been denied permission to attend by the U.S. State Department. See Doctorow's original complaint, "Shultz and PEN," *Nation*, 18 January, 37; 85.1, 85.2, 85.6, 85.8, 85.9 and 1986 entries.

86.6 "Shultz Heckled at PEN Meeting." Article by unidentified writer. *Newsday*, 13 January. Another article on the appearance of Secretary of State Shultz at the PEN Congress. See 85.1, 85.2, 85.6, 85.8, 85.9 and 1986 entries.

86.7 "Shultz Issue Dominates PEN Congress Sessions." Article by Edwin McDowell. *New York Times*, 14 January, Sec. C, p. 12. Another report on the Shultz issue, with several quotes from Mailer. See 85.1, 85.2, 85.6, 85.8, 85.9 and 1986 entries.

86.8 "UNESCO Director Speaks at PEN, Uneventfully." Article by unidentified writer. *New York Times*, 15 January, Sec. C, p. 15. Mailer is quoted on the appearance of UNESCO Director Amadou-Mahtar at the PEN Congress. See 85.1, 85.2, 85.6, 85.8, 85.9 and 1986 entries.

86.9 "PEN Talks on Freedom of the Word." Article by Edwin McDowell. *New York Times*, 16 January, Sec. C, p. 17. At a PEN Congress panel on censorship, Mailer is quoted on the possibility of the Reagan administration working to repeal the McCarran-Walter Act. See 85.1, 86.2, 85.6, 85.8, 85.9 and 1986 entries.

86.10 "Women at PEN Caucus Demand a Greater Role." Article by Edwin McDowell. *New York Times*, 17 January, Sec. C, p. 26. First of several articles about a protest, led initially by Betty Friedan, about the underrepresentation of women on various PEN Congress panels. Mailer is quoted, as is Friedan. See 85.1, 85.2, 85.6, 85.8, 85.9 and 1986 entries.

86.11 "PEN Congress Ends with a Protest." Article by Edwin McDowell. *New York Times*, 18 January, 11. Another article on the issue of underrepresentation of women on PEN Congress panels. Mailer, who was both praised and criticized for his work in organizing the conference, called for a vote on removing him: "the votes were solidly in his favor." Mailer, Erica Jong, Nadine Gordimer and Cynthia Macdonald (a PEN executive board member) are quoted. See 85.1, 85.2, 85.6, 85.8, 85.9 and 1986 entries.

86.12 "At PEN, a Feeling of Community." Article by Walter Goodman. *New York Times*, 20 January, Sec. C, p. 25. Overview article on the PEN Congress. Mailer is quoted briefly. See 85.1, 85.2, 85.6, 85.8, 85.9 and 1986 entries.

86.13 "Shultz Sparks Dispute at Start of International PEN Congress." Article by Madalynne Reuter. *Publishers' Weekly*, 24 January, 18. Mailer and Shultz are quoted in this round-up article on the controversy surrounding Secretary of State Shultz's appearance at the 12 January PEN Congress opening session at the New York Public Library. See 85.1, 85.2, 85.6, 85.8, 85.9 and 1986 entries.

86.14 "Independent States of Mind." Article by R.Z. Sheppard, Dean Brelis and Amy Wilentz. *Time*, 27 January, 74-75. Summary article on the

PEN Congress; Mailer is quoted briefly. See 85.1, 85.2, 85.6, 85.8, 85.9 and 1986 entries.

86.15 "Mailer Offers a PEN Post-Mortem." Article-interview by Walter Goodman. *New York Times*, 27 January, Sec. C, p. 24. Summary of the PEN Congress from Mailer's perspective. He discuses the conference's theme, "The Writer's Imagination and the Imagination of the State"; his invitation of Secretary of State Shultz; and the way the panels were chosen by standing committees (six of eight headed by women). See 85.1, 85.2, 85.6, 85.8, 85.9 and 1986 entries.

86.16 "Mightier than the Sword." Article by David Lehman and Ray Sawhill. *Newsweek*, 27 January, 60-61. Another round-up on the PEN conference. Mailer, "who masterminded the Congress," is quoted briefly. See 85.1, 85.2, 85.6, 85.8, 85.9 and 1986 entries.

86.17 "When Worlds Collide: A Report from the PEN Congress." Article by Geoffrey Stokes. *Village Voice*, 28 January, 18-22, 24, 26, 54-55. Overview with quotes set off in boxes from Mailer, George P. Shultz, Omar Cabezas, Margaret Atwood, Meredith Tax, Elizabeth Janeway, Grace Paley, Günter Grass, Salman Rushdie, John Updike, Sandor Csoóri, Ryszard Kapuscinski and Toni Morrison. See 85.1, 85.2, 85.6, 85.8, 85.9 and 1986 entries.

86.18 "Bad Manners and Bad Faith." Article by Maria Margaronis and Elizabeth Pochoda. *Nation*, 1 February, 116-19. Angry piece on the PEN Congress in which Mailer is described as "unruly," "overbearing," "authoritarian," displaying "a fat and fateful rudeness," "foolish" and so on. The authors reprint the letter protesting Secretary of State Shultz's appearance. Pochoda is one of the signers. See 85.1, 85.2, 85.6, 85.8, 85.9 and 1986 entries.

86.19 "At Play in the Fields of the Word." Article by Rhoda Koenig. *New York*, 3 February, 40-47. One of the longest summary articles on the PEN Congress with quotes from all and caricatures of several. See 85.1, 85.2, 85.6, 85.8, 85.9 and 1986 entries.

86.20 "'The Writer's Imagination and the Imagination of the State': Two Views." *New York Review of Books*, 13 February, 23-25. Consists of Mailer's 12 January address at the opening of the PEN Congress, and Nadine Gordimer's statement given on 13 January at the PEN Congress's panel, "How Does the State Imagine?" See George Steiner's criticism of the theme: "Language Under Surveillance: The Writer and the State," *New York Times Book Review*, 12 January, 12, 36; 85.1, 85.2, 85.6, 85.8, 85.9 and 1986 entries.

86.21 "Lead Me Not into PEN Station." Article by Edward Rothstein, *New Republic*, 24 February, 20-23; cover portrait of Mailer, Kurt Vonnegut and Günter Grass. Analytic article on the debate and dissension at the PEN conference. Mailer is quoted briefly. See 85.1, 85.2, 85.6, 85.8, 85.9 and 1986 entries.

86.22 "The First Sitting." Article by James Atlas. *Vanity Fair*, April, 58-62; cover photograph of Kate Mailer as Marilyn Monroe with the blurb:

154

"Mailer's New Marilyn: It's His Daughter." Report on the Actors Studio staging of "Strawhead," a play by Mailer and Richard Hannum adapted from *Of Women and Their Elegance* (80.15). Accompanied by 86.25. See 73.30, 81.4, 83.11.

86.23 "A PEN Scrapbook." Article by James Atlas. *Vanity Fair*, April, 32. Zippy piece on the PEN Congress focusing on a party at the apartment of Saul and Gayfryd Steinberg. Mailer is quoted briefly. See 85.1, 85.2, 85.6, 85.8, 85.9 and 1986 entries.

86.24 "The Prisoner of Sexism: Mailer Meets His Match." Article by Miriam Schneir. *Ms.*, April, 82-83. Late addition to the list of summary articles on the PEN Congress. Mailer is quoted throughout this piece, which is only slightly less outraged than 86.18. See 85.1, 85.2, 85.6, 85.8, 85.9 and 1986 entries.

86.25 "Strawhead: An Extract from Act One." *Vanity Fair*, April, 63-66. Produced only at Actors Studio, New York, in Boston and in Provincetown, in brief experimental runs, "Strawhead" has never been published. Accompanied by 86.22. See 73.30, 80.15, 81.4, 83.11.

86.26 "What Makes Writers Run." Article by Barbara Probst Solomon. *Partisan Review* 53 (no. 2), 183-89. This number of *Partisan Review* was on magazine stands on 30 April. Solomon rebuts some of the feminist criticisms of Mailer's words and deeds at the PEN Congress made in 86.18 and 86.24. See 85.1, 85.2, 85.6, 85.8, 85.9 and 1986 entries.

86.27 "When PEN Pals Collide." Article by David Lehman. *Partisan Review* 53 (no. 2), 190-99. Balanced overview of the PEN Congress, including comment on the media coverage of the event. Mailer is quoted throughout. Two other articles on the PEN Congress appear in this number of *Partisan Review*, by Czeslaw Milosz and Adam Zagajewski, respectively. Mailer is not quoted in either. See 85.1, 85.2, 85.6, 85.8 and 1986 entries.

86.28 "Throwing Punches: Mailer on Mailer." Interview by Jennifer L. Farbar. *Esquire*, June, 238-40, 243-44, 247-50. Mailer discusses a string of related topics with the daughter of his friend, Buzz Farbar: machismo, birth control, the 60s, homosexuality and the sexual revolution, with asides on J.F.K., "The White Negro" (57.1) and *The Executioner's Song* (79.14). Rpt: 88.6.

86.29 "Page Six: Filmmakers Beard Norman Mailer." Column by unidentified writer. *New York Post*, 30 August, 6. Provides quotes from an unlocated Carole Mallory interview in *L.A.* magazine on Mailer's deal with Cannon Films to star, along with his daughter Kate, in Jean-Luc Godard's version of "King Lear," and then direct the movie version of *Tough Guys Don't Dance* (84.17). Mailer wrote the screenplays for both films, and both were produced, although Godard didn't use Mailer's script for "King Lear." See 1986 and 1987 entries.

86.30 "Penned In." Article by Richard Stern. Photographs by Inge Morath. *Critical Inquiry* 13 (autumn), 1-32; cover photographs of Mailer,

Stern, Secretary of State Shultz and Grace Paley. Long first-person account of the major public (and some of the private) debate and discussion at the PEN Congress. Stern gives the best report on Shultz's speech on the opening day of the PEN Congress, and the only one on Mailer's argument (with Saul Bellow as witness) with E.L. Doctorow. See 85.1, 85.2, 85.6, 85.8, 85.9 and earlier 1986 entries.

86.31 "Norman Mailer: The Author as Social Conscience." Article-interview by Charlotte Buak, Gwen Thomas and Angela R. Dickey. *Pencil Press Quarterly* 1 (fall), 4, 6-7. Mailer talks to the editors of this new magazine after speaking at the University of Florida at Gainesville. Most of his comments concern the writerly life.

86.32 "He's Putting His 'Guys' on Film." Article-interview by Gregory Katz. *USA Today*, 12 November, Sec. D, pp. 1-2. Interviewed on the set of "Tough Guys Don't Dance" in Provincetown, Mailer compares filmmaking and writing, and describes his film: "a study of American passions, a horror story, a murder mystery, a comedy and offbeat." See 84.17, other 1986 and 1987 entries.

86.33 "Accountability for Sale, Cheap." Article by Willard Gaylin. *New York Times*, 16 November, Sec. 4, p. 23. Examination of the nature of responsibility with reference to various criminal cases, including Jack Abbott's. Mailer is quoted briefly. See 1982 entries.

86.34 "'Three Cheers for Good Marks': Writers on Their Prizes." *New York Times Book Review*, 16 November, 3, 46. Excerpts from the National Book Awards acceptance speeches of William Faulkner, W.H. Auden, Philip Roth, Saul Bellow, Adrienne Rich, Joyce Carol Oates, Gloria Naylor and Mailer, who won the 1969 award in the arts and letters category for *The Armies of the Night* (68.8). His speech provided the title for this piece. The full speech appears in *Existential Errands* (72.7). See 69.3, 69.4.

86.35 "'Tough Guy' Mailer Shows He Can Dance with the Big Boys: Novelist Directs First Major Film." Article-interview by Roger Ebert. *Chicago Sun-Times*, 23 November, 6-8. Another on-the-set interview in Provincetown, perhaps the best. Mailer recalls in detail the arrangement with Cannon Films under which he came to direct the film version of *Tough Guys Don't Dance* (84.17), and discusses his scripts, his actors, his marriage, his mother, his God and the films made from his novels. Accompanied by an Ebert article-interview, "Prospects are Good for Debra Sandlund," who plays Patty Lareine in the film. Rpt: 88.6, 86.43 (partial). See other 1986 and 1987 entries.

86.36 "People: Tough Guys Do Make Movies: Mailer in Provincetown." Article-interview by G.D.G. *Time*, 1 December, 58-59. Brief piece, with a few quotes from Mailer, that reveals the budget for the film version of 84.17 to be $5 million, and the shooting schedule to be seven weeks. See 1986 and 1987 entries.

86.37 "Movie Beats Writing." Article-interview by Tim Miller. *Cape Cod Times*, 5 December, 1, 15. Mailer again compares writing and filmmaking in this piece, which also reports that Mailer's Commercial Street home was used as Tim Madden's home in the film version of 84.17. See 1986 and 1987 entries.

86.38 "At the Movies." Article-interview by Nina Darnton. *New York Times*, 12 December, Sec. C, p. 10. Very brief piece on the filming of 84.17 containing one fine quote from Mailer: "When I write a novel I try not to think of a plot—I am much more concerned with character. But in a movie the plot is the motor, it is essential. It took me two months to write the novel. The screenplay took six months." See 1986 and 1987 entries.

86.39 "Mailer Makes a Movie." Article-interview by Constance Gorfinkle. (Quincy, Mass.) *Patriot-Ledger*, 16 December, 21-22. On the Provincetown set of "Tough Guys Don't Dance" near the final day (13 December) of shooting, Mailer talks about the play he was almost in at Harvard, his longtime affiliation with Actors' Studio and, again, speaks comparatively of writing novels and directing films. See 84.17, 1986 and 1987 entries.

86.40 "Mailer's Stamp on the Movies." Article-interview by Joseph Gelmis. *Providence Sunday Journal*, 21 December, Sec. I, p. 3. Mailer tells Gelmis that if the movie version of 84.17 is a success, he'd like to make more films. Quotes from Ryan O'Neal and other members of the cast are included. See 1986 and 1987 entries.

86.41 Comments at the National Arts Club Award dinner for Allen Ginsberg, 22 February 1979. Introduced and excerpted by Victor Bockris. In *Best Minds: A Tribute to Allen Ginsberg*, edited by Bill Morgan and Bob Rosenthal, 28-29, 184. New York: Lospecchio Press. Rpt: The comments of Mailer and the other speakers at the dinner are excerpted from a transcript of the evening's proceedings, later assembled in a booklet, with a preface by Bockris, titled *A Buddhist Apocalypse Banquet with Allen Ginsberg, Norman Mailer, William Burroughs, John Ashbery and Ted Berrigan*. Photographs by Marcia Resnik. No date, no publisher.

86.42 "Mailer: The Avenger and the Bitch." Article-interview by Martin Amis. In *The Moronic Inferno and Other Visits to America*, by Martin Amis, 57-73. London: Jonathan Cape; New York: Viking, 1987. The English edition appeared in 1986. Amis's chapter on Mailer (which contains excerpts from two conversations he had with him), consists of three short pieces from the (London) *Observer* (1981, 1982, 1985) cobbled together. Valuable for its representative British combination of indignation and awe in the face of genuine American phenomena.

86.43 Comments. In *Two Weeks in the Midday Sun: A Cannes Notebook*, by Roger Ebert, passim. Kansas City, Mo.: Andrews and McMeel. Rpt: Ebert's memoir includes comments by Mailer from 86.35 (partial); 88.6 (partial). See 87.5.

PROVINCETOWN
A R T S
VOLUME 3, NUMBER 1   SUMMER 1987 $3.50

1987

"*This is a town you could see yourself digging in and fighting for.*"
NORMAN MAILER

Photograph by
Joel Meyerowitz
87.9

87.1 Chatter. Column by Tim Allis. *People Weekly*, 5 January, 92. Allis quotes Mailer from the Italian newspaper *La Republica* on the film he is poised to direct, "Tough Guys Don't Dance." The quotes, however, were made up; the interview never took place, as Mailer explained in a letter to the editor, the published version of which has not been located. See 84.17, 1986 and 1987 entries.

87.2 "Tough Guys Make Movie." Article-interview by Dinitia Smith. *New York*, 12 January, 32-37. Report on the final days of shooting "Tough Guys Don't Dance" in Provincetown. Mailer, Ryan O'Neal, producer Tom Luddy and Lawrence Tierney are quoted. Provides a good explanation of the arrangement with Cannon Films which resulted in Mailer writing the screenplay (five drafts) and directing the film. Mailer also collaborated with Angelo Badalamonti on one of the songs in the film: "You'll Come Back (You Always Do)." See 84.17, 1986 and 1987 entries.

87.3 "Medium-Boiled Mailer." Article-interview by Gerald Peary. *Sight and Sound*, spring, 104-7. Mailer speaks of his earlier films, the pleasures of filmmaking, with an aside on how Charles Laughton had to give up his plan to direct the movie version of *The Naked and the Dead* (48.2). Debra Sandlund and Lawrence Tierney are also quoted. See 76.21, 84.17, 1986 and 1987 entries.

87.4 "Mailer Gives Film Another Fling with 'Guys.'" Article-interview by Todd McCarthy. *Variety*, 4 May, 2, 13, 14. Mailer discusses the various screenplays he has written: "King Lear" for Jean-Luc Godard, "Once Upon a Time in America" for Sergio Leone, one on mobster Meyer Lansky for producer Martin Starger at Universal, and Henry Miller's "Sexus" for Interscope and producers Joe Wizan and Marcia Nasatir. The possibility that Sidney Lumet might direct a screenplay of *The Deer Park* (55.4) by Joan Didion and John Gregory Dunne is also discussed in this useful piece. See 84.17, 1986 and 1987 entries.

87.5 "The Calm Comes to Cannes: But Not Entirely, as Norman Mailer Brings Out His 'Tough Guys.'" Article-interview by Rita Kempley. *Washington Post*, 18 May, Sec. C, pp. 1, 3. Mailer is quoted briefly on "Tough Guys Don't Dance" (which was screened outside the competition at Cannes because Mailer was a juror) in this potpourri on the festival. See 84.17, 1986 and 1987 entries.

87.6 "Mailer, [Jean-Luc] Godard, [Lillian] Gish Bask in the Spotlight." Article-interview by Jay Carr. *Boston Globe*, 18 May, 24, 27. Another article on the Cannes Film Festival with Mailer again comparing directing and writing: "My idea of an ideal life at this time is to write a book, direct a movie, and so on." Mailer was a juror in the film competition. See 84.17, 1986 and 1987 entries.

87.7 "Mailer Hangs Tough Despite the Critics." Article-interview by Jeannie Williams. *USA Today*, 18 May, Sec. D, p. 7. Early, negative reviews of the film version of *Tough Guys Don't Dance* (84.17) are cited in this piece about Mailer at Cannes. Mailer says, "I think my film lies somewhere in a no-man's land between a murder mystery, a suspense tale, a film of horror and a comedy of manners." See 1986 and 1987 entries.

87.8 "Pialat Film Gets Top Prize at Cannes." Article by Vincent Canby. *New York Times*, 20 May, Sec. C, p. 24. Canby praises "Tough Guys Don't Dance" in this overview of the Cannes Film Festival. Mailer is quoted briefly. See 84.17, 1986 and 1987 entries.

87.9 "Camera Angles: Reporters on the Set of 'Tough Guys.'" Article-interview by Bonnie Barber and Gregory Katz. *Provincetown Arts* 3 (summer), 18-20, 116-17; cover photograph of Mailer by Joel Meyerowitz. Interleaved perspectives by Barber and Katz about the filming of "Tough Guys Don't Dance" in Provincetown. One of the best of the on-the-set pieces, with long quotes from Mailer and Ryan O'Neal, who compares Mailer's directorial style to Stanley Kubrick's. See 84.17, 1986 and 1987 entries.

87.10 Comment on James Jones. In "Glimpses: James Jones, 1921-1977." By J. Michael Lennon and George Plimpton. *Paris Review*, no. 103 (summer), 205-36. This portrait of Mailer's friend, comprised of excerpts from Lennon's interviews with Jones's family and friends, including four with Mailer, are taken from those done for "James Jones: From Reveille to Taps," a 60-minute television documentary produced by Lennon and Jeffrey Van Davis for Sangamon State University (now University of Illinois, Springfield). It appeared on PBS in 1985 and 1986.

87.11 "Mailer's Minuet: 'Tough Guys' Two Left Feet." Article-interview by Karen Jaehne. *Film Comment* 23 (July-August), 11-17. Mailer says more on filmmaking , and says it well, in this interview than in any other, and dissipates, to some extent, Jaehne's initial skepticism about his abilities. He also discusses his resistance to "categories" which are "just critics' attempt to bring order to a complex aesthetic universe." "Forms," he says should "be explored, not obeyed." Tom Luddy, Wings Hauser and Frances Fisher are also quoted. See 84.17, 1986 and 1987 entries.

87.12 "Proud Father: Mailer Pleased with 'Tough Guys.'" Article-interview by Tim Miller. *Cape Cod Times*, 14 August, 35, 38. Notable mainly for revealing that "Tough Guys Don't Dance" will arrive at movie theaters on 18 September (New York premier, 16 September). See 84.17, 1986 and 1987 entries.

87.13 "Norman Mailer Directs 'Tough Guys' on Film." Interview by unidentified interviewer. *Brooklyn Heights Press and Cobble Hill News*, 10 September, 1, 16. Mailer speaks again of how his film cuts across categories, his previous films, the acting of Ryan O'Neal; he also compares literature and film. A cast list is given. Rpt: *L.A. Alive*, 18 September, 25, and in a Cannon Films publication booklet, which also contains a full crew list and biographies of the leading actors, the director and producers. See 84.17, 1986 and 1987 entries.

87.14 "Film-Goers' Parties Bring Out the Strangest Mix." Article by Deirdre Kelly. *Globe and Mail* (Toronto), 14 September, Sec. C, p. 12. In Canada for a film festival, Mailer is quoted briefly on Ryan O'Neal and the similarities between "Tough Guys Don't Dance" and David Lynch's "Blue Velvet." Accompanied by 87.15. See 84.17, 1986 and 1987 entries.

87.15 "Mailer Flees from Decades of Yuppiedom." Article-interview by Rick Groen. *Globe and Mail* (Toronto), 14 September, Sec. C, p. 12. After a press conference at Toronto's Festival of Festivals, where "Tough Guys Don't Dance" was shown, Mailer spoke to Groen about the 80s, yuppies, the coming end of communism in Russia, and called Oliver North "a young Ronald Reagan, who can press every sentimental button and sit on every pious pot." Accompanied by 87.14. See 84.17, 1986 and 1987 entries.

87.16 "Tough Guys Keep Writing." Article-interview by Jay Carr. *Boston Globe*, 17 September, 85, 88. In an expansive mood, Mailer talks about his first visit to Provincetown in the early 40s, Jean-Luc Godard, actors, screenplays, Raymond Chandler, machismo, feminism, and the darkness in *Tough Guys Don't Dance* (84.17). Accompanied by Carr's positive review. See 1986 and 1987 entries.

87.17 "Dance of a Tough Guy." Article-interview by Michael Ventura. *L.A. Weekly*, 18-24 September, 14-21; cover photograph of Mailer. Ventura combines a fine interview in California with his remembrance of Mailer lecturing at University of California, Berkeley in 1972, some well-chosen quotes from Mailer's books, and his final reflections on how Mailer "is

160

going down slow, like the old blues [song] says, but he is going down smart." Mailer's elaboration of the distinction between "soul" and "psyche" is only one of several thoughtful exchanges with Ventura. Rpt: 88.6. See 84.17, 1986 and 1987 entries.

87.18 "Mailer and the Movies: Tough Guy Gives Film Another Shot." Article-interview by Peter Rainer. *Weekend Magazine, Los Angeles Herald Examiner*, 18 September, 6-7; cover photograph of Mailer. Interviewed in his attic study in Provincetown, Mailer talks about "Tough Guys Don't Dance," which opened nationwide on 18 September, and his year (1949-50) in Hollywood: "I had a hard time getting out of Los Angeles, even with nothing happening. I hated to leave with a failure and so I kept staying and staying and getting into more and more conversations about making a movie myself. And finally I gave up and said to myself, 'Get Out.'" Accompanied by a largely negative review by Deborah J. Kunk, and a full-page ad for the film. See 84.17, 1986 and 1987 entries.

87.19 "A New Direction: Norman Mailer Makes His First Mainstream Film." Article-interview by Marshall Fine. *Gannet Westchester Newspapers*, 18 September, Sec. B, pp. 1, 12. Mailer again discusses "Tough Guys Don't Dance": how it straddles categories, his future in filmmaking, and his early films. See 84.17, 1986 and 1987 entries.

87.20 "Mailer, 64, Stays Tough." Article-interview by James Verniere. *Boston Sunday Herald*, 20 September, Sec. 3, pp. 1-2. Humdrum piece based on an interview with Mailer in Toronto where "Tough Guys Don't Dance" was screened as part of that city's Festival of Festivals. See 84.17, 1986 and 1987 entries.

87.21 "Norman Mailer the Director Hangs Tough." Article-interview by Edward Guthmann. *Datebook, San Francisco Chronicle*, 20 September, 19-20; cover photograph of Mailer. Another piece based on Mailer's Toronto visit. Mailer again discusses "Blue Velvet," the uncertain category of his film, Ryan O'Neal, and audience response to the film. See 84.17, 1986 and 1987 entries.

87.22 "Norman Mailer 'Tough' Enough?" Article-interview by Bob Lardine. *Close-Up* (New York) *Daily News*, 20 September, 1-2; cover photograph of Mailer. Most of Mailer's comments are given over to his relations with the cast of "Tough Guys Don't Dance," but he also lists the four stages of knowing a woman: "(1) living with her, (2) marrying her, (3) having children with her, and (4) divorcing her. You really know nothing about a woman until you meet her in court." See 84.17, 1986 and 1987 entries.

87.23 "A Mellower Mailer Has a Mystery Movie." Article-interview by Luaine Lee. *Chicago Tribune*, 21 September, Sec. 2 ("Tempo"), p. 3. Mailer talks more about the problems of celebrity than "Tough Guys Don't Dance" in this brief piece. See 84.17, 1986 and 1987 entries.

87.24 "Semi-'Tough' Mailer." Article-interview by Stephen M. Silverman. *New York Post*, 21 September, 31. Mailer credits John Bailey, his cinematographer for "Tough Guys Don't Dance," with improving "the director's vision." He also contrasts cinematic and novelistic pace, and discusses "Blue Velvet" in his conversation with Silverman at Toronto's Festival of Festivals. See 84.17, 1986 and 1987 entries.

87.25 "Norman Mailer's 'Extreme' Situations." Article-interview. Information provided by Luaine Lee of Knight-Ridder newspapers; by Candice Burk-Block, in a dispatch of the New York Times Syndication Sales Corp.; and by Barbara Bright of Reuter News Service. *St. Louis Post-Dispatch*, 30 September, 1, 4. Expansion of material in 87.23, including Mailer's comments on good and evil: "My idea of an awful person is one who is 35 percent good and 65 percent evil. A hero is perhaps a reverse percentage. I'm fascinated by the good that is in evil people." See 84.17, 1986 and 1987 entries.

87.26 "His Brilliant (New).Career?" Article-interview by Daphne Merkin. Photographs by Adam Bartos. *American Film*, October, 42-49. In this insider piece, which captures the mood of the shoot better than any other, Merkin gets comments on the set of "Tough Guys Don't Dance," not only from Mailer, but from set designer Armin Ganz, the mixer, Drew Kunin, the makeup artist, Don, the costume designer, Michael Kaplan, and actors Lawrence Tierney, Ryan O'Neal, Debra Sandlund and Frances Fisher. She also reveals that the film used six interior sets, 59 locales, and had a crew of 97. See 84.17, 1986 and 1987 entries.

87.27 "Words and Pictures: A Conversation with Norman Mailer about Directing the Movie of His Own Novel, *Tough Guys Don't Dance* [87.17]." Article by unidentified writer. *Vanity Fair*, October, 68, 72, 76. Mailer reveals here that Warren Beatty was his first choice to play Tim Madden in his film. He also speaks at length on the director's relationship to his crew, comparing making a film with being in the army. See 1986 and 1987 entries.

87.28 "No Longer Such a Tough Guy, Norman Mailer Frets over His Shaky Career as a Filmmaker." Article-interview by Alan Richman. *People Weekly*, 5 October, 40-42. Mailer says little new about his film in this piece, but he does discuss the writing life: "I'm not morbid, but anything I do could be the last thing. I've become more serious naturally. It's a biological process." The first weekend gross for "Tough Guys Don't Dance" is reported: "a disappointing $421,390." The film went on to make a profit. See 84.17, 1986 and 1987 entries.

87.29 "The Electronic Mailer." Article-interview by Peter O. Whitmer. In *Aquarius Revisited: Seven Who Created the Sixties Counterculture That Changed America: William Burroughs, Allen Ginsberg, Ken Kesey, Timothy Leary, Norman Mailer, Tom Robbins, Hunter S. Thompson*, by Peter O. Whitmer, 55-65. New York: Macmillan, 10 October. Whitmer's piece is based on an 80s interview with Mailer focusing on "The White Negro" (57.1). Along the way, Mailer provides opinions on Hunter Thompson, William Burroughs, Allen Ginsberg, James Dean, Ken Kesey and Robert Lindner.

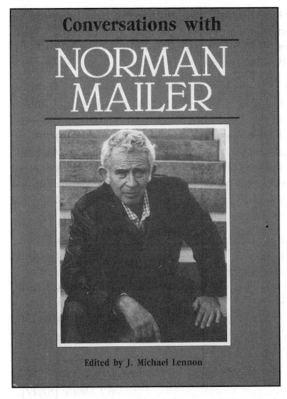

Conversations with

NORMAN MAILER

Edited by J. Michael Lennon

1988

Photograph by Petra Lukoschek
88.6

88.1 "A Conversation with Norman Mailer." By Barry H. Leeds. *Connecticut Review* 10 (spring), 1-15. In a revealing interview with the author of the first book-length study of Mailer's work (*The Structured Vision of Norman Mailer*, New York University Press, 1969), Mailer discusses a number of topics surrounding the violence of modern life: AIDS, cancer, the Bernard Goetz case, prize-fighting, the police and criminals. Further, he discusses several writers: Mario Puzo, Ernest Hemingway, James Jones, Ken Kesey, Joan Didion and Harry Crews. Mailer also gives his fullest answer to the question of why he abandoned the trilogy of which *Ancient Evenings* (83.18) was to have been the first volume. Finally, he discusses moviemaking, his own and Clint Eastwood's. Rpt: 88.6.

88.2 "Jackson Is a Friend of Life's Victims." *New York Times*, 18 April, 23. Endorsement of Jesse Jackson in the New York Democratic presidential primary. Mailer's most considered discussion of Jewish-black relations.

88.3 "Writer Needs 'Stability' Novelist Mailer Advises." Article by George Smith. *Times-Leader* (Wilkes-Barre, Pa.), 11 May, Sec. B, p. 1. Report on a visit to the University of Scranton on 10 May. Mailer's remarks on novel-writing are quoted briefly.

88.4 "No, PEN Decides, It Won't Invite the Pope to Join." Article by Walter Goodman. *New York Times*, 17 May, Sec. C, p. 20. Mailer is only paraphrased in this piece, which describes his attempt to convince the American Chapter of PEN to offer an honorary membership to Pope John Paul II, based on his recent encyclical, "On Social Concern," and other writings. He was opposed by PEN's president Susan Sontag (who succeeded him) and novelist Maureen Howard, and the proposal never made it formally onto the floor.

88.5 "A Piece of *Harlot's Ghost.*" *Esquire,* July, 80-82, 84-90; cover photograph of Mailer. First advance excerpt from then-unpublished novel (91.26) of the same name about the CIA. Rpt: This excerpt, a much-compressed and altered version of chapters 2 and 3 of "Early Years, Early Training," part 1 of "The Alpha Manuscript," describes the Maine rock-climbing of Hubbard and Harlot. The excerpt is accompanied by boxed photographs of Mailer and notes on his career, including the comment that this is "his first fiction for *Esquire* since *An American Dream.*" See 64.2-64.9.

88.6 *Conversations with Norman Mailer,* edited by J. Michael Lennon. Jackson, Miss.: University Press of Mississippi, 31 July. Collection of 37 previously published interviews, including three self-interviews, 396 pp., $26.95. Contains introduction, chronology of Mailer's life and index.

88.7 "Fury, Fear, Philosophy: Understanding Mike Tyson." *Spin,* September, 40-44, 78. Mailer explains Tyson by reference to his "spiritual father, surrogate father, coach, and training philosopher," Cus D'Amato.

88.8 "Lipton's." *Antaeus,* no. 61 (autumn), 259-65. Twenty entries from a private journal prefaced with this statement: "The Journal from which these excerpts are taken went on for close to one hundred thousand words. I would usually write in it on Mondays and Tuesdays after a heavy pot weekend—marijuana was referred to by the not very opaque alias of Lipton's. Begun on December 1, 1954, the Journal has entries until March 4, 1955. Anyone more curious about the origins might take a look at the Fourth Advertisement in my book *Advertisements for Myself* [59.13](Putnam's, New York, 1959)." Rpt: 17 December 1954 entry in *Self,* May 1990, 192.

88.9 "Norman Mailer Burning as His Democrats Fiddle." Article-interview by Mary Ann Grossmann. *St. Paul Pioneer Press Dispatch,* 24 October. Telephone interview in advance of Mailer's 24 October appearance at the Guthrie Theater in Minneapolis. Mailer comments briefly on novelwriting, movie-making, and politics in this error-laden piece. "I thought the '80s were going to have a little spark," he said. "Ronald Reagan took care of that. We've had watered-down maple syrup for eight years."

88.10 "Novelists Get the Credits: Mailer, Kennedy Have Reel Clout in Adaptations." Article-interview by Michael Kilian. *Chicago Tribune,* 4 November, Sec. 2 ("Tempo"), 2. Mailer and William Kennedy discuss adaptations of their novels to screen at the Virginia Film Festival in Charlottesville, Va. Mailer notes that he hopes *Harlot's Ghost* (91.26) will be done in two years.

88.11 "The Changing of the Guard." *Playboy*, December, 86-88, 196-98. Advance excerpt from *Harlot's Ghost* (91.26). Rpt: This excerpt (taken from the first pages of chapter 2, in "Omega-2,") is an account of Hubbard's affair with Chloe. A comparison with the final, book version demonstrates Mailer's editorial scalpel; hardly a paragraph is untouched.

1989

89.1 "Norman Mailer Chills Out." Article-interview by Janet Barker. *Daily Breeze* (Los Angeles County), 30 January, Sec. C ("Life/Arts"), pp. 1-2. On the occasion of a lecture at Congregation New Tamid in Rancho Palos Verdes, Cal., Mailer spoke with Barker about his life as a writer. He said he was more than 1,000 pages into *Harlot's Ghost* (91.26) and explained, "When I'm writing a novel, I work at least 200 days a year, maybe 250. I write about five or six pages a day."

89.2 "We Must Be Willing to Die for Ideas." *USA Today*, 23 February, Sec. A, p. 9. Excerpt from statement read in New York on 22 February at a meeting of hundreds of writers protesting the death threat against Salman Rushdie, author of *The Satanic Verses*. Rpt: 89.8. See 89.3-89.5, 93.9.

89.3 "U.S. Muslims Urge Ban." Article by Edwin McDowell. *New York Times*, 4 March, 3. At a 3 March news conference at United Nations Plaza called by the American Muslim Action Committee and by American writers who were supporting Salman Rushdie's free speech, but were also seeking conciliation with the Muslims, Mailer, Robert K. Massie, J. Anthony Lukas and Letty Cottin Pogrebrin represented the writers. Mailer read a statement drafted by him expressing the position of the PEN American Center and the Authors Guild. Accompanied by Craig R. Whitney's article, "Iran Rebuffs Britain on Rushdie's Novel." See 89.2, 89.4, 89.5, 89.8, 93.9.

89.4 "U.S. Writers, Moslems Meet." Article by Vivienne Walt. *Newsday*, 4 March. A second report on the meeting of U.S. writers and Muslims seeking common ground on the Salman Rushdie affair. See 89.2, 89.3, 89.5, 89.8, 93.9.

89.5 "Words for Salman Rushdie." *New York Times Book Review*, 12 March, 1, 28-29. In response to the Salman Rushdie crisis, 28 writers from 21 countries, offer words of support to him. Mailer, Ralph Ellison, Thomas Pynchon and Susan Sontag represent the U.S. Mailer says: "'My country, right or wrong,' Stephen Decatur said. That is faith. It seems all we writers who have no faith have been led back to one by your nightmare. The irony is that we have had it all along. We believe in freedom of expression as an absolute. How dangerous to use the word absolute, but you have pulled it forth from us—your health!" See 89.2-89.4, 89.8, 93.9.

89.6 "Outrageously Fond of [Samuel] Goldwyn." Letter to the editor. *New York Times Book Review*, 30 April, 24. Mailer corrects errors in Mordecai Richler's 26 March review of Scott Berg's *Goldwyn*, explaining that he did not pattern Herman Teppis in *The Deer Park* (55.4) on Goldwyn, "but L.B. Mayer (whom, in fact, I never met, but took pleasure in imagining)." Goldwyn, he continues, "treated me well—if eccentrically—and I remain outrageously fond of his memory."

89.7 "Books: Moonraker." Interview by Tom Piazza." *Omni*, July, 18, 78. Mailer revisits some of the questions he raised in *Of a Fire on the Moon* (71.1), including the ultimate one: was Apollo 11 a noble or an insane venture?

89.8 "A Folly Repeated: On Conviction and Creative Freedom, as Reflected by the Salman Rushdie Controversy." *Writer's Digest*, July, 80, 78-79. Full statement read in New York on 22 February at a meeting of hundreds of writers in support of Salman Rushdie. Some of the writers present were Larry McMurtry, Don DeLillo, E.L. Doctorow, Susan Sontag, Gay Talese, Joan Didion, Diana Trilling, John Gregory Dunne, Edward Said, Mary Gordon, Robert Stone and Robert Caro. Rpt: 89.2; *Salman Rushdie: Sentenced to Death*, by W.J. Weatherby. New York: Carroll and Graf, 1990 (partial); 98.7. See 89.3-89.5, 93.9.

89.9 "Checking In with Norman Mailer." Interview with Carole Mallory. *Smart*, September-October, 96-102. Wide-ranging interview: his novel-in-progress, *Harlot's Ghost* (91.26), Tom Wolfe's *Bonfire of the Vanities*, E.L. Doctorow's *Billy Bathgate*, the media, greed and wealth in the 80s, his directorial aspirations, Ronald Reagan, George Bush, and abortion.

89.10 "*Harlot's Ghost*: An Excerpt." *Story* 37 (Autumn), 10-13. Advance excerpt from novel of same title (91.26). In a note prefacing this excerpt (which erroneously notes that Mailer was a chemistry major at Harvard), Mailer is quoted on the importance of winning the *Story* college short story contest in 1941: "Obviously it was one of the most important experiences of my life up to then. In those days, for a young writer to be published in *Story* was enough to give you the beginning of a real certainty that perhaps you were meant to be a writer." Rpt: This excerpt (taken from the conclusion of chapter 1, part 1, "Early Years, Early Training," of "The Alpha Manuscript") describes a lunch at "21." In the final version, Mailer makes several small but significant changes. See 41.1.

89.11 "Cosmic Ventures: A Meditation of God at War." *Esquire*, December, 156-57. Mailer refines his ideas on the nature of God first given in "Hip, Hell and the Navigator" (59.2): "It has occurred to me since, despite my reputation as a male chauvinist, that God may be referred to as 'She' as legitimately (for all we know) as 'He,' or, even better, as 'They,' if one can conceive of divinity as marriage between a godlike Male and Female, a marriage, indeed that may not work a great deal better than the majority of ours!" Rpt: *Living Philosophies: The Reflections of Some Eminent Men and Women of Our Time*, edited by Clifton Fadiman. New York: Doubleday, 1990. See 75.2, 75.11, 82.15, 83.45.

89.12 "Norman Mailer Complains about Mention in 'Tru.'" Article by Glenn Collins. *New York Times*, 21 December, 28. Report on a disagreement between Mailer and Jay Presson Allen, author of "Tru," a one-man Broadway play about Truman Capote, starring Robert Morse.

90.1 "Norman Mailer: The Power of Sex." Interview by Carole Mallory. *M: The Civilized Man,* February, 79-83, 146; cover photograph of Mailer. Discussion of marriage, sex and ego with asides on Henry Miller, D.H. Lawrence, Clint Eastwood, Sarah Ferguson and George Bush. Asked what is the chief difference between men and women, Mailer says, "If you're talking about middle-class urban professional intellectuals who go to offices and work, the difference between them is 2 on a scale of 100."

90.2 Letter to Peter Balbert (31 January 1989). Rpt: In Balbert's essay, "From *Lady Chatterly's Lover* to *The Deer Park*: Lawrence, Mailer, and the Dialectic of Erotic Risk." *Studies in the Novel* 22 (spring 1990), 67-81. Mailer explains his "spoof" of identifying a passage from *The Deer Park* (55.4) as being from Lawrence in one of his *Esquire* Big Bite columns (63.11), reprinted in *Existential Errands* (72.7).

90.3 "A Doctor Is No Better than His Patient: An Interview with Norman Mailer." Self-interview. *Cosmopolitan,* May, 332-33, 404. Mailer explains in a headnote that the questions he answers are a mixture of his own and those submitted by the editors of *Cosmopolitan.* One of Mailer's most detailed discussions of sexual matters: timed orgasm, guilt, promiscuity, sex aids, loneliness and "the lost art of cleavage." Asked if he has ever felt disloyal, he says, "Oh, yes. Absolutely. I'm haunted by it. When you have children, you feel your disloyalties more. There's an indefinable integument that surrounds children." See 73.40, 81.23.

90.4 "In P-Town, a Night of Mailer and Memories." Article by Jeff McLaughlin. *Living, Boston Globe,* 20 August, 44. Report on a benefit for the Provincetown Art Association and Museum at the home of Reggie Cabral, art collector and owner of the Atlantic House in Provincetown. Mailer read from his poems and *Tough Guys Don't Dance* (84.17).

90.5 "Library Hosts 1990 Hemingway Conference." Article by unidentified writer. *John F. Kennedy Library Newsletter,* Fall, 3-4. At a conference at the J.F.K. Library, Mailer said of Hemingway, "He was maybe the most competitive American writer who ever lived. And that is an enormous remark."

91.8

91.1 "Children of the Pied Piper." *Vanity Fair*, March, 154-59, 220-21. Review of *American Psycho*, by Bret Easton Ellis. The review's lead-in notes that Mailer had accepted the position of writer-at-large at *Vanity Fair*. Rpt: 98.7. See 92.8.

91.2 "How the Wimp Won the War." *Vanity Fair*, May, 138-43, 184, 186. Essay on the Gulf War. Discarded title: "Cleaning the Augean Stables." Rpt: 92.13, 98.7 (partial).

91.3 "Mailer and Vidal: The Big Schmooze." Interview by Carole Mallory. *Esquire*, May, 105-6, 108-12. Less of an interview than a Mailer-Gore Vidal conversation, this piece moves rapidly and humorously over a lot of ground. It is focused as much on the end of the American century as it is on purely literary matters. They discuss LaRochefoucauld, Herman Melville, J.F.K. (at some length), L.B.J., George Bush, John Cheever, Tennessee Williams, Truman Capote, Saddam Hussein and Eugene McCarthy. Mailer states, "I'm not saying that I write as well as Melville, but my style was absolutely shaped by his love of long , rolling sentences that contain inversions and reverses and paradoxes and ironies and exclamation points and dashes." See 77.4-77.9, 85.6.

91.4 "Norman Mailer: *Harlot's Ghost*, Part I: In Berlin, CIA Agent Harry Hubbard Gets His First Taste of Sex and Treachery." *Rolling Stone*, 11-25 July, 56-60, 126, 128-30, 132-33. Excerpt from novel of same name (91.26).

Illustrated by Philip Burke and John Collier. Rpt: Appearing three months before the novel, this excerpt (first of three in *Rolling Stone*) deals with Hubbard's exploits with Dix Butler in the bars and brothels of Berlin; it is taken with very minor changes (the excision of some CIA code names) from "The Omega" Manuscript," part 2, "Berlin," most of chapter 3 and all of chapter 7.

91.5 "Norman Mailer: *Harlot's Ghost,* Part II: CIA Agent Harry Hubbard Invades the Privacy of an Indiscreet Stewardess." *Rolling Stone,* 8 August, 46-47, 49, 52, 54, 56, 90, 92, 94-95. Excerpt from novel of same name (91.26). Illustrated by C.F. Payne. Rpt: Appearing less than two months before the novel, this excerpt (taken with a few very minor changes from "The Alpha Manuscript," part 5, "The Bay of Pigs, May 1960-April 1961: Miami," chapters 5 through 9) deals with Hubbard's assignment to seduce Modene Murphy, lover of J.F.K., Frank Sinatra and Sam Giancana.

91.6 "Norman Mailer: *Harlot's Ghost,* Part III: In the Shadow of Nuclear War, CIA Man Harry Hubbard Risks Death in Cuba." *Rolling Stone,* 22 August, 46-47, 49-52, 79-80, 82, 84. Excerpt from novel of same name (91.26). Illustrated by Daniel Zakroczemski. Rpt: Appearing five weeks before the novel, this excerpt (taken with a few very minor changes from "The Alpha Manuscript," part 6, "Mongoose, 1961-1963: Miami, Washington, Paris," most of chapter 19 and all of chapter 20) deals with Hubbard, Dix Butler and the invasion of Cuba in 1962.

91.7 "Elusive Mailer 'Older, Wiser' on Eve of New Novel's Release." Article-interview by Carrie Izard Richardson. *Boston Sunday Herald,* 15 September, 31, 49. Interviewed in Provincetown, Mailer explains his motives and intentions for *Harlot's Ghost* (91.26): "Because of my left politics all these years, I never really had conversations and dialogues with these people [the CIA]—and they've been running the country. So I thought about them....'What's good about them, what's not good about them, in what ways can I respect them, in what ways can I bring in an honest, moral judgment on them.'" Mailer also notes that he is now at work on a short book about Pablo Picasso, "a biographical sketch, an interpretation of his character" (95.38).

91.8 "From *Harlot's Ghost.*" *Paris Review,* no. 120 (fall), 95-105. Excerpt from novel of same name (91.26). Rpt: Appearing at approximately the same time as the novel, this excerpt (taken with three or four small changes from "The Omega Manuscript," part 1, "Early Years, Early Training," chapters 8 and 9) deals with Hubbard's CIA course on world communism.

91.9 "Harlot's Lady." *Partisan Review* 53 (fall), 607-19. Excerpt from 91.26. Rpt: Appearing at approximately the same time as the novel, this excerpt (taken with no changes from "The Alpha Manuscript," part 1, "Early Years, Early Training," chapter 5) deals with Hubbard's first meeting with Hadley Kittredge Gardiner in Maine and her explanation of her Alpha-Omega dualist theory of personality.

91.10 "The Old Man and the Novel." Article-interview by Scott Spencer. *New York Times Magazine,* 22 September, 28-31, 40, 42, 47; cover photograph of Mailer by Joel Meyerowitz. On the eve of the publication of *Harlot's Ghost* (91.26), Mailer spends two sessions with Spencer, who records Mailer's comments along with his ambivalent feelings toward the man and the novel. Mailer talks on several of his favorite topics: identity and celebrity, the CIA as a bureaucracy, the Women's Liberation movement, his competitiveness with other writers, fiction vs. nonfiction and the American establishment: "I'll never be completely part of the establishment, because the establishment will never be completely comfortable with me. The establishment is not comfortable with anyone whose dimensions have not been calibrated." Rpt: *Guardian Weekend* (London), 5-6 October, 19-22.

91.11 "Books." *New York,* 23 September, 106-7. Advance excerpt from 91.26. This brief excerpt, dealing with Hubbard's relationship to Kittredge and her first husband Hugh Montague, is taken from the opening chapter of the novel.

91.12 "Norman Mailer, Company Man." Article-interview by Charles Trueheart. *Washington Post,* 23 September, Sec. C, pp. 1, 4. Focused interview on 91.26 in which Mailer explains that, initially, "I was going to write about [James Jesus] Angleton," and he planned a "huge feud" between him and Hugh "Harlot" Montague, but he decided against it because to use a real person, you must "know him so well that you won't misrepresent him." Also revealed is the price of the novel: $30, a new high for hardcover fiction.

91.13 "The Espionage Lesson." *New York Review of Books,* 26 September, 17-18, 20-21. Advance excerpt from 91.26. Rpt: Tenth advance excerpt (taken with a few minor changes from "The Alpha Manuscript," part 3, "Washington," last half of chapter 1 and all of chapter 2) which describes "High Thursday" seminars given to novice CIA agents by Hugh Montague.

91.14 "Maternal Jodie; Mailer's CIA." Column by Jeannie Williams. *USA Today,* 26 September, Sec. D, p. 2. Mailer comments on 91.26: "I wasn't writing this book to expose the CIA"; and John Simon's review in the *New York Times Book Review,* 29 September: Simon "liked the book more than he wanted to." Williams says the novel "could be the longest hard-cover novel Random House (or anyone) has printed." See 91.15, 91.16, 91.19, 91.43, 91.48.

91.15 "A Fjord in George Will's Future." (New York) *Daily News,* 27 September, 8. Column by Richard Johnson. Mailer is quoted on his response to John Simon's review of 91.26: "I'm impressed that John Simon, the Adolf Eichmann of theater critics, now promoted, or demoted, to book reviewer, was obliged grudgingly and against his grain to give *Harlot's Ghost* a grossly favorable reception." See 91.14, 91.16, 91.19, 91.43, 91.48.

91.16 "Harlot Militant." *New York Times Book Review,* 29 September, 25. Brief excerpt (244 words) from 91.26 consisting of Hugh Montague's comparison of Communism and Christianity. Accompanied by John Simon's negative review. See 91.14, 91.15, 91.19, 91.43, 91.48.

91.17 "Mailer's America." Interview by J. Michael Lennon. *Chicago Tribune*, 29 September, Sec. 13 ("Arts"), pp. 18-19, 27. Fact and fiction in 91.26 is the heart of this interview, conducted in Provincetown, in mid-July, with additional comment on epistolary and epistemological aspects of the novel: "[Henry] James frightened me forever with his dictum that one must never put information into a novel unless it is digested through the lens of a protagonist's perceptions."

91.18 "The Softer Norman Mailer." Article-interview by Tim Warren. (Baltimore) *Sun*, 29 September, Sec. H, pp. 1, 8. Warren records some of Mailer's comments at a Random House meeting with reporters just prior to the publication of 91.26. See 91.31, 91.32.

91.19 "Between the Covers: Mailer Goes the Distance." Column by Matthew Flamm. *New York Post*, 30 September, 23. Flamm serves up the responses of several individuals to John Simon's "mixed-to-negative review" of 91.26 in the 29 September *New York Times Book Review*, including Mitchell Ivers, Random House managing editor, Simon, Mailer and daily *Times* book reviewer Christopher Lehmann-Haupt, whose positive review of 91.26 Simon called "a typical, miserable, toadying, cowardly review." Mailer says, "The mark of Simon's incapacity to be a literary reviewer—as a theater reviewer he's vicious but very often interesting—is that he knows very little about the novel." Accompanied by 91.20. See 91.14-91.16, 91.43, 91.48.

91.20 "The Mail-est Tries Kinder." Article-interview by Matthew Flamm. *New York Post*, 30 September, 23-24. Over breakfast at Random House, Mailer talks about 91.26: "My goal would be that half the people who read this book say: 'Let's abolish the goddam thing' [the CIA] and the other half says: 'Gee, I'd like to join.'" Accompanied by 91.19.

91.21 "His Punch Is Better than Ever." Interview by Bonnie Angelo. *Time*, 30 September, 68-69. Mailer speaks more of politics than literature, touching on George Bush, the Clarence Thomas nomination, the Women's Liberation movement, reincarnation, and the men's movement led by Robert Bly: "I believe Bly and I are thinking on parallel lines. He may be a touch too mystical to my taste, but I think there are great mysteries to masculine psychology." Accompanied by Paul Gray's negative review of 91.26.

91.22 *The Lives of Norman Mailer* by Carl Rollyson. New York: Paragon House, October. Mailer was not interviewed for this biography (which Paragon House published to appear at the same time as 91.26), nor were most of his family and friends. Rollyson provides more purely literary analysis—much of it very thoughtful—than his predecessors, but overall the book is quite derivative. Over 55 percent of his secondary references are to three books: the biographies of Hilary Mills (82.23) and Peter Manso (85.13), and *Conversations with Norman Mailer* (88.6); only a bit more than five percent of the references are to the author's original interviews, although some of these—with William Styron, John W. Aldridge, Norman Rosten and Rust Hills—are unique and valuable. See 91.38.

91.23 "Mailer's Alpha and Omega." Article-interview by Toby Thompson. *Vanity Fair*, October, 150, 152, 154, 156, 158, 160, 162. The keel of this piece is Mailer's Alpha-Omega personality theory from 91.26. Thompson interviews Mailer at least three times, and also speaks with Robert F. Lucid, Richard Stratton, Gay Talese, Camille Paglia, Tom McGuane, Larry McMurtry, his editor at Random House, Jason Epstein, his sister Barbara Wasserman, and his wife Norris Church.

91.24 "Norman Mailer: America's Literary Lion, Still Roaring." Interview by Anka Radakovich. *Details*, October, 132. The interviewer attempts to be provocative, but only elicits several curt replies from Mailer in this brief, unmemorable interview focused on television and sex.

91.25 "Stormin' Norman." Article-interview by Christopher Hitchens. *Vogue*, October, 311-12, 366-67. Contains a thoughtful dialogue on 91.26 and the nature of the CIA. Mailer calls the novel a "comedy of manners," and explains the contradiction he sees at the heart of the CIA: "the interface between bureaucracy and unprecedented action."

91.26 *Harlot's Ghost.* New York: Random House, 2 October. London: Michael Joseph, late October; Novel, 1310 pp., $30. Dedication: "To Jason Epstein." Rpt: Advance excerpts appeared in *Esquire* (88.5), *Playboy* (88.11), *Story* (89.10), *Rolling Stone* (91.4-91.6), *Paris Review* (91.8), *Partisan Review* (91.9), *New York* (91.11), *New York Review of Books* (91.13), *New York Times Book Review* (91.16); 16 separate excerpts, more than from any other work, are reprinted in *The Time of Our Time* (98.7). See 76.9, 91.27, 91.48, other 1991 entries, 92.5, 98.9.

Mailer: "There is a very unspoken drama in the CIA. Obviously no one is ever going to write about indiscretion in the ranks; they will feel it within the ranks, but it's never going to get out if they can help it. I've always been amused by CIA novels that have this absolute immaculate secrecy governing operations. Maybe there's one traitor, but he's absolutely uncharacteristic of the whole. But it seems to me that the way these things really work is with the mixture of high secrecy and violations of that secrecy" (91.17).

91.27 "Norman Mailer on *Harlot's Ghost.*" Random House Publicity Flyer. Adapted and expanded version of two question-and-answer periods conducted by Norman Mailer at the Poetry Center of the 92nd Street YM-YWHA, New York, on 25 February. No date; probably appeared just before or on publication date (2 October) of 91.26. Mailer explains why he used the real names for some characters in 91.26, and fictional names for others, his sources, and the working title of the sequel: *Harlot's Grave.*

91.28 "The Mellower Mailer." Article-interview by Josh Getlin. *Los Angeles Times*, 3 October, Sec. E, pp. 1, 9. The conversation revolves around 91.26, including comments on J.F.K., and a conversation about conservatism he once had with Arthur Miller.

91.29 "Mailer: Man of God." Article-interview by Mashey Bernstein. *Jewish Chronicle*, 4 October. Interesting profile of Mailer the Jew, centering on a Passover Seder Bernstein conducted at Mailer's home. See 83.44, 97.3.

91.30 "The Last Tough Guy in America." Article by Martyn Harris. *Telegraph Magazine* (England), 5 October, 19-20, 22. Mailer is quoted only briefly in this somewhat disapproving piece on 91.26 and his religious beliefs.

91.31 "Norman's Conquest." Article-interview by Ruth Pollack Coughlin. *Detroit News*, 5 October, Sec. C ("Accent"), pp. 1, 4. Coughlin and five other reporters meet Mailer at Random House. Brief piece centered on her own reactions to Mailer. Accompanied by David Walton's positive review. See 91.18, 91.32.

91.32 "Norman Mailer: Larger than Life." Article-interview by Jocelyn McClurg. *Hartford Courant*, 6 October, Sec. G, pp. 1, 6. Like 91.31, this piece is based on a Random House meeting of six reporters and Mailer in late September to discuss 91.26. Asked if Kittredge was a response to his female critics, he says, "I wanted to say to women, 'Look, if you can't recognize that I am trying to create a woman who is completely a woman, a woman who can talk to all of you, the hell with it, let's cease having a dialogue altogether.'" See 91.18.

91.33 "Norman Mailer Returns to the Arena." Article-interview by Dana Kennedy. *Houston Post*, 6 October, Sec. C, p. 6. This brief Associated Press piece, drawn from a meeting at Random House, contains a few Mailer comments on 91.26 and how it feels to be getting old.

91.34 "Mailer Raises Sword against Critics' Pens." Article-interview by Carlin Romano. *Philadelphia Inquirer*, 11 October, Sec. F, pp. 1, 8. Several of Romano's quotes come from earlier interviews with other writers on the subject of 91.26. The piece ends with Mailer's comment on self-pity: "Who ever committed murder or incest without [first] being drenched in self-pity? Self-pity is the core of it all. If one spent every day cleaning the self-pity out, the way animals take pests out of their hide, we'd each be that inch closer to where we want to be." Quotes, positive and negative, from five reviews of 91.26 are given by Romano.

91.35 "Soft Spots in a Tough Guise." Article-interview by Peter Stothard. *Times Saturday* (London), 12 October, 16-17; cover photographs of Mailer by Graham Wood. In preparation for the British publication of 91.26, Mailer talks (in New York) about the novel, the CIA, capitalism, Fidel Castro, alcohol and drugs and the U.S.: "Are we a good country or a bad one? I mean, are we a good country with all sorts of hideous things wrong with us, or are we essentially a bad country with lots of superficially positive aspects?"

91.36 "He's Back to the Old Haunts." Article-interview by Bill Bell. (New York) *Daily News*, 16 October, 1, 40; cover photograph of Mailer. Light piece with brief quotes from Mailer on 91.26, drinking, fame, the Brooklyn Dodgers, his reading habits and the questions of reporters: "They ask the same questions," he says, "and I give them different answers."

91.37 "Mailer's American Dream." Article-interview by Patricia Holt. *San Francisco Chronicle*, 17 October, Sec. E ("Datebook"), pp. 1, 4. Mailer sticks closely to the nature of the CIA and his motives for writing 91.26 in this relatively brief piece: He says that the CIA is "the nearest thing Americans have to sophisticated evil. Of course, the paradox is that the *best* people working for the government work for the CIA. So I wanted to explore the American establishment at its top and at its best."

91.38 "Page Six: Knife? Nice! Norm Told Styron." Column by Frank DiGiacomo and Joanna Molloy. *New York Post*, 21 October, 6. Mailer and William Styron deny that Mailer, in 1954, spoke with admiration about an acquaintance stabbing a woman, as reported in Carl Rollyson's biography of Mailer (91.22). Mailer says, "My reaction was not admiration, but awe. I was bewildered. I felt that it was absolutely outside my compass. I wondered, 'How does anyone get to that feverpitch?' The irony is that I learned how." See 60.11.

91.39 "Mailer Muzzles His Mouthpiece." Article-interview by Bruce Cook. *L.A. Life*, 22 October, 18-19. Cook's by-line is followed by "Special to the [New York] *Daily News*," indicating where this piece first appeared. Cook, an old Mailer hand, places *Harlot's Ghost* (91.26) in the context of Mailer's long career, and gets him to talk about his protagonist, Harry Hubbard.

91.40 "Advertisements: On the Publicity Trail with Norman Mailer." Article-interview by Maureen O'Brien. *Publishers' Weekly*, 25 October, 22-24. O'Brien sticks with Mailer throughout 7 October as he moves through a dizzying round of interviews accompanied by Random House publicist, Peter Vertes: the "Today" show; WCBS News Radio's "Book Beat"; a local talk show, "New York and Co."; the *Miami Herald*; National Public Radio's "All Things Considered"; for a Canadian television documentary on Henry Miller; and, in the evening, on Debra Norville's syndicated talk show. O'Brien notices that "he never answers the same question the same way twice." Mailer says that "he plans to start writing the sequel to *Harlot's Ghost* [91.26] this summer ('All I have now are a lot of notes') after he puts the finishing touches on his 'short, interpretive biography' of Picasso" (95.38).

91.41 "Life's Like That." Article-interview by unidentified writer. *Economist*, 26 October, 115. In London to promote the British publication of 91.26, Mailer meets the press at Brown's Hotel and talks about the architecture of his novel. It has "an excluded middle," he says. "That's good because it gives the reader some scope. The missing part shapes up in his mind. Life is like that."

91.42 "Mailer Likes That Dangling Participle in His New Novel." Article by unidentified writer. (Illinois) *State Journal-Register*, 26 October, 2. After quoting the first sentence of *Harlot's Ghost* (91.26), this article gives Mailer's faxed response to criticism of it in a 25 October Associated Press story in the paper. The sentence reads: "On a late winter evening in 1983, while driving through fog along the Maine coast, recollections of old campfires began to drift into the March mist, and I thought of the Algonquin tribe who dwelt near Bangor a thousand years ago." In reply, Mailer says: "Let's not put the blame on the copy editor. The dangling modifier in the first sentence of *Harlot's Ghost* was my decision, repeated several times over several months, to keep the sentence intact. I like the rhythm as it stands. I could not find a better one by fixing the sentence grammatically. For that matter, the meaning is clear. We often live in recollections while driving a car; it can even seem as if the recollections are steering the vehicle. Dangling participles can offend a few readers intensely, but the damage caused might add up to less than the rupture occasioned by straightening out the grammar and wrecking the mood. I hope I learned a long time ago from Melville, Mark Twain, and Faulkner, among others, that syntax is what you obey until there is some better reason to ignore it. Future editions will appear with the sentence unchanged." Grammarians may legitimately disagree on whether this is a bonafide dangling participle.

91.43 "Mailer Gets to Talk Back to *N.Y. Times.*" Article by David Streitfeld. *Washington Post*, 30 October. Report on Mailer's meeting with *New York Times Book Review* editor, Rebecca Sinkler, and *Times* managing editor, Joseph Lelyveld, on 28 October to seek a chance to reply to John Simon's 29 September review of 91.26. Mailer was successful and his response (91.48) appeared on 17 November. A *Times* spokesman, William Adler, said Mailer's piece "is unusual but I don't believe it's unprecedented. It's in the context of a literary dialogue." Simon said if he were running a book review, "I would publish whatever review I published and that would be it. If the author didn't like it, tough." Mailer described the session at the *Times* in one word: "transmogrificational." See 91.14-91.16, 91.19.

91.44 "Mailer: He's 'Not Finished Yet.'" Article-interview by Lloyd Sachs. *Chicago Sun-Times*, 30 October, Sec. 2 ("Lifestyle"), 31. Mailer compares his work to that of a cobbler—"You're doing your best to make good shoes for the sheer sake of the craft"—in this breezy piece with a few comments on 91.26, and a rehearsal of the high points of Mailer's life and career.

91.45 "The Warren Report." *Vanity Fair*, November, 174-80, 224, 226, 228, 230, 232-33. Long interview with Warren Beatty, conducted in the summer of 1991.

91.46 "Mr. Mailer's Love-Fest." Column by Liz Smith. *Newsday*, 3 November. Report on party at New York's "21" given by Random House chief, Harry Evans, to celebrate the publication of 91.26. Mailer was extolled by Evans, Richard Snyder of Simon and Schuster and Salman Rushdie, whose letter was read. Rushdie called Mailer "literature's chief gladiator," and said he "has to be judged by the highest standards. To hell with buts and maybes." The column also reported that 91.26 was on the bestseller lists nationwide. Mailer is quoted briefly.

91.47 "Mailer Dubbed Big Apple's Author." Article by Associated Press writer. *Newport* (R.I.) *Daily News*, 14 November. Mailer is quoted briefly in this report on his 13 November appointment by Governor Mario Cuomo as New York State Author, which came with a $10,000 prize. Audre Lorde was appointed state poet on the same day, the report notes. On the occasion, Mailer was introduced by William Kennedy, who reprinted his introduction in his collection, *Riding the Yellow Trolley Car: Selected Nonfiction* (New York: Viking, 1993).

91.48 "A Critic with Balance: A Letter from Norman Mailer." *New York Times Book Review*, 17 November, 7. Mailer's 1500-word response to John Simon's 29 September review of 91.26 provides quotes from other, earlier negative reviews of Mailer's books by Simon, as well as his negative review of Kate Mailer's 1988 performance in Peter Brook's version of Anton Chekov's "The Cherry Orchard." Simon replies to what he calls Mailer's "irrelevant hue and cry" on p. 38 of the *Review*; Rebecca Sinkler, *Review* editor, adds her comments on the same page, noting that the editors were not aware of all the previous Simon reviews of Mailer's work when they assigned the review to him, after four others turned down the assignment. See 91.14-91.16, 91.19, 91.43.

91.49 "Norman Mailer: Stormin' No More." Article-interview by Joan Smith. *San Francisco Examiner*, 24 November, Sec. D ("Style"), pp. 1, 4. In San Francisco on the publicity tour for 91.26, Mailer talks to the media in his suite at the Ritz-Carlton Hotel.

91.50 "A Talk with Norman Mailer." Article-interview by W. David Atwood. *Book-of-the-Month Club Book News*, December, 11. Brief piece in which Mailer says, "It was my intention to write a novel that would give the reader a good and detailed sense of what it might be like to live and work in the CIA."

91.51 "A Letter from Norman Mailer." In *Hockney's Alphabet*, edited by Stephen Spender, 17-19. Drawings by David Hockney. New York: Random House in Association with the American Friends of AIDS Crisis Trust. Mailer and 25 other writers provide reflections on the letters of the alphabet. Mailer is given "F" and says, "I am sure you are aware what a compliment you are paying me with that letter—ahhh, the fonts of fucking."

92.1 "Mailer's Many Lives." Article-interview by Julia Braun Kessler. *Life: The World and I*, January, 332-39. Mailer comments on *Harlot's Ghost* (91.26) in this piece, which contains several errors, the most notable being that Mailer served four years as a rifleman in WWII (he served a little over two years in the army); and that *The Naked and the Dead* (48.2) was accepted by Little, Brown (they turned it down). Mailer says that his "own key experiences are exactly what I will not use directly. They can instead form crystals in the mind and the heart so that metaphorically I can shine a light through them. I can get one story if the light points in one direction, and yet another for the opposite. That is why I have always wanted to do books not too near me, books that take me out to distant, alien landscapes, places where I have an insight and where the event can have a life, a psychological reality within my imagination."

92.2 "Chronicle: David Frost Goes a Round with Norman Mailer." Column by Marvine Howe. *New York Times*, 17 January, Sec. B, p. 6. Consists of a couple of brief quotes taken from the transcript of Mailer's television interview with David Frost. When Frost suggested that Mailer was "a sort of literary Frank Sinatra," Mailer laughed and said, "That's a remark that will make Sinatra as unhappy as it makes me." "Talking with David Frost" aired on PBS a week later on 24 January. See 92.3.

92.3 "TV Weekend: Mailer Plugs Himself Instead of His Book." Article by Walter Goodman. *New York Times*, 24 January, Sec. C, p. 28. Another advance report on Mailer's 24 January television interview with David Frost. Goodman provides a few quotes and a summary of topics: the stabbing of his second wife, Adele, the Jack Abbott affair, his notion of an embattled God, feminism, sex, AIDS, the 60s, and American politics. Of the interview, one of the very best Mailer has given on television, Goodman says: "There is a high intelligence operating along with a sometimes original perspective; at his most engaging, he manages to be off the wall and on the mark at the same time." See 92.2.

92.4 "Footfalls in the Crypt." *Vanity Fair*, February, 124-29, 171. Review of "J.F.K.," directed by Oliver Stone. One of two movie reviews by Mailer. Rpt: *JFK: The Book of the Film, The Documented Screenplay*, by Oliver Stone and Zachary Sklar. New York: Applause Books, 1992. See 73.12, 92.7.

92.5 "Mailer Visits CIA and Finds He's in Friendly Territory. Really." Article-interview by Elaine Sciolino. *New York Times*, 3 February, Sec. A, p. 10. Report of Mailer's visit to the CIA in Washington where he gave a standing-room-only lecture to 500 officials, and then later met with top officials in the private conference room of Robert M. Gates, CIA Director. Various

CIA officials are quoted on the accuracy of *Harlot's Ghost* (91.26), and Mailer tells Sciolino that with the end of the Cold War, "the CIA can get out of the beartrap of ideology and begin to provide serious and needed intelligence on the rest of the world."

92.6 "Norman Mailer Blames Reagan for Economy." Article by Jack Crager. *The Park Slope Reader*, 28 February-5 March. Report of a 20 February meeting of the Brooklyn Heights Association at which Mailer spoke and answered questions from the audience. His comments ranged from topics such as the horrors of modern architecture, to the Cold War and Russia, to the Democratic presidential candidates.

92.7 "What Debt Does Hollywood Owe to Truth." Article by William Grimes. *New York Times*, 5 March, Sec. C ("Arts"), pp. 15, 22. Report of a 3 March panel debate at Town Hall in New York, convened under the auspices of several educational and cultural organizations, to discuss "the duty of art to history, fiction to fact." Victor Navasky moderated the panel consisting of Mailer, Nora Ephron, Edward Jay Epstein and Oliver Stone, whose film, "J.F.K.," was the centerpiece. Mailer, "who embraced, perhaps embodied, the historical complexities and ambiguities heaped up throughout the evening," spoke both of J.F.K.'s assassination ("the mind-stultifying myth of the lone assassin"), and Stone's film ("should be seen not as history but myth," the story of "a huge and hideous event in which the gods warred, and a god fell"). See 92.4.

92.8 "Earl and Lyndon: An Imaginary Conversation." *Vanity Fair*, April, 200-203, 260. Illustrated by Philip Burke. One-act play, a conversation between Chief Justice Earl Warren and President Lyndon B. Johnson, shortly after J.F.K.'s assassination. Mailer's final contribution to *Vanity Fair* as writer-in-residence. See 59.9, 91.1.

92.9 Preface to *The JFK Assassination: The Facts and the Theories*, by Carl Oglesby, 9. New York: New American Library, May, softcover. In 189 words, Mailer praises Oglesby for his "crucial" contribution to illuminating the J.F.K. case.

92.10 "By Heaven Inspired: Republican Convention Revisited." *New Republic*, 12 October, 12, 24, 26-27, 30-35. Nonfiction narrative on the August Republican Convention in Houston. Except for his poem "Gladiators: For Hemingway" (74.16), this is Mailer's only contribution to the *New Republic*. His report on the 1992 Democratic Convention has never been published. Rpt: 98.7 (partial). See 76.5.

92.11 Preface to *A Driving Passion*, by Marco Vassi, 9-12. Sag Harbor, N.Y.: Permanent Press, November. Mailer's preface is also an eulogy for Vassi, who was passionately devoted to all varieties of sex, and died of AIDS.

92.12 Comments. In *Girls Lean Back Everywhere: The Law of Obscenity and the Assault on Genius*, by Edward de Grazia, passim. New York: Random

House. de Grazia quotes from Mailer's published work, from his 1965 court testimony on behalf of William Burroughs's *Naked Lunch*, from his comments on Burroughs at the 1962 Edinburgh conference on the current state of the novel, and from interviews he conducted with Mailer for this book, a comprehensive and brilliant study. Mailer's longest quote is an overview of the obscenity problems he faced with *The Naked and the Dead* (48.2), *An American Dream* (65.7) and *The Armies of the Night* (68.8). See 49.3, 62.24, 65.1, 65.13, 65.21, 68.31, 69.82, 81.21, 95.53, 96.7.

92.13 *How the Wimp Won the War*. Northridge, Cal.: Lord John Press. Essay on the Gulf War, 28 pp., $75. No dedication. Limited edition of 301 copies. Rpt: 91.2.

93.1 "Chronicle: Mailer Is Presenting 'Don Juan in Hell' with an All-Star Literary Cast." Article by unidentified writer. *New York Times*, 9 February, Sec. B, p. 6. Report on upcoming (15 February) reading at Weill Recital Hall at Carnegie Hall of "Don Juan in Hell," which is a large part of the third act of George Bernard Shaw's "Man and Superman." Mailer (standing in for the ill Kurt Vonnegut) as the Commander, Susan Sontag as Dona Ana, Gay Talese as Don Juan, and Gore Vidal as the Devil comprised the cast. Mailer conceived of and directed this one-time benefit performance for the Actors Studio in New York. The event was also an homage to the 1951 reading of "Don Juan" at Carnegie by Charles Boyer, Charles Laughton, Agnes Moorehead and Sir Cedric Hardwicke. See 93.2 and Bruce Weber's "The Devil and the Commander," *New York Times*, 19 February, Sec. B, p. 2.

93.2 "Satanic Verses: Literary Lions." Article by Philip Gourevitch. *New York*, 15 February, 20. A second report on the staged reading of "Don Juan in Hell" at Carnegie Hall. Mailer, Gore Vidal and Gay Talese are quoted. Mailer says, "I know Gore well enough to know the Devil would be a role that would appeal to him, as it has all along." Vidal answers, "I'll take Norman's compliment; I'll play the Devil. I will make that Devil, that Lucifer, so noble that he will rise above all of the towers of Manhattan in that glorious evening." See 93.1.

93.3 "Chapter Two: In Which Author Norman Mailer Offers Up Drawings He Says Exhibit Not a Lot of Talent, but Plenty of Flair." Article-interview by Hamilton Kahn. *Cape Cod Times*, 23 July, Sec. C ("Capestyle"), pp. 1, 3. Mailer provides commentary on his line drawings, which were shown at the Berta Walker Gallery in Provincetown through 3 August as a fundraiser for the Fine Arts Work Center in Provincetown. Mailer donated half of the proceeds from the sale of 25 of his drawings to the Center, which was celebrating its 25th anniversary. Mailer's inspiration was the work of Pablo Picasso, whose work he had analyzed in a completed but unpublished book (95.38). "I can't draw; I certainly can't paint, and I have no illusions that either one is feasible for me. But what I could do was just sort of let my hand, in a sense, lead me—that is, draw without preconception." The article also notes that Mailer is at work on a nonfiction book "about Lee Harvey Oswald in the Soviet Union" (95.16). See 93.4, 93.5.

93.4 "Mailer's Latest Lines: The Well-known Author Makes His Debut as a Visual Artist in Provincetown." Article-interview by Robert Taylor. *Boston Globe* ("Living/Arts"), 23 July, 39, 44. A second report on the exhibition of Mailer's drawings in Provincetown. Mailer speaks about his artistic inclinations, but says more about his completed but unpublished biography of the young Picasso (95.38), then titled "Pablo and Fernande: A Portrait of Picasso as a Young Artist." Doubleday was then expected to publish the book (Atlantic Monthly Press finally did), because Random House was the publisher of Picasso's authorized biographer, John Richardson. See 93.3, 93.5, 94.8.

93.5 "Picasso Biographer in a Blue Period: Has Mailer Painted Him into a Corner?" Article-interview by Doris Athineos. *New York Observer*, 30 August-6 September, 1, 23. Account of the dispute between Mailer and John Richardson, authorized biographer of Pablo Picasso, over Mailer's desire to quote from the first volume of Richardson's biography and Richardson's refusal to let him. Mailer says that he had written "a one-volume interpretive biography [95.38], and I have things to say about Picasso that will open new arguments—that's my hope." Besides Mailer and Richardson, Jason Epstein, Random House editor of both, is quoted, as is Nan Talese, who supported Mailer, and Robert Rosenblum, an art history professor, who supported Richardson. See 93.3, 93.4.

93.6 "The Best Move Lies Very Close to the Worst." *Esquire*, October, 60-62, 64, 186. Essay on boxing and Mailer's relationship with Ryan O'Neal, with appearances by José Torres and Sylvester Stallone. Rpt: 98.7.

93.7 "Does Fashion Matter?" Symposium, edited by Eric P. Nash. *New York Times Magazine*, 24 October, 46, 52, 58, 64, 72. As part of this issue, "How Fashion Broke Free: A Special Report on a Half-Century of Fashion in the *Times*," 56 individuals were asked "Does fashion matter?" Some of those joining Mailer in answering were: Roy Blount Jr., Rev. Al Sharpton, Betty Friedan, Joan Rivers, Liz Smith, Gay Talese, David Dinkins and Susan Faludi. Mailer's reply: "I have the uneasy feeling that fashion matters a good deal but in all the years I've been asking myself how and why, my questions remain more lively than my findings."

93.8 "Big Dealy: Dallas Postcard." Article by Doug Smith. *New Republic*, 13 December, 11-12. Report on the Third Assassination Symposium on John F. Kennedy (ASK) held in Dallas in late November 1992, including quotes from Mailer's keynote address. Smith notes that Mailer is working on a new book on the assassination, published as *Oswald's Tale: An American Mystery* (95.16).

93.9 Letter to Salman Rushdie. In *The Rushdie Letters: Freedom to Speak, Freedom to Write*, edited by Steve MacDonogh in association with Article 19 [of the United Nations Charter], p. 73. Lincoln: University of Nebraska Press. See 89.2-89.5, 89.8.

93.10 Foreword to *Bay/Sky*, by Joel Meyerowitz, no pagination. Boston: Bullfinch Press, Little, Brown. Mailer adds 276 words of praise to Meyerowitz's haunting photographs of the Cape Cod shoreline.

Mailer on Madonna

1994

THE MAGAZINE FOR MEN   AUGUST 1994 · $2.50

WOMEN WE LOVE

Photograph by
Wayne Maser
94.7

94.1 "Who Are You?" Article-interview by James Baron. *New York Times*, 13 February, Sec. 9 ("Style"), pp. 1, 7. In the wake of a national *New York Times/*CBS poll that asked 1,136 adults to describe themselves in one word, 26 "prominent people," including Mailer, were asked the same question. Some of the others were former mayors of New York Ed Koch ("candid") and David Dinkins ("caring"), Mary Gordon, novelist ("seeing"), David Lynch, film director ("confused") and Camille Paglia, feminist social critic ("ambition"). Mailer's answer: "Improvisational." He continued, saying, "In a time when all ideologies...have significantly failed us as guides to a reasonable inner life, it helps to treat each situation before us as novel, just born, without guide or precedent."

94.2 Letter to the editor. *New Yorker*, 18 April, 10. Mailer responds to a comment by Pauline Kael in the 21 March issue that he once offered to butt heads with her. He says if he did, it was a joke. "You have to feel kinship with somebody to butt his head."

94.3 Comments. In *Shot in the Heart*, by Mikal Gilmore [brother of Gary Gilmore], passim. New York: Doubleday, June. See 79.14.

94.4 "On Eddie's First Collection of Stories." *Provincetown Arts* 10 (July), 59. Mailer's 1977 blurb for *The Wine Cellar*, a collection of stories by his late friend, Eddie Bonetti, is included in a memorial article. Mailer says that the collection "is a work about Italians living in America that begins where *The*

Godfather ends," and compares Bonetti's prose with that of Ernest Hemingway and John Steinbeck.

94.5 "Mailer's Side." Letter to the editor. *Arkansas Times*, 7 July, 6. Mailer corrects comments by Crescent Dragonwagon, daughter of Maurice Zolotow, concerning "a host of accusations against my book, *Marilyn* [73.30], speaking of libel, invasion of privacy and plagiarism." These accusations were later withdrawn by Zolotow after the publishers of *Marilyn* paid him $22,500 for permission to quote from his biography of Marilyn Monroe, instead of the "pittance" (according to Mailer) he had been previously paid. Mailer puts Dragonwagon on notice about "disseminating a canard against my literary reputation."

94.6 "Mailer: Wills is Full of Bile." Letter to the editor. *New York Post*, 25 July, 20. Mailer responds to a 21 July column by Garry Wills in which he speaks of Mailer as "supporting a gaggle of children from his huddle of various wives." Mailer says, "For shame, Garry Wills. You sound like George Will."

94.7 "Like a Lady." *Esquire*, August, 40-56; cover story. Interview with Madonna. Wide-ranging interview on sex, AIDS, the media, and artistic growth. Rpt: Several long excerpts from this interview appeared in a 12 July Liz Smith column, subtitled "Mailer-Madonna Gush Fest," in *Newsday*, A4, A11; 98.7 (partial).

94.8 "New York Intelligencer: Norman Mailer's Non-Self Portrait." Column by Pat Wechsler and Roger D. Friedman. *New York*, 19 September, 13. Mailer is quoted briefly in this piece, which explains why Random House will not be publishing his next book, a biography, *Portrait of Picasso as a Young Man* (95.38). See 93.4.

See 95.20

95.1 "Literati Probing Oswald's Days in Minsk." Article-interview by James P. Gallagher. *Chicago Tribune*, 17 January, 1, 10. Several people who knew Lee Harvey Oswald when he lived in Minsk (then part of the U.S.S.R., now capital of Belarus) gave Gallagher comments about him. Mailer is quoted briefly only to say that he cannot discuss his book-in-progress, *Oswald's Tale: An American Mystery* (95.16).

95.2 "Looking for Inspiration for His New Book, Mailer Visits Campus." Article by Tammy Polonsky. *Daily Pennsylvanian*, 21 March, 1, 5. Visiting the University of Pennsylvania for four days of lectures and class visits, Mailer began with a dialogue with students focusing on communism, capitalism, and U.S. race relations. Robert F. Lucid, English professor and Mailer's authorized biographer, joined him in conducting the 20 March dialogue in Meyerson Hall. Urging President Clinton to make race relations the keynote of his re-election campaign, Mailer said that until black-white tensions are resolved, "nothing else will get better." See spring 1983 entries, 95.3-95.7, 95.12.

95.3 "Mailer Gives Sneak Peek at New Book." Article by Andrea Ahles. *Daily Pennsylvanian*, 23 March, 1, 7. Brief report on Mailer's 22 March reading at University of Pennsylvania's Harrison Auditorium, one of a series of events included in his 20-23 March visit to the campus. Mailer gave his first reading from *Oswald's Tale: An American Mystery* (95.16). In response to a question about his conclusions as to Oswald's complicity in J.F.K.'s assassination, he said, "He was perfectly capable of committing the crime alone. But whether he did or not is another question." See spring 1983 entries, 95.2, 95.4-95.7, 95.12.

95.4 "Mailer Talks on the Ills of Advertising." Article by Tammy Polonsky. *Daily Pennsylvanian*, 24 March, 1. Report on a 23 March symposium titled "Advertising in America" in Meyerson Hall, University of Pennsylvania, moderated by Kathleen Hall Jamieson, dean of the Annenberg School of Communication. Besides Mailer, two Penn professors took part: Law School Professor Ed Baker and Communication Professor Joseph Turow. See spring 1983 entries, 95.2, 95.3, 95.5-95.7, 95.12.

95.5 "A New Generation at Penn Meets Norman Mailer." Article by Howard Goodman. *Philadelphia Inquirer*, 24 March, Sec. B ("Metro"), pp. 1, 4. Report on Mailer's conversation with the students in Professor Bruce Kuklick's class, who had just read *The Armies of the Night* (68.8). Mailer spoke on several topics, including the misrepresentations of history, the possibility of fascism coming to America, the miseries of airplane travel, television, and Lee Harvey Oswald. Several students and Professor Kuklick are also quoted. Rpt: As "Norman Who? Mailer on Campus" in *Providence Journal-Bulletin*, 28 March, Sec. E ("Lifebeat"), pp. 1-2. See spring 1983 entries, 95.2-95.4, 95.6, 95.7.

95.6 "Does Norman Mailer Know the Way to San Jose?" Article by Kirby F. Smith. *Compass* (Philadelphia), 30 March, 3. Report on Mailer's visit to the "Urban Visions" class of Professor Witold Rybczynski at University of Pennsylvania where discussion focused on two books: Jane Jacobs's *The Death and Life of Great American Cities*, and Joel Garreau's *Edge City: Life on the New Frontier*. See spring 1983 entries, 95.2-95.5, 95.7, 95.12.

95.7 "The Critic's Choice: Norman Mailer Talks about Journalism and Millennialism." Interview by Jorie Green and Tammy Polonsky. *Daily Pennsylvanian*, 4 April, 3. Three topics dominate this discussion: the millennium, the fact/fiction debate, and the media: "The daily news is a delusion. It's a dream. The idea that you're getting something as it's happening and you know what's happening is absurd." See spring 1983 entries, 95.2-95.6, 95.12.

95.8 "Oswald in the U.S.S.R.: Annals of Surveillance." *New Yorker*, 10 April, 56-99. Nonfiction narrative excerpt from *Oswald's Tale: An American Mystery* (95.16). Rpt: Appearing about a month before 95.16, this excerpt is a much compressed version of parts 2 and 4-9 of volume 1, "Oswald in Minsk with Marina," with an epilogue from chapter 5, part 8, of volume 2, "Oswald in America," dealing with Marina Oswald at age 52. It is titled "A Widow's Elegy" in the book.

95.9 "No Ordinary Secret Agent: Mailer Talks about Lee and the KGB." Interview with Ray Sawhill. *Newsweek*, 24 April, 60. In this very brief interview on the forthcoming *Oswald's Tale* (95.16), Mailer says, "I think he did it by himself, but I think he was leaned on by the FBI and CIA, which is why there was that tremendous effort at cover-up."

95.10 "An Exclusive Talk with Norman Mailer." Article-interview by André Bernard and Joseph Cummins. *Book-of-the-Month Club News*, May, 3. Mailer says that he'll never forgive Oswald "because we'll never get over the tragedy that a man who could have been a great president, or could not have been, didn't live long enough to fulfill our notion of history." See 95.11.

95.11 "Interview with Norman Mailer." Article-interview by Joseph Cummins. *BOMC Insights*, May, 1. A second piece drawn from the same January visit to Mailer's home in Brooklyn Heights. Mailer describes Marina Oswald, whom he interviewed for five days in Texas: "She's only in her early 50s, but she's bent over as if she were holding a stone on her back....She has this obsessive question: 'How much of this is my fault?'" See 95.10.

95.12 "Toward a Concept of Norman Mailer." Article-interview by Samuel M. Hughes. *Pennsylvania Gazette* (Alumni Magazine of the University of Pennsylvania), May, 20-27. Detailed report of Mailer's 20-23 March visit to the University of Pennsylvania, with comments from Hughes's interview with Mailer interspersed. In the course of four days of lectures, class visits and readings from his work, Mailer spoke of race relations in America, advertising, literary style, the worsening "spiritual ecology" of modern times, capitalism and communism, his sole foray into commercial advertising, corporations, and his forthcoming book, 95.16. Hughes is both skeptical and admiring in this fine portrait—one of the best—of Mailer the dialectician, looking for action in academe. See spring 1983 entries, 95.2-95.7.

95.13 "Norman Mailer Tells 'Oswald's Tale.'" Article-interview by Patricia Holt. *San Francisco Chronicle*, 1 May, Sec. E ("Datebook"), pp. 1-2. Interviewed at Random House in New York, Mailer talks about 95.16, with emphasis on the sexuality of Lee Harvey and Marina Oswald.

95.14 "Mailer Obsessed." Article-interview by Wil Haygood. *Boston Globe*, 2 May, 59, 68. Mailer says that he is "75 percent sure" that Oswald killed J.F.K. Haygood attempts, unconvincingly, to link Mailer and Oswald: "Both were dreamers. Both were U.S. Marines who felt unappreciated in the Marines." Mailer was in the U.S. Army.

95.15 "The Amateur Hit Man." *New York Review of Books*, 11 May, 52-59. Advance excerpt from *Oswald's Tale: An American Mystery* (95.16). Rpt: Appearing just before the official publication date of 95.16, this excerpt, dealing with Oswald's murderer, Jack Ruby, consists of the whole of part 7, "The Amateur Hit Man," of volume 2, "Oswald in America," with only a few minor changes. See 67.2.

95.16 *Oswald's Tale: An American Mystery*. New York: Random House, 12 May; London: Little, Brown, 7 September. Nonfiction narrative, 828 pp., $30. A signed, leather-bound "limited first edition" appeared simultaneously carrying a two-page preface, "A Special Message for the First Edition from Norman Mailer." Franklin Center, Pa.: Franklin Library, $75. Dedication: "To Norris, my wife, for this book and for the other seven that have been written through these warm years, these warm twenty years we have been together." Appreciation: "To Larry Schiller, my skilled and wily colleague in interview and investigation, for the six months we labored side by side in Minsk and Moscow, and then again in Dallas, feeling as close as family (and occasionally as contentious); and to Judith McNally, my incomparable assistant, whose virtues are so numerous it would weigh upon one's own self-regard to list them—yes, to Schiller and McNally, a full and unconditional appreciation. Without them there might have been no tale to tell." Rpt: A lengthy advance excerpt appeared in *New Yorker* (95.8), a shorter one in *New York Review of Books* (95.15), and, shortly after publication, another brief one in *Parade* (95.17); eight excerpts are reprinted in *The Time of Our Time* (98.7). See 83.58, 93.8, 1995 entries, 96.2, 97.26.

Mailer: "The intent of *Oswald's Tale*, you see, is not to solve the case—that's beyond my means—but to delineate for the reader what kind of man he was (that is to say, what kind of character Oswald would be in a novel), and thereby enable the reader to start thinking about which plots, conspiracies, or lone actions Oswald would have been capable of, as opposed to all the ones he would never fit" (95.27).

95.17 "What American Haunts Us More?" *Parade*, 14 May, 4-7; cover story. Excerpt from 95.16. Rpt: Appearing just after the book, this excerpt deals with Oswald's culpability in J.F.K.'s assassination, taken from chapters 3 and 4 of part 8, "Oswald's Ghost," of volume 2, "Oswald in America."

95.18 "Mailer on Oswald: 'An American Mystery.'" Article by Joan Smith. *San Francisco Examiner*, 22 May, Sec. B ("Style"), pp. 1, 3. In this report on his appearance in a City Arts and Lectures program with Wendy Lesser, editor of *Threepenny Review*, Mailer discusses his collaboration with Lawrence Schiller on 95.16, his former status as a conspiracy theorist, and his ideas about Oswald's character. Mailer says Oswald was "a psychopathic liar," but he respects him for his guts, concluding by saying, "John Updike once said of the Kennedy assassination that it was as if God had removed his sanction from America....It's as if all the troubles have come to us since then, as if we were no longer a blessed nation."

95.19 "Norman M. Praises Norman R." *New York Newsday*, 24 May, Sec. B, p. 7. Excerpt from letter read at a 17 May memorial ceremony for Brooklyn poet laureate, Norman Rosten, whom Mailer called "the quintessence" of the "good guy" from Brooklyn.

95.20 Commencement Address, Wilkes University, Wilkes-Barre, Pa., 27 May. In a speech of approximately 1,000 words, Mailer focused on the Cold War and the way it affected the lives of nearly all Americans over the past 40 years. "Looking back on it," he said, "we were like magnetic filings in the power of a huge electromagnet, the Cold War, and almost all of us pointed in the same direction. When the Cold War ended, it was as if the great switch on this huge electromagnet was released and now all the fragments went in all directions." Mailer ended his speech by challenging the graduates "to anticipate the glorious, and exciting, and fearful, and incredible days and years that await you." Rpt: His speech appeared, in part, over the next few days in an Associated Press story in at least 70 newspapers. Longer reports of his speech appeared in the (Scranton, Pa.) *Sunday Times*, 28 May, Sec. B, pp. 11, 13; the (Wilkes-Barre, Pa.) *Citizens' Voice*, 28 May, 5, 18; the (Hazelton, Pa.) *Standard-Speaker*, 30 May; and the *Wilkes University Alumni Journal*, July-August, 3. See 95.21.

95.21 "Activism Dormant, Not Dead, Says Author." Article-interview by Anthony Colarossi. (Wilkes-Barre, Pa.) *Times Leader*, 28 May, Sec. A, p. 3. Interviewed after receiving an honorary doctor of humane letters degree at Wilkes University, Mailer said that if President Bill Clinton based his 1996 election campaign on bringing whites and blacks together, it might generate an activist movement. The administration, he added, "is just not passionate enough. And Clinton is not ready to die [politically] for a political idea." See 95.20.

95.22 "Mailer Back in the Arena, Pushing 'Oswald.'" Article-interview by Carol McCabe. *Providence Journal*, 28 May, Sec. E ("Sunday Brunch"), pp. 1, 9. Report of a meeting with three reporters, including McCabe, in a Cambridge, Mass., hotel room as Mailer was concluding his 12-city tour on behalf of 95.16. Besides speaking of Oswald's character ("he is a tragic *figure*, not a tragic *hero*"), Mailer comes up with a new metaphor for the fact/fiction opposition: "Most people think the line between fiction and nonfiction is a Berlin Wall. I think, on the contrary, that it's a barely marked boundary. I like working back and forth on that boundary....being a range rider on that line." Accompanied by Margaria Fichtner's mixed review. See 95.24, 95.32.

95.23 "Mailer Takes Look into Mind of Assassin." Article by Coply News Service writer. *Washington Times*, 2 June. In this brief piece, Mailer says he sees "a huge difference" between Lee Harvey Oswald and Timothy McVeigh, suspect in the Oklahoma City bombing: "Oswald saw himself as a creator....McVeigh, or whoever did the bombing, is a symbol of a destroyer."

95.24 "Norman Mailer Takes Aim at the Oswald Riddle." Article-interview by Nicholas A. Basbanes. *Milwaukee Journal Sentinel*, 4 June, 1-2. Another discussion of the fictive nature of Mailer's nonfiction narratives, including 95.16 and *The Executioner's Song* (79.14), and drawn from the same interview session as 95.22 and 95.32.

95.25 "Discovering Lee Harvey Oswald: Norman Mailer's Biography Reveals an Extraordinary Risk-Taker." Article-interview by Alan Dumas. *Rocky Mountain News*, 5 June, Sec. D ("Arts and Entertainment"), pp. 6, 8. Based on a telephone interview, this piece reveals little new about 95.16. Dumas does report, however, that Mailer said he was thinking of writing a novel about a concentration camp after finishing the sequel to *Harlot's Ghost* (91.26). See 95.26.

95.26 "For a Draft of Reality, It's Mailer Time." Article-interview by Louise Continelli. *Buffalo News*, 11 June, Sec. E ("Lifestyles"), pp. 1-2. Based on the same telephone interview as 95.25, this piece gives more space to Mailer's comments comparing Oswald to Timothy McVeigh. He says, "There's a tendency to ignore the depth of commitment in evil people. For instance, President Clinton spoke of the bombing of Oklahoma City as a cowardly, evil act. Well, it seems to me that it was certainly an evil act. But it does take a kind of guts, finally, just to drive with that much explosives in the back of your car."

95.27 "America's Obsessions: Norman Mailer Talks about Lee Harvey Oswald, J.F.K., the KGB, O.J. Simpson, and the Nasty Nineties." Interview by Sean Abbott. *At Random*, no. 11 (summer), 12-19. Longest and best interview on 95.16, covering all major aspects of the book, including Mailer's lucid explanation of his six months with Lawrence Schiller in Minsk in 1992-93, and a good exchange on J.F.K.'s diminished stature in American life. Mailer ends by saying of the sequel to *Harlot's Ghost* (91.26): "I'm working on it."

95.28 "Norman Mailer." Article-interview by Wendy Smith. *US Air Magazine*, July, 12, 14, 16. Interviewed at Random House in New York, Mailer explains how he came to see Lee Harvey Oswald: "He was not just a passive, Dreiserian character that life just worked upon; he did a great deal to create his own destiny."

95.29 "Norman Mailer Replies." Letter to the editor. *New York Review of Books*, 13 July, 61. Mailer replies to the letter (in the same issue) of J. Herbie DiFonzo concerning Mailer's explanations in 95.15 of Jack Ruby's movements just before he killed Lee Harvey Oswald. Mailer points out that while Ruby's movements "are epistemologically dysfunctional," the key fact "is that Ruby was not only an amateur hit man but was scared stiff of the task before him."

95.30 "A Tribute to the United Nations." *Wall Street Journal*, 25 July, Sec. A, p. 3. Quarter-page photograph of Mailer by Nancy Crampton (same as on dustwrapper of 95.16) with the following statement: "The United Nations has endured through all the massive maneuvers of the Cold War and all the chaos that has followed. If our hope of peace is to be achieved, it can probably not be realized without the presence of the United Nations as mediator." The statement was paid for by Swissair.

95.31 "Character Assassination." Article-interview by Clive Davis. *Sunday Times* (London), 3 September, 12-13. Round-up of new doings on the Oswald/J.F.K./conspiracy front, with quotes from Mailer and Gerald Posner, author of *Case Closed: Lee Harvey Oswald and the Assassination of J.F.K.*, and snippets from the Internet. Davis reports that the English edition of 95.16 would appear the same week as this article.

95.32 "Norman Mailer: Tough Fights." Interview by Harvey Blume. *Boston Book Review*, September, 3, 33-34. Blume's interview on *Oswald's Tale* (95.16) comes from the same Cambridge, Mass., session several months earlier as 95.22 and 95.24.

95.33 "Callow Young Genius." Interview by Barbara Probst Solomon. *New York*, 11 September, 81-84. First (and one of the best) interviews on *Portrait of Picasso as a Young Man* (95.38). Solomon leads Mailer into a thoughtful discussion of the young Picasso, sex, narcissism, science and painting. Mailer also anticipates, correctly, the response of art critics to 95.38: "Art jargon is one of the most offensive critical languages, and it certainly seals the subject off from the onlooker. So the art critics who are making a living out of the subject without real penetration will absolutely detest what I am trying to do here. Because I am trying to say, here's a man, an immensely complicated man, and incredibly talented, but he is not beyond our reach."

95.34 "Page Six: Mailer's Ex-Lover Writes It Down." Column by Richard Johnson, with Jeane MacIntosh and Sean Gannon. *New York Post*, 15 September, 6. Mailer responds to comments by Carole Mallory that she is writing a biography, titled "On Mailer," detailing her affair with him. In his statement, Mailer says, "I am guilty of a few extramarital episodes over the years, and Carole is one of them. Now, at the age of 72, these are matters to regret since I adore my wife and was much in love with her even when I was being unfaithful."

95.35 "I Ask the Questions (Such as: What's an Old Warhorse like You Doing Drinking Iced Tea?)." Article-interview by Dermot Purgavie. *Mail on Sunday* (London), 24 September. Brief piece based on an interview at Mailer's Brooklyn Heights apartment. In a somewhat valedictory mood, he says, "Writers aren't taken seriously any more, and a large part of the blame must go to the writers of my generation, including me. We haven't written the books that should have been written. We've spent too much time exploring ourselves. We haven't done the imaginative work that could have helped define America, and as a result we're not a nation that has characteristics or form."

95.36 "Why Picasso Biography Quotes So Fully." Letter to the editor. *New York Times*, 3 October, Sec. C, p. 24. Mailer complains that Michiko Kakutani "not only gave a very bad review to my last book, *Oswald's Tale* [95.16], but rushed to put it into print....Now, she has done it once more. Ms. Kakutani (Arts pages, Sept. 29) has rushed into print to attack my new book, *Portrait of Picasso as a Young Man* [95.38], and is again two weeks early." Kakutani did it again in 1997 when she blasted *The Gospel according to the Son* (97.13) on 14 April, more than two weeks before it was published. Mailer's letter is dated, Provincetown, Mass., 2 October.

95.37 "Mailer on Mailer." Interview by Michael Mailer. Photograph by Frank W. Ockenfels. *Time Out* (New York), 11-18 October, 20-21, 23. Thoughtful exploration of 95.38 with his eldest son, including discussion of Picasso as a celebrity, narcissist, and explorer of the secrets of the universe, and his relations with women. Mailer also reveals that his three self-interviews of the early 60s came out of his effort to write a biography of Picasso: "I started to write and thought I would go in for an introductory chapter on questions of form and function, and before I got done I spent the entire summer writing a dialogue between an imaginary interviewer and myself. It was influenced completely by Picasso." See 59.8, 61.10, 88.6.

95.38 *Portrait of Picasso as a Young Man: An Interpretive Biography.* New York: Atlantic Monthly Press, 15 October; London: Little, Brown. 284 illustrations, including 48 color plates, 400 pp., $35. Dedication: "To Judith McNally; For her insights and her labors large and small that contributed so much to the publication of this work." Discarded title: "Pablo and Fernande: Portrait of Picasso as a Young Artist." See 59.8, 61.10, 93.4, 93.5, 94.8, 1995 entries, 96.3.

Mailer: "Picasso wished to penetrate into more and more secrets of the universe. Now, you have to understand that he considered himself an atheist. He had a tremendous animosity toward the church. But he was also, and this is the argument in my book, immensely aware of the presence of God in almost everything he did. He saw himself as on a parapet, if you will, daring God" (95.37).

95.39 "Black and White Justice." Interview by Michael Mailer. *New York*, 16 October, 28-32. Exploration of the O.J. Simpson case, shortly after the not-guilty verdict. Mailer says that "blacks can see themselves as inhabitants, willy-nilly of a powerful, vain, imperial-minded country that's shooting itself in the foot. Only they are the foot."

95.40 "Norman Mailer: Literary Tough Guy Takes on Picasso's High-Stakes Cubist Gamble." Article-interview by Michael Hollett. *Now* (Toronto), 19-25 October, 32-33; cover photograph of Mailer. Mailer discusses 95.38 at the Algonquin Hotel in New York, focusing on Picasso's relationship with women, with asides on Lee Harvey Oswald.

95.41 "Picasso Couldn't Box, but He Could Paint Like Hell, Says Norman Mailer." Article-interview by Bruce Barcott. *Seattle Weekly*, 25 October, 19. Mailer, in Provincetown, is interviewed by telephone in anticipation of his appearance at the Seattle Art Museum on 28 October, where he lectured on Picasso and read from 95.38. He explains how he spent two months in 1962 looking at every page in Christian Zervos's 33-volume collection of Picasso's paintings and drawings.

95.42 Statement on Herman Melville's Captain Ahab. *New York Times Magazine*, 29 October, 51. Accompanying a full-page color photograph of Mailer costumed as Ahab is this statement by Mailer: "Many a novelist has a touch of the monomaniac and Ahab is the monster of us all."

95.43 "Questions about Mailer's Artistry Arise after Publication of Picasso." Article-interview by Regina Hackett of the *Seattle-Post-Intelligencer*. *Vancouver Sun*, 31 October. In Seattle to promote 95.38, Mailer discusses his credentials for writing an interpretive biography.

95.44 "Kindred Spirits: Mailer and Picasso." Article-interview by Pete Hamill. *Art News*, November, 208-13. Mailer talks about his relationship with the painters of Provincetown and Greenwich Village in this long, easy, Provincetown conversation with Hamill, an old friend, who wrote about Mailer's influence on him in his memoir, *A Drinking Life* (Boston: Little, Brown, 1994). After Picasso, Hans Hoffman and Andy Warhol are the two artists Mailer says the most about.

95.45 "Norman Conquest." Article-interview by Mary Ann Grossman. *Saint Paul Pioneer Press*, 4 November, "Showtime" Sec., p. 1. Prior to speaking at Macalester College, Mailer spoke to Grossman about 95.38. The piece is most memorable for a surprising error: she writes that Mailer spoke of his close relationship with James Joyce; he was referring to James Jones.

95.46 "Art Attack: Norman Mailer Fires Back at Critics of His *Portrait of Picasso*." Article-interview by Mary Voelz Chandler. *Rocky Mountain News*, 6 November, Sec. D ("Arts and Entertainment"), pp. 5, 7. Mailer responds, in general terms, to the art critics who wrote negative reviews of 95.38.

95.47 "Author to Author: Norman Mailer Talks with Jay McInerney." Interview. *Providence Phoenix*, 10 November, Sec. 1, pp. 10-11, 15; cover story. One of the best interviews on *Portrait of Picasso as a Young Man* (95.38). Mailer tells McInerney that he feels "more street smart after I've looked at a lot of Picasso drawings or paintings. He understood people so well. He had the gifts of one of the greatest draftsmen who ever lived, but he had the mind of a novelist in a funny way. His eye for character is incredible." Other matters discussed include John Richardson, Picasso's view of sex, fame, James Jones, Ernest Hemingway, and the response of reviewers to 95.38. Accompanied by an excerpt from part 6 of the biography, "Gertrude Stein."

95.48 "Norman Conquest: Mailer Profiles Picasso as a Young Man." Article-interview by Rebecca Ascher-Walsh. *Entertainment Weekly*, 10 November. Little more than a squib based on Mailer's tour of the Museum of Modern Art with the author, who quotes him briefly.

95.49 "Mailer vs. Picasso at Harvard." Article-interview by M.R. Montgomery. *Boston Globe*, 14 November, 77, 82. In Boston to promote 95.38, Mailer visits Harvard's Fogg Museum for the first time since 1943 when he took a course on modern art in the Fogg. He notes that the reviews of 95.38 are "the worst I've ever gotten for a book," which is accurate, although *Barbary Shore* (51.1) and *Tough Guys Don't Dance* (84.17) received equally bad reviews.

95.50 "Artistic License? Norman Mailer Paints a Controversial Picture of Picasso." Article-interview by Alan G., Artner. *Chicago Tribune*, 19 November, Sec. 7 ("Arts and Entertainment"), pp. 1, 20. Artner, art critic for the *Tribune*, finds fault with Mailer's methods and conclusions in 95.38, but quotes him fully and fairly on these matters.

95.51 "At last, a Norman Conquest." Article-interview by Alan W. Petruceli. *Cape Cod Times*, 20 November, Sec. C, pp. 1-2. Mailer again speaks of the painters he knew in Provincetown—Franz Kline, Hans Hoffman, Robert Motherwell and Helen Frankenthaler—and his love of the town in this interview centered on 95.38. "Provincetown," he says, "may be a joke to the rest of the Cape, but it's perhaps the most generous small town in America, full of wonderfully goofy aspects and sweet freedom." Mailer also notes that 95.38 was completed in 1992, but it took three years to obtain the needed permissions.

95.52 "Self-Propelled: Mailer—with Ego Intact—Looks at Picasso's Early Years." Article-interview by John Barron. *Chicago Sun-Times*, 26 November. Besides commenting on his interest in Picasso's early life in this piece, Mailer discusses political parties, Newt Gingrich, religion in America and the decline of interest in good novels.

95.53 "Dysfunctionally Literate." Column by Brad Wieners. *Bay Guardian*, December, 3. Encountering Mailer at a cocktail party on 6 November in San Francisco, Wieners tells him that he just read (in *The F-Word* by Jesse Sheidlower) that he had been forced to change "fuck" to "fug" in *The Naked and the Dead* (48.2). Mailer explains that he had used "fug" from the outset. See 49.3, 65.21, 68.31, 92.12.

95.54 "Scholarship Gets Boost from Mailer's Speech." Article by unidentified writer. *Atkins* (Arkansas) *Chronicle*, 6 December, 1. Visiting the hometown of his wife Norris Church, Mailer spoke at Arkansas Tech on 4 December, answering questions on various current events, including the O.J. Simpson trial, the war in Bosnia, welfare reform and the end of the Cold War. He says, "The United States used the Cold War to push the U.S.S.R. into bankruptcy, while President Reagan tripled the U.S. national debt." Mailer donated his speaking fee to the Francis Gwaltney scholarship fund at Arkansas Tech, where Gwaltney taught before his death in 1981. Gwaltney served in the army with Mailer and was, according to Mailer, his oldest friend. Mailer met his sixth wife, Norris Church, through Gwaltney.

95.55 "Homage to Faulkner." *New Yorker*, 11 December, 42. Poem.

95.56 Interview by Michael K. Glenday, 21 October 1991; letter to him, 10 December 1993. In *Norman Mailer*, by Michael K. Glenday, 130, 138, respectively. New York: St. Martin's, 1995. Two quotes from one of Mailer's press conference interviews during a British publicity tour for *Harlot's Ghost* (91.26), and one from a later letter, all dealing with the novel and the Cold War.

95.57 Preface to *Writers: Photographs*, by Sally Soames, 9. San Francisco: Chronicle Books; London: Deutsch. Mailer praises Soames, who uses only available light, in his 454-word preface to this collection of photographs of 83 writers, accompanied by a quote from the work of each. Mailer's quote is the opening paragraph of *Advertisements for Myself* (59.13). See Soames's comments on the writers she photographed, including Mailer, in Lesley White's article, "Open Books," (London) *Sunday Times Magazine*, 7 May.

Photograph by
Michael Comte
96.5

96.1 [The Flea Market]. *Pharaon* (Paris), March-April, 3. In 335 words, Mailer extols the virtues of the flea market over the shopping mall in this French art and antique magazine.

96.2 "Oswald's Ghost: An Interview with Norman Mailer." By Peter DePree. *Bloomsbury Review*, March-April, 3, 10. Mailer reveals who he was with when he first heard J.F.K. had been shot (Norman Podhoretz), and who he was with when he heard Lee Harvey Oswald had been shot (George Plimpton), and his reactions on both occasions. Accompanied by 96.3.

96.3 "About Picasso." Interview by Peter DePree. *Bloomsbury Review*, March-April, 3, 10-11. Discussion of Mailer's sources, his knowledge of painters and modern art, Picasso's sexuality and other matters related to *Portrait of Picasso as a Young Man* (95.38). Accompanied by 96.2 and DePree's positive review of 95.38.

96.4 "Mailer and Me." Memoir by Barry Leeds. *Connecticut Review* 18 (spring), 5-12. A long-time Mailer scholar remembers his meetings with Mailer over 30 years, and quotes from their wide-ranging conversations and correspondence.

96.5 "Searching for Deliverance." *Esquire*, August, 54-61, 118-27. Slugged on the cover as "Norman Mailer: Armies of the Right." Essay-interview with Patrick J. Buchanan. Long, thoughtful discussion of the populist roots of the Right and Left and the possibilities of an alliance between factions of both against corporate excess and big government. See 68.8.

96.6 Statement on F. Scott Fitzgerald. In *F. Scott Fitzgerald: 24 September 1996 Centenary Celebration*, edited by Matthew J. Bruccoli, 34. Columbia, S.C.: Thomas Cooper Library, University of South Carolina, 24 September. Mailer and 26 other writers, including Margaret Atwood, Vance Bourjaily, Don DeLillo, James Dickey, Annie Dillard, William Maxwell, Budd Schulberg and Tony Tanner contributed statements on the man and the work in this tribute, limited to 750 softcover presentation copies. Mailer's full statement: "What would any of us have been without Fitzgerald? A little less, for certain. Literary pleasures of the most special sort would have been withheld, and some of his errors in life, God bless him, would soon have been ours."

96.7 Comment on William Burroughs. In *With William Burroughs: A Report from the Bunker*, by Victor Bockris, xxii. Revised edition. New York: St. Martin's, November. Brief approving comment by Mailer on Burroughs. The first edition (New York: Seaver Books, distributed by Grove Press, 1981) was not examined. See 62.24, 65.1, 65.13, 81.21, 92.12.

96.8 "War of the Oxymorons." *George*, November, 128-39, 164, 166, 168-70, 172-73. Mailer's first appearance in *George*. Nonfiction narrative on the Republican and Democratic conventions of 1996. Rpt: *Observer Life* (London), 10 November, 6-7, 9-10, 12, 14-15, 17-18, 20-21, 23-24; 98.7 (partial). See 76.5, 97.1.

96.9 Statement on John Dos Passos. In "John Dos Passos: A Centennial Commemoration." In *Dictionary of Literary Biography Yearbook: 1996*, edited by Samuel W. Bruce and L. Kay Webster, 173. Detroit: Bruccoli Clark Layman, Gale Research. In 44 words Mailer praises Dos Passos's novel *U.S.A.* as the "most successful portrait of America in the first half of the twentieth century."

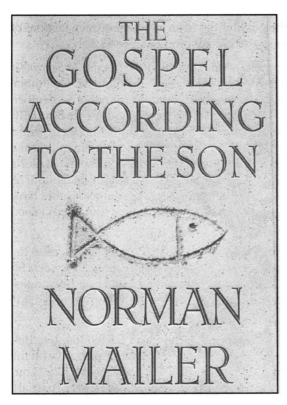

Illustration by John
Sposato
97.13

97.1 "How the Pharaoh Beat Bogey." *George*, January, 54-60, 82-86. Issued with two different covers; one titled "Special Collector's Edition" with a black-and-white cover photograph of Claudia Schiffer; the other cover has a color photograph of her. Nonfiction narrative on the 1996 presidential campaign. Rpt: 98.7 (partial). See 76.5, 96.8.

97.2 "Narrator of Mailer's Next Novel: Jesus." Article-interview by Dinitia Smith. *New York Times*, 4 February, Sec. B ("Living Arts"), p. 7. First report on Mailer's forthcoming novel *The Gospel according to the Son* (97.13). In a statement quoted by Smith, Mailer says, "My intent is to be neither pious nor satirical; it is instead to make comprehensible for myself what Fulton Oursler called *The Greatest Story Ever Told*. I'm going to say no more because the book's publication is still three months away and I don't wish to arouse interest that cannot be satisfied at this point." Carol Schneider, director of publicity at Random House, and Jason Epstein, Mailer's longtime editor, are also quoted in this piece.

97.3 "Mailer Goes to the Mountain." Interview by Sean Abbott. *At Random*, no. 17 (spring-summer), 48-55. First and best interview on *The Gospel according to the Son* (97.13). Interviewed in New York just before Christmas 1996, Mailer discusses his Jewishness, the causes, source materials and language of the novel, his first-person point of view, miracles and his personal religious beliefs. He says, "I would say this book was written to fill an empty space in my mind. What's almost never discussed, because it's too tough a subject, is how it feels to be Jewish growing up in a benign Christian country." See 83.44, 91.29.

97.4 "You Are the Boss!" In *Pierian Spring: The Literary Anthology of Berrien Springs High School,* edited by David Chaudoir, 7. Berrien Springs, Mich.: Berrien Springs High School, April-May. Essay. Mailer and several other professional writers, including Sara Paretsky, T. Coraghessan Boyle, Sue Grafton and George Plimpton, contributed to this anthology of high school writing. Mailer's 134-word contribution deals with the joys of reading.

97.5 "Gospel according to Mailer: The Greatest Story Ever Retold." Article-interview by Charles W. Bell. (New York) *Daily News,* 13 April, 7. Mailer explains his reasons for writing 97.13, especially his desire to improve the committee prose of the synoptic gospels. Accompanied by 97.6.

97.6 [Chapters 1-7 of] *The Gospel according to the Son.* (New York) *Daily News,* 13 April, 8-9. Advance excerpt from 97.13. Rpt: Appearing about three weeks before the novel, these excerpts follow the published novel faithfully. Accompanied by 97.5. The remaining 42 chapters appeared in 18 parts in the *Daily News* 14 April to 1 May.

97.7 "The Gospel of Mailer: Hubris, but without Limits." Article-interview by Bruce Weber. *New York Times,* 24 April, Sec. A ("New York Report"), p. 21. Mailer, after discussing chutzpah as a "vulgar and endearing" quality that is "very much a part of New York," goes on to "assure the New York world—the rest of America will never believe me—that I do not think of myself as Jesus Christ." The piece also reveals: 1) that Mailer had originally wished to publish 97.13 anonymously, but Random House demurred because of problems encountered by Joe Klein when he published *Primary Colors* anonymously; and 2) that Random House would publish a literary retrospective of Mailer's work of about 1,500 pages to commemorate his 75th birthday and the 50th anniversary of *The Naked and the Dead* (48.2) on 6 May 1998. *The Time of Our Time* (98.7) did appear on this date. Accompanied by 97.8. Weber's article appeared in truncated form in at least two other newspapers: *Oakland Tribune* (5 May) and *Tampa Tribune* (10 May).

97.8 "First Person Singular: A Look Inside." *New York Times,* 24 April, Sec. A ("New York Report"), p. 21. Advance excerpt from 97.13. Rpt: Appearing about a week before 97.13, this brief excerpt from chapter 29 deals with Christ's dreams before going to Jerusalem to preach in the Great Temple. Accompanied by 97.7.

97.9 "Jesus Feeds the Multitudes: Two Versions." *Chicago Sun-Times,* 24 April, 35. Advance excerpt from 97.13. Rpt: Appearing a week before 97.13, this brief excerpt from chapter 27 deals with the miracle of the loaves and fishes; it is contrasted with the version in Mark, 6:37-45, New King James Version. Accompanied by Tom Sheridan's mainly positive review and 97.10.

97.10 "Mailer's Gospel Tempts Critics." Article-interview by John Barron. *Chicago Sun-Times*, 24 April, 35, 39. Interviewed by telephone from his home in Brooklyn Heights, Mailer spoke about forthcoming response to 97.13. Accompanied by Tom Sheridan's mainly positive review and 97.9.

97.11 Quotations. In *The Last Party: Scenes from My Life with Norman Mailer*, by Adele Mailer, passim. New York: Barricade Books, late April. Mailer disputes the accuracy and tone of this memoir by his second wife.

97.12 "The Gospel according to Norman Mailer." Article-interview by Stephanie Schorow. *Boston Herald*, 2 May. Mailer comments on 97.13 in this brief interview, including a comment on the Gospels: "The writing is extraordinary and intensely poetic and the great lines of Jesus remain the great lines. But a good deal of writing in between was rather pedestrian."

97.13 *The Gospel according to the Son*. New York: Random House, 2 May; London: Little, Brown, 18 September. Novel, 224 pp., $22. Dedication: "To Susan, Danielle, Elizabeth, Kate, Michael, Stephen, Maggie, Matthew, and John Buffalo." Acknowledgments: "I would like to give an acknowledgment to my wife, Norris; to my assistant, Judith McNally; to my friends Michael Lennon and Robert Lucid; to Veronica Windholz; and to James and Gaynell Davis, who all offered signal contributions to this work. And not least, to Jason Epstein, Joy de Menil, and Andrew Wylie." Rpt: All of 97.13 was published in the (New York) *Daily News* (97.6) in 19 parts before book publication. Advance excerpts also appeared in the *New York Times* (97.8) and the *Chicago Sun-Times* (97.9). Seven excerpts are reprinted in *The Time of Our Time* (98.7). See 1997 entries.
     Mailer: "So I thought: If I can write about Osiris and Ra, then certainly the New Testament is not going to be that difficult to do. And in a sense, it wasn't. In contrast to the complexity of the ancient Egyptian myth of Isis and Osiris, this is simpler and more beautiful. And far more cohesive. It was perfectly conceivable to me that one could have a character in a novel who's the son of God. Novelists are supposed to look into the eye of the tiger" (97.3).

97.14 "The Gospel according to Norman." Article-interview by Margaria Fichtner. *Miami Herald*, 4 May, Sec. I ("Arts"), pp. 1-2. Interviewed at Random House in New York, Mailer gives full measure in this piece, speaking of the myriad aesthetic, philosophical and historical issues he faced in writing 97.13, which he says he wrote "for those people who are like myself, who don't have a clear idea of what Jesus is."

97.15 "Mailer Agrees His 'Gospel' Is an Audacious Book." Article-interview by Nicholas A. Basbanes. (Quincy, Mass.) *Patriot Ledger*, 10 May. In this relatively brief piece Mailer tells Basbanes that his greatest risk in writing 97.13 was the prospect of "ridicule and dismissal as a person playing the fool, exactly the sort of risk that all writers face whenever they want to do something particularly ambitious." Sometimes truncated, this piece also appeared in the following newspapers: (Worcester, Mass.) *Sunday Telegram*

(11 May); *Knoxville News-Sentinel* (18 May); *Grand Rapids Press* (18 May); (Toledo) *Blade* (18 May); (Jackson, Miss.) *Clarion-Ledger* (25 May); (Allentown, Pa.) *Morning Call* (25 May); (Madison) *Wisconsin State Journal* (1 June); *Salt Lake Tribune* (8 June).

97.16 "The Gospel according to Norman." Article-interview by Doug Riggs. *Providence Journal*, 11 May. Based on a telephone interview in early May with 20 book reviewers and editors, this brief piece adds little to earlier articles on 97.13. See 97.18, 97.20, 97.21.

97.17 "Courage in Profiles: Attacked by Critics for His Hubris, Norman Mailer Nonetheless Tackles the Tough Topics." Article-interview by Paul Galloway. *Chicago Tribune*, 12 May, Sec. 5 ("Tempo"), pp. 1, 5. In Chicago to promote 97.13, Mailer talks to Galloway and appears on WGN radio's "Extension 720" with interviewer Milt Rosenberg. Again he discusses the first person point of view used in 97.13, and his admiration for the Jesus story, which he calls "the keel of western civilization."

97.18 "Latest Retelling of Jesus' Life Is by 'Reckless Talent.'" Column by Ina Hughes. *Knoxville News-Sentinel*, 18 May. Mailer's brief remarks in this column seem to be taken from the same telephone conversation reported in 97.16. See 97.20, 97.21.

97.19 "Mailer Defends Novel in Spirited Dowagiac Lecture." Article by Miles White. *South Bend Tribune*, 18 May. Report on Mailer's appearance at the Dogwood Fine Arts Festival in Dowagiac, Ind. on 16 May.

97.20 "Mailer's Not So Bad after All." Column by Lois Blinkhorn. *Milwaukee Journal Sentinel*, 1 June. Another piece based on a telephone interview with journalists around the country. See 97.16, 97.18, 97.21.

97.21 "The Gospel...according to Mailer." Article-interview by Julie Irwin. (Elmira, N.Y.) *Star-Gazette*, 20 August, Sec. 5 ("Twin Tiers Life"), p. 5. Still another report based on a telephone interview with Mailer. Accompanied by a brief excerpt (the miracle of the loaves and fishes) from 97.13. See 97.16, 97.18, 97.20.

97.22 "The Martyrdom of Mailer." Profile-interview by Andrew O'Hagen. *Guardian Weekend* (London), 30 August, 10-12, 14, 17-19; cover photograph of Mailer by Frank Ockenfels. Despite several errors in his profile, O'Hagen does provide some thoughtful Mailer quotations: on *The Naked and the Dead* (48.2), immigrants to America and the identity crises they faced, current literary criticism, Vietnam, *Harlot's Ghost* (91.26), socialism and Christianity, *The Gospel according to the Son* (97.13), and Ernest Hemingway: "I once wrote that for years he hadn't written anything that would bother an eight-year old....I might have felt what I said, but, after all, the man had been working in the vineyard all his life, and you wouldn't say that of an old grape-picker. But now it's my turn in the barrel." Accompanied by the first of three excerpts from 97.13; parts two and three appeared on 31 August and 1 September, respectively.

200

97.23 "Mailer Retells the Greatest Story Ever." Article-interview by Bob Minzesheimer. *USA Today*, 8 September. Mailer comments on 97.13, listing some of the theologians he read (Elaine Pagels, Robert Funk, John Meyer), and announces that he is working on a retrospective, the best of his fiction and nonfiction (98.7).

97.24 Interview with George Plimpton. In *Truman Capote: In Which Various Friends, Enemies, Acquaintances, and Detractors Recall His Turbulent Career*, by George Plimpton, passim. New York: Random House, December. Mailer (along with most of the New York literary world) is quoted several times in this oral biography of Capote, which uses the same method as Plimpton's and Jean Stein's *Edie: An American Biography* (82.17).

97.25 "Struggling with God: A Conversation with Norman Mailer." Interview by Barbara Probst Solomon. *Culturefront* 6 (winter 1997-1998), 36-41. Thoughtful interview by a veteran Mailer interviewer, focusing on the religious ideas behind 97.13.

97.26 "Norman Mailer." Interview by Brian Lamb. In *Booknotes: America's Finest Authors on Reading, Writing, and the Power of Ideas*, by Brian Lamb, 162-65. New York: Random House. Included are interviews with 47 "reporters," 26 "public figures," and 46 "storytellers," including Mailer. The latter include Shelby Foote, Doris Kearns Goodwin, Simon Schama, Daniel Boorstin, Henry Louis Gates Jr., Peggy Noonan and Charles Kuralt. The host of C-Span's "Booknotes" interviewed Mailer on the air on 25 June 1995 on *Oswald's Tale: An American Mystery* (95.16). Lamb leaves his questions out of his interviews with 119 writers collected in this volume. Mailer's comments deal mainly with the six months (1992-93) he spent in Minsk, researching Lee Harvey Oswald's two years there. He also describes his writing routine.

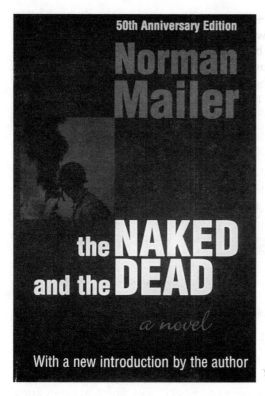

98.6. See 98.2

98.1 "Clinton for Pres. No, Not You Bill." *Observer* (London), February, 1, 4. Essay charging President Clinton with betraying the poor and enriching the wealthy. See 98.2.

98.2 "Norman Mailer, Visiting Philadelphia, Shows He Can Still Work a Crowd." Article-interview by Thomas J. Brady. *Philadelphia Inquirer*, 27 March. Speaking as part of the "Rebuilding the Future" series at the Central Library on Logan Square in Philadelphia, Mailer read from 98.1 and answered questions from Brady. Speaking of the Internet, he said that "there are going to be very few people who are going to read novels on a monitor. Or printed out....In a small way, a book does have an immanence. It has a presence. It has a sense of the past about it." The article also notes that Henry Holt and Co. intends to reissue *The Naked and the Dead* (48.2) in hardcover and softcover, with a new introduction by Mailer, to coincide with the novel's 50th anniversary. See 98.6.

98.3 "Life and Letters: The Contender." Article-interview by David Denby. Photographs by Richard Avedon. *New Yorker*, 20 April, 60-66, 68-71. Denby's piece is simultaneously an interview, a review of *The Time of Our Time* (98.7), an overview of Mailer's career, a thoughtful analysis of his staying power and, overall, one of the finest appreciations of Mailer published in the 90s. When Denby suggests that organizing the selections in 98.7 in the order of composition might have resulted in a "spiritual autobiography," Mailer says, "I've been waiting to write an autobiographical novel all these years, but I've been waiting to become the hero of my own life in order to write it. I have never become the hero of my own life." During his visit to Mailer's home in Provincetown, Denby engages him on several topics: President Clinton, "The White Negro" (57.1), his weight and diet, Provincetown, reincarnation, the media, Gore Vidal, corporations and the Women's Liberation movement. Asked how he felt when the movement "began to gather steam, roughly thirty years ago," he says, "Like the British when they lost India."

98.4 "1958-1967: Rounding Camelot." In *A Century of Arts and Letters: The History of the National Institute of Arts and Letters and the American Academy of Arts and Letters as Told, Decade by Decade, by Eleven Members*, edited by John Updike, 156-97. New York: Columbia University Press, early May. Along with Mailer, the following ten individuals contributed chapters to this 1898-1997 history: Louis Auchincloss, Jack Beeson, Hortense Calisher, Ada Louise Huxtable, Wolf Kahn, R.W.B. Lewis, Richard Lippold, Cynthia Ozick, Arthur Schlesinger Jr. and John Updike. See 84.31.

98.5 "The Joy of Bricks." Article by Anthony Lane. *New Yorker*, 4 May, 96-98, 100, 102-3. Mailer is quoted briefly in this article on Lego bricks, and a color photograph of his Lego construction, "Vertical City," opens the piece. The same photograph appears on the dustwrapper of *Cannibals and Christians* (66.11). See 65.2.

98.6 Introduction to *The Naked and the Dead*. New York: Henry Holt, 6 May, simultaneously in softcover, xi-xiii. Mailer wrote this new introduction for an edition issued on the 50th anniversary of the first edition (48.2). See 79.36, 98.2.

98.7 *The Time of Our Time*. New York: Random House, 6 May; London: Little, Brown, November. Retrospective anthology, 1286 pp., $39.50. Dedication: "To Robert F. Lucid and J. Michael Lennon." Organized not by dates of composition, but by the dates of the events described, this huge collection contains 139 excerpts from 26 of Mailer's books, and from uncollected periodical pieces. In almost every excerpt, as Mailer notes in the "Acknowledgments and Appreciations," he deleted old references, and took "the liberty of improving old sentences," not to "alter an idea to conform to a new time," but to "improve the prose an agreeable bit." Besides the foreword and "Acknowledgments and Appreciations," the only original piece in the collection is "The Shadow of the Crime: A Word from the Author," a one-page reflection on the 1960 stabbing of his second wife Adele. In it, Mailer explains the impact the event had on him, his wife, and his family, and the enforced delay it caused in sending a November 1960 letter to Fidel Castro, later published in the *Village Voice* (61.5) and *The Presidential Papers* (63.37). Mailer signed 25,000 copies of 98.7, and the dustwrapper of these bears the line, "A Signed First Edition." See 60.11, 74.19, 97.7, 97.23, 1998 entries.

Mailer: "Re-reading the bulk of my work in the course of a spring and summer, one theme came to predominate—it was apparent that most of my writing was about America. How much I loved my country—that was evident—and how much I didn't love it at all! Our noble ideal of democracy was forever being traduced, sullied, exploited, and downgraded through a non-stop reflexive patriotism. And every decade our great land lay open more and more to all the ravages of greed. So, yes, the question was alive—would greed and the hegemony of the mediocre—the media—triumph over democracy? Or could we also celebrate some happy reading—well, yes, we could!" (98.7).

98.8 "View from Writing's Heights: Time Arrives for Mailer to Mark 50 Years in Publishing." Article-interview by Bob Minzesheimer. *USA Today*, 6 May, Sec. D ("Life"), 1-2; cover story. Mailer discusses 98.7 and reveals that the first printing was 25,000 copies. Besides discussing the collection, Mailer talks about his working methods, boxing, corporations, architecture and the Women's Liberation movement, which he says was "welcomed by the corporation that now hires women at every level but the very top and pays them 90% of what it pays men."

98.9 "After Half a Century, Still Writing, Still Questing." Article-interview by Rick Lyman. *New York Times*, 7 May, Sec. E, pp. 1, 8. The chief theme of this piece, based on Lyman's visit to Mailer's home in Brooklyn Heights, is religion: "For the last 50 years, my preoccupation has been religion. What might God be? I am searching for a notion of God that is alive to me." Mailer also compares New York and Provincetown as places to work, reveals his summer reading plans (Cormac McCarthy and Don DeLillo), lauds Warren Beatty's new film "Bulworth," discusses abortion, fiction vs. nonfiction, the nature of 98.7, his plans for a sequel to *Harlot's Ghost* (91.26), and J.F.K., who, he says, "is as vivid to me as Bill Clinton, and he's been gone all these years." In sum, a typical Mailer interview, wide-ranging, pungent and self-revealing.

98.10 The Talk of the Town: "Ink: Two Fighting Legends Reminisce and Ruminate over the Cheese Puffs." Column by Lillian Ross. *New Yorker*, 18 May, 31. Ross reports on the publication party for *The Time of Our Time* (98.7) at the Rainbow Room / Pegasus Suite in Rockefeller Center, New York, including Mailer's conversation with Muhammad Ali, who attended. Mailer was accompanied by his wife Norris, and eight of his nine children.

98.11 "Fine Distinctions: Norman Mailer on Fiction, Non-Fiction and the Differences between Them." Interview by Elizabeth Taylor. *Chicago Tribune*, 24 May, Sec. 14 ("Books"), p. 3. Besides discussing fiction and nonfiction, Mailer comments on John Dos Passos, James T. Farrell and the organizational scheme for 98.7.

98.12 "In Prose, in Person, Mailer's Still the Tough Guy." Interview by Susan Salter Reynolds. *New Hampshire Sunday News*, 7 June, Sec. E, p. 4. Reynolds's piece, in which Mailer recalls his mother and her family loyalty, appeared first in the *Los Angeles Times*.

98.13 "Mailer: At Age 75, Lauded Author Mourns That Marvelous Madness." Article-interview by Hillel Italie, Associated Press. (Wilkes-Barre, Pa.) *Times-Leader*, 5 July, Sec. G, p. 5. Brief comments by Mailer on the writing life in a 4 May Brooklyn interview in connection with the publication of 98.7.

98.14 "Making Books: 'Private Ryan' Reviews a Genre." Article-interview by Martin Arnold. *New York Times*, 30 July, Sec. E, p.3. Discussion of the "concentrated carnage" in Stephen Spielberg's film, "Saving Private Ryan" and how it parallels *The Naked and the Dead* (48.2), which Arnold calls "arguably the greatest combat novel ever written by an American." Mailer says, "The Second World War was a watershed. Everything is of it, before it or after it. It is a point of reference. It's still my point of reference."

98.15 "Writer Norman Mailer Talks about Religion, Abortion, Clinton." Article-interview by Joshua Karetny. *Daily Pennsylvanian*, 3 November, 11. Report on Mailer's keynote address at the Jewish Book Festival at the Gershwin YM-YWHA in Philadelphia.

98.16 "A Man Half Full." *New York Review of Books*, 17 December, 18, 20-23. Review of *A Man in Full*, by Tom Wolfe. Contains some of Mailer's most considered and thoughtful comments on novel-writing.

98.17 "Mailer Charms Central Students." Article-interview by Anthony R. Cannela. *Hartford Courant*, 6 December, Sec. B, pp. 1, 3. Report, with brief Mailer quotes, of his 4 December visit to Barry Leeds's Mailer course at Central Connecticut State University in New Britain.

A Chronology of Mailer's Appearances

in (English Language) Periodicals,
Excluding Interviews, Symposia, Questionnaires
and (Routine) Letters to the Editor:
1941-1998

First Appearance	Title	Number of Appearances
1941	_Harvard Advocate_	5
1941	_Story_	2
1948	_Book Find News_	1
1948	_New York Post_	2
1948	_National Guardian_	1
1952	_Partisan Review_	8
1952	_Discovery_	1
1953	_Esquire_	42
1953	_World Review_ (London)	1
1953	_Cornhill_	1
1954	_Dissent_	11
1955	_One: The Homosexual Magazine_	1
1956	_Village Voice_	36
1959	_Provincetown Annual_	1
1959	_Big Table_	1
1961	_Journal for Protection of All Beings_	1
1961	_Paris Review_	4
1961	_New Yorker_	4
1961	_New Statesman_	2
1962	_Atlantic_	2
1962	_Queen Magazine_ (London)	1
1962	_Nugget_	1
1962	_Evergreen Review_	3
1962	_Commentary_	8
1963	_New York Review of Books_	12
1963	_Way Out_	2
1963	_Playboy_	12
1963	_Book Week_	2
1964	_Architectural Forum_	1
1964	_Cleft_ (Edinburgh)	1
1964	_Fuck You: A Magazine of the Arts_	1
1965	_New York Times Magazine_	3
1965	_Realist_	1
1966	_East Side Review_	1
1967	_New York Times Book Review_	5
1967	_Poetry Bag_	1
1968	_Harper's_	3
1968	_Newsweek_	1
1969	_Look_	1

1969	*New York Times*	3
1969	*Life*	5
1973	*Ladies Home Journal*	3
1973	*Rolling Stone*	4
1974	*New Republic*	2
1975	*Counter-Spy*	1
1976	*Los Angeles Times Book Review*	1
1976	*New American Review*	3
1976	*Cosmopolitan*	1
1976	*New York*	3
1976	*Chic*	1
1978	*Stone Age*	1
1979	*Boston*	1
1979	*U.S. News and World Report*	1
1981	*Parade*	3
1981	*Book Digest Magazine*	1
1981	*Shooter's Bible*	1
1982	*Video Review*	1
1983	*House and Garden*	1
1983	*Vogue*	1
1983	*Proceedings of the American Academy and Institute of Arts and Letters*	1
1983	*Mail on Sunday*	3
1984	*Vanity Fair*	7
1984	*Pen American Center Newsletter*	1
1985	*Michigan Quarterly Review*	1
1988	*Spin*	1
1988	*Antaeus*	1
1989	*Writer's Digest*	1
1994	*Provincetown Arts*	1
1996	*Pharaon* (Paris)	1
1996	*George*	2
1997	*Pierian Spring: The Literary Anthology of Berrien Springs High School*	1
1997	*Daily News*	19
1997	*Guardian Weekend*	1
1998	*Observer*	1

Total number of periodicals: 74

Number of Entries by Year

1941	1	
42	2	
44	1	
48	13	
49	4	
		Total 1940s: 21
1951	5	
52	3	
53	5	
54	3	
55	8	
56	26	
57	2	
58	8	
59	19	
		Total 1950s: 79
1960	12	
61	23	
62	24	
63	40	
64	23	
65	24	
66	15	
67	24	
68	32	
69	83	
		Total 1960s: 300
1970	15	
71	32	
72	24	

73	47	
74	20	
75	16	
76	23	
77	14	
78	7	
79	36	
		Total 1970s: 234
1980	26	
81	23	
82	26	
83	59	
84	35	
85	16	
86	43	
87	29	
88	11	
89	12	
		Total 1980s: 280
1990	5	
91	51	
92	13	
93	10	
94	8	
95	57	
96	9	
97	26	
98	17	
		Total 1990s: 196
		Grand Total: 1110

Days

1891   Isaac Barnett "Barney" Mailer born in Lithuania.

1891   Fanny "Fan" Schneider born in Lithuania.

Fanny Schneider, 1922

Isaac B. Mailer, 1922

by G. Maillard Kesslere   by G. Maillard Kesslere

1922   Barney and Fan marry in Manhattan on 12 February.

1923   Norman Kingsley Mailer born in Long Branch, New Jersey on 31 January. Mailers live with Fan's family in Long Branch, at first with them on Morris Ave., and then in "Kingsley Court," a cluster of three large beach "cottages" at Beach and Ocean Avenues, owned by Fan's parents.

Norman and Barbara, 1932

1925   In the fall, Mailers move to Cortelyou Road in the Flatbush section of Brooklyn, but continue to summer in Long Branch.

1927   Barbara Jane, Mailer's sister, born on 6 April.

1928 In September, Mailer enters Public School 181, Flatbush.

1933 Mailers move to Crown Heights section of Brooklyn in January. Mailer transfers to Public School 161, where he skips two half-year terms. In the summer he writes a long science fiction story, "The Martian Invasion."

1935 Graduates from P.S. 161 in June, and in September, enters Boy's High School in Brooklyn.

P. S. 161 graduation, 1935

1936 Celebrates his Bar Mitzvah on 15 February.

1939 Graduates from Boy's High School in June, and in late September enters Harvard planning to study aeronautical engineering.

1941 In April, is taken onto the board of the college's literary magazine, *The Harvard Advocate*, which that same month publishes his short story, "The Greatest Thing in the World." In late spring, it wins *Story* magazine's eighth annual college contest and a $100 prize. In September, completes "No Percentage," a novel (408 manuscript pages), still unpublished.

1939

1943 Graduates from Harvard in June with a S.B. degree (with honors) in engineering sciences; most of his electives are English writing courses. Moves to his parents' apartment on Pierrepont Street in Brooklyn.

1944 Drafted into the U.S. Army in January. On 7 January, he marries Beatrice "Bea" Silverman. In February, completes his second novel, *A Transit to Narcissus*, which is not published until 1978. In late March, is inducted into the army. His novella, "A Calculus at Heaven," is included in Edwin Seaver's *Cross-Section: A Collection of American Writing*, published in April. In August, after five months

Dunster House, Harvard, where Mailer lived, September 1941-June 1943

of training at Fort Bragg, North Carolina, he is sent to Fort Ord, California as an artillery trainee. In early December, he ships out from San Francisco on a troop ship, arriving in Leyte Gulf, the Philippines, on 29 December.

1945 In mid-January, joins the 112th Cavalry Regimental Combat Team in Leyte. He serves in the Luzon campaign in the Philippines as a clerk and then a rifleman, and in Japan after the war ends he becomes a cook. Meets Francis Irby "Fig" Gwaltney (same outfit), who in 1975 introduces him to his sixth wife, Norris Church.

Fort Bragg, N. C.,
Summer 1944

Barbara, 1944

by G. Maillard Kesslere

211

1945-46 See 59.13

1946 Discharged from the Army on 2 May, rents a small apartment in North Truro, near Provincetown, Massachusetts in June, and begins work on his war novel. He will spend the greater part of most summers for the next half-century in Provincetown at the tip of Cape Cod. Mailer's friend Adeline Lubell, an editor at Little, Brown, reads 186 pages of his manuscript, but no contract is offered by Little, Brown because of the novel's alleged obscenity. Mailer then turns to the New York firm of Rinehart. In November, they offer and Mailer accepts a $1250 advance for *The Naked and the Dead*.

1947 Completes *The Naked and the Dead* while living on Remsen Street in Brooklyn, around the corner from his parents' home. Turns in the completed manuscript to Rinehart in September. In early October, he and Bea leave for Paris to study at the Sorbonne on the GI Bill. In Paris, he begins *Barbary Shore*, and meets Jean Malaquais, who later becomes his mentor and lifelong friend.

1947 dust wrapper photograph
48.2

1948 On 6 May *The Naked and the Dead* is published. It tops the *New York Times* best seller list for 11 straight weeks during the spring and summer, and remains on the list for a total of 61 weeks, including 19 in the top position and 43 in the top five. The novel is nominated for the Pulitzer Prize and the Gutenberg Award, and the Associated Press names Mailer "Man of the Year" in literature. Mailer returns from Europe in late July to campaign for Progressive Party presidential candidate Henry Wallace. He moves to a rented house in Jamaica, Vermont shortly after Harry S. Truman's election.

1948   by John H. Popper

1949   Mailer resumes work on *Barbary Shore*. From 25 to 27 March he attends and speaks at the Cultural and Scientific Conference for World Peace (Waldorf Conference) in New York, which is attacked as a Communist front in *Life* magazine (4 April). In June, the Mailers move to Hollywood, where they are joined by Jean Malaquais. Susan born to Bea 28 August. Finishes first draft of *Barbary Shore*. Mailer and Malaquais work on scripts for Samuel Goldwyn.

1950   In June, the Mailers return to Provincetown. He completes work on the final version of *Barbary Shore* in Putney, Vermont, where the Mailers move in October.

1951   Having met Adele Morales on a visit to New York City, Mailer separates from Bea in the winter, and begins living with her on the lower

1952

with   Mickey Knox   Adele Mailer   James Jones

213

East Side. Bea and Susan move to Mexico. *Barbary Shore* is published on 24 May to almost unanimously bad reviews.

1952   Mailer and Bea divorce in February. Begins work on *The Deer Park*.

1953   In April, "The Language of Men," a short story, is published in *Esquire*, the first of over 40 Mailer appearances in this magazine.

1953   with Fan and Susan

Mailer and Adele visit New Orleans and Mexico in the summer and early fall.

1954   Publishes his first piece, "The Meaning of 'Western Defense,'" in *Dissent*, and joins its editorial board, remaining on it until the 80s. In the spring, completes *The Deer Park*, marries Adele, and visits Mexico for several months. Upon their return to New York City in November, they move into a duplex on East 55th Street. In the same month, with publication less than three months away, Rinehart stops publication of *The Deer Park* because of six lines describing *fellatio*. The novel is subsequently rejected by six publishers before being accepted by G.P. Putnam's Sons.

1955   Mailers visit Barcelona and Rome in the summer. *The Deer Park* is published on 14 October and on 13 November climbs to number six on the *New York Times* bestseller list. With Edwin Fancher and Daniel Wolf, Mailer founds *The Village Voice*, and gives the new paper its name. The first issue is 26 October. For a time he is circulation manager of the *Voice*.

1956   Village Voice offices

1956   Publishes 17 weekly columns, the first 14 titled "Quickly: A Column for Slow Readers," and the last three, "The Hip and the Square," in *The Village Voice* from 11 January through 2 May, at which point he resigns from active participation because of editorial differences with his partners. In early May, "The Man Who Studied Yoga" is published in *New Short Novels* 2. The Mailers spend the summer in Paris where they meet James Baldwin. In the fall, they move to Bridgewater, Connecticut near the homes of William Styron and John W. Aldridge.

1957   Danielle born to Adele 16 March. "The White Negro" is published in the summer number of *Dissent*.

July 1957   Lady Jeanne Campbell
Daily Express (London)

1958   The Mailers move from Connecticut to Perry Street in Greenwich Village. In the fall, spends a week at the University of Chicago and meets Robert F. Lucid, who later becomes his authorized biographer. He is invited to join the Actors' Studio (Playwright and Directors Unit) in New York City.

1959   Elizabeth Anne born to Adele 28 September. *Advertisements for Myself* is published on 6 November.

1960   On 25 May, receives a $1,500 award from the National Institute of Arts and Letters. In July, covers the Democratic National Convention in Los Angeles for *Esquire*, and publishes "Superman Comes to the Supermarket" in the November issue. On 20 November, stabs his wife Adele with a penknife after a party at their apartment on West 94th Street; he is committed briefly to Bellevue for 17 days of psychiatric observation.

1961   On 9 March, pleads guilty to assault charges; later that month he separates from Adele. During that same month, meets Lady Jeanne Campbell. On 13 November receives a suspended sentence and is placed on probation.

1962   *Deaths for the Ladies (and Other Disasters)* is published on 30 January. In early spring, divorces Adele in Juarez, Mexico. In April, marries Jeanne Campbell, and in late spring they move into 142 Columbia Heights, Brooklyn, a brownstone he had purchased and renovated in 1960. Mailer has lived there continuously since, except for his

215

August 1965   with Muhammad Ali, San Juan, PR   See 65.17

sojourns in Provincetown, where he has spent the majority of the year since the mid-1980s. Kate born to Jeanne on 18 August. Attends the International Writers' Conference in Edinburgh, 20-24 August. On 25 September, covers the Sonny Liston-Floyd Patterson fight in Chicago for *Esquire*. In November, begins a column, "The Big Bite," in *Esquire* (through December 1963), and a bi-monthly column, "Responses and Reactions," in the December *Commentary* (through October 1963). In late fall, separates from Jeanne Campbell.

1963 In March, meets Beverly Bentley and marries her in December, shortly after divorcing Jeanne Campbell. *The Presidential Papers* is published on 8 November. In addition, he publishes more than thirty pieces (poems, book reviews, essays, interviews, columns, letters, debates and a short story) in a dozen different places, the acceleration of a periodical blizzard that began in 1959 and continues until abating somewhat in the mid-1970s. Scott Meredith becomes his literary agent in the fall.

1964 Serialization in eight installments of *An American Dream* in *Esquire*, January-August. Michael Burks born to Beverly 17 March. In August, covers the Republican Convention in San Francisco for *Esquire*. "In the Red Light," his account, appears in the November issue.

1965 In January, testifies on behalf of William Burroughs's novel, *Naked Lunch*, at its Boston obscenity trial. *An American Dream* (revised) is published on 15 March. On 21 May, speaks against the Vietnam War at the Berkeley campus of the University of California. In December, addresses the Modern Language Association in Chicago.

1966 Stephen McLeod born to Beverly on 10 March. In June, purchases a house in Provincetown on Commercial Street. *Cannibals and Christians* is published on 29 August.

1967 "The Deer Park: A Play" opens at Theatre DeLys in New York on 31 January; it closes 21 May after 127 performances. On 24 May, he is inducted into the National Institute of Arts and Letter. Publishes four books: *The Short Fiction of Norman Mailer* (11 May); *The Deer Park: A Play* (7 August); *Why Are We in*

March 1966   New York City
Demonstration against Vietnam War

Vietnam? (15 September); *The Bullfight* (mid-November); makes two experimental films, "Wild 90" and "Beyond the Law." On 21 October, is arrested at an anti-war protest at the Pentagon. *Why Are We in Vietnam?* is nominated for the National Book Award.

1968 "Wild 90" premieres on 8 January. "Beyond the Law" premieres on 2 April. Preceded by long excerpts in *Harper's* and *Commentary*, *The Armies of the Night* is published on 6 May, 20 years to the day after

April 1967   with Gwen Verdon   Princess Lee Radziwell

217

The Naked and the Dead. In July, makes his third experimental film, "Maidstone," on Long Island. In August, covers the national political conventions, and publishes his account, *Miami and the Siege of Chicago*, first in *Harper's* and then in book form on 24 October.

June 1969   On the campaign trail   See 70.7
Mailer with   Elizabeth   Fan   Danielle   Joe Flaherty
Stephen   Michael

1969   *The Armies of the Night* wins several awards: National Book Award in arts and letters (12 March); George Polk Memorial Award for magazine reporting (27 March); Pulitzer Prize for general nonfiction (5 May). In addition, *Miami and the Siege of Chicago* is a finalist for the National Book Award in the history and biography category. On 1 May, he announces his candidacy for the Democratic primary for mayor of New York (with Jimmy Breslin as his running mate); he comes in fourth in a field of five. Awarded honorary Doctor of Letters by Rutgers University on 4 June. Also in June, running as an "insurgent" candidate for the Harvard Board of Overseers, he is defeated in an alumni election. In July, he begins coverage of the Apollo 11 mission for *Life*. Separates from Beverly Bentley in late summer.

May 1969   Wall Street   Mayoral Campaign See 69.44

1970   In January, testifies at the trial of the "Chicago Seven." On 18 April,
is awarded Harvard University's Signet Society Medal for Achievement in the Arts. In early May, he serves a three-day sentence for
his 1967 arrest at the Pentagon. He summers in Maine with five of
his children and Carol Stevens. In August, "Maidstone" is shown
at the Venice Film Festival.

1969   with other Democratic mayoral candidates
          James Scheuer   Robert Low
Robert Wagner   Mario Proccacino   Herman Badillo

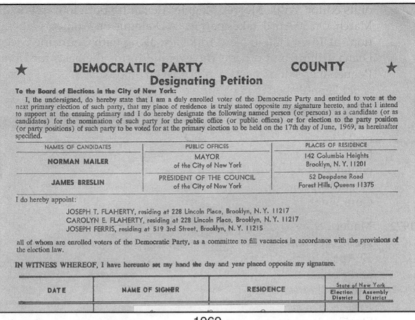

★ **DEMOCRATIC PARTY**   **COUNTY**   ★

Designating Petition

To the Board of Elections in the City of New York:

I, the undersigned, do hereby state that I am a duly enrolled voter of the Democratic Party and entitled to vote at the next primary election of such party, that my place of residence is truly stated opposite my signature hereto, and that I intend to support at the ensuing primary and I do hereby designate the following named person (or persons) as a candidate (or as candidates) for the nomination of such party for the public office (or public offices) or for election to the party position (or party positions) of such party to be voted for at the primary election to be held on the 17th day of June, 1969, as hereinafter specified.

NAMES OF CANDIDATES	PUBLIC OFFICES	PLACES OF RESIDENCE
NORMAN MAILER	MAYOR of the City of New York	142 Columbia Heights Brooklyn, N. Y. 11201
JAMES BRESLIN	PRESIDENT OF THE COUNCIL of the City of New York	52 Deepdene Road Forest Hills, Queens 11375

I do hereby appoint:

JOSEPH T. FLAHERTY, residing at 228 Lincoln Place, Brooklyn, N. Y. 11217
CAROLYN E. FLAHERTY, residing at 228 Lincoln Place, Brooklyn, N. Y. 11217
JOSEPH FERRIS, residing at 519 3rd Street, Brooklyn, N. Y. 11215

all of whom are enrolled voters of the Democratic Party, as a committee to fill vacancies in accordance with the provisions of the election law.

IN WITNESS WHEREOF, I have hereunto set my hand the day and year placed opposite my signature.

DATE	NAME OF SIGNER	RESIDENCE	State of New York	
			Election District	Assembly District

1969

1971   Preceded by three excerpts in *Life*, *Of a Fire on the Moon* is published on 11 January by Little, Brown, the first of eight books by Mailer to be published by this firm. It is later nominated for the National Book Award in the sciences category. "The Prisoner of Sex" is published in the March *Harper's*, which contributes to the resignation

5 May 1969   See 68.8

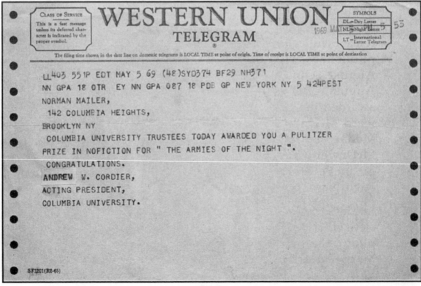

WESTERN UNION

TELEGRAM

LL403 551P EDT MAY 5 69 (48)SYD374 BF29 NH371
NN GPA 18 OTR EY NN GPA 087 18 PDB GP NEW YORK NY 5 424PEST
NORMAN MAILER,
142 COLUMBIA HEIGHTS,
BROOKLYN NY
COLUMBIA UNIVERSITY TRUSTEES TODAY AWARDED YOU A PULITZER
PRIZE IN NOFICTION FOR " THE ARMIES OF THE NIGHT ".
CONGRATULATIONS.
ANDREW W. CORDIER,
ACTING PRESIDENT,
COLUMBIA UNIVERSITY.

SF1201(R2-65)

220

of its editor, Willie Morris. Maggie Alexandra born to Carol on 21 March. On 30 April, takes part in "A Dialogue on Women's Liberation" at Town Hall in New York City, along with Germaine Greer, Diana Trilling and others. The evening forms the basis for Donn Pennebaker's documentary film, "Town Bloody Hall." *The Prisoner of Sex* is published in book form on 27 May, and is later nominated for the National Book Award in the arts and letters category. "Maidstone" premieres at the Whitney Museum in New York City on 23 September, and is published as *Maidstone: A Mystery* in October. *The Long Patrol: 25 Years of Writing from the Work of Norman Mailer*, edited by Robert F. Lucid, is published on 25 October. On 2 December, he appears on the "Dick Cavett Show" with Janet Flanner and Gore Vidal.

1972 Mailer begins work on "the Egyptian novel." During the year, he speaks at more than 20 colleges. *Existential Errands* is published on 17 April. In the summer, covers the national political conventions, and publishes his account of them, *St. George and the Godfather*, in late October (with excerpts appearing earlier in *Life* and *New York Review of Books*). In September, he and Carol Stevens move to Stockbridge, Massachusetts where he purchases a house. On 12 October his father dies. In November, he begins working on a biography of Marilyn Monroe.

1973 At his 50th birthday party (celebrated on 5 February), he announces his idea for "The Fifth Estate," a citizen watchdog group to keep tabs on the FBI and CIA. Preceded by excerpts in *Ladies Home Journal, Atlantic* and *New York Review of Books, Marilyn: A Biography* (with photographs assembled by Lawrence Schiller) is published on 1 August. On 18 August, he is awarded the Edward McDowell Medal at the McDowell Colony in Peterborough, New York.

1974 In May, *The Faith of Graffiti* (with photographs by Mervyn Kurlan-

Summer 1976   Maine
with either Matthew or Stephen

221

sky and Jon Naar) is published simultaneously in *Esquire* and book form. In October, he covers the Muhammad Ali-George Foreman fight in Zaire.

1975 In March, meets Barbara Norris (later Norris Church Mailer) in Arkansas through "Fig" Gwaltney. *The Fight* is published on 21 July, after long excerpts appear in *Playboy*. During the summer—spent largely in Mt. Desert, Maine—he separates from Carol Stevens and begins living with Norris Church and her son Matthew at 142 Columbia Heights in Brooklyn. In December, excerpts from *The Fight* in *Playboy* win the magazine's Best Nonfiction Award.

1976 On 25 February, he is awarded the 1976 Gold Medal for Literature by the National Arts Club. *Some Honorable Men: Political Conventions, 1960-1972*, is published on 1 April. In September, he profiles presidential candidate Jimmy Carter for the *New York Times Magazine*. Preceded by an excerpt in *American Review*, *Genius and Lust: A Journey through the Major Writings of Henry Miller* is published in October. In December, receives *Playboy's* Best Major Work in Fiction Award for "Trial of the Warlock."

1977 Continues work on "the Egyptian novel." Summers in Mt. Desert, Maine.

1978 A facsimile of the manuscript of Mailer's unpublished novel from the 40s, *A Transit to Narcissus*, is published in January. John Buffalo born to Norris on 16 April. Summers in Provincetown and Mt. Desert, Maine.

1979 *The Executioner's Song* is published on 15 October, with excerpts appearing in *Playboy*, October-December. It climbs to number three on the *New York Times* bestseller list in January 1980. In late October, he meets Jack Henry Abbott at the Marion Federal Penitentiary in Illinois. In

1976   Alta, Utah
with Norris Church Mailer

222

December, *The Executioner's Song* is nominated for the National Book Critics Circle award, and wins the Best Major Work in Fiction Award from *Playboy*.

1980 On 14 April, *The Executioner's Song* wins the Pulitzer Prize for fiction. In November, he divorces Beverly Bentley, marries and divorces Carol Stevens, and marries (on 11 November) Norris Church. *Of Women and Their Elegance* is published on 26 November, the same month that he and Norris play cameo roles in Milos Foreman's film, "Ragtime."

November 1980   See 80.20
As Stanford White in Milos Forman's film
"Ragtime"

1982   with Michael and Norris   by Renate Ronsold

1983   with Matthew   John Buffalo   Stephen   by Kelly Wise

1981 In late June, he writes the introduction for and helps arrange the publication of *In the Belly of the Beast: Letters from Prison* by Jack Henry Abbott. On 18 July, Abbott stabs to death Richard Adan in New York City. Abbott is subsequently convicted and sentenced for the crime. Mailer attends his trial.

1982 *Pieces and Pontifications* is published on 21 June. *The Essential Mailer* is published on 1 August.

1983 Preceded by advance excerpts in *Playboy*, *Vogue*, *House and Garden* and *Paris Review*, *Ancient Evenings* is published on 4 April. It climbs to number six on the *New York Times* bestseller list in mid-May. In August, he moves from Little, Brown to Random House. In late September, Mailer is nominated for an Emmy for his screenplay based on *The Executioner's Song*. In October, purchases his current home on Commercial Street, Provincetown.

1984 Visits Russia for the first time in March; returns with Norris in June. On 11 July, he is elected president of the PEN American Center for a two-year term. Preceded by excerpts in *Vanity Fair*, *Tough Guys Don't Dance* is published on 20 August. Inducted into the American Academy of Arts and Letters on 7 December. Begins work on *Harlot's Ghost*.

Fall 1985   PEN Celebration   See 85.1
with John Irving and William F. Buckley, Jr.   by Jack Kaminsky

1985   On 28 August Mailer's mother dies. On 20 November, he receives Lord and Taylor's annual Rose Award for public accomplishment.

1986   Presides over the PEN International Congress meeting in New York, 12-18 January. In the same month, "Strawhead," a play adapted from *Of Women and Their Elegance*, is staged by the Actors Studio in New York with Kate Mailer as Marilyn Monroe. From 14 October to 13 December, in Provincetown, directs his own filmscript based on *Tough Guys Don't Dance*.

1987   In May, "Tough Guys Don't Dance" is screened (outside the competition) at the Cannes Film Festival. On 16 September, it premieres in New York.

1988   *Conversations with Norman Mailer*, edited by J. Michael Lennon, is published on 31 July.

1989   In February and March, attends meetings and writes statements in support of Salman Rushdie. On 11 October, he receives the Emerson-Thoreau Medal for distin-

1992   Wilkes University
with J. Michael Lennon by Curtis Salonick

225

1992 Norris   1992 Kate

guished achievement in literature from the American Academy of Arts and Sciences.

1990 Continues work on *Harlot's Ghost*.

1991 In March, accepts the position of writer-at-large at *Vanity Fair*. In late October, *Harlot's Ghost* is published after advance excerpts appear in nine publications, including *Esquire*, *Playboy*, *Rolling Stone* and *Partisan Review*. On 13 November, he receives the New York State Edith Wharton Citation of Merit. Begins work on *Portrait of Picasso as a Young Man*.

1992 Covers the August Republican Convention and publishes his account in the 12 October *New Republic*. Begins six months of research in Minsk, Belarus (1992-93) on Lee Harvey Oswald. Andrew Wylie becomes Mailer's literary agent after the death of Scott Meredith.

1993 Along with Susan Sontag, Gay Talese and Gore Vidal, Mailer takes part in a 15 February reading (which he directs) of George Bernard Shaw's "Don Juan in Hell" at Carnegie Hall. In late July, his line drawings are shown at the Berta Walker Gallery in Provincetown. In late November, gives the keynote address at the Third Assassination Symposium on

1995   Univ. of Pennsylvania
See 95.2   with Robert F. Lucid

226

August 1993   Provincetown
Norris Mailer with Donna Pedro Lennon

John F. Kennedy in Dallas. Continues work on *Oswald's Tale: An American Mystery*.

1994 On 23 April, receives (for the second time) Harvard University's Signet Society Medal for Achievement in the Arts.

November 1995   Munich

30 December 1996   Shickshinny, Pennsylvania
with Robert F. Lucid   Joanne Lucid   Norris Mailer

1995 Preceded by excerpts in *The New Yorker* and *New York Review of Books*, *Oswald's Tale: An American Mystery* is published on 12 May. Receives honorary Doctor of Humane Letters from Wilkes University in Wilkes-Barre, Pennsylvania on 27 May. *Portrait of Picasso as a Young Man: An Interpretive Biography* is published on 15 October. Begins work on *The Gospel according to the Son.*

1996 Covers the 1996 political conventions in the summer. His report on them appears in the November issue of *George*. He then covers the campaign of Senator Dole and President Clinton in the fall.

1997   John Buffalo   Matthew
by Elke Rosthal

1997 Mailer's article on the 1996 campaign appears in the January issue of *George*. In the spring, he begins work on *The Time of Our Time*. Preceded by serial publication (19 parts) in the *New York Daily News*, *The Gospel according to the Son* is published on 18 September.

1998 On 6 May, 50 years to the day after the publication of *The Naked and the Dead*, Mailer's anthology of his work, *The Time of Our Time*, is published.

1997   Maggie

August 1999
Stephen and Callan Marx Mailer
(Norman Mailer's grandson)

Dustwrapper photograph for
95.16   By William Majeski

229

Select Secondary Bibliography

The following secondary references are divided into five sections: 1) primary and secondary bibliographies; 2) biographies; 3) cultural backgrounds; 4) key reviews of 27 Mailer books; and 5) critical essays and books. There is some unavoidable overlapping between some of the items in this section and "Works" because a number of critical essays and books, as well as memoirs and biographical writings, contain Mailer quotations not found elsewhere. The secondary items refer back to "Works," but not vice versa. The web of cross-reference may be drawn tighter by users of this volume; we have gone as far as seemed useful.

The cultural backgrounds section contains many items that arguably could be better placed with the critical materials. Their location is an attempt to identify key references to the worlds (and *demimondes*) Mailer has moved in, sometimes with reference to him, sometimes not. This section is far from exhaustive and is more a reflection of our Mailer library than any comprehensive plan.

The volume of reference to Mailer grows, if not exponentially, then constantly and quite rapidly. We are confident that the forthcoming accretions, and the inevitable omissions, will prompt future addenda and corrigenda to this volume. We request that you help us with your comments, corrections and discoveries.

BIBLIOGRAPHIES

Adams, Laura. *Norman Mailer: A Comprehensive Bibliography*. Metuchen, N.J.: Scarecrow Press, 1974. Primary and secondary, including partial list of Mailer's unpublished manuscripts and dissertations about his works..

Ahearn, Allen, and Patricia Ahearn. "Norman Mailer: Author Price Guide 114.2." Dickerson, Md.: Quill and Brush, 1997. 14 pp. Authoritative price guide to first editions with identifying "points" for same.

Fiske, Thomas. "A Collector's Bibliography of the Writings of Norman Mailer, 1938-1993." Unpublished manuscript. Contains annotated list of Mailer's published work through 1993, a list of unpublished screenplays, playscripts and ephemera, and all or part of four unpublished Mailer letters.

Lennon, J. Michael. "Norman Mailer." In *Contemporary Authors Bibliographical Series: American Novelists*, edited by James J. Martine, 219-60. Detroit: Bruccoli Clark/Gale Research, 1986. Primary (including key interviews) and secondary with essay on secondary sources.

_____. "Norman Mailer." In *Facts on File Bibliography Series: American Fiction, 1919-1988*, 306-10. New York: Facts on File, 1991. Primary and secondary, including biographical sources.

Lucid, Robert F. "A Checklist of Mailer's Published Works." In *Norman Mailer: The Man and His Work*, edited by Robert F. Lucid, 299-310. Boston: Little, Brown, 1971. The foundation stone of Mailer bibliographies.

Shepard, Douglas. "Norman Mailer: A Preliminary Bibliography of Secondary Comment." *Bulletin of Bibliography* 29 (April-June 1972), 37-45. Thorough, if not exhaustive, list of reviews of Mailer's books through *Miami and the Siege of Chicago* (68.25), and other critical comment.

Sokoloff, B.A. *A Bibliography of Norman Mailer*. Darby, Penn.: Darby Books, 1969. Primary and secondary with many omissions, but including obscure early reviews.

BIOGRAPHIES

Atlas, James. "Life with Mailer." *New York Times Magazine*, 9 September 1979, 52-55, 86, 88, 90, 92, 94, 96, 98, 102, 104, 107. See 79.9.

Baldwin, James. "The Black Boy Looks at the White Boy." In *Nobody Knows My Name: More Notes of a Native Son*, 216-41. New York: Dial, 1961. Rpt: Lucid (1971), Braudy (1972). See 57.1.

Brower, Brock. "Norman." In *Other Loyalties: A Politics of Personality*, 105-37. New York: Atheneum, 1968. See 65.20.

Christian, Frederick. "The Talent and the Torment." *Cosmopolitan*, August, 63-67. See 63.34.

Cohen, Marcia. "Town Bloody Hall." In *The Sisterhood: The True Story of the Women Who Changed the World*, 288-306. New York: Simon and Schuster, 1988. See 71.20.

Cook, Bruce. *The Beat Generation*, 93-98, 168-69. New York: Scribner's, 1971. See 61.4.

_____. "Aquarius Rex." *National Observer*, 4 November 1972, 1, 15. Rpt: Adams (1974). See 61.4.

Denby, David. "The Contender." *New Yorker*, 20 April 1998, 60-66, 68-71. Best recent profile. See 98.3.

Flaherty, Joe. *Managing Mailer*. New York: Coward-McCann, 1970. Account of Mailer's 1969 campaign for the Democratic nomination for mayor of New York by his campaign manager. See 70.7.

Greer, Germaine. "My Mailer Problem." In *The Madwomen's Underclothes: Essays and Occasional Writings*, 78-89. New York: Atlantic Monthly Press, September 1987. Rpt: Bloom (1986). See 71.27.

"Harvard: America's Great University Now Leads World." *Life*, 5 May 1941, 89-99. Journalistic sketch, with many photographs, appearing at the end of Mailer's sophomore year.

Hayden, Hiram. *Words and Faces*, 234-35, 263-64. New York: Harcourt Brace Jovanovich, 1974. Comment on the rejection of *The Deer Park* (55.4) by Random House.

Krim, Seymour. *Shake It for the World Smartass*, 89-99, 111-19, 125-51. New York: Dial, 1970. Three essays on Mailer's powerful presence in the literary world. See 61.23.

Land, Myrick. "Mr. Norman Mailer Challenges All the Talent in the Room." In *The Fine Art of Literary Mayhem: A Lively Account of Famous Writers and Their Feuds*, 228-44. San Francisco: Lexikos, 1983. See 63.40.

Lennon, J. Michael. "Norman Mailer." In *Concise Dictionary of American Literary Biography, Volume 6: Broadening Views, 1968-1988*, 162-83. Detroit:

Bruccoli Clark Layman/Gale Research, 1989.

Lucid, Robert F. "Prolegomenon to a Biography of Mailer." In *Critical Essays on Norman Mailer*, edited by J. Michael Lennon, 174-84. Boston: G.K. Hall, 1986. Invaluable overview. See 71.29.

Macdonald, Dwight. "Massachusetts vs. Mailer." In *Discriminations: Essays and Afterthoughts*, 194-209. Introduction by Norman Mailer. New York: Grossman, 1985. Rpt: Lucid (1971). See 60.8, 83.57.

Mailer, Adele. *The Last Party: Scenes from My Life with Norman Mailer*. New York: Barricade Books, 1997. Memoir by Mailer's second wife. See 97.11.

Manso, Peter, editor. *Running Against the Machine: A Grass Roots Race for the New York Mayoralty by Norman Mailer, Jimmy Breslin, Peter Maas, Gloria Steinem and Others*. New York: Doubleday, 1970. See 69.80.

_____. *Mailer: His Life and Times*. New York: Simon and Schuster, 1985. Oral biography. See 85.13.

Martien, Norman. "Norman Mailer at Graduate School or, One Man's Effort." *New American Review, No. 1*, edited by Theodore Solotaroff, 233-41. New York: New American Library, 1967. Account of a Mailer university visit. Rpt: Lucid (1971).

Mills, Hilary. *Mailer: A Biography*. New York: Empire Books, 1982. First book-length biography. See 82.23.

Morris, Willie. *New York Days*, 210-22. New York: Little, Brown, 1993. See 71.10.

Newfield, Jack. "On the Steps of a Zeitgeist." In *Bread and Roses Too: Reporting About America*, 385-90. New York: Dutton, 1971, 385-90. Rpt: Lennon (1986). See 68.10.

Pell, Edward. "His Childhood Was a Happy Time: Norman Mailer Remembers Long Branch." *Daily Register* (Red Bank, N.J.), 12 December 1966, Sec. 2, p. 13. See 66.15.

Plimpton, George. *Shadow Box*, passim. New York: Putnam's, 1977. See 77.13.

Podhoretz, Norman. *Ex-Friends: Falling Out with Allen Ginsberg, Lionel and Diana Trilling, Lillian Hellman, Hannah Arendt, and Norman Mailer*, 178-220 and passim. New York: Free Press, 1999.

_____. *Making It*, passim. New York: Random House, 1967. See 68.4.

Rembar, Charles. *The Law of the Land: The Evolution of Our Legal System*, 370-75. New York: Simon and Schuster, 1980. See 80.24.

Roddy, Joseph. "The Latest Model Mailer." *Look*, 27 May 1969, 22-28. Rpt: 88.6. See 69.43.

Rollyson, Carl. *The Lives of Norman Mailer*. New York: Paragon House, 1991. See 91.22.

Seaver, Edwin. *So Far, So Good: Recollections of a Life in Publishing*, passim. Westport, Conn.: Lawrence Hill, 1986. See 48.1.

"A Shaky Start." *Time*, 27 October, 1967, 25. Brief, unfriendly description of Mailer speaking at the Ambassador Theater in Washington, D.C. prior to the March on the Pentagon. Mailer used it in the opening of *The Armies of the Night* (68.8).

Sokolov, Raymond A. "Flying High with Mailer." *Newsweek*, 9 December 1968, 84, 86-88. See 68.29.

Soll, Rick. "Norman Mailer: A Man, an Artist, a Cultural Phenomenon." *Chicago Sun-Times*, 7 August 1983, "Living" Section, 1, 6-7, 12. See 83.47.
Spencer, Scott. "The Old Man and the Novel." *New York Times Magazine*, 22 September 1991, 28-31, 40, 42, 47. See 91.10.
Stern, Richard G. "Report from the MLA." *New York Review of Books*, 17 February 1966, 26-28. See 66.7.
Toback, James. "At Play in the Fields of the Bored." *Esquire*, December 1968, 150-55, 22, 24, 26, 28, 30, 32, 34, 36. Rpt: (partial) 71.28. See 68.28.
Trilling, Diana. "The Prisoner of Sex." In *We Must March My Darlings: A Critical Decade*, 199-210. New York: Harcourt Brace Jovanovich, 1977. Rpt: Lennon (1986). See 77.14.
Truscott, Lucian K., IV. "Mailer's Birthday." *Village Voice*, 8 February 1973, 1, 24-26. See 73.6.
Vidal, Gore. "Norman Mailer's Self-Advertisements." In *United States: Essays, 1952-1992*, 31-40. New York: Random House, 1993. Rpt: Lucid (1971), Bloom (1986). See 60.3.
Weatherby, W.J. *Squaring Off: Mailer vs. Baldwin*. New York: Mason/Charter, 1977. The Mailer-Baldwin rivalry is exaggerated in this largely derivative study, which nevertheless provides insights on their relationship.
Willingham, Calder. "The Way It Isn't Done: Notes on the Distress of Norman Mailer." *Esquire*, December 1963, 306-8. Rpt: Lucid (1971). See 63.9.

CULTURAL BACKGROUNDS

Aldridge, John W. *The Devil in the Fire: Retrospective Essays on American Literature and Culture, 1951-1971*. New York: Harper's Magazine Press, 1972. Historical chronicle of major literary developments and critiques of the most significant post-World War II writers, including Mailer.
Anderson, Elliott, and Mary Kinzie. *The Little Magazine in America: A Modern Documentary History*. Yonkers, N.Y.: Pushcart Press, 1978. Forty-two chapters on the great literary magazines and Peter Martin's detailed, annotated bibliography of 85 of them, including *Big Table, Evergreen Review, Fuck You, New American Review, Paris Review, Partisan Review* and *Story*. Definitive.
Beach, Joseph Warren. *American Fiction: 1920-1940*. New York: Macmillan, 1941. Classic study of eight writers—John Dos Passos, William Faulkner, Erskine Caldwell, John P. Marquand, Ernest Hemingway, Thomas Wolfe, James T. Farrell and John Steinbeck—which Mailer "devoured" in college, as he explains in "Last Advertisement for Myself before the Way Out" in 59.13.
Bloom, Alexander. *Prodigal Sons: The New York Intellectuals and Their World*. New York: Oxford University Press, 1986. Standard work on the subject.
Bowers, John. *The Colony*. New York: E.P. Dutton, 1971. Memoir of James Jones's writing colony in Illinois, including Mailer's 1954 visit.
Bradbury, Malcolm. *The Modern American Novel*. revised edition. New York: Viking, 1992. Balanced and insightful overview of the American novel from the 1890s to the 1990s.

Broyard, Anatole. *Kafka Was the Rage: A Greenwich Village Memoir*. New York: Crown, 1996. The Village in the late 1940s.

Burgess, Anthony. *99 Novels: The Best in English since 1939*. New York: Summit Books, 1984. *The Naked and the Dead* (48.2) and *Ancient Evenings* (83.18) are included.

Cawelti, John G. "The Writer as a Celebrity: Some Aspects of American Literature as Popular Culture." *Studies in American Fiction* 5 (spring 1977), 161-74. Careful, detached discussion of celebrity and fame in the careers of nineteenth and twentieth century American writers, including Poe, James, Hemingway and Mailer.

Charters, Ann, editor. *The Portable Beat Reader*. New York: Viking Penguin, 1992. Perhaps the best collection of the work of the Beat writers, including Jack Kerouac, Allan Ginsberg, William Burroughs, John Clellon Holmes and many others. Mailer's "The White Negro" (57.1) is included.

Cox, James M. "Autobiography and America." In *Aspects of America: Selected Papers from the English Institute*, edited by J. Hillis Miller, 143-72. New York: Columbia University Press, 1971. Lucid discussion of the forebears of Mailer and other 1960s autobiographical-political writers: Ben Franklin, Henry David Thoreau and Henry Adams.

de Grazia, Edward. *Girls Lean Back Everywhere: The Law of Obscenity and the Assault on Genius*. New York: Random House, 1992. Comprehensive account of the century-long struggle against censorship. See 92.12.

Dickstein, Morris. *Gates of Eden: American Culture in the Sixties*. New York: Basic Books, 1977. Mailer is a touchstone in this major cultural history.

Eisinger, Chester E. *Fiction of the Forties*. Chicago: University of Chicago Press, 1963. Survey of the emotional temper of the decade with extended discussions of Mailer, Budd Schulberg, Irwin Shaw, John Dos Passos, Mary McCarthy, Truman Capote, Saul Bellow, Nelson Algren, Lionel Trilling and others.

Feldman, Gene, and Marx Gartenberg, editors. *The Beat Generation and the Angry Young Men*. Secaucus, N.J.: Citadel Press, 1958. First anthology of the Beat writers and first to reprint "The White Negro" (57.1).

Fiedler, Leslie A. *Waiting for the End*. New York: Stein and Day, 1964. Essays on the shift in the U.S. from "a whiskey culture to a drug culture."

Frankfort, Ellen. *The Voice: Life at "The Village Voice."* New York: William Morrow, 1976. Account of the newspaper's movement away from its more radical origins. See 56.1-.17.

Geismar, Maxwell. *American Moderns: From Rebellion to Conformity*. New York: Hill and Wang, 1958. Essays on American fiction at mid-century, from Theodore Dreiser and William Faulkner to Mailer, James Jones and William Styron. See 48.3.

Girgus, Sam B. *The New Covenant: Jewish Writers and the American Idea*. Chapel Hill: University of North Carolina Press, 1984. Historical overview of Jewish writers and American culture, with close readings; Mailer and Abraham Cahan are the key figures.

Gitlin, Todd. *The Sixties: Years of Hope, Days of Rage*. New York: Bantam, 1987. Benchmark examination of the New Left.

Green, Martin. "Norman Mailer and the City of New York: Faustian Radical-
    ism." In *Cities of Light and Sons of the Morning: A Cultural Psychology for an
    Age of Revolution*, 58-89. Boston: Little, Brown: 1972. Green's Mailer is a
    Jewish Faust, epitome of 1960s New York. Rpt: Partial in Lennon (1986).
Hamill, Pete. *A Drinking Life*. Boston: Little, Brown, 1994. Crisp memoir of
    New York in the 1950s and 1960s, with asides on Mailer.
Hayes, Harold, editor. *Smiling through the Apocalypse: Esquire's History of the
    Sixties*. New York: McCall, 1969. From the pages of the decade's indis-
    pensable magazine, the best collection on the 1960s. Two of Mailer's
    most important pieces (60.9 and 63.8) from the period are included.
Hellman, John. *American Myth and the Legacy of Vietnam*. New York: Co-
    lumbia University Press, 1986. Examination of the reflection of the Viet-
    nam War in American history, literature, film and popular culture.
    Mailer's *Why Are We in Vietnam?* (67.15) is discussed.
Hoffman, Abbie. *The Best of Abbie Hoffman*, edited by Daniel Simon and
    Hoffman. New York: Four Walls Eight Windows, 1989. Mailer provided
    an introduction to this collection of the writings of the mad genius of
    the counterculture. See 80.26.
Hoffman, Daniel, editor. *Harvard Guide to Contemporary American Writing*.
    Cambridge: Harvard University Press, 1979. Critical survey of the most
    important American writing from the end of World War II through the
    1970s.
Holmes, John Clellon. *Passionate Opinions: The Cultural Essays*. Fayetteville,
    Ark.: University of Arkansas Press, 1988. Essays on the Beat writers by
    their unofficial scribe.
Johnson, Michael L. *The New Journalism: The Underground Press, the Artists of
    Nonfiction, and Changes in the Established Media*. Lawrence: University
    Press of Kansas, 1971. Rpt: Partial in Adams (1974). Pioneering study.
Jones, Howard Mumford, and Richard M. Ludwig. *Guide to American Litera-
    ture and Its Backgrounds since 1890*. 4th edition, revised and enlarged. Cam-
    bridge: Harvard University Press, 1972. Select bibliography and outline
    of American literature in its intellectual, social and cultural contexts.
Jones, Peter G. *War and the Novelist: Appraising the American War Novel*.
    Columbia: University of Missouri Press, 1976. Comprehensive study
    of World War II novels, including those by Mailer, James Jones, Irwin
    Shaw, James Gould Cozzens and Kurt Vonnegut.
Jumonville, Neil. *Critical Crossings: The New York Intellectuals in Postwar
    America*. Berkeley and Los Angeles: University of California Press, 1991.
    The debates and dilemmas of the cultural elites. Fine opening chapter
    on the 1949 Waldorf conference.
Klein, Holger, editor (with John Flower and Eric Homberger). *The Second
    World War in Fiction*. London: Macmillan, 1984. Contains chapters on
    the U.S., Britain, France, Germany, the Soviet Union and Japan. *The
    Naked and the Dead* (48.2) is given careful analysis, especially the "un-
    easy" liberalism of Lt. Hearn.
Klein, Marcus, editor. *The American Novel since World War II*. New York:
    Fawcett, 1969. One of the best collections on this topic to date. Includes

Mailer's 1965 address to the Modern Language Association. See 66.5.

Kazin, Alfred. *Bright Book of Life: American Novelists and Storytellers from Hemingway to Mailer*. Boston: Little, Brown, 1973. Major study by our finest postwar critic.

_____. *Contemporaries*. Boston: Little, Brown, 1962. Rich collection of Kazin's reviews and essays from the 1940s through the early 1960s including his review of *Advertisements for Myself* (59.13).

Kerrane, Kevin, and Ben Yagoda, editors. *The Art of Fact: A Historical Anthology of Literary Journalism*. New York: Scribner's, 1997. Most comprehensive collection of its kind, extending from Daniel Defoe and Jack London through Mailer, Michael Herr and Rosemary Mahoney.

Lasch, Christopher. *The New Radicalism in America, 1889-1963: The Intellectual as a Social Type*. New York: Random House, 1965. The roots of American radicalism and a critique of "the isolation of American intellectuals, as a class, from the main currents of American life." Mailer is the chief whipping boy.

Lois, George. *Covering the 60s: George Lois, the "Esquire" Era*. New York: Monacelli Press, 1996. Full reproduction of 70 of George Lois's covers for *Esquire* in the 1960s and 1970s, with commentary. See 71.27.

Macdonald, Dwight. *The Memoirs of a Revolutionist: Essays in Political Criticism*. New York: Farrar, Straus and Cudahy, 1957. Political essays and reports by an iconoclastic critic, including a memoir of Macdonald's debate on Russia with Mailer at Mt. Holyoke College in the winter of 1952. See 60.8, 83.57.

Madden, David, editor. *American Dreams, American Nightmares*. Carbondale: Southern Illinois University Press, 1970. Nineteen original critical essays on fiction dealing with dream and nightmare themes, including Ihab Hassan's essay on *Why Are We in Vietnam?* (67.15).

Malin, Irving, editor. *Contemporary American-Jewish Literature*. Bloomington: Indiana University Press, 1973. One of the best collections on these writers, including both general essays and individual appreciations of Mailer, Saul Bellow, Lionel Trilling, I.B. Singer, Leslie Fiedler and others, with an extensive bibliography.

McAuliffe, Kevin Michael. *The Great American Newspaper: The Rise and Fall of "The Village Voice."* New York: Scribner's, 1978. Standard history.

McDarrah, Fred W., editor. *Kerouac and Friends: A Beat Generation Album*. New York: William Morrow, 1984. Collection of key historical articles and essays on the Beat movement by a veteran *Village Voice* photographer, with 190 of his photographs.

Millett, Kate. *Sexual Politics*. Garden City, N.J.: Doubleday, 1970. Feminist critique of Mailer, D.H. Lawrence, Sigmund Freud, Henry Miller and others. Mailer responded in *The Prisoner of Sex* (71.20).

Millgate, Michael. *American Social Fiction: James to Cozzens*. Edinburgh: Oliver and Boyd, 1964. Elegant study of American novelists from 1887 to the late 1950s, including Mailer.

Mills, Nicolaus, editor. *Legacy of "Dissent": 40 Years of Writing from "Dissent" Magazine*. New York: Simon and Schuster, 1994. See 54.1.

_____. *The New Journalism: A Historical Anthology*. New York: McGraw-Hill, 1974. One of the earliest collections of literary journalism, with useful prefatory matter.

Panichas, George A., editor. *The Politics of Twentieth-Century Novelists*. New York: Hawthorn Books, 1971. Essays on British, continental and American novelists, including Mailer, with an important introduction by John W. Aldridge.

Phillips, William. *A Partisan View: Five Decades of the Literary Life*. New York: Stein and Day, 1983. Memoir by *Partisan Review*'s long-time editor. See 52.1, 68.4.

Podhoretz, Norman, editor. *The Commentary Reader: Two Decades of Articles and Stories*. New York: Atheneum, 1966. Contains Alfred Kazin's important introduction, "The Jew as Modern American Writer," and many other significant essays. See 62.22, 68.4.

Polsgrove, Carol. *It Wasn't Pretty Folks, but Didn't We Have Fun: "Esquire" in the Sixties*. New York: W.W. Norton, 1995. The serial publication of *An American Dream* (64.2-.9) is but one strand in this history, which focuses on editor Harold Hayes.

Rader, Dotson. *Blood Dues*. New York: Knopf, 1973. Memoir of the counterculture in the 1960s, including the rise and fall of the SDS. See 72.18.

Rahv, Philip. *Essays on Literature and Politics, 1932-1972*, edited by Arabel J. Porter and Andrew J. Dvosin. Boston: Houghton Mifflin, 1978. Contains the most important essays of Rahv, a long-time editor of *Partisan Review*, including those from his influential 1949 collection, *Image and Idea*, and his review of *An American Dream* (65.7).

Reed, T.V. *Fifteen Jugglers, Five Believers: Literary Politics of American Social Movements*. Berkeley and Los Angeles: University of California Press, 1992. Argument for the synchronicity of literary theory and political action via an examination of writings by Mailer, James Agee, Ralph Ellison and others.

Rideout, Walter B. *The Radical Novel in the United States, 1900-1954*. New York: Hill and Wang, 1956. Still the finest critical survey of these novels, including Mailer's first two.

Scholes, Robert, and Robert Kellog. *The Nature of Narrative*. New York: Oxford University Press, 1968. Comprehensive and stimulating historical overview.

Smith, Richard Norton. *The Harvard Century: The Making of a University to a Nation*. New York: Simon and Schuster, 1986. History of Harvard, focusing on five of its greatest presidents.

Solotaroff, Theodore. *The Red Hot Vacuum and Other Pieces on the Writing of the Sixties*. New York: Atheneum, 1970. Solid collection of literary journalism about Mailer and his contemporaries: Philip Roth, Saul Bellow, Flannery O'Connor, William Burroughs, Seymour Krim and others.

Tabbi, Joseph. *Postmodern Sublime: Technology and American Writing from Mailer to Cyberpunk*. Ithaca, N.Y.: Cornell University Press, 1995. Ambivalent attitudes to technology in the writings of Mailer, Don DeLillo and Joseph McElroy.

Tanner, Tony. *City of Words: American Fiction, 1950-1970*. New York: Harper and Row, 1971. The finest twentieth-century British critic of American fiction examines the work of 25 novelists, including Ralph Ellison, Thomas Pynchon, Susan Sontag, Ken Kesey, Philip Roth and Saul Bellow. His chapter on Mailer, "On the Parapet," is unlikely to be surpassed. Rpt: Partial in Adams (1974), Bloom (1986).

Tytell, John. *Naked Angels: The Lives and Literature of the Beat Generation*. New York: McGraw-Hill, 1976. The origins of the Beat sensibility in the culture of the 1950s.

Vogelgesang, Sandy. *The Long Dark Night of the Soul: The American Intellectual Left and the Vietnam War*. New York: Harper and Row, 1974. Early and excellent overview of the New Left's involvement in the anti-war movement, including Mailer's.

Wakefield, Dan. *New York in the Fifties*. Boston: Houghton Mifflin, 1992. New York City during the decade in which American society began its transmogrification.

_____. *Supernation at Peace and War: Being Certain Observations, Depositions, Testimonies, and Graffiti Gathered on a One-Man Fact-and-Fantasy Tour of the Most Powerful Nation in the World*. Boston: Little, Brown, 1968. Account of Wakefield's trip around the United States and his assessment of a nation moving deeper into the Vietnam War.

Weber, Ronald, editor. *The Reporter as Artist: A Look at the New Journalism Controversy*. New York: Hastings House, 1974. Early and valuable anthology of 26 reprinted pieces that debate the New Journalism.

Whitmer, Peter O. (with Bruce VanWyngarden). *Aquarius Revisited: Seven Who Created the Sixties Counterculture that Changed America: William Burroughs, Allen Ginsberg, Ken Kesey, Timothy Leary, Norman Mailer, Tom Robbins, Hunter S. Thompson*. New York: Macmillan, 1987. Based on interviews with all seven.

Wolfe, Tom. *The New Journalism, with an Anthology*, edited by Tom Wolfe and E.W. Johnson. New York: Harper and Row, 1973. The editors' selections are as important as Wolfe's apology for literary journalism and his attack on the contemporary novel.

Wolf, Daniel, and Edwin Fancher. *The Village Voice Reader: A Mixed Bag from the Greenwich Village Newspaper*. New York: Doubleday, 1962. The first anthology of essays and columns from the *Voice*, including several of Mailer's, and Kenneth Tynan's review of *Advertisements for Myself* (59.13). See 56.1-.17.

Wreszin, Michael. *A Rebel in Defense of Tradition: The Life and Politics of Dwight Macdonald*. New York: Basic Books, 1994. Standard biography of Mailer's longtime friend (1949 to 1983), which includes accounts of the 1949 Waldorf conference and the 1968 march on the Pentagon. See 49.1.

REVIEWS

The reviews listed below were chosen because of: 1) representative quality; 2) intrinsic interest; 3) reviewer's reputation and/or relationship with

Mailer; or 4) subsequent comment by Mailer. Obviously, some reviews meet more than one criteria.

The Naked and the Dead (48.2)

Geismar, Maxwell. "Nightmare on Anopopei." *Saturday Review*, 8 May 1948, 10-11. Positive. See 48.3.

Lardner, John. "Pacific Battle, Good and Big." *New Yorker*, 15 May 1948, 115-17. Positive.

"Men in War." *Newsweek*, 10 May 1948, 86-87. Positive.

Prescott, Orville. Books of the Times. *New York Times*, 20 December 1948, 23. Positive. Rpt: Lennon (1986).

Pritchett, V.S. "Kinsey's Army." *New Statesman and Nation* (London), 14 May 1949. Positive.

Smith, Harrison. "Sizing Up the Comers." *Saturday Review*, 12 February 1949, 9-11. Negative.

Barbary Shore (51.1)

Howe, Irving. "Some Political Novels." *Nation*, 16 June 1951, 568-69. Negative. Rpt: Lennon (1986).

"Last of the Leftists?" *Time*, 28 May 1951, 110. Negative.

Rolo, Charles. "A House in Brooklyn." *Atlantic*, June 1951, 82. Mixed.

West, Anthony. "East Meets West, Author Meets Allegory." *New Yorker*, 9 June 1951, 106-9. Negative. Rpt: (partial) 59.13.

The Deer Park (55.4)

Cowley, Malcolm. "Mr. Mailer Tells a Tale of Love, Art, Corruption." *New York Herald Tribune Book Review*, 23 October 1955, 5. Positive.

Gill, Brendan. "Small Trumpet." *New Yorker*, 22 October 1955, 173-75. Mixed. Rpt: Lennon (1986).

Lindner, Robert. Review of *The Deer Park*. *Village Voice*, 9 November 1955. Positive. See 56.9.

"Love among the Love-Buckets." *Time*, 17 October 1955, 122, 124. Negative. Rpt: 59.13.

Nichols, Dudley. "Secret Places of the Groin." *Nation*, 5 December 1955, 393-96. Negative.

"Norman Mailer's Despair." *Newsweek*, 17 October 1955, 122-23. Positive. Rpt: 59.13.

Advertisements for Myself (59.13)

Davis, Robert Gorham. "Norman Mailer and the Trap of Egotism." *Story* 33 (spring 1960), 117-19. Negative.

Kazin, Alfred. "How Good is Norman Mailer?" *Reporter*, 26 November 1959, 40-41. Positive. Rpt: Kazin (1962), Lucid (1971).

Steiner, George. "Naked but Not Dead." *Encounter*, December 1961, 67-70. Positive. Rpt: Lennon (1986).

Tynan, Kenneth. Review of *Advertisements for Myself*. *Village Voice*, 18 November 1959. Positive. Rpt: Wolf and Fancher (1962). See 56.1-56.17.

Vidal, Gore. "The Norman Mailer Syndrome." *Nation*, 2 January, 1960, 13-16. Mixed. Rpt: Lucid (1971), Bloom (1986), Vidal (1993). See 60.3.

Deaths for the Ladies (and Other Disasters) (62.3)

Macdonald, Dwight. "Art, Life and Violence." *Commentary*, August 1962, 169-72. Mixed.

[Simmons, Charles]. "Running Down." *Time*, 30 March 1962, 84. Negative. Rpt: 71.31.

The Presidential Papers (63.37)

Decter, Midge. "Mailer's Campaign." *Commentary*, February 1964, 83-85. Positive. Rpt: Lucid (1971).

Galbraith, John Kenneth. "The Kennedys Didn't Reply." *New York Times Book Review*, 17 November 1963, 6. Negative.

Wills, Garry. "The Art of Not Writing Novels." *National Review*, 14 January 1964, 31-33. Negative.

An American Dream (65.7)

Aldridge, John W. "The Big Comeback of Norman Mailer." *Life*, 19 March, 12. Positive. Rpt: 65.9 (partial); in an expanded form in: Aldridge (1966), Braudy (1972).

Bersani, Leo. "The Interpretation of Dreams." *Partisan Review* 32 (fall 1965), 603-8. Positive. Rpt: Lucid (1971), Braudy (1972).

Didion, Joan. "A Social Eye." *National Review*, 20 April 1965, 329-30. Positive.

Epstein, Joseph. "Norman X: The Literary Man's Cassius Clay." *New Republic*, 17 April 1965, 22, 24-25. Negative.

Hardwick, Elizabeth. "Bad Boy." *Partisan Review* 32 (spring 1964), 291-94. Negative. Rpt: Lucid (1971). See 65.9.

Wolfe, Tom. "Son of Crime and Punishment, or: How to Go Eight Fast Rounds with the Heavyweight Champ and Lose." (*Washington Post*) *Book Week*, 14 March 1965, 1, 10, 12-13. Negative. Rpt: Lucid (1971).

Cannibals and Christians (66.11)

Fremont-Smith, Eliot. "A Nobel for Norman?" *New York Times*, 22 August 1966, 31. Positive.

Handlin, Oscar. Review of *Cannibals and Christians*. *Atlantic*, October 1966, 144. Negative.

Tanner, Tony. "In the Lion's Den." *Partisan Review* 34 (summer 1967), 465-71. Positive. Rpt: Lennon (1986).

Wain, John. "Mailer's America." *New Republic*, 1 October 1966, 19-20. Positive.

Why Are We in Vietnam? (67.15)

Donoghue, Denis. "Sweepstakes." *New York Review of Books*, 28 September 1967, 5-6. Positive.

Hicks, Granville. "Lark in the Race for the Presidency." *Saturday Review*, 16 September 1967, 39-40. Negative.

"Hot Damn." *Time*, 8 September 1967, D12-D13. Negative.

Glenn, Eugene. Review of *Why Are We in Vietnam?* *Village Voice*, 28 September 1967, 6-7, 41. Positive.

Lehmann-Haupt, Christopher. "Norman Mailer as Joycean Punster and Manipulator of Language." *Commonweal*, 8 December 1967, 338-39. Positive.

The Armies of the Night (68.8)

Gilman, Richard. "What Mailer Has Done." *New Republic*, 8 June 1968, 27-31. Positive. Rpt: Braudy (1972).

Kazin, Alfred. "The Trouble He's Seen." *New York Times Book Review*, 5 May 1968, 1-2, 26. Positive. Rpt: Lennon (1986).

Macdonald, Dwight. Politics. *Esquire*, May 1968, 41-42, 44, 194, 196; June 1968, 46, 48, 50, 183. Positive. Rpt: Macdonald (1985). See 83.57.

O'Brien, Conor Cruise. "Confessions of the Last American." *New York Review of Books*, 20 June 1968, 16-18. Positive.

Puzo, Mario. "Generalissimo Mailer: Hero of His Own Dispatches." (*Chicago Tribune*) "Book World," 28 April 1968, 1, 3. Negative.

Simon, John. "Mailer on the March." *Hudson Review* 21 (autumn 1968), 541-45. Negative.

Miami and the Siege of Chicago (68.25)

Buckley, Priscilla L. "Seeing It like Mailer Does." *National Review*, 11 February 1969, 129-30. Negative.

Fremont-Smith, Eliot. "Family Report." *New York Times*, 28 October 1968, 45. Positive.

Richardson, Jack. "The Aesthetics of Norman Mailer." *New York Review of Books*, 8 May 1969, 3-4. Positive. Rpt: Lucid (1971), Bloom (1986).

Shaw, Peter. "The Conventions, 1968." *Commentary*, December 1968, 93-96. Positive.

Of a Fire on the Moon (71.1)

DeMott, Benjamin. "Inside Apollo 11 with Aquarius Mailer." *Saturday Review*, 16 January 1971, 25-27, 57-58. Mixed. See 71.8.

Dickstein, Morris. "A Trip to Inner and Outer Space." *New York Times Book Review*, 10 January 1971, 1, 42-43, 45. Positive.

Poirier, Richard. "Ups and Downs of Mailer." *New Republic*, 23 January 1971, 23-26. Mixed. Rpt: Braudy (1972); partial in Poirier (1972).

Sisk, John P. "Aquarius Rising." *Commentary*, May 1971, 83-84. Positive.

The Prisoner of Sex (71.20)

Brophy, Brigid. "Meditations on Norman Mailer, by Norman Mailer, against the Day a Norman Mailest Comes Along." *New York Times Book Review*, 23 May 1971, 1, 14, 16. Negative. See 71.22.

Broyard, Anatole. "Norman Writes a Dithyramb." *New York Times*, 27 May 1971, 41. Positive.

Lodge, David. "Male, Mailer, Female." *New Blackfriars* (London), December 1971, 558-61. Mixed.

Oates, Joyce Carol. "With Norman Mailer at the Sex Circus I: Out of the Machine." *Atlantic*, July 1971, 42-45. Mixed. Rpt: Adams (1974), Bloom (1986).

Pritchett, V.S. "With Norman Mailer at the Sex Circus II: Into the Cage." *Atlantic*, July 1971, 40-42. Positive.

Existential Errands (72.7)

Buchanan, Cynthia. "We Read Him because He Is Our Genius." *New York Times Book Review*, 16 April 1972, 27-28. Positive.

Oberbeck, S.K. "Like an Ahab Hunting Many Whales." *Washington Post Book World*, 30 April 1972, 5. Positive.

St. George and the Godfather (72.17)

Solotaroff, Robert. "The Glop of the Wad." *Nation*, 15 January 1973, 87-89. Positive.

Wills, Garry. "Aquarius Returns to Miami." *New York Times Book Review*, 15 October 1972, 1, 22. Positive.

Marilyn: A Biography (73.30)

Bengis, Ingrid. "Monroe according to Mailer: One Legend Feeds on Another." *Ms.*, October 1973, 44-47. Mixed. Rpt: Lennon (1986).

Fuller, Edmund. "Mailer's Sexploitation of Marilyn." *Wall Street Journal*, 24 September 1973, 14. Negative.

Kael, Pauline. "A Rip-Off with Genius." *New York Times Book Review*, 22 July 1973, 1-3. Mixed. See Mailer's comment on Kael in 73.12.

The Fight (75.12)

Higgins, George V. "Another View of Foreman-Ali." *Boston Globe*, 3 August 1975, Sec. A, p. 15. Positive.

Wood, Michael. "Mohammad Ali versus George Foreman via Norman Mailer." *New York Times Book Review*, 27 July 1975, 1-2. Positive.

Genius and Lust: A Journey through the Major Writings of Henry Miller (76.12)

Crews, Frederick. "Stuttering Giant." *New York Review of Books*, 3 March 1977, 7-9. Negative.

Gilman, Richard. "Norman Mailer Searches the Tropics—'Mr. Miller, I Presume.'" *Village Voice*, 4 October 1976, 43-44. Positive.

The Executioner's Song (79.14)

Balz, Douglas. "Gilmore Story Shows Mailer at His Finest." *Miami Herald*, 21 October 1979. Positive.

Didion, Joan. "'I Want to Go Ahead and Do It.'" *New York Times Book Review*, 7 October 1979, 1, 26-27. Positive. Rpt: Lennon (1986).

Lodge, David. "From a View to a Death." *Times Literary Supplement*, 11 January 1980, 27-28. Positive.

Lucid, Robert F. "A Man Sought Death and, Too Late, Found It." *Philadelphia Inquirer*, 21 October 1979, Sec. M, p. 14. Positive.

McMurtry, Larry. "Review of *The Executioner's Song*." *New West*, 22 October 1979, 82. Positive.

Stern, Richard. "Where is That Self-Mocking Literary Imp?" *Chicago*, January 1980, 108. Mixed.

Pieces and Pontifications (82.16)

Feeney, Mark. "Not Mailer's Best, but Brilliant Anyway." *Boston Globe*, 25 June, 84. Positive.

Leonard, John. Books of the Times. *New York Times*, 3 June 1982, 25. Positive.

Ancient Evenings (83.18)

Bloom, Harold. "Norman in Egypt." *New York Review of Books*, 28 April 1983, 3-4, 6. Mixed. Rpt: Bloom (1986).

Burgess, Anthony. "Magical Droppings. " (London) *Observer*, 5 June 1983, 30. Positive.

Fiedler, Leslie. "Going for the Long Ball." *Psychology Today*, June 1983, 16-17. Negative.

Poirier, Richard. "In Pyramid and Palace." *Times Literary Supplement*, 10 June 1983, 591-92. Positive. Rpt: Lennon (1986).

Wolcott, James. "Enter the Mummy." *Harper's*, May 1983, 81-83. Negative.

Tough Guys Don't Dance (84.17)

Lennon, J. Michael. "Mailer Spins a Spellbinding Tale." (Springfield, Ill.) *State Journal-Register*, 26 August 1984, 21. Positive.

Manning, Margaret. "From Mailer, a Little Mayhem in P-town." *Boston Globe*, 5 August 1984, Sec. B, p. 11. Negative.

Ricks, Christopher. "Rectum." *London Review of Books*, 18-31 October 1984, 15. Positive.

Harlot's Ghost (91.26)

Burgess, Anthony. "A Secret History of Our Time." *Washington Post Book World*, 29 September 1991, 1, 10. Positive.

Koenig, Rhoda. "Devil's Party." *New York*, 7 October 1991, 108-9. Positive.

Rushdie, Salman. "God Squad versus the King Brothers." *Independent on Sunday* (London), 20 October 1991. Positive.

Sheed, Wilfred. "Armageddon Now?" *New York Review of Books*, 5 December 1991, 41-48. Positive.

Simon, John. "The Company They Keep." *New York Times Book Review*, 29 September 1991, 1, 24-26. Negative. See 91.48.

Oswald's Tale (95.16)

Aldridge, John W. "Documents as Narrative." *Atlantic*, May 1995, 120-25. Positive.

Kakutani, Michiko. "Oswald and Mailer: The Eternal Basic Questions." *New York Times*, 25 April 1995, Sec. C, p. 19. Negative. See 95.36.

Massie, Allan. "The Road from Minsk to Dallas." *Daily Telegraph* (London), 2 July 1995. Positive.

Stone, Robert. "The Loser's Loser." *New York Review of Books*, 22 June 1995, 7-10. Positive.

Portrait of Picasso as a Young Man **(95.38)**

du Plessix Gray, Francine. "Stud Wars." *Los Angeles Times Book Review*, 15 October 1995, 1, 15. Negative.

Shattuck, Roger. "Brinksmanship." *New York Review of Books*, 11 January 1996, 4-8. Negative.

Taylor, Robert. "Mailer Conjures a Mailer-Like Picasso." *Boston Globe*, 25 October 1995. Positive.

The Gospel according to the Son **(97.13)**

Kakutani, Michiko. "Norman Mailer's Perception of Jesus." *New York Times*, 14 April 1997, Sec. B, p. 7. Negative. See 95.36.

Kermode, Frank. "Advertisements for Himself." *New York Review of Books*, 15 May 1997, 4, 6-8. Positive.

Review of *The Gospel according to the Son*. *Publisher's Weekly*, 31 March 1997, 59. Positive. Rpt: On the dust jacket of the second impression and the back cover of the subsequent Random House softcover edition.

Updike, John. "Stones into Bread." *New Yorker*, 12 May 1997, 92-94, 96-97. Positive.

The Time of Our Time **(98.7)**

Denby, David. "The Contender." *New Yorker*, 20 April 1998, 60-66, 68-71. Positive. See 98.3.

Menand, Louis. "Beat the Devil." *New York Review of Books*, 22 October 1998, 27-30. Positive.

Shapiro, James. "Advertisements for Himself." *New York Times Book Review*, 10 may 1998, 16-17. Positive.

Silver, Daniel J. "His American Nightmare." *Wall Street Journal*, 6 May 1998, Sec. A, p. 20. Negative.

CRITICAL ESSAYS AND BOOKS

Adams, Laura. *Existential Battles: The Growth of Norman Mailer*. Athens: Ohio University Press, 1976. Good discussion of themes and techniques, especially early narrators; includes description of extra-literary activities.

_____, editor. *Will the Real Norman Mailer Please Stand Up*. Port Washington, N.Y.: Kennikat Press, 1974. Fourteen essays and reviews and one interview examining Mailer's protean activities. Includes two essays on Mailer's cosmology, a long bibliography and Adams's useful introduction.

Aldridge, John W. *Classics and Contemporaries*. Columbia: University of Missouri Press, 1992, 54-58, 186-97. Contains Aldridge's reviews of *Genius and Lust* (76.12), *The Long Patrol* (71.29), and *Harlot's Ghost* (91.26).

_____. "Mailer, Burns, and Shaw." In *After the Lost Generation: A Study of the Writers of Two Wars*. 1951. Reprint, with an introduction by Norman Mailer, New York: Arbor House, 1985, 133-56. In his introduction Mailer says, "Aldridge was the nearest guideline to absolute truth that the working novelist had in my young days." See 85.14.

_____. "Norman Mailer: The Energy of New Success." In *Time to Murder and Create: The Contemporary Novel in Crisis*, 149-63. New York: David McKay, 1966. Expanded version of Aldridge's influential review of *An American Dream* (65.7). See 65.9.

Algren, Nelson. "New York: Rapietta Greensponge, Girl Counselor Comes to My Aid." In *Who Lost An American*, 1-29. New York: Macmillan, 1963. Satirical portrait of Mailer (Norman Manlifellow) and James Baldwin (Giovanni Johnson) and other New York literary figures. See 63.10.

Amis, Martin. "The Avenger and the Bitch." In *The Moronic Inferno and Other Visits to America*, 37-43. New York: Viking, 1987. See 86.42.

Anderson, Chris. "Norman Mailer: The Record of a War." In *Style as Argument: Contemporary American Nonfiction*, 82-132. Carbondale: Southern Illinois University Press, 1987. Concrete reading of Mailer's "rhetoric of self-dramatization," with deft discussion of Mailer's "Left-conservatism."

Apple, Max. "Inside Norman Mailer." In *The Oranging of America and Other Stories*, 49-60. New York: Grossman, 1976. One of the best comic fantasy struggles with a larger-than-life Mailer.

Arlett, Robert M. "The Veiled Fist of a Master Executioner." *Criticism* 29, no. 2 (1987), 215-32. Examination of free indirect speech in *The Executioner's Song* (79.14).

Bailey, Jennifer. *Norman Mailer: Quick-Change Artist*. New York: Harper and Row, 1979. Provides extended summaries of his work from a feminist perspective. Bailey sees *Advertisements for Myself* (59.13) as the key transitional work.

Balbert, Peter. "From *Lady Chatterly's Lover* to *The Deer Park* [55.4]: Lawrence, Mailer, and the Dialectic of Erotic Risk." *Studies in the Novel* 22 (spring 1990), 67-81. Best study of Lawrence's influence. See 90.2.

Barnes, Hazel. "The Negative Rebels: The Apolitical Left." In *An Existential Ethics*, 56-96. Chicago: University of Chicago Press, 1967. Professional philosopher's sympathetic examination of Mailer's existential credentials.

Begiebing, Robert J. *Acts of Regeneration: Allegory and Archetype in the Works of Norman Mailer*. Columbia: University of Missouri Press, 1980. Close reading of major works from *Barbary Shore* (51.1) on; fine discussion of Mailer's "heroic consciousness."

_____. "Norman Mailer: The Magician as Tragic Hero." In *Toward a New Synthesis: John Fowles, John Gardner, Norman Mailer*, 87-125. Ann Arbor, Mich.: UMI Research Press, 1989. Demonstration of how Mailer uses metafictional technique but rejects postmodern negativism. Important study of *Ancient Evenings* (83.18).

Berthoff, Warner. "Witness and Testament: Two Contemporary Classics." In *Aspects of Narrative: Selected Papers from the English Institute*, edited by J. Hillis Miller, 173-98. New York: Columbia University Press, 1971. One of the first extended treatments of *The Armies of the Night* (68.8), which Berthoff places—along with *The Autobiography of Malcolm X*—in the American tradition of personal witness and "the saving counterforce of personality."

245

Bloom, Harold, editor. *Norman Mailer: Modern Critical Views*. New York: Chelsea House, 1986. Sixteen reviews and essays covering Mailer's major works and emphasizing the influence of Hemingway, with Bloom's brief introduction.

Booth, Wayne. *The Company We Keep: An Ethics of Fiction*, 207-10, 327-36. Berkeley and Los Angeles: University of California Press, 1988. Useful to gauge how Mailer's public image has alienated an important critic.

Braudy, Leo. "*Maidstone: A Mystery* by Norman Mailer." In *Native Informant: Essays on Film, Fiction and Popular Culture*, 60-63, 145-51. New York: Oxford University Press, 1991. Rpt: Adams (1974). Informed comment on Mailer's film and the Mailer-Pynchon dichotomy.

_____, editor. *Norman Mailer: A Collection of Critical Essays*. Englewood Cliff, N.J.: Prentice-Hall, 1972. Thirteen essays on Mailer's work through *Of a Fire on the Moon* (71.1); includes Steven Marcus interview (64.1) and a thoughtful introduction with useful insights into *Miami and the Siege of Chicago* (68.25).

Brookeman, Christopher. "Norman Mailer and Mass America." In *American Culture and Society Since the 1930s*, by Christopher Brookeman, 150-70. New York: Schocken, 1987. Staid overview of Mailer as "a personal index of American history since the Second World War."

Bryant, Jerry H. "The Moral Outlook. In *The Open Decision: The Contemporary American Novel and Its Intellectual Background*, 369-94. New York: Free Press, 1970. Authenticity, courage and the belief that "self-discovery must precede the establishment of satisfactory societies" in the early novels of Mailer.

Bufithis, Philip M. *Norman Mailer*. Modern Literature Monographs. New York: Ungar, 1978. Rpt: Partial in Lennon (1986). Perhaps the most readable and reliable study of Mailer's early work.

Busch, Frederick. "The Whale as Shaggy Dog." In *When People Publish: Essays on Writers and Writing*, 65-82. Iowa City: Iowa University Press, 1986. Argues persuasively for the influence of *Moby-Dick* on "The Man Who Studied Yoga" (56.25). See 51.2.

Capote, Truman. *Conversations with Capote*, edited by Lawrence Grobel, 112-16 and passim. New York: New American Library, 1985. Capote criticizes *The Executioner's Song* (79.14).

_____. Preface to *Music for Chameleons*, xii-xix. New York: Random House, 1980. Capote comments on how Mailer "realized the value of my experiment": *In Cold Blood*.

_____. *Truman Capote: Conversations*, edited by M. Thomas Inge, 108-9, 232-33, 288-99 and passim. Jackson: University Press of Mississippi, 1987. Reveals Capote's shifting opinions of Mailer and his work.

Carson, Tom. "The Time of His Prime Time." *Village Voice Literary Supplement*, no. 14 (February 1983), 1, 10-12. Marvelous, personalized overview.

Cleaver, Eldridge. "Notes on a Native Son." *Ramparts*, June 1966, 51-56. Negative comment on Baldwin's *Nobody Knows My Name*; positive on *The White Negro* (58.8).

Coale, Samuel Chase. "Melville to Mailer: Manichean Manacles." In *In Hawthorne's Shadow: American Romance from Melville to Mailer*, 22-45. Lexington: University Press of Kentucky, 1985. Extended attack on Melville and Mailer as dualists.

Cooley, John R. *Savages and Naturals: Black Portraits by White Writers in Modern American Literature*, 137-60. Newark: University of Delaware Press, 1982. Argues that Mailer's images of blacks are stereotypical, excepting Shago in *An American Dream* (65.7).

Cowan, Michael. "The Quest for Empowering Roots: Mailer and the American Literary Tradition." In *Critical Essays on Norman Mailer*, edited by J. Michael Lennon, 156-74. Boston: G.K. Hall, 1986. Revised and expanded version of his essay in Leo Braudy's 1972 collection. Exhaustive recording of Melville's influence and transcendental perception in Mailer. Indispensable.

Dienstrefy, Harris. "The Fiction of Norman Mailer." In *On Contemporary Literature*, edited by Richard Kostelantz, 422-36. New York: Avon, 1964. Sympathetic study of Mailer's first three novels and "The Man Who Studied Yoga" (56.25).

Dupee, F.W. "The American, Norman Mailer." *Commentary*, February 1960, 128-32. Rpt: Braudy (1972). A fine critic tries to get a fix on a writer changing fast.

Early, Gerald. "The Unquiet Kingdom of Providence: The Patterson-Liston Fight." In *Culture of Bruising: Essays on Prizefighting, Literature, and Modern American Culture*, 46-65. Hopewell, N.J.: Ecco Press, 1994. The 1963 fight as interpreted by Mailer and James Baldwin. See 63.3.

Ehrlich, Robert. *Norman Mailer: The Radical as Hipster*. Metuchen, N.J.: Scarecrow Press, 1978. Focus on Mailer's work through *Marilyn* (73.30) as an expression of the hipster philosophy of *The White Negro* (58.8).

Eisinger, Chester E. Introduction to *The Naked and the Dead* (48.2), vii-xxv. softcover edition. New York: Holt, Rinehart and Winston, 1968. One of the best introductions, which notes echoes from Whitman in Mailer.

Ellmann, Mary. *Thinking about Women*, passim. New York: Harcourt Brace Jovanovich, 1968. Early feminist critique of Mailer, Sigmund Freud, Mary McCarthy and others.

Fetterly, Judith. "*An American Dream*: 'Hula, Hula,' Said the Witches." In *The Resisting Reader: A Feminist Approach to American Fiction*, 154-89, 197-98. Bloomington: Indiana University Press, 1978. Rpt: Partial in Lennon (1986). Delineation of "Mailer's fantasy of female power and male powerlessness" in *An American Dream* (65.7).

Finholt, Richard. "Mailer's Cosmology." In *American Visionary Fiction: Mad Metaphysics as Salvation Psychology*, 112-27. Port Washington, N.Y.: Kennikat Press, 1978. Rpt: Adams (1974). First extended treatment of Mailer's cosmology, which is linked to medieval and Elizabethan systems.

Foster, Richard. "Mailer and the Fitzgerald Tradition." *Novel* 1 (spring 1968), 219-30. Rpt: Braudy (1972). Exploration of the striking similarities between the fictional male characters of the two writers.

_____. *Norman Mailer*. University of Minnesota Pamphlets on American Writers, no. 73. Minneapolis: University of Minnesota Press, 1968. Rpt: Lucid (1971); partial in Bloom (1986). This monograph, one of the first extended treatments of Mailer's work, is still one of the best. Excellent on Mailer's urgent, "forcing style."

Fuller, Edmund. *Man in Modern Fiction: Some Minority Opinions on Contemporary American Writing*, 154-62. New York: Random House, 1958. Dreary comment from one of Mailer's most disapproving critics.

Gerson, Jessica. "Sex, Creativity and God." *Mosaic*, 15 (June 1982), 1-16. Rpt: Bloom (1986). Argues that Mailer's attitudes toward sexuality are based in mystical Judaism.

Gilman, Richard. "Norman Mailer: Art as Life, Life as Art." In *The Confusion of Realms*, 81-153. New York: Random House, 1969. Often disparaging, but well-developed essay on Mailer as a "new kind of American Romantic."

Glenday, Michael K. *Norman Mailer*. New York: St. Martin's Press, 1995. Examines Mailer's novels in a socio-political context. Contains one of the finest discussions of *Why Are We in Vietnam* (67.15), which he deftly relates to the issues of the day.

Glickman, Susan. "The World as Will and Idea: A Comparative Study of *An American Dream* [65.7] and *Mr. Sammler's Planet*." *Modern Fiction Studies* 28 (winter 1982-83), 569-82. Amazing parallels of theme and narrative strategy.

Godden, Richard. *Fictions of Capital: The American Novel from James to Mailer*, ch. 7-9, pp. 183-250. Cambridge: Cambridge University Press, 1990. Leftist economic history in the service of analyses of *Why Are We in Vietnam?* (67.15) and *The Armies of the Night* (68.8).

Goodhart, Eugene. "Lawrence and American Fiction." In *The Legacy of D.H. Lawrence*, edited by Jeffrey Meyers, 135-55. New York: St. Martin's Press, 1987. Focus is on Mailer's appreciation of Lawrence in *The Prisoner of Sex* (71.20).

Gordon, Andrew. *An American Dreamer: A Psychological Study of the Fiction of Norman Mailer*. Cranbury, N.J.: Associated University Presses, 1980. Thoroughly Freudian study of Mailer's work through *The Armies of the Night* (68.8); notable for its cataloging of imagery patterns.

Grace, Matthew. "Norman Mailer at the End of the Decade." *Etudes Anglaises* 24 (January-March 1971), 50-58. Rpt: Adams (1974). Mailer and the apocalyptic 1960s.

Graff, Gerald. *Literature against Itself: Literary Ideas in Modern Society*, 216-20. Chicago: University of Chicago Press, 1979. Sharp leftist attack on Mailer's "schematism."

Green, Martin. "Mailer's *Why Are We in Vietnam?*" (67.15). In *The Great American Adventure*, 199-215. Boston: Beacon Press, 1984. Shows the novel's parallels in the works of Herman Melville, Ernest Hemingway, Mark Twain and William Faulkner.

Gross, Theodore L. "Norman Mailer: The Quest for Heroism." In *The Heroic Ideal in American Literature*, 272-95. New York: Free Press, 1971. The author sees Mailer as a "Quixotic hero."

Guttman, Allen. "The Apocalyptic Vision of Norman Mailer." In *The Jewish Writer in America*, 153-72. New York: Oxford University Press, 1971. Guttman sees Mailer as "a non-Jewish Jew."

Guttman, Stanley T. *Mankind in Barbary: The Individual and Society in the Novels of Norman Mailer*. Hanover, N.H.: University Press of New England, 1975. Able discussions of early novels; links to Emersonian tradition explored.

Harap, Louis. "The Jew Manqué: Norman Mailer." In *In the Mainstream: The Jewish Presence in Twentieth-Century American Literature, 1950s-1980s*, by Louis Harap, 151-60. Although Mailer resides in "a limbo of indifference" regarding his Jewishness, Harap could not leave him out of this study, which includes comment on Saul Bellow, Bernard Malamud, Philip Roth, Alfred Kazin, Leslie Fielder, Irving Howe and others.

Harper, Howard M. "Norman Mailer—A Revolution in the Consciousness of Our Time." In *Desperate Faith: A Study of Bellow, Salinger, Mailer, Baldwin and Updike*, 96-136. Chapel Hill: University of North Carolina Press, 1967. Competent discussion of the novels through *An American Dream* (65.7).

Hassan, Ihab. "Encounter with Necessity, III." *Radical Innocence: Studies in the Contemporary American Novel*, 140-51. Princeton: Princeton University Press, 1961. Rpt: Lennon (1986). Hassan sees Lt. Hearn in *The Naked and the Dead* (48.2) as an ironist and scapegoat who both links and opposes Gen. Cummings and Sgt. Croft.

_____. "Focus on Norman Mailer's *Why Are We in Vietnam?* (67.15) In *American Dreams, American Nightmares*, edited by David Madden, 197-203. Carbondale: Southern Illinois University, 1970. Orphic meditation.

Healey, Robert C. "Novelists of the War: A Bunch of Dispossessed." In *Fifty Years of the American Novel, 1900-1950: A Christian Appraisal*, edited by Harold C. Gardiner, S.J., 257-71. New York: Scribner's, 1952. *The Naked and the Dead* (48.2) makes if difficult, the author says, "to believe that Western civilization ever existed." Valuable for revealing the doctrinaire in the early 1950s.

Hellman, John. "Journalism as Metafiction: Norman Mailer's Strategy for Mimesis and Interpretation in a Postmodern World." In *Fables of Fact: The New Journalism as New Fiction*, 55-65. Urbana: University of Illinois Press, 1986. Pioneering study of Mailer's nonfiction.

Hendin, Josephine. "American Rebels are Men of Action." In *Vulnerable People: A View of American Fiction Since 1945*, 117-44. New York: Oxford University Press, 1978. Feminist critique focusing on the "fixed principles" of Mailer's work: "anger and the adversary relation."

Hersey, John. "The Legend on the License." *Yale Review* 70 (October 1980), 1-25. Attack on the veracity of *The Executioner's Song* (79.14).

Hesla, David. "The Two Roles of Norman Mailer." In *Adversity and Grace: Studies in Recent American Literature*, edited by Nathan Scott, Jr., 211-38. Chicago: University of Chicago Press, 1968. Argues that Mailer fails as a thinker and ignores earlier intellectual leaders.

Hicks, Granville. *Literary Horizons: A Quarter Century of American Fiction*, 273-90. New York: New York University Press, 1970. Reviews of four Mailer narratives by *Saturday Review*'s longtime literary reviewer and Mailer misconstruer.

Hollowell, John. "Mailer's Vision: History as a Novel, The Novel as History." In *Fact and Fiction: The New Journalism and the Nonfiction Novel*, 87-125. Chapel Hill: University of North Carolina Press, 1977. First major appraisal of Mailer as a New Journalist, with excellent bibliography.

Horn, Bernard. "Ahab and Ishmael at War: The Presence of *Moby-Dick* in The Naked and the Dead" (48.2). *American Quarterly* 34 (fall 1982), 379-85. Definitive. See 51.2.

Jameson, Fredric R. "The Great American Hunter, or Ideological Content in the Novel." *College English* 34 (November 1972), 180-99. Marxist critique which argues that Mailer is dependent on the very diseases and poisons of technology that he condemns.

Johnson, Diane. "Death for Sale: Norman Mailer on Gary Gilmore." *Terrorists and Novelists*, 87-96. New York: Knopf, 1982. One of the few commentators to question the truthfulness of *The Executioner's Song* (79.14).

Karl, Frederick P. *American Fictions, 1940-1980*, 12-14, 579-82 and passim. New York: Harper and Row, 1983. Extravagant praise for *Why Are We in Vietnam?* (67.15) and delineation of Mailer's concern for a schizophrenic America.

Kaufmann, Donald L. *Norman Mailer: The Countdown (The First Twenty Years)*. Carbondale: Southern Illinois University Press, 1969. Pioneering discussion of the beast-seer conflict in the early work which overlooks Mailer's political interests.

Kellman, Steven G. "Mailer's Strains of Fact." *Southwest Review* 68 (spring 1983), 126-33. Richly allusive generic discussion of *The Executioner's Song* (79.14).

Kernan, Alvin B. "The Taking of the Moon: The Struggle of the Poetic and Scientific Myth in Norman Mailer's *Of a Fire on the Moon* [71.1]." In *The Imaginary Library: An Essay on Literature and Society*, 130-61. Princeton: Princeton University Press, 1982. Rpt: Bloom (1986). Perhaps the best thing written on Mailer's narrative of the Apollo 11 mission.

Kuberski, Philip. "The Metaphysics of Postmodern Death: Mailer's *Ancient Evenings* [83.18] and Merrill's *The Changing Light at Sandover*." *English Literary History* 56 (spring 1989), 229-54. Mailer and Merrill against Cartesian mechanism and postmodern despair.

Landow, George P. *Elegant Jeremiahs: The Sage from Caryle to Mailer*, 101-4, 128-29, 144-50. Ithaca, N. Y.: Cornell University Press, 1986. Careful tracing of the pattern of definition, revilement, warning and visionary promise in Mailer, Joan Didion, Tom Wolfe and earlier writers such as John Ruskin and Henry David Thoreau.

Langbaum, Robert. "Mailer's New Style." In *The Modern Spirit: Essays on the Continuity of Nineteenth and Twentieth Century Literature*, 147-63. New York: Oxford University Press, 1970. Rpt: Bloom (1986). Important essay on the evolution of Mailer's "hallucinated realism."

Leeds, Barry H. "Boxing as a Moral Paradigm in the Works of Norman Mailer." *The New Review* 1 (September-October 1992), 12-16. The most complete discussion of the topic.

———. "Mailer and Marilyn: Prisoners of Sex." *North Dakota Quarterly* (winter 1991), 110-17. "The coherence of Mailer's vision of [Marilyn] Monroe, of women, and of heterosexual love."

———. *The Structured Vision of Norman Mailer*. New York: New York University Press, 1969. First major study of Mailer's work; valuable for its analysis of *An American Dream* (65.7), and consideration of *The Armies of the Night* (68.8) and *Deaths for the Ladies (and Other Disasters)* (62.3).

———. "Tough Guy Goes Hollywood: Mailer and the Movies." In *Take Two: Adapting the Contemporary American Novel to Film*, edited by Barbara Tepa Lupack, 154-68. Bowling Green, Ohio: Bowling Green State University Popular Press, 1994. Most nuanced discussion of the adaptation of *Tough Guys Don't Dance* (84.17) to the screen.

Lehan, Richard. *A Dangerous Crossing: French Literary Existentialism and the Modern American Novel*, 81-95. Carbondale: Southern Illinois University Press, 1973. Mailer's cosmology as an existential recreation.

Leigh, Nigel. "Getting It Wrong: The Cinema of Norman Mailer." *Journal of American Studies* 24, no. 3 (1990), 399-413. Comment on Mailer's films and those made from his novels.

———. *Radical Fictions and the Novels of Norman Mailer*. New York: St. Martin's Press, 1990. Leigh writes about Mailer and power from a Foucauldian perspective, but ignores the nonfiction narratives. Excellent readings of *Why Are We in Vietnam?* (67.15) and *Ancient Evenings* (83.18). Many misquotations, typos, incorrect page numbers.

Lennon, J. Michael, editor. *Critical Essays on Norman Mailer. Critical Essays on American Literature*. Boston: G.K. Hall, 1986. Ten reviews and ten essays, including two original ones: Robert F. Lucid's overview of his forthcoming biography and Michael Cowan's on Mailer's Americanness. Introduction summarizes critical response to Mailer's work.

———, and Charles B. Strozier. "Empathy and Detachment in the Narratives of Erikson and Mailer." *Psychohistory Review* 10 (fall 1981), 18-32. Comparison of the introspective-empathic narratives of Mailer and Erik Erikson.

———. "Mailer's Cosmology." *Modern Language Studies* 12 (summer 1982), 18-29. Rpt: Lennon (1986). Delineation of the "three linked strands" of Mailer's cosmology: 1) universe in process 2) intensified free will 3) intensified presence of evil.

———. "Mailer's Radical Bridge." *Journal of Narrative Technique* 7 (fall 1977), 170-88. Discussion of point of view in Mailer as it relates to his thought.

———. "Mailer's Sarcophagus: The Artist the Media, and the 'Wad.'" *Modern Fiction Studies* 23 (summer 1977), 179-87. How Mailer's view of his audience helps shape his work.

Lodge, David. "The Novelist at the Crossroads." In *The Novelist at the Crossroads and Other Essays on Fiction and Criticism*, 3-34. Ithaca, N. Y.: Cornell University Press, 1971. Masterful delineation of the origins and possibilities of the nonfiction novel, including *The Armies of the Night* (68.8).

Lounsberry, Barbara. "Norman Mailer's Ages of Man." In *The Art of Fact: Contemporary Artists of Nonfiction*, 139-89. New York: Greenwood Press, 1990. Careful exploration of the parallels between *Advertisements for Myself* (59.13) and Whitman's "Song of Myself."

Lowell, Robert. "A Conversation with Ian Hamilton." *American Poetry Review*, September/October, 1978, 23-27. Lowell says Mailer's portrait of him in *The Armies of the Night* (68.8) is "the best, the only thing written about me as a living person."

Lucid, Robert F. Introduction to *The Long Patrol: 25 Years of Writing from the Work of Norman Mailer*, xi-xxvii. New York: World, 1971. "The Ambition of Norman Mailer" could serve as the title to this brilliant recapitulation of Mailer's career through *Of a Fire on the Moon* (71.1). See 71.29.

_____. "Norman Mailer: The Artist as Fantasy Figure." *Massachusetts Review* 15 (autumn 1974), 581-95. How increasingly greater demands on Mailer have made him disassemble himself into various avatars and employ new narrative strategies. Indispensable.

_____, editor. *Norman Mailer: The Man and His Work*. Boston: Little, Brown, 1971. First major collection of essays: 13 on his work, four on his life and Paul Carroll's interview (68.1). Contains checklist of his work and important introduction in which Lucid attempts to resolve the apparent conflict between Mailer's public and artistic activities.

_____. "Three Public Performances: Fitzgerald, Hemingway, Mailer." *American Scholar* 43 (summer 1974), 447-66. Subtle exploration of the love-hate relationship of three public writers and their audiences.

Macdonald, Dwight. "The Bright Young Men in the Arts." *Esquire*, September 1958, 38-40. Besides Mailer, Macdonald chooses James Baldwin in the prose category and mentions Truman Capote, Norman Podhoretz, John Updike and Flannery O'Connor. Macdonald says Mailer's failures are "more interesting than the successes of less-talented writers" and praises "his enthusiasm for general ideas."

Marks, Barry A. "Civil Disobedience in Retrospect: Henry Thoreau and Norman Mailer." *Soundings* 2, 62 (1979), 144-65. Inevitable and careful comparison.

Marx, Leo. "'Noble Shit': The Uncivil Response of American Writers to Civil Religion in America." *Massachusetts Review* 14 (autumn 1973), 709-39. The virtues of the American vernacular in Mailer, Walt Whitman, Ralph Waldo Emerson, Mark Twain and others.

Matz, Charles. "Mailer's Opera." *Opera News* 34 (21 February 1970), 14-16. See 70.4.

Maud, Ralph. "Faulkner, Mailer, and Yogi Bear." *Canadian Review of American Studies* 2, no. 2 (fall 1971), 69-75. *Why Are We in Vietnam?* (67.15) and William Faulkner's "The Bear" are related to Indian stories, with an ecological emphasis.

McConnell, Frank D. "Norman Mailer and the Cutting Edge of Style." In *Four Postwar American Novelists: Bellow, Mailer, Barth and Pynchon*, 58-107.

Chicago: University of Chicago Press, 1977. Traces the shift from ideological to "visionary" politics in Mailer's work.

McCord, Phyllis Frus. "The Ideology of Form: The Nonfiction Novel." *Genre* 19 (spring 1986), 59-79. Convincingly sorts out the generic status of *The Executioner's Song* (79.14) by comparing/contrasting it with Truman Capote's *In Cold Blood*.

Meredith, Robert. "The 45-Second Piss: A Left Critique of Norman Mailer and *The Armies of the Night*" (68.8). *Modern Fiction Studies* 17 (autumn 1971), 433-48. Forceful and detailed critique.

Merrill, Robert. "*The Armies of the Night*: The Education of Norman Mailer." *Illinois Quarterly* 37 (September 1974), 30-44. Rpt: Bloom (1986). Sound analysis of point of view and structure in 68.8.

_____. *Norman Mailer*, revised edition. Twayne's United States Authors Series. Boston: Twayne, 1992. Thoughtful examination of the formal structure of Mailer's novels and nonfiction narratives; contains perhaps best analysis of *The Executioner's Song* (79.14). Includes biographical chapter. Most comprehensive study to date.

_____. "Norman Mailer's Early Nonfiction: The Art of Self-Revelation." *Western Humanities Review* 28 (winter 1974), 1-12. A shrewd study of Mailer's emerging persona in the essays preceding *The Armies of the Night* (68.8).

Middlebrook, Jonathan. *Mailer and the Times of His Time*. San Francisco: Bay Books, 1976. Extended personal essay on Mailer's ties to American romantics, including a comic account of his first meeting with Mailer.

Muste, John M. "Norman Mailer and John Dos Passos: The Question of Influence." *Modern Fiction Studies* 17 (autumn 1971), 361-74. Raises serious doubts about the specific influence of John Dos Passos's *U.S.A.* on *The Naked and the Dead* (48.2).

New Orleans Review 3, no. 3 (1973). Special Mailer number. Contains three essays and an interview by Matthew Grace and Steve Roday. See 73.14.

Newlove, Donald. "Dinner at the Lowells." *Esquire*, September 1969, 128-29, 168, 170-78, 180, 184. Lowell comments on his portrait in *The Armies of the Night* (68.8).

Oates, Joyce Carol. "The Teleology of the Unconscious: The Art of Norman Mailer." In *New Heaven, New Earth: The Visionary Experience in Literature*, 170-92. New York: Vanguard Press, 1974. Discussion of Mailer's dualisms in *Why Are We In Vietnam?* (67.15) and *Of a Fire on the Moon* (71.1) by a novelist who "disagree[s] with nearly every one of Mailer's stated or implied ideas."

Olster, Stacey. "The Transition to Post-Modernism: Norman Mailer." In *Reminiscence and Re-creation in Contemporary American Fiction*, 36-71. Cambridge: University of Cambridge Press, 1989. Mailer is seen as a transitional figure between modernism and postmodernism; focus is on his writings of the 1960s.

Ostriker, Dane Proxpeals. "Norman Mailer and the Mystery Woman or, The Rape of the C—k." *Esquire*, November 1972, 122-25. Pseudonymous attack in rhymed couplets on Mailer as male chauvinist.

253

Parker, Hershel. "Norman Mailer's Revision of the *Esquire* Version of *An American Dream*: The Authority of 'Built-in' Intentionality." In *Flawed Texts and Verbal Icons: Literary Authority in American Fiction*, 181-212. Evanston, Ill.: Northwestern University Press, 1984. Argues that the magazine version of 65.7 is superior to the book version. See 83.6.

Pease, Donald E. "Citizen Vidal and Mailer's America." *Raritan* 11 (spring 1992), 72-98. Argues for Vidal as an ignored genius who prefigured the New Historicism and Mailer as anti-homosexual. Tendentious.

Pizer, Donald. "Norman Mailer: *The Naked and the Dead*" (48.2). In *Twentieth-Century American Literary Naturalism*, 90-144. Carbondale: Southern Illinois University Press, 1982. Arguably the best essay on Mailer's first novel.

Podhoretz, Norman. "Norman Mailer: The Embattled Vision." In *Doings and Undoings: The Fifties and After in American Writing*, 179-204. New York: Farrar, Straus, 1964. Rpt: Lucid (1971). One of the first essays to examine Mailer's shifting ideologies and idiosyncratic existentialism.

Poirier, Richard. *Norman Mailer*. Modern Masters Series. New York: Viking, 1972. Rpt: Partial in Bloom (1986). Still considered to be most intelligent study of Mailer. Contains three chapters: on Mailer's career, his relation to history, and his dualisms. Poirier's Mailer is perhaps too postmodern, but Poirier is acute on Mailer's endlessly modulating rhetoric, even if he is incredulous about Mailer's cosmology.

_____. "The Performing Self." In *The Performing Self: Compositions and Decompositions in the Languages of Contemporary Life*, 86-111. New York: Oxford University Press, 1971. Prelude to his 1972 volume on Mailer.

Pratt, William C. "Mailer's 'Barbary Shore' and His Quest for a Radical Politics." *Illinois Quarterly* 44 (winter 1982), 48-56. Ideological context for Mailer's second novel (51.1). Excellent sources.

Radford, Jean. *Norman Mailer: A Critical Study*. New York: Harper and Row, 1975. General survey of Mailer's work from a feminist perspective. Her study is marred by its focus on ideology and lack of interest in stylistic nuance; contains a fine analyses of the Eitel-Esposito affair in *The Deer Park* (55.4).

Raleigh, John Henry. "History and Its Burdens: The Example of Norman Mailer." In *Uses of Literature*. Harvard English Studies 4, edited by Monroe Engel, 163-86. Cambridge: Howard University Press, 1973. Mailer's historical sense, use of the small town and the "dynamic, orgiastic, explosive accelerating city."

Ross, Mitchell S. "Norman Mailer." In *The Literary Politicians*, 166-216. Garden City, N.J.: Doubleday, 1978. Lacking notes and an index, this vicious diatribe is valuable to help understand the depth of anger among Mailer's detractors. Ross is the Babe Ruth of Mailer revilers.

Rother, James. "Mailer's 'O'Shaugnessy Chronicle': A Speculative Autopsy." *Critique* 19, no. 3 (1978), 21-39. Contends that Lawrence Durrell's *Alexandria Quartet* caused Mailer to rethink his plans.

Schaub, Thomas Hill. "Rebel without a Cause: Mailer's White Negro and Consensus Liberalism." In *American Fiction in the Cold War*, 137-62.

Madison: University of Wisconsin Press, 1991. Attempt to deconstruct "The White Negro" (58.8) into consensus liberalism.

Scheffler, Judith A. "The Prisoner as Creator in Norman Mailer's *The Executioner's Song*" (79.14). *Midwest Quarterly* 24 (summer 1983), 400-11. Rpt: Bloom (1986). Focus on Gilmore's self-definition.

Schickel, Richard. "Super Hero, Super Victim," "The Politics of Illusion." In *Intimate Strangers*, 88-208. Garden City, N.Y.: Doubleday, 1985. Discussion of Mailer's insights about Marlon Brando, Marilyn Monroe, Ernest Hemingway and John F. Kennedy.

Schrader, George Alfred. "Norman Mailer and the Despair of Defiance." *Yale Review* 51 (December 1961), 267-80. Rpt: Braudy (1972). Argues that hipsterism is not existentialism, but a violent variant of romanticism based on "libidinal urges."

Schulz, Max F. "Norman Mailer's Divine Comedy." In *Radical Sophistication: Studies in Contemporary Jewish-American Novelists*, 69-109. Athens: Ohio University Press, 1969. Rpt: Adams (1974). Examination of Mailer's novels, with only modest procrusteanism, in a Dantesque framework.

Schwenger, Peter. *Phallic Critiques: Masculinity and Twentieth-Century Literature*, 24-36, 103-7 and passim. London: Routledge and Kegan Paul, 1984. Worthy exploration of Mailer's rhetoric and obscenity.

Scott, Nathan A., Jr. "Norman Mailer—Our Whitman." In *Three American Moralists: Mailer, Bellow, Trilling*, 15-97. Notre Dame, Ind.: University of Notre Dame Press, 1973. In detailed readings, Scott makes the case that Mailer, like Whitman, is a "spokesperson for the American conscience."

Seib, Kenneth A. "Mailer's March: The Epic Structure of *The Armies of the Night* [68.8]." *Essays in Literature* 1 (spring 1974), 89-95. Surprising parallels.

Shechner, Mark. "Memoirs of a Revolutionist." In *After the Revolution: Studies in the Contemporary American Imagination*, 159-79. Bloomington: Indiana University Press, 1987. Examination of Mailer's post-Marxist revolutionary impulses through *Advertisements for Myself* (59.13). Contains extensive discussion of influence of Wilhelm Reich and Robert Lindner. See 56.9.

Sheed, Wilfrid. "Norman Mailer: Genius or Nothing." In *The Morning After: Selected Essays and Reviews*, 9-17. New York: Farrar, Straus and Giroux, 1971. Tribute to Mailer as a weather vane: "As Mailer goes, so goes the nation."

Shloss, Carol. "Norman Mailer and Combat Photography." In *In Visible Light: Photography and the American Writer, 1840-1940*, 233-49. New York: Oxford University Press, 1987. Interesting consideration of the subjective-objective dilemma in *The Naked and the Dead* (48.2).

Shoemaker, Steve. "Norman Mailer's 'White Negro': Historical Myth or Mythical History." *Twentieth Century Literature* 37 (fall 1991), 242-60. Important reconsideration via the "New Historicism" of Stephen Greenblatt.

Silverstein, Howard. "Norman Mailer: The Family Romance and the Oedipal Fantasy." *American Imago* 34 (fall 1977), 277-86. Triangular relationships in the early work.

255

Smolla, Rodney A. *"Harlot's Ghost* [91.26] and 'JFK': A Fictional Conversation with Norman Mailer, Oliver Stone, Earl Warren, and Hugo Black." *Suffolk University Law Review* 26 (fall 1992), 587-613. Discussion of aesthetics and conspiracy.

Solotaroff, Robert. *Down Mailer's Way.* Urbana: University of Illinois Press, 1974. Rpt: Partial in Lennon (1986). General survey containing a comprehensive and penetrating examination of Mailer's existentialism and its debts to European philosophers. Contains one of the best critiques of "The White Negro" (58.8) in print.

Stade, George. "Mailer and Miller." *Partisan Review* 44, no. 4 (1972), 616-24. Thoughtful comparison.

Stark, John. *"Barbary Shore* [51.1]: The Basis of Mailer's Best Work." *Modern Fiction Studies* 17 (autumn 1971), 403-8. The Hollingworths of Mailer and Nathaniel Hawthorne are considered.

Stone, Albert E. "Factual Fictions: Experiments in Autobiography by Norman Mailer, Frank Conroy, Lillian Hellman." In *Autobiographical Occasions and Original Acts: Versions of American Identity from Henry Adams to Nate Shaw,* 265-90, 340-42. Philadelphia: University of Pennsylvania Press, 1982. Valuable examination of *The Armies of the Night* (68.8) as part of the American autobiographical tradition.

"Studies of Norman Mailer." *Modern Fiction Studies* 17 (autumn 1971), 345-463. Special issue containing nine essays on Mailer's writings, and Laura Adams's pioneering checklist of criticism.

Styron, William. "Aftermath of 'Aftermath.'" In *This Quiet Dust and Other Writings,* 137-42. New York: Random House, 1982. Styron empathizes with Mailer on the Jack Abbott affair. See 81.10.

Taylor, Gordon O. "Of Adams and Aquarius." *American Literature* 46 (March 1974), 68-82. Best essay on the influence of Henry Adams on Mailer's nonfiction. See 81.16.

Toback, James. "Norman Mailer Today." *Commentary,* October 1967, 67-76. Examination of Mailer's religious commitments, and the role of existential dread.

Trilling, Diana. "The Radical Moralism of Norman Mailer." In *Claremont Essays,* 175-202. New York: Harcourt, Brace and World, 1964. Rpt: Lucid (1971), Braudy (1972). Best developed and most intelligent examination of Mailer's work through *Advertisements for Myself* (59.13). Sensitive mediation between extremes of Mailer's sensibility with praise for his "high political consciousness" and "moral affirmation."

Vidal, Gore, and Robert J. Stanton, editors. *Views from a Window: Conversations with Gore Vidal,* passim. Secaucus, N.J.: Lyle Stuart, 1980. Vidal's rivalry with Mailer is palpable here.

_____. "Women's Liberation Meets Miller-Mailer-Manson Man." In *Homage to Daniel Shays,* 398-402. New York: Random House, 1972. Cause of Mailer's fight with Vidal on the Dick Cavett television show in December 1971. See 77.7.

Vogelgesang, Sandy. *The Long Dark Night of the Soul: The American Intellectual Left and the Vietnam War,* 9-10, 131-33, 149-51, 178-79. New York:

Harper and Row, 1974. The powerful influence of *The Armies of the Night* (68.8) on the anti-Vietnam War movement.

Volpe, Edmond L. "James Jones—Norman Mailer." In *Contemporary American Novelists*, edited by Harry T. Moore, 106-19. Carbondale: Southern Illinois University Press, 1964. Two existentialists compared.

Waldron, Randall H. "The Naked, the Dead and the Machine: A New Look at Norman Mailer's First Novel." *PMLA* 87 (March 1972), 271-77. Rpt: Bloom (1986). The U.S. Army as the epitome of technology in *The Naked and the Dead* (48.2).

Weber, Ronald. *The Literature of Fact*, 80-87, 166-71, passim. Athens: Ohio University Press, 1980. Examination of *The Armies of the Night* (68.8) and *The Executioner's Song* (79.14) from an American Studies perspective.

Weinberg, Helen A. "The Heroes of Norman Mailer's Novels." In *The New Novel in America: The Kafkan Mode in Contemporary Fiction*, 108-40. Ithaca, N. Y.: Cornell University Press, 1970. Emergence of Mailer's "activist hero" from *Barbary Shore* (51.1) to *An American Dream* (65.7).

Wenke, Robert. *Mailer's America*. Hanover, N.H.: University Press of New England, 1987. Wenke's focus is almost completely thematic. Contains first extended treatment of *Ancient Evenings* (83.18).

Werge, Thomas. "An Apocalyptic Voyage: God, Satan, and the American Tradition in Norman Mailer's *Of a Fire on the Moon* [71.1]." *The Review of Politics* 34 (October 1972), 208-28. Rich discussion of Mailer's "conviction of the essential religious drama of man's experience," focusing on 71.1 as a continuation of the vision of Herman Melville.

Whalen-Bridge, John. "Adamic Purity as Double-Agent in *Harlot's Ghost* [91.26]." In *Political Fiction and the American Self*, 103-30. Urbana: University of Illinois Press, 1998. Subtle examination of "Mailer's dual aptitude for representing and resisting American mythologies."

Widmer, Kingsley. "Several American Perplexes." *The Literary Rebel*, 175-98. Carbondale: Southern Illinois University Press, 1965. Comparison of Mailer and Paul Goodman.

Zavarzadeh, Mas'ud. *The Mythopoeic Reality: The Postwar American Nonfiction Novel*, 153-76 and passim. Urbana: University of Illinois Press, 1976. Attempts to prove, unconvincingly, that *The Armies of the Night* (68.8) has a "zero degree of interpretation" of reality.

Norman Mailer: Key Publications, 1948-1998

Following are two lists: 1) Mailer's 27 books, in rank order high to low, by average review rating; 2) the 25 reviewing publications in rank order high to low, by average rating of reviews of his books which will be found on page 262. Another presentation of these ratings, with notes, will be found on pages 260-261.

Average Ratings, Books

Number of Reviews	Title	Item Number	Average Ratings
20	The Armies of the Night	68.8	4.100
16	The Naked and the Dead	48.2	4.031
14	Miami and the Siege of Chicago	68.25	3.821
9	Existential Errands	72.7	3.777
10	The Fight	75.5	3.700
20	The Executioner's Song	79.14	3.650
21	Of a Fire on the Moon	71.1	3.571
8	St. George and the Godfather	72.17	3.500
10	The Time of Our Time	98.7	3.300
17	Cannibals and Christians	66.11	3.176
21	Why Are We in Vietnam?	67.15	3.143
8	Genius and Lust	76.12	3.125
16	Oswald's Tale	95.16	3.125
13	The Prisoner of Sex	71.20	3.000
18	Harlot's Ghost	91.26	2.833
17	Advertisements for Myself	59.13	2.647
11	Pieces and Pontifications	82.16	2.636
23	Marilyn: A Biography	73.30	2.609
12	The Presidential Papers	63.37	2.500
20	An American Dream	65.7	2.400
8	Deaths for the Ladies	62.3	2.375
19	Ancient Evenings	83.18	2.368
17	The Gospel according to the Son	97.13	2.236
18	The Deer Park	55.4	2.278
16	Tough Guys Don't Dance	84.17	2.188
12	Portrait of Picasso as a Young Man	95.38	2.000
18	Barbary Shore	51.1	1.944

Review Ratings

Item Number	Rating Averages	Atlantic	Boston Globe	Chicago Tribune	Christian Sci. Monitor	Commentary	Commonweal	Esquire	Harper's	Los Angeles Times	Nation	National Review	New Leader	New Republic	New York	N.Y. Rev. of Books	New York Times	N.Y. Times Book Rev.	New Yorker	Newsweek
Total Reviews		16	18	17	13	15	12	10	8	18	18	19	12	17	8	18	24	27	13	19
98.7	3.300						3			2	1	2	1	4		4	4	4	5	
97.13	2.236	2	4	3			3			1	1	2	1	1		3	4	1	3	2
95.38	2.000	5	4	4						1	3	3		2			2	1		
95.16	3.125	4	3	2				2	2	4		3	3	4		2	4	4	N	
91.26	2.833		3	5	1					2	3	2		3	3	3	4	4	1	2
84.17	2.188	1	1	4	1						2			2	1		2	2		3
83.18	2.368		1					3	1	1	2	3	2	5	1	1	3	2		4
82.16	2.636		4	2						4	2	1	2		2	2	4	3		
79.14	3.650	3				2	5	4		5	4	4	4	4	5	5	2	3	1	5
76.12	3.125									4	4	4		3		3	1	1		3
75.5	3.700		4	1												4	4	4	4	
73.30	2.609	N	4	3		4	3	2	2	3	1	2	1	4		2	2	3	2	3
72.17	3.500					3	4				4				N	4	4	4	3	
72.7	3.777				4	4	3				4	3	4	3	4	3	4	3	3	
71.20	3.000	2	4		3		2	2		4	4				5	5	1	5	4	4
71.1	3.571	5		2	4	2		1	N	4	4	5	2	2	2	3	4	5	4	5
68.25	3.821			3					N	4	3	3	3	5	5	5	4	3		
68.8	4.100		4	1	4	N		5/5	N	5	5	1	4	4	4	5	5	5	3	
67.15	3.143	3	4	4	3	4	4	5	5	1	2	1	2	2	2	5	5	2	5	5
66.11	3.176	1	3	2	3	5		4		1	5	1		5	2	4	5	3	4	
65.7	2.400	2	3	3	1	2	N	N	N	5	1	2		1	1	X	2	4	3	
63.37	2.500	3		3	5	5	N	N	2	4	1	1		2	2	X	1	2	2	
62.3	2.375			1		4				1	1	1			X	X	X	3	4	
59.13	2.647	1	3		5	4	3			1	3	1	3	4	2	X	3	4	2	
55.4	2.278	3	1	2	4	4	3			2	2	3	2	4	3	X	1	3	4	
51.1	1.944	3	1	1	3	2				3	2	1	2	3	3	X	1	2	4	
48.2	4.031	4	4	4	3	4			4		5	X	X	4	X	X	4	5	4	5
Rating Averages		2.938	3.056	2.765	3.000	3.800	3.250	3.100	2.500	2.777	2.889	2.211	2.167	3.118	3.375	3.167	2.920	3.111	2.846	3.526

260

Publication	Avg	98.7	97.13	95.38	95.16	91.26	84.17	83.18	82.16	79.14	76.12	75.5	73.30	72.17	72.7	71.20	71.1	68.25	68.8	67.15	66.11	65.7	63.37	62.3	59.13	55.4	51.1	48.2	Total
San Fran. Chronicle	2.625			2	2	2		1				4	3	2	4		4	5	4	4	3	1	2	1	2	1	2	5	16
Saturday Review	2.738		3	3	4	X	4	3		5	4	4	2	4	4	5	3	3	5	1	4	1	2	1	1	1	2	5/2	21
Time	2.478			2	2	4	2	3	2	3	3	3	3	3		2	4	3	3	1	2	3	3	1	1	1	1	3	23
Village Voice	3.929	2	X	X	X	X	2				5						4		5	5	N	5	N	4	5	5	X	X	14
Wall Street Journal	2.500	1	2	2	2	1	4			4			1		5	5		5			3	1			1	1	2		14
Washington Post	3.023	4	2	2	2	5	1	5	4	2		5	3		5	3		4/1	5	4	2	1				1	2	3	22
Total Reviews		16	18	18	17	8	12	20	17	21	14	21	23	9	8	13	9	10	23	16	11	19	16	18	16	12	17	10	412

Notes

A. Numbers 1–5 refer to the rating of the review, negative to positive.

B. X = no review because publication was not in existence (24 instances).

C. 5/2 (example) = ratings of two reviews in the same publication; an average is used in the three instances where this occurs.

D. N = no review because excerpt(s) from the book in question appeared in the publication (10 instances).

E. The top row of numbers in the chart refer to the corresponding item numbers in "Works," beginning with *The Naked and the Dead* (48.2) and ending with *The Time of Our Time* (98.7).

F. The second row of numbers is the average rating for each of 27 books.

G. The number next to each of 25 publications is the average review rating given by that publication.

H. The number at the end of each column, and at the bottom of each column, is the total number of located reviews for each of 25 publications and 27 books, respectively. No book was reviewed by all 25 publications. *Marilyn* (73.30), with 23 reviews, had the most. Only the *New York Times Book Review* reviewed all 27 books.

I. A total of 412 reviews were rated (counting the double reviews as one), or 64.27% of 641 possible reviews (the number 641 was determined by subtracting 24 [numbers of Xs] plus 10 [number of Ns] from 675, the maximum potential number of reviews: 27 books times 25 publications = 675). More reviews remain to be discovered, of course, but our conservative estimate is that at least 95 percent of existing reviews have been located and rated. No major changes in the average scores of individual books or publications is therefore likely.

J. The cumulative average of all reviews is 2.947.

K. The 12 books from 1966 to 1979 received a cumulative average of 3.431, with *The Armies of the Night* (68.8) receiving 4.100, the highest of all 27 books.

261

Average Ratings, Publications

Number of Reviews	Magazine Title	Average Ratings
14	Village Voice	3.929
15	Commentary	3.800
19	Newsweek	3.526
8	New York	3.375
12	Commonweal	3.250
18	New York Review of Books	3.167
17	New Republic	3.118
27	New York Times Book Review	3.111
10	Esquire	3.100
18	Boston Globe	3.056
13	Christian Science Monitor	3.000
22	Washington Post	3.023
16	Atlantic	2.938
24	New York Times	2.920
18	Nation	2.889
13	New Yorker	2.846
18	Los Angeles Times	2.777
17	Chicago Tribune	2.765
21	Saturday Review	2.738
16	San Francisco Chronicle	2.625
8	Harper's	2.500
14	Wall Street Journal	2.500
23	Time	2.478
19	National Review	2.211
12	New Leader	2.167

Index of Persons in "Works"

Baudelaire, Charles: 64.23
Bauer, Jerry: 84.22
Bean, Orson: 63.33
Bean, Judge Roy: 74.2
Beatty, Warren: 87.27, 91.45, 98.9
Beauman, Sally: 68.17, 71.28
Beaverbrook, Lord: 62.9
Beckett, Bill: 72.8
Beckett, Samuel: 56.17, 56.26
Beckmann, Max: 79.14
Beeson, Jack: 98.4
Begiebing, Robert: 83.10
Belfrage, Cedric: 49.1
Bell, Bill: 91.36
Bell, Charles W.: 97.5
Bellow, Saul: 59.10, 63.8, 65.3, .4, .6, .10, 76.18, 81.3, .16, 83.46, 85.1, 86.30, .34
Berg, Scott: 89.6
Bernard, André: 95.10
Bernhard, Gabrielle: 65.1
Bernstein, Mashey: 91.29
Berrigan, Ted: 86.41
Bertolucci, Bernardo: 73.12
Beyette, Beverly: 80.18
Bezner, Kevin: 80.1
Billy the Kid: 67.23
Blades, John: 84.6
Blinkhorn, Lois: 97.20
Bloom, Harold: 71.27
Blount Jr., Roy: 93.7
Blue, Adrianne: 79.34, 83.43
Blume, Harvey: 95.32
Bly, Robert: 91.21
Bockris, Victor: 86.41, 96.7
Bode, Winston: 61.22
Bogan, Louise: 52.1
Boland, Maura: 83.16
Bonetti, Eddie: 71.8, 94.4
Bonn, Thomas L.: 55.4
Boorstin, Daniel: 97.26
Borders, William: 80.20, .21
Borges, Jorge Luis: 74.18, 81.16
Bosworth, Patricia: 73.8
Boudart, Mimi: 72.5
Bourjaily, Tina: 82.23
Bourjaily, Vance: 52.2, .3, 59.10, 63.7, .8, .40, 82.23, 96.6

Bova, Ben: 72.24
Bowden, Mark: 84.30
Bowles, Paul: 59.10
Boyer, Charles: 93.1
Boyle, T. Coraghessan: 97.4
Bradford, Larned G. "Ned": 74.10, 79.5, 83.18, .24
Bradley, Van Allen: 59.16
Brady, James: 79.1, 83.37
Brady, Thomas J.: 98.2
Bragg, Melvyn: 73.46, 79.26, 83.42
Brando, Marlon: 84.12
Bras, Juan Mari: 67.24
Braudy, Leo: 64.1
Braziller, George: 48.4
Brecht, Bertold: 55.2
Breit, Harvey: 51.2, 67.7
Breit, Luke: 84.2
Brelis, Dean: 86.14
Brenner, Marie: 83.13
Breslin, Jimmy: 69.7, .10, .12, .14, .17, .18, .21, .23, .24, .27, .28, .33, .37, .38, .44, .45, .52, .56, .65, .70, .73, .76, .80, 71.24, 82.23
Bright, Barbara: 87.25
Brodin, Pierre: 64.23
Brook, Peter: 91.48
Brophy, Brigid: 71.22
Brossard, Chandler: 59.10, 63.40
Brower, Brock: 65.20, 79.9
Brower, Millicent: 59.5, 63.29
Brown, Claude: 65.3
Browne, Nick: 69.13, .46
Brownmiller, Susan: 78.6
Broyard, Anatole: 59.10
Bruccoli, Matthew: 96.6
Bruce, Samuel W.: 96.9
Bryan, Bill: 75.7
Buak, Charlotte: 86.31
Buber, Martin: 62.22, 63.16-.20
Buchanan, Patrick J.: 96.5
Buck, Joan Juliet: 81.18
Buckley, Tim: 72.24
Buckley, William F., Jr.: 63.3, .15, .22, .27, 65.14, .23, .24, 79.32, 85.1
Burk-Block, Candice: 87.25
Burke, Philip: 91.4, 92.8
Burks, Edward C.: 69.42

Burnett, Hallie: 41.1, 75.14
Burnett, Whit: 41.1, 70.14, 75.14
Burroughs, Edgar Rice: 71.24
Burroughs, William: 61.3, 62.24, 63.8,
    64.18, 65.1, .10, .13, 68.18, 74.3,
    81.21, 85.15, 86.41, 87.29, 92.12,
    96.7
Bush, Barbara: 81.17
Bush, George H.: 89.9, 90.1, 91.3, .21
Butler, Dix: 91.4, .6
Byrne, Evelyn B.: 71.32
Byrnes, Sean: 77.12

C

Cabezas, Omar: 86.2, .17
Cabral, Reggie: 90.3
Calder, Alexander: 84.31
Caldwell, Erskine: 84.31
Califano, Joseph A.: 74.11
Calisher, Hortense: 98.4
Callaghan, Morley: 63.1
Calta, Louis: 57.2
Campbell, Gary: 67.13
Campbell, James: 83.46
Canby, Vincent: 68.26, 87.8
Cannela, Anthony R.: 98.17
Capote, Truman: 49.2, 59.3, .4, .10,
    73.22,   75.1, 77.7, 79.1, 80.1, .10,
    81.8, 84.21, 85.15, 89.12, 91.3,
    97.24
Carmody, Deirdre: 74.1
Caro, Robert: 89.8
Carr, Jay: 87.6, .16
Carroll, Paul: 68.1
Carson, Johnny: 72.16
Carter, Jimmy: 76.11
Cary, Joyce: 61.17
Castro, Fidel: 61.5, 91.35, 98.7
Cavett, Dick: 72.16, 77.7, 79.27, .29,
    80.6, 82.10
Ceballos, Jacqueline: 71.16
Chamberlain, Wilt: 74.2
Chambers, Andrea: 84.20
Chancellor, John: 72.9
Chandler, Mary Voelz: 95.46
Chandler, Raymond: 87.16
Charlebois, Sandy: 68.8
Chaudoir, David: 97.4

Cheever, John: 66.3, 81.3, 91.3
Chekov, Anton: 70.11, 83.13, 91.48
Child, Julia: 74.1
Chinlund, Stephen: 59.19
Chloe: 88.11
Chomsky, Noam: 75.10
Christ, Jesus: 97.2, .7-.9, .12, .14, .17,
    .18
Christian, Frederick: 63.34
Christy, Marian: 80.17
Churchill, Winston: 48.13
Chusmir, Janet: 72.1
Ciardi, John: 65.1
Claiborne, Craig: 81.15
Clampitt, Amy: 85.3
Clark, Kenneth: 85.6
Clark, Marsh: 73.20
Clark, Walter Van Tilburg: 84.6
Clarke, Arthur C.: 72.9
Clay, Cassius [see Ali, Mohammad]
Cleaver, Eldridge: 80.09
Clines, Francis H.: 69.28
Clinton, Bill: 95.2, .21, .26, 98.1, .3,
    .9, .15
Cobb, John: 49.2
Cober, Alan E.: 79.36
Coburn, Marcia Froelke: 83.56
Cocks, Jay: 71.30
Colacello, Bob: 77.12
Colarossi, Anthony: 95.21
Coleman, Terry: 84.27
Coles, Robert: 68.3
Collier, John: 91.4
Collin, Dorothy: 59.15
Collins, Glenn: 89.12
Collins, Nancy: 77.6
Colodro, Valentina (granddaughter):
    83.59
Conrad, Harold: 82.26
Conroy, Frank: 67.12
Continelli, Louise: 95.26
Cook, Bruce: 61.4, 72.21, 91.39
Cook, Molly Malone: 76.5
Coppola, Lee: 67.9
Cortes, Pedro: 67.20
Cott, Jonathan: 80.22
Coughlin, Ruth Pollack: 91.31
Cousins, Norman: 48.13

265

266

Eckman, Fern Marja: 62.9
Ehrlichman, John: 76.15
Eichmann, Adolf: 62.2, 91.15
Eisenberg, Lee: 83.54
Eisenhower, Dwight D.: 59.9, 61.3
Eitel, Charles Francis: 68.11
Ekstand, Karl L.: 56.13
El Cordobes: 67.20
El Loco (see Ramirez, Amado)
Eldred, Stanley: 65.1
Elkin, Stanley: 83.4
Ellis, Bret Easton: 91.1
Ellison, James Whitfield: 73.27
Ellison, Ralph: 59.10, 59.18, 66.3,
    83.10, 89.5
Engle, Paul: 59.18
Engstrom, John: 83.11
Enzmann, Robert D.: 72.24
Ephron, Nora: 92.7
Epstein, Barbara: 63.1
Epstein, Edward Jay: 92.7
Epstein, Jason: 79.17, 82.23, 83.48,
    91.23, .26, 93.5, 97.2, .13
Ervin, Sam J., Jr.: 74.1
Esposito, Meade: 69.50
Evans, Harry: 91.46
Every-Mae: 63.37

F

Fadiman, Clinton: 89.11
Fagen, Cynthia R.: 82.5
Fairchild, Margaret: 67.13
Fallaci, Oriana: 68.21, 70.5
Faludi, Susan: 93.7
Fancher, Edwin: 56.1-56.17
Farbar, Bernard "Buzz": 67.13, .15,
    .20, 71.28, 73.40, 75.1, 82.23,
    83.21, 84.20, 86.28
Farbar, Jennifer L.: 86.28
Farber, M.A.: 81.13
Farley, Elizabeth: 67.13
Farnol, Jeffrey: 71.32, 79.30
Farrell, James T.: 79.30, 83.35, 98.11
Farrell, Warren: 74.17
Farrell, William E.: 69.72
Faulkner, William: 42.2, 55.6, 63.7,
    68.24, 76.12, 81.6, 83.5, 84.12,
    86.34, 91.42, 95.55

Faye, Marion: 58.4
Feiffer, Jules: 60.2, 63.33
Feldman, Gene: 57.1
Feldman, Paul: 68.3
Ferguson, Sarah: 90.1
Ferlinghetti, Lawrence: 61.5
Ferraro, Geraldine: 84.19, .27
Ferretti, Fred: 85.7
Ferris, Timothy: 73.11
Fertig, Howard: 67.11, 78.2, 80.23
Fiandaca, Alfred: 79.8
Fichtner, Margaria: 95.22, 97.14
Fiedler, Leslie: 52.1, 69.2
Figes, Eva: 77.4
Fine, Donald: 65.7
Fine, Marshall: 87.19
Finn, Huckleberry: 84.32, 85.12
Fisher, Frances: 87.11, .26
Fisher, Stanley: 59.8
Fishkin, Shelley Fisher: 85.16
Fitzgerald, F. Scott: 84.12, 96.6
FitzGerald, Frances: 68.10, 85.5
Fitzpatrick, Tom: 73.31
Flaherty, Joe: 69.10, .70, 70.7, 82.23
Flamm, Matthew: 91.19, .20
Flander, Judy: 73.41
Flaubert, Gustave: 64.23
Foffé, Alfredo: 81.22
Foote, Shelby: 97.26
Foreman, George: 75.8, .9, .12, 77.13
Forman, Milos: 80.20, 81.18, .19, .20
Forster, E.M.: 48.13, 59.4
Foster, William: 68.24
Francke, Linda: 73.7
Frankenthaler, Helen: 95.51
Frazier, Joe: 71.14, .15, 83.46
Fremont-Smith, Eliot: 76.8
Freud, Sigmund: 51.3, 55.6, 83.31
Friedan, Betty: 86.10, 93.7
Friedman, Robert: 65.17
Friedman, Roger D.: 94.8
Fripp, Bill: 73.13, .15
Froelke, Marcia: 83.56
Frost, David: 71.2, 92.2, .3
Frost Robert: 74.18

267

Fulford, Bob: 68.22
Funk, Robert: 97.23

G

Galbraith, John Kenneth: 60.2, 74.11, 86.5
Gallagher, James P.: 95.1
Galloway, Paul: 97.17
Gannett, Lewis: 48.13
Gannon, Sean: 95.34
Ganz, Armin: 87.26
Gardiner, Hadley Kittredge: 91.9
Gardner, William: 49.2
Garelik, Sanford D.: 69.22
Garen, Leo: 67.13
Garland, Judy: 80.15
Garreau, Joel: 95.6
Garrett, James: 69.58
Gartenberg, Max: 57.1
Gates, Gary Paul: 73.19
Gates, Henry Louis, Jr.: 97.26
Gates, Robert M.: 92.5
Gay, Peter: 69.2
Gaylin, Willard: 86.33
Geiger, H. Jack: 68.19
Geismar, Maxwell: 48.3
Gelber, Jack: 51.1
Gelmis, Joseph: 70.15, 86.40
Genet, Jean: 61.6, 68.18
Gervais, Marty: 83.24
Getlin, Josh: 91.28
Giacometti, Alberto: 74.3
Giancana, Sam: 91.5
Gide, André: 64.23
Gilmore, Gary: 79.1, .10, .12, .14, .16, .19, .25, .26, .31, .32, .33, 80.1, .10, 94.3
Gilmore, Mikal: 94.3
Gilroy, Harry: 65.4
Gimbel, Mary: 80.22
Gingrich, Arnold: 53.2, 59.18
Gingrich, Newt: 95.52
Ginsberg, Allen: 60.2, 64.18, 65.10, .13, 68.18, 74.18, 85.5, 86.41, 87.29
Girson, Rochelle: 49.2
Gish, Lillian: 87.6
Gittelson, Natalie: 71.23
Glenday, Michael K.: 95.56

Glenn, John: 62.19
Gobel, George: 56.7
Godard, Jean-Luc: 86.29, 87.4, .6, .16
Goetz, Bernard: 88.1
Gold, Herbert: 56.26, 59.10, 63.40
Goldwyn, Samuel: 89.6
Goodman, Howard: 95.5
Goodman, Mark: 75.15, .16
Goodman, Michael Barry: 81.21
Goodman, Walter: 86.5, .12, .15, 88.4, 92.3
Goodwin, Doris Kearns: 76.20, 97.26
Goodwin, Richard: 76.20
Gordimer, Nadine: 86.11, .20
Gordon, Mary: 89.8, 94.1
Gorfinkle, Constance: 86.39
Gottesman, Ronald: 76.12
Gould, Donna: 67.24
Goulden, Mark: 73.16
Gourevitch, Philip: 93.2
Grace, Matthew: 73.14
Grafton, Sue: 97.4
Graham, Jorie: 85.3
Grant, Ulysses S.: 67.19, 75.2
Grass, Günter: 86.17, .21
Graves, Ralph: 69.81, 76.5
Gray, Paul: 83.21, 84.13, 91.21
Green, Blake: 83.19
Green, Jorie: 95.7
Greenberg, Daniel: 70.6
Greene, Amy: 80.12, .15
Greene, Graham: 48.13, 61.17
Greene, Milton: 80.12, .14, .15, 82.23
Greenfield, Jeff: 79.32
Greer, Germaine: 71.16, .27, 80.2, 84.26
Gregory, Dick: 65.12, 68.18
Gregory, Paul: 58.3, 76.21
Griffin, Merv: 68.10
Griffith, Tom: 76.5
Griffiths, David: 61.18
Grimes, William: 92.7
Groen, Rick: 87.15
Gross, Kenneth: 69.44
Grossman, Richard: 61.9
Grossmann, Mary Ann: 88.9, 95.45
Grosvenor, Peter: 79.25
Guerard, Albert: 75.14
Guiles, Fred Lawrence: 73.16

Gussow, Mel: 66.6, 73.2
Guthmann, Edward: 87.21
Guthrie, William: 79.5, .17
Gwaltney, Francis Irby "Fig": 55.3, 85.13, 95.54

H

Haber, Joyce: 73.36
Hackett, Regina: 95.43
Hackney, Sheldon: 83.35
Haley, Alex: 85.3
Hall, Donald: 42.2
Hamill, Pete: 65.23, 67.7, 68.10, 82.23, 95.44
Hamilton, Charles V.: 68.3, 69.22
Hamilton, Edward A.: 58.7
Hamilton, William: 78.3
Hannum, Richard: 83.11, 86.22
Hansberry, Lorraine: 61.7
Harcourt, William: 60.2
Hardwick, Elizabeth: 65.9, 66.2, 68.9, 75.10, 86.5
Hardwicke, Cedric: 93.1
Hardy, Thomas: 79.30
Harlot (see Montague, Hugh)
Harlow, Jean: 67.23
Harrington, Stephanie: 67.1, .10
Harris, Mark: 59.18
Harris, Martyn: 84.25, 91.30
Harvey, Joseph M.: 65.1
Harvey, Robert: 73.43
Hauser, Wings: 87.11
Hayden, Tom: 68.10
Hayes, Harold: 60.9, 65.7, 71.27, 82.23
Haygood, Wil: 95.14
Hearst, Patti: 75.2
Hearst, Will: 79.31
Heep, Uriah: 70.8, .9, .10
Hefner, Hugh M.: 67.17
Heinlein, Robert: 72.24
Heller, Joseph: 63.8, 85.15
Heller, Karen: 84.21
Hellman, Lillian: 80.6
Hemingway, Ernest: 55.6, 56.12, 62.18, .19, 63.1, .7, 67.20, 68.24, 74.16, .18, 75.13, 76.12, .21, 79.22, 81.6, 82.14, 83.13, 84.12, 29, 88.1, 90.4,

92.9, 94.4, 95.47, 97.22
Hemingway, Gregory H.: 76.22
Henderson, Randi: 72.12
Henriques, Darryl: 63.31
Henry, Jan: 63.28
Hentoff, Nat: 67.12, 68.9
Hepburn, Audrey: 80.15
Herman, Jan: 79.13
Herres, David: 69.38
Hersey, John: 80.4
Hershey, Lenore: 80.12
Hewitt, Don: 73.19
Higham, Charles: 76.21
Hills, L. Rust: 53.2, 74.19, 82.23, 91.22
Hillyer, Robert: 44.1
Hilton, James: 48.13
Hirschkop, Phil: 70.11
Hiss, Alger: 60.2, 76.6
Hitchcock, Alfred: 41.1
Hitchens, Christopher: 84.26, 91.25
Hoagland, Paul: 81.7
Hockney, David: 91.51
Hodenfield, Jan: 73.3
Hoefler, Sandy: 83.23
Hoffman, Abbie: 68.3, 70.3, 80.26, 82.23
Hoffman, David G.: 72.6
Hoffman, Hans: 95.44, .51
Hoffman, Julius J.: 70.2, .3, .6
Hoffman, Paul: 69.39
Hohenberg, John: 74.20
Holland, Norman H.: 65.1
Hollander, John: 67.12
Hollander, Paul: 65.1
Hollander, Ron: 69.56
Hollett, Michael: 95.40
Holloschutz, Don: 69.12
Holt, Patricia: 91.37, 95.13
Hook, Sidney: 54.2
Hoopes, Townsend: 79.17
Hoover, J. Edgar: 63.33
Horn, Bernard: 51.2
Howard, Anthony: 84.26
Howard, Lorilee: 83.33
Howard, Maureen: 88.4
Howard, Pamela: 69.74
Howard, Peter E.: 84.14
Howard, Richard: 84.23, .24

270

272

56.4, 63.37, 67.20, .22, 71.1, 72.7,
83.18, 84.2, 97.13
Malaquais, Jean: 51.1, 58.1, 64.23,
69.2, 74.14, 81.16, 82.23
Malina, Judith: 64.18
Mallory, Carole Wagner: 86.1, .29,
89.9, 90.1, 91.3, 95.34
Malraux, André: 44.1, 64.23
Mann, Roderick: 81.19
Mann, Thomas: 80.8
Manso, Peter: 69.58, .80, 85.13, 91.22
Manson, Charles: 75.1
Marchi, John J.: 69.62, .66, .68
Marcus, Stephen: 64.1
Marcuse, Herbert: 68.9, 69.22
Margaronis, Maria: 86.18
Marlowe, Hugh: 67.13, .20
Márquez, Gabriel García: 74.18,
77.11, 79.30, 81.16
Martine, Darrell: 79.8
Marx, Karl: 51.3, 59.7
Mason, Marsha: 67.13
Massie, Robert K.: 89.3
Match, Richard: 48.13
Matusow, Harvey: 68.23
Matz, Charles: 70.4
Maxwell, William: 96.6
Mayer, L.B.: 89.6
McAuliffe, Kevin Michael: 78.7
McCabe, Carol: 95.22
McCarthy, Cormac: 98.9
McCarthy, Eugene: 68.23, 91.3
McCarthy, Mary: 62.24, 63.36, 75.10,
80.6
McCarthy, Todd: 87.4
McCarthy, W.J.: 65.15
McClure, Michael: 61.5, 64.18, 65.3,
67.23, 83.19
McClurg, Jocelyn: 91.32
McDonald, Erroll: 81.11
McDonald, William: 81.8
McDowall, Roddy: 66.14
McDowell, Edwin: 84.8, 85.5, .8, .9,
86.7, .9-.11, 89.3
McElroy, Joseph: 81.7
McFadden, Marian: 80.11
McGovern, George: 72.23
McGrady, Mike: 67.18

McGuane, Tom: 91.23
McInerney, Jay: 95.47
McLaughlin, Jeff: 90.4
McLuhan, Marshall: 68.22
McManus, Doyle: 82.4
McMurtry, Larry: 89.8, 91.23
McNally, Judith: 83.18, 95.16, .38,
97.13
McNamee, George C.: 70.6
McNeeley, Tom: 65.17
McNeil, Legs: 79.7
McVeigh, Timothy: 95.23, .26
McWherter, Joe: 67.13
Mead, Margaret: 52.1
Medwick, Cathleen: 80.16, 83.30, .34
Mejías, Ignacio Sánchez: 67.20, .22,
84.2
Melcher, Fredric: 48.13
Meltzer, David: 61.5
Melville, Herman: 51.2, 76.12, 91.3,
.42, 95.42
Menenhetet: 83.17, .28
Meras, Phyllis: 67.19
Meridith, Scott: 65.7, 69.34, 74.10,
79.14, 82.23, 83.18, .21, .48, 84.17
Merkin, Daphne: 87.26
Merrill, Robert: 73.43
Meskil, Paul: 69.27
Meyer, John: 97.23
Meyerowitz, Joel: 84.17, 91.10, 93.10
Michaelson, Jeffrey: 81.23
Michaelson, Judy: 61.20, 69.14
Michener, James: 85.1
Miller, Arthur: 80.12, 85.1, 91.28
Miller, Henry: 66.14, 68.11, 76.3, .4,
.12, .18, 77.11, 83.19, 87.4, 90.1,
91.40
Miller, Merle: 49.2
Miller, Tim: 86.37, 87.12
Mills, C. Wright: 52.1, 60.2
Mills, Hilary: 81.2, 82.23, 83.31, .50,
84.5, 91.22
Milosz, Czeslaw: 86.27
Minton, Walter: 55.4, 65.5, .7, 74.19,
82.23
Minzesheimer, Bob: 97.23, 98.8
Mitgang, Herbert: 76.18, 80.5, 83.6,
84.31, 86.2

273

274

Ozick, Cynthia: 98.4

277

Styron, William: 59.10, 63.8, .40,
65.3, 79.14, 80.4, 82.6, .22, .23,
83.13, 85.1, 91.22, .38
Suess, Dr.: 79.30
Sullivan, Barbara: 83.55
Sullivan, Tom: 78.4, 79.2
Suplee, Curt: 83.22
Susskind, David: 59.3, 73.22

T

Talese, Gay: 86.5, 89.8, 91.23, 93.1,
.2, .7
Talese, Nan: 93.5
Tallmer, Jerry: 67.5, 69.3
Tanner, Tony: 96.6
Tax, Meredith: 86.17
Taylor, Elizabeth: 98.11
Taylor, Robert: 80.8, 83.5, 93.4
Teppis, Herman: 68.11, 89.6
Terry, Clifford: 73.39
Thatcher, Margaret: 84.27, .29
Thernstrom, Stephen: 68.3
Theroux, Paul: 85.15
Thomas, Clarence: 91.21
Thomas, Gwen: 86.31
Thomas, Norman: 60.2
Thomas, Robert McG., Jr.: 82.10
Thompson, Hunter: 77.13, 87.29
Thompson, Toby: 91.23
Thornhill, Arthur: 83.18
Thurman, Tedi: 80.15
Tierney, Lawrence: 87.2, .3, .26
Tinkle, Lon: 48.13
Toback, James: 68.28, 71.28
Tobin, Greg: 83.41
Tolstoy, Leo: 54.2, 68.24, 81.6
Toomey, Philippa: 79.28
Topp, Sylvia: 73.47
Torn, Rip: 67.13, 71.28
Torres, José: 65.17, 67.15, 68.10,
71.26, 82.23, 83.21, 93.6
Tory, Rosemary: 67.13, .20
Trecker, Barbara: 71.12
Treisman, Dan: 84.29
Trilling, Diana: 71.16, 77.14, 89.8
Trilling, Lionel: 52.1
Trollope, Anthony: 83.6
Troy, George: 65.8

Trueheart, Charles: 91.12
Truman, Harry S.: 74.13, 75.13
Truscott, Lucian K., IV: 73.6
Tuers, Raymond J.: 69.49
Tully, Paul: 69.52
Turner, Alice K.: 76.17
Turner, Joseph: 76.12
Turow, Joseph: 95.4
Twain, Mark: 82.25, 83.6, 91.42
Tyler, Anne: 82.22
Tynan, Kenneth: 60.2
Tyson, Mike: 88.7

U

Underwood, Peter: 61.16
Updike, John: 63.8, 73.9, .43, 75.13,
83.13, .21, 84.5, 85.1, 86.17, 95.18,
98.4

V

Valentin, Gilberto Gerena: 67.24
Vanocur, Sander: 63.38
Vassi, Marco: 92.11
Ventura, Michael: 87.17
Verniere, James: 87.20
Vertes, Peter: 91.40
Vespa, Mary: 81.12
Vibbert, Spencer: 79.5
Vidal, Gore: 59.10, 60.3, 63.7, .40,
68.20, 72.16, 75.10, 77.4, .6-.9,
82.23, 83.3, .33,
85.1, .6, .15, 86.4, 91.3, 93.1, .2, 98.3
Voltaire, Francois: 72.17
Vonnegut, Kurt: 73.9, 76.17, 82.25,
85.1, 86.5, .21, 93.1

W

Wagner, Robert F.: 69.35, .39, .50, .68,
.72
Walcott, Derek: 74.18
Walker, Berta: 93.3
Walker, Joe: 69.75
Wallace, George: 68.23
Wallace, Henry: 48.9, 48.11-.13, 49.4,
74.20
Wallace, Mike: 58.2, .7, 73.19, .21,
.24, .26, .45, 77.7

The first edition of this book consists of 490 numbered copies, 80 of which are hors commerce copies; and 26 lettered copies bound in leather and signed by Norman Mailer and the authors.

This is copy ___*86*___ .